SENSORY QUALITY IN FOODS AND BEVERAGES:
Definition, Measurement and Control

ELLIS HORWOOD SERIES IN FOOD SCIENCE AND TECHNOLOGY

This publishing programme provides an organised coverage on food science for professional technologists, research workers, and students in universities and polytechnics.

Series Editors:
Professor I. D. Morton, Head of Food Science, Queen Elizabeth College, University of London;
Dr. R. Scott, formerly Reading University

FUNDAMENTALS OF FOOD CHEMISTRY
    W. Heimann, Director, Institute for Food Chemistry, University of Karlsruhe, Germany
HYGIENIC DESIGN AND OPERATION OF FOOD PLANT
    Edited by R. Jowitt, National College of Food Technology, University of Reading
SERVICES, HEATING AND EQUIPMENT FOR HOME ECONOMISTS
    D. Kirk, Sheffield City Polytechnic and A. Milson, The Queen's College, Glasgow
PRINCIPLES OF DESIGN AND OPERATION OF CATERING EQUIPMENT
    A. Milson, The Queen's College, Glasgow and D. Kirk, Sheffield City Polytechnic
TECHNOLOGY OF BISCUITS, CRACKERS AND COOKIES
    J. R. Manley, Consultant, Peterborough
SENSORY QUALITY IN FOOD AND BEVERAGES
    A. A. Williams and R. K. Atkin, Long Aston Research Station, Bristol
PHYSICAL PROPERTIES OF FOODS AND FOOD PROCESSING SYSTEMS
    M. J. Lewis, University of Reading
FLAVOUR OF DISTILLED BEVERAGES
    J. R. Piggott, University of Strathclyde
ENERGY MANAGEMENT IN FOODSERVICE
    N. Unklesbay and K. Unklesbay, University of Missouri, Columbia, Missouri, USA
THE PSYCHOBIOLOGY OF HUMAN FOOD SELECTION
    L. M. Barker, Baylor University, Waco, Texas, USA
ADVANCED SUGAR CHEMISTRY
    R. S. Shallenberger, Cornell University, Geneva, New York, NY, USA
HANDBOOK OF SENSORY EVALUATION OF FOOD
    G. Jellinek, formerly University of Berlin and University of Stuttgart
FISH PROCESSING: Its Science and Technology
    S. W. Hanson and W. F. A. Horner, Grimsby College of Technology
MODERN FOOD PROCESSING
    J. Lamb, University of Leeds
BATTER AND BREADING TECHNOLOGY
    D. R. Sudermann, Durkee Foods, Strongsville, Ohio, U.S.A. and F. E. Cunningham, Kansas State University, Manhattan, Kansas, U.S.A.
SUSTAINABLE FOOD SYSTEMS
    D. Knorr, University of Delaware, Delaware, U.S.A.
FOOD OILS AND THEIR USES
    T. J. Weiss, Hunt-Wesson Foods Inc., Fullerton, California, U.S.A.
WORLD VEGETABLES: PRODUCTION AND UTILIZATION
    M. Yamaguchi, University of California at Davis, California, U.S.A.

SENSORY QUALITY
IN FOODS AND BEVERAGES:
Definition, Measurement
and Control

Editors:

A. A. WILLIAMS B.Sc., Ph.D
R. K. ATKIN B.A., Ph.D
Long Ashton Research Station
Principal Scientific Officers

Published for the
SOCIETY OF CHEMICAL INDUSTRY, London

by **ELLIS HORWOOD LIMITED**
Publishers · Chichester

First published in 1983 by
ELLIS HORWOOD LIMITED
Market Cross House, Cooper Street, Chichester, West Sussex, PO19 1EB, England

The publisher's colophon is reproduced from James Gillison's drawing of the ancient Market Cross, Chichester.

Distributors:

Australia, New Zealand, South-east Asia:
Jacaranda-Wiley Ltd., Jacaranda Press,
JOHN WILEY & SONS INC.,
G.P.O. Box 859, Brisbane, Queensland 40001, Australia

Europe, Africa:
JOHN WILEY & SONS LIMITED
Baffins Lane, Chichester, West Sussex, England.

The Americas, Japan, The Phillipines:
VERLAG CHEMIE INTERNATIONAL, INC.
1020 N.W. 6th Street, Deerfield Beach, Florida, 33441, USA.

© 1983 Society of Chemical Industry/Ellis Horwood Ltd.

British Library Cataloguing in Publication Data
Williams, A.A.
Sensory quality in foods and beverages.–
(Ellis Horwood series in food science and technology)
1. Flavours – congresses
I. Williams, A.A.   II. Atkin, R.K.
664   TP418

Library of Congress Card No. 83-8420

ISBN 0-85312-480-9 (Ellis Horwood Ltd., Publishers-Library Edn.)
ISBN 0-89573-130-4 (Verlag Chemie International Inc.)

Printed in Great Britain by Unwin Brothers of Woking.

Table of Contents

Preface   11

**Section 1 – UNDERSTANDING AND DEFINING
         SENSORY QUALITY**

1.1 What is sensory quality?
     D. G. LAND   15
1.2 Integrating needs – from grower to consumer
     T. R. GORMLEY   30
1.3 Industrial approaches to defining quality
     J. L. SIDEL, H. STONE and J. BLOOMQUIST   48
1.4 Understanding and interpreting consumer answers in
     the laboratory
     NICOLE DAGET   58

**Section 2 – MEASUREMENT OF SENSORY QUALITY:
         SENSORY METHODS, STATE OF
         THE ART**

2.1 Adapting short cut signal detection measures to the
     problem of multiple difference testing: the R-Index
     M. A. P. D. O'MAHONY   69
2.2 Flavour description and flavour classification
     J. F. CLAPPERTON and J. B. HARWOOD   82
2.3 The application of Procrustes statistics to sensory profiling
     S. P. LANGRON   89
2.4 Is there an alternative to descriptive sensory assessment?
     D. M. H. THOMSON and H. J. H. MACFIE   96

Posters:

2.5   A tasting procedure for assessing bitterness and
astringency
G. M. ARNOLD   109

2.6   Use of micro-computer with card reader system for flavour
profile data handling and storage
A. M. DUFFIELD and J. J. STAGG   115

**Section 3 – MEASUREMENT OF SENSORY QUALITY:
INSTRUMENTAL METHODS
AND THEIR VALIDATION**

3.1   Instrumental assessment of the appearance of foods
D. B. MACDOUGALL   121

3.2   Colour in beverages
C. F. TIMBERLAKE and P. BRIDLE   140

3.3   Correlating instrumental measurements with sensory
evaluation of texture
M. C. BOURNE   155

3.4   Measurement of particular textural characteristics of some
fruits and vegetables
J. G. BRENNAN   173

3.5   Measuring of sensory quality: assessing aroma by gas
chromatography
P. DURR   188

3.6   Headspace gas-chromatography as a means of assessing the
effect of non-volatile food components on volatile flavour
compounds
BONNIE M. KING and J. SOLMS   196

3.7   Bitterness, astringency and the chemical composition of
ciders
A. G. H. LEA and G. M. ARNOLD   203

Poster:

3.8   Two instruments designed to measure texture or related
properties in food products
G. LAMBERT   213

**Section 4 – SENSORY AND INSTRUMENTAL METHODS
AND THEIR APPLICATION TO SPECIFIC
PRODUCTS**

(a)   Vegetables

4.1   Quality appraisal of processed fruits and vegetables
D. H. LYON   219

4.2   Relationships between sensory and chemical quality
criteria for carrots studied by multivariate data analysis
M. MARTENS, B. FJELDSENDEN, H. RUSSWUM JR,
and H. MARTENS   233

4.3   Quality assessment of watercress
       R-M. SPENCE and O. G. TUCKNOTT   247

Posters:

4.4   Texture profile analysis studies of stored common beans
       (Phaseolus vulgaris L.)
       R. dos SANTOS GARRUTI and
       D. dos SANTOS GARRUTI   259
4.5   Relationship between the capsaicoids content and the
       Scoville Index of Capsicum oleoresins
       L. J. VAN GEMERT, L. M. NIJSSEN,
       A. T. H. J. DE BIE and H. MAARSE   266
4.6   Descriptive sensory analysis of soy sauce
       S. M. TAN and J. R. PIGGOTT   272

(b)   Fruit and Fruit Products

4.7   Enzymes as indices of ripening
       P. W. GOODENOUGH   279
4.8   Flavour quality evaluation and specifications for
       non-alcoholic beverages
       R. DOBBS   287
4.9   Comparison between direct similarity assessments and
       descriptive profiles of certain soft drinks
       J. CHAUHAN, R. HARPER and
       W. KRZANOWSKI   297
4.10   Objective and hedonic sensory assessment of ciders and
       apple juices
       A. A. WILLIAMS, S. P. LANGRON and
       G. M. ARNOLD   310
4.11   Descriptive analysis and quality of Bordeaux wines
       A. C. NOBLE, A. A. WILLIAMS and
       S. P. LANGRON   324

Posters:

4.12   Influence of storage conditions on the organoleptic quality
       of apple juice
       L. POLL   336
4.13   Sensory and instrumental measurement of quality
       attributes in apples
       S. M. SMITH and A. CHURCHILL   341
4.14   Colour measurement in red wines
       P. BRIDLE   347
4.15   Browning in white wines
       L. F. BURROUGHS and A. G. H. LEA   350
4.16   Evaluating wine quality by the application of statistical
       methods to analytical GC data
       M. BERTUCCIOLI, P. DADDI and
       A. SENSIDORI   353

(c)   Fish and Meat

4.17   Quality of deboned fish flesh
       P. HOWGATE   361
4.18   Sensory and instrumental methods in meat aroma analysis
       A. M. GALT and G. MACLEOD   374

Posters:

4.19   Effect of processing changes on the quality of broiler
       chickens
       N. M. GRIFFITHS and J. M. JONES   387
4.20   Firmness of pig carcass backfat – sensory and instrumental
       measurements
       R. C. D. JONES and E. DRANSFIELD   392
4.21   Some observations on the role of lipids in meat flavour
       D. S. MOTTRAM   394

(d)   Dairy Products

4.22   Aspects of sensory quality in milk and unfermented milk
       products
       M. J. A. SCHRODER   401
4.23   Flavoured dairy products: sensory and stability problems
       W. GRAB   412

Poster:

4.24   Potato-like off flavour in smear coated cheese: a defect
       induced by bacteria
       J-P. DUMONT, R. MOURGES and J. ADDA   424

**Section 5 – INFLUENCE OF SENSORY QUALITY ON
           FOOD CHOICE AND INTAKE**

5.1   Sensory qualities, palatability of food and overweight
       J. E. R. FRIJTERS   431
5.2   Marketing and sensory quality
       D. LESSER   448
5.3   Future trends in the evaluation of sensory quality
       R. HARPER   467

Index   483

Preface

This book contains papers presented at an international Symposium "Sensory Quality in Foods and Beverages: its Definition, Measurement and Control", held at the University of Bristol between 4th – 8th April 1982. The meeting was organised jointly by the Society of Chemical Industry's Food Group (Sensory Panel) and Long Ashton Research Station as part of the Food Group's Jubilee Year Celebrations. Nearly 140 scientists from 15 countries attended the Symposium, which comprised invited papers and posters covering topics relevant to current concerns of researchers in industry and academic institutions.

What makes food acceptable to the consumer is one of the fundamental questions being asked by the food industry. If established products are to maintain their market position and new products are to succeed, it is essential that food scientists and technologists know more precisely what the consumer wants, not merely in general terms but in terms of the chemical and physical parameters of such products.

Acceptance, however, is a complex response with many factors interacting to influence a person's decision to purchase or consume a food. These considerations may be physiological, psychological, cultural, sensory, nutritional, economical, social and practical. Sensory aspects – just one facet – may form an equally complex picture in which aroma, flavour and texture attributes interact.

This Symposium attempts to explore the state of our knowledge and understanding of sensory quality in foods and beverages, and how we interpret information about consumer preferences in relation to chemical and physical measurements pertinent to food quality.

This book is a record of the proceedings of the Symposium, and comprises a blend of review papers and original unpublished data, concerning specific products, recent developments in methodology, and the application of statistical techniques. These proceedings emphasise the need for multidisciplinary approaches to be adopted to resolve problems associated with food and beverage quality, and conclude by outlining areas where further research may be useful.

We acknowledge the permission given to reproduce the following illustrations as indicated in the text: Figrues 3, 5 and 6 in Dr. D. G. Land's paper, and Figures 1-8 in Professor M. C. Bourne's paper.

Many people contributed to the success of the Symposium and the organisers thank all who attended in particular H. P. Bulmer plc, Farley Health Products Ltd. and Golden Spring Cress Ltd. for financial help; Dr. J. J. Wren, Mr. J. M. Harries, Dr. H. Maarse, Dr. F. W. Beech, Mr. P. A. Halstead, Mr. A. B. Haddon, Dr. J. Adda and Dr. W. F. J. Cuthbertson for chairing the sessions; Mr. E. G. R. Chenoweth for redrawing several of the illustrations; and Mrs. L. Houlden and Mrs. B. R. Courtice for their excellent secretarial help.

A. A. Williams
R. K. Atkin

UNDERSTANDING AND DEFINING SENSORY QUALITY

Chapter 1.1

What is sensory quality?

D.G. Land
ARC Food Research Institute, Colney Lane, Norwich NR4 7UA, UK

SUMMARY

Quality may be defined as fitness for purpose, and,
in the case of food, consists of safety, nutritional
value and acceptability, all of which are interrelated.
Sensory quality may be defined as those attributes of
quality which are perceived through the senses. This
paper provides a broad outline of the multiple aspects
of sensory quality and the ways in which they are
interrelated. It shows, for example, that factors
ranging from those influencing plant breeding and
husbandry to those affecting consumer food choice at
the level of cooking and eating should all be considered as potential influences on sensory quality. It
also considers the various levels at which measurements of sensory quality may be made, whether as
direct sensory/behavioural information or as related
instrumental measures, and the relevance of the resulting information.

INTRODUCTION

This opening paper sets the stage for the following
more specialised papers and poster contributions that
follow. My task is also to provide a skeleton frame-
work to facilitate an integration of aspects ranging
from breeding and growing to marketing, consumer
behaviour, and health; from specific sensory and
instrumental methods of data analysis; and from gen-
eralised techniques to specific food products. Such

is the diversity of sensory quality.

What is sensory quality? This must be defined
first in terms of quality of food and beverages.
Quality may be defined as degree of excellence or
fitness for purpose [1] and, in the case of complex
products or materials, is a composite of many contributory attributes. Sensory quality is therefore the
degree of excellence or fitness for eating in those
contributory attributes which are perceived via the
senses of sight, smell, taste, touch and hearing. It
impinges on several aspects of the three main areas
of food quality. These are:

(i)   Nutritional, e.g. protein, energy or trace
       factors which are positive quality factors
       (i.e. good for us).

(ii)   Safety, e.g. micro-organisms, toxins, contamin-
       ants or genetic aberrations which are negative
       (i.e. bad for us), and

(iii) Acceptability, e.g. appearance, smell, taste,
       texture, after-effects, etc. which are positive
       (i.e. satisfy us) or negative (i.e. do not sat-
       isfy us).

Nutritional quality of food is not directly
influenced by sensory quality, but indirectly it is
totally dependent upon it. However good a food may
be in nutrient composition, if it is not acceptable
it is not eaten, and until food is eaten its practical
nutrient value is zero. Sensory quality is thus an
essential prerequisite for nutrition.

Safety is also not directly influenced by sensory
quality in some cases, e.g. if a food is contaminated
with traces of lead, polychlorinated biphenyls or
Botulinum toxin, this will not influence any of the
sensory attributes. However, in other cases the presence of an agent which reduces safety in food is
associated with changes in sensory quality. Microbial
growth on meat and other foods is frequently accompanied by formation of odours which warn us not to
eat the food, and the presence of high levels of toxic
glycoalkaloids in a new potato variety Lenape was
accompanied by increased bitterness [2,3,4]. Indeed,
bitterness has been associated with toxic effects for
centuries and may be regarded as a basic biological
protection mechanism.

The major area in which sensory quality is directly concerned is acceptability, although it should

be noted that it is also influenced by factors other than sensory ones (e.g. price, availability). A product which costs more than we can afford, or are prepared to pay at that time is unacceptable to us however good its sensory quality. So what is this sensory quality in functional terms? How do we measure it? What are the factors which influence it?

First of all, sensory quality is perceived by man as a result of a stimulus or usually many stimuli. It is behavioural response to those stimuli. It must therefore be measured in the first place by sensory techniques using people.

STIMULUS ——————▶ | PEOPLE | ——————▶ RESPONSES
(FOOD or DRINK)   (BEHAVIOUR)

These measures may in turn be related to chemical or physical components in the food and may then result in the development of instrumental measures which may be used, *under conditions defined by the original validation*, to predict sensory responses. Such instrumental methods must only be used after validation; they arise as a result of understanding the basis in the food of the sensory responses which can only come from research, the continuation of which is essential if the food industry is to maintain and improve the sensory quality of its products.

Sensory quality is not a single entity - it covers an area in which there are three major contributing variables which must be clearly understood. These variables are:

(i)   of food origin,
(ii)   in measurement techniques and level, and
(iii) in people.

VARIABLES OF FOOD ORIGIN

These variables are basic and usually taken into consideration. There are extensive plant and animal breeding programmes in several countries which aim to produce breeds or cultivars which show improved yield, disease resistance, suitability for mechanical harvest, composition, etc. Unfortunately, sensory quality is sometimes not considered until a very late stage because it cannot be simply and easily quantified. This omission can be very expensive. There are many examples, of which the potato Lenape, already referred to [3,4], and stringless beans, which were

also flavourless, are but two. Although several
papers at this Symposium (see Lea and Arnold; Lyon; and
Martens et al.) refer to assessment of different cultivars, no paper seems to deal with assessment of
sensory quality as part of the breeding programme.
The screening of new Brussels sprouts varieties by
analytical and sensory methods though illustrates one
approach to this problem [5].

Most studies, however, involve developed cultivars or breeds and frequently examine the influence of
location and husbandry treatments; see, for example,
Martens et al in this Symposium. I should like to
illustrate the effect of environment (i.e. growing
site) on the flavour of carrots, because it shows the
interactions with both method and with people variables.
Growing site includes both differences in soil type and
nutrients with climatic (e.g. rainfall) differences.
Autumn King Red-cored carrots were grown at four sites,
and flavour differences compared with a labelled control were assessed in triplicate by a panel of 10
using a coded control (Fig. 1) [6]. Marked differences were found which, on descriptive analysis
(Table 1), were shown to be caused by lack of carrot
flavour with an unpleasant note in those grown on peat
soils. The scaling method used was shown to have the
properties of a true interval scale and therefore parametric methods of statistical analysis could be validly
used. The small but highly significant difference
Shown at Cawston was caused by increased sweetness,
which preference tests showed was liked by 60% and
disliked by 33% of the panel. Note how few responses
were "no difference" in preference, although two-
thirds of responses to the hidden control were "no
difference". These results illustrate a marked effect
of growing site on sensory quality, the different
types of information obtained using different methods
and the existence of people variables. The last two
factors are discussed further below.

Other food variables which may influence sensory
quality are harvesting (i.e. state of maturity) which
is very important in many crops for processing (e.g.
peas for freezing), and also conditions and length of
storage (see, for example, paper by Spence and
Tucknott, this Symposium). Processing variables (see,
for example, paper by Griffiths and Jones, this Symposium) may also have a marked influence, as will
packaging methods. The packaging materials used have
a dual function; firstly, protection (e.g. catalytic
effects of light or lipid oxidation [7] or bacterial

or chemical contamination); and secondly, in the
expectation that the pack creates in the consumer.
The latter is covered by people variables. Cooking
methods and adjuncts (condiments, spices and sauces)
may also have a marked influence on sensory quality.
It is most important to realise that changes in any
of these food variables should not be made without
testing for effects on sensory quality. This requires
consideration of the second major variable, that of
sensory methodology and level of measurement.

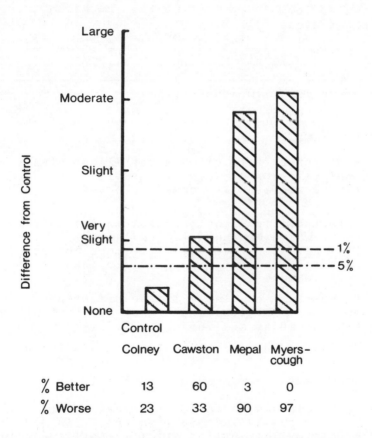

	Control			
	Colney	Cawston	Mepal	Myers-cough
% Better	13	60	3	0
% Worse	23	33	90	97

Fig. 1 — Flavour differences between Autumn King carrots grown at four
centres using Colney as reference. 10 assessors 3x.

Table 1 — **Characterisation of flavour differences between Autumn King carrots grown at four centres using Colney as reference.**

Description	Centre			
	Colney*	Cawston	Mepal	Myerscough
No difference	17	0	2	0
Sweeter	4	26	0	1
Less sweet	0	0	7	5
Unpleasant, low carrot flavour	3	2	16	20
Bitter	1	0	2	3
Stale, musty	1	0	2	3
Others	4	1	4	3

* Coded control;   10 assessors 3x.

SENSORY VARIABLES

The example on carrots given above illustrates some aspects of all four classes of sensory techniques which may be applied to foods and beverages. These are:

(i)   Detectability - may be absolute (Is there anything which can be detected?) or differential (Is there a detectable difference between two samples?), although in practice the latter is most common.

(ii).   Intensity - how large is the difference? How much of a particular attribute is present? Also known as scaling.

(iii).   Quality - what is the nature, character or description of the attributes present?

(iv)   Reactions - how much do we like it or not?

These classes, each of which has several different methods available, are frequently confused because they may be applied at different levels in the sequence of perception from food stimulus to resultant behaviour (Fig. 2). The first level is that of detection and measurement of intensity of specific sensory attributes, and includes difference detection in these attributes (see O'Mahony, this Symposium). However, usually implicit in intensity measurement is characterisation or description of the attribute to be measured and its importance is

reflected in the many papers which describe or use
the techniques of profiling (see Clapperton, Chauhan
et al ; Williams et al ; Noble et al ; this Symposium),
its data analysis (see Langron) or even alternative
approaches (see Thomson and MacFie, Chauhan et al).
A simple example of information at this level is
'How salty is this product?' and the information
obtained would lie somewhere between zero and extreme
saltiness. However, this information, at a simple
level, can also be evaluated in terms of 'How well do
I like this amount of saltiness in this product?'
This provides information on a scale which may range
from dislike, or neutral through an optimum for
liking, to extreme dislike as saltiness increases.
At this level of measurement, control is more difficult as feedback from prior experience may be very
strong and the data is therefore more complex. In
fact it is multivariate although usually few of the
variables can be specified.

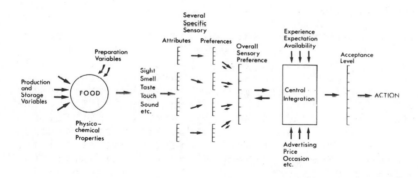

Fig.2 — Variables — measurement levels of sensory quality.

        The next level (Fig. 2) considers 'How well do
I like the product overall?' and again it contains an
even larger contribution from past experience and is
even more complex and context dependent. For example,
a small excess of saltiness may ruin the flavour of
an otherwise good quality product and show a relatively larger reduction in liking than the same excess
of saltiness in a poor product, where it may even

give some flavour or mask an off-flavour and thus be
better liked than the unsalted material. Here, responses are more complex than at the first level and
reflect much feed-back from experience. It may be
argued that such information is superfluous but it
may prove to be an important link in understanding
the relationships between sensory data in terms of
attributes and acceptance behaviour.

Finally (Fig. 2), there is the major test at
the marketing stage, where the degree of like or dislike changes to acceptance level. Here many factors
other than immediate sensory quality may substantially
influence the resultant behaviour. These include
prior experience of this and similar products, expectations for the product, with or without the influence
of recent advertising pressure, availability, convenience, price, appropriateness for the occasion and
many more. These factors and marketing strategies to
influence behaviour all fall into the area of the
third variable, which I have called people.

PEOPLE VARIABLES

As already stated, sensory quality is excellence or
fitness for eating as perceived by people. The
primary sensor is therefore a person or more usually
a group of people. Thus far I have referred to
sensory quality in its various contributory measures,
components and levels as something implied to be absolute. This would be a very convenient situation if
it were true - it would mean that for most measures,
responses of one person would reflect that of all the
population. The single expert assessor is still used
in a few specialised commodities, but in general it
is recognised that sensory quality should be measured
using panels. The reasons for this, however, are
frequently ignored and sensory attributes are often
referred to as properties only of the food. People
are frequently surprised when someone reacts differently to them in response to a stimulus 'You can't
taste it!' (when I can) certainly implies that something is wrong with you.

The reality is that biological variation is the
norm and applies to what people perceive as sensory
quality at all levels.

Let us start with detectability, or sensitivity.
The work of Zoeteman [8] in Holland illustrates the
range of sensitivity within a population of 120 people

to four widely different odorous chemicals in water
(Fig. 3). The concentrations of each chemical are
all expressed•as a ratio of that detectable by 50% of
the population for that chemical. What is noteworthy
is the spread of sensitivity; 20% differ by more than
200-fold in sensitivity, and half of those differ by
nearly 2000-fold! There is no reason to believe that
this population is unrepresentative, and there are
more extreme examples such as 2-methylpropanal, where
8.6% of a population of 222 differed by more than
16 000-fold[9]. Thus, differences in sensitivity may
account for some differences in perception and therefore in behaviour. We should remember also that in
selecting members of a sensory panel the less sensitive are frequently omitted. However, both extremes
of sensitivity exist in consumer populations and
could be demonstrated if we took sufficiently large
samples.

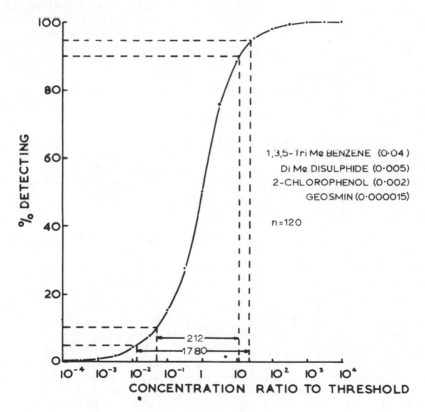

Fig.3 — Distribution of population sensitivity to four odorants in water (after
        Zoeteman, 1973).

Diversity of response also occurs at the level
of preference. Previous work at Norwich on odours
confirmed the original observation of the Swedish bot-
anist Linnaeus that some odours are pleasant to some
people and unpleasant to others [10,11]. The four
odours (Fig. 4) show preference distributions which
are predominantly pleasant, unpleasant, neutral, and
pleasant to some, unpleasant to others with a bimodal
distribution respectively. There is some evidence to
support the idea that people at each end of the response scale perceive these odours as quite different
in character [12]. However, these differences also
apply to foods. Work by Rose Marie Pangborn at Davis
shows great individual diversity in hedonic response
to varying the amount of sugar in coffee (Fig. 5)
which is not reflected in the mean response [13].
None of the eight individual response curves shown
corresponds to that of the mean for the 30 subjects,
which shows very little change of liking with sucrose
concentration. All possible behaviour patterns except
a high level of liking for all concentrations of
sucrose were found in the original data [14] demonstrating the loss of information on individual behaviour by using means. We must never forget that consumers are individuals! The use of methodology,
including data analysis, which identifies sub-groups
of populations is very important.

A method of identifying foods which display
such divergent responses has recently been proposed
[15]; it recognises those to which the old adage
'One man's meat is another's poison' applies and which
has its application in marketing techniques in which
target populations are identified.

Like/dislike also varies within the individual
and, for example, is influenced by what we have already eaten. The work of Cabanac [16] shows how the
pleasantness of smell of orange juice very rapidly
declines after a drink containing 100 g of glucose
(Fig. 6). It is then a very small step towards liking
or disliking foods because of other after-effects.
Why do we like drinks such as coffee or beer which are
bitter and should be unpleasant? There are many
social factors involved but one can speculate that we
accept the bitterness because we like the after-effects
[17] and become conditioned to like those drinks -
they are in fact acquired tastes [18]. This situation
then leads us to eating for health and problems such
as obesity - if we know something is bad for us to
eat, does it make us want it more, or do we rational-

ise our behaviour by convincing ourselves we like it
less? (see paper by Frijters, this Symposium).

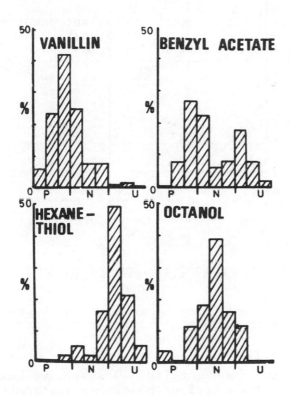

Fig.4 — Distribution of hedonic responses to four odorants using a 9-point scale.

Thus, there are many aspects of the 'people
variables' and these should be considered in attempt-
ing to understand perception of sensory quality.

INSTRUMENTAL METHODS RELATING TO SENSORY QUALITY

As referred to above, it is essential to understand
the basis in the food of factors influencing sensory
quality. This, together with the wish to increase the
use of automated methods of quality control, is why
there is a strong interest in analytical methods.
Further research into these factors in the food will
undoubtedly improve our ability to efficiently produce

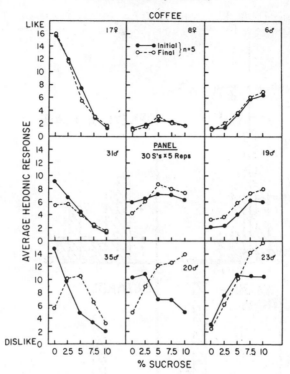

Fig. 5 — Variation of hedonic responses to varying sucrose in coffee (from
Pangborn (1981) [13]).

and control our food quality. However, we must not
forget that for control purposes any instrumental
method is at best secondary. It can only predict the
sensory consequences of those defined parameters which
it measures. It cannot respond to those contributing
factors which are not being measured. It is clear
that sensory quality is in almost all cases the resultant of extremely complex multicomponent stimuli, the
interactions between which are still only poorly understood. At worst, instrumental methods may be a simple,
convenient and arbitary indicator of constancy of some
factor, but may well be grossly misused as a replace-
ment for sensory methods which directly measure the
perceived attributes. Any instrumental method to be
used as a predictor of sensory attributes must be
subjected to thorough and critical evaluation, using
as wide a range of variables as practicable and validated thoroughly against sensory methods. To do less
is to court disaster.

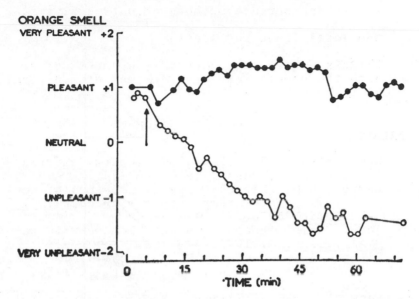

Fig.6 — Variation in hedonic response to orange drink odour before (closed circles) and after (open circles) consuming glucose (at arrow) (from Cabanac [16]).

CONCLUSIONS

I have attempted to illustrate the diversity of influences on sensory quality. Some aspects have been given greater emphasis than others because they are less widely recognised. In conclusion, I would like to summarise the following points, many of which are discussed further in the papers in this Symposium.

(i)   Sensory quality is a perceived response by people - primary measurements using people may then be related to other secondary measurements but such relationships must be well validated under the conditions to be used.

(ii) It is essential to recognise the existence of the three main variables of food, methods and people in defining operations involving sensory quality. Variables do not occur *only* in the food.

(iii) In interpreting *data* we must know what we are measuring, the strengths and limitations of the methods used, and we must accept the multivariate nature of many of the responses and be prepared to use appropriate methods of data analysis,

and lastly, but not least

(iv)   Fitness for eating by whom? - we must define
both the populations used for measurements and
as targets.

REFERENCES

1.   Webster's New Collegiate Dictionary.   Merrian,
Springfield, Mass.   1977, pp. 944.
2.   Barnes, E.M.   Microbiological problems of poultry
at refrigerator temperature - a review. J. Sci.
Fd Agric. 1976, 27, 777-782.
3.   Anon.   Name of potato variety Lenape withdrawn.
Amer. Pot. J. 1970, 47, 103.
4.   Zitnac, A.; Johnson, G.R.   Glycoalkaloid content
of B5141-6 potatoes.   Amer. Pot. J. 1970, 47,
256-60.
5.   Fenwick, G.R.; Griffiths, N.M.; Heaney, R.K.
Sprouts: causes of bitterness in frozen
samples.   Grower 1982, April 15, 43-45.
6.   Land, D.G.   Some aspects of the measurement of
flavour.   Proc. Nutr. Soc. 1970, 29, 309-317.
7.   Chan, H.W-S; Levett, G.; Griffiths. N.M.   Light
induced flavour deterioration.   Exposure of
potato crisps to light and its effect on subsequent storage in the dark.   J. Sci. Fd Agric.
1978, 29, 1055-1060.
8.   Zoeteman, B.C.J.; Piet, G.J.   Drinkwater is nog
geen water drinken. H_2O 1973, 6, (7), 174.
9.   Amoore, J.E.; Forrester, L.J.; Pelosi, P.
Specific anosmia to isobutyraldehyde: the
malty primary odor.   Chem. Senses and Flavor
1976, 2, 17-25.
10.   Harper, R.; Bate-Smith, E.C.; Land, D.G.;
Griffiths, N.M.   A glossary of odour stimuli
and their qualities.   Perfum. Essent. Oil
Rec. 1968, 59, 22-37.
11.   Harper, R.; Land, D.G.; Griffiths, N.M. Bate-
Smith, E.C.   Odour qualities: a glossary of
usage.   Br. J. Psychol. 1968, 59, 231-252.
12.   Land, D.G.   Hedonic response and perceived
characteristics of odours in man.   In"Preference
Behaviour and Chemoreception" (Kroeze, J.H.A.,
Ed)   Information Retrieval Ltd, London. 1979,
93-106.
13.   Pangborn, R.M.   Individuality in responses to
sensory stimuli.   In "Criteria of Food Accept-

ance" (Solms,J.; Hall, R.L. Eds). Forster
Verlag A.G. Zurich, 1981, 177-219.

14.   Sontag, A.M. Comparison of sensory methods:
discrimination, intensity and hedonic responses in four modalities. M.S. Thesis, Univ.
of California, 1978.

15.   Land, D.G.; Piggott, J.R. Criteria for identifying stimuli with diverse hedonic responses.
In "Olfaction and Taste VII" (van der Starre,
H. Ed). Information Retrieval Ltd, London,
1980, 389-392.

16.   Cabanac, M. Physiological role of pleasure.
Science 1971, 173, 1103-1107.

17.   Hawthorn, J. Pharmacologically-active substances in food. *In* "Criteria of Food Acceptance" (Solms, J.; Hall, R.L. Eds) Forster
Verlag A.G., Zurich, 1981, 370-378.

18.   Rozin, P.; Fallon, A.E. The acquisition of
likes and dislikes for foods. *In* "Criteria
of Food Acceptance" (Solms, J.; Hall, R.L.
Eds). Forster Verlag A.G., Zurich, 1981,
35-48.

Chapter 1.2

Integrating needs – from grower to consumer

T.R. Gormley
The Agricultural Institute, Kinsealy Research Centre, Malahide Road, Dublin 5, Ireland

SUMMARY

In the 1980s, growers require higher crop yields for
economic reasons while consumers demand value for
money and greater variety in their foods. Satisfying
these demands can cause problems throughout the food
chain.

Fruit and vegetable processors are seeking
energy conservation through reduced or avoidance of
blanching, higher frozen storage temperatures and
the use of processing techniques such as irradiation
or gas packaging; these factors may influence sensory
quality of the product.

Consumer demand for fast foods, convenience
foods, and new products has resulted largely from
the ingenuity of the food industry in making such
products available coupled with aggressive marketing
and good advertising.

INTRODUCTION

The grower does not have direct access to the
consumer, except in the case of pick-your-own, or
farm shop outlets, and so his produce must pass
through a "middle-man" to the consumer. The term
"middle-man" as used here refers to anyone in the

food chain between the grower and the consumer, i.e.
wholesalers, processors, millers, bakers, cold
storage companies, retailers, caterers and others.
Whatever the route, the grower, the "middle-man" and
the consumer have ever-changing needs and requirements which must be integrated for better overall
efficiency and for the benefit of all.

In this paper only the needs and requirements
of growers, "middle-men" and consumers that relate
directly to, or impinge upon, the sensory quality of
the product will be considered; and discussion is
limited to foods of plant origin.

Sensory quality of food is often illustrated in
circular form [1] to accommodate the necessary overlap between the three dimensions of sensory quality
i.e. appearance, flavour and texture. Appearance
can be subdivided into shape, size, defects,
viscosity, colour and gloss; texture, into hand and
mouth feel; and flavour, into taste and aroma.

NEEDS OF THE GROWER

The grower's main requirement is high yield with
accompanying good quality [2]. If selling directly
to a processor or retailer, he must have a contract;
if selling fresh produce, he must have a good
produce market and/or wholesaler. Achieving these
criteria should mean good returns for the grower.
The pick-your-own concept is becoming more widespread
especially for strawberries and other fruits, and
this usually ensures excellent integration between
grower and consumer needs.

NEEDS OF THE "MIDDLE-MEN"

Volume and continuity of supply of produce/products
together with acceptable quality are essential
elements in the profitable running of a food
processing or retailing operation. Other
considerations of the "middle-men" include energy
saving during processing, transporting and storage
of food and its implications for the sensory quality
of the product. He should also have a capability
for process and product modification and for market
appraisal. A range of produce/product types is
essential to success.

The quality requirement for fruit and vegetables

depends on circumstances; for example, a processor freezing peas requires a lower tenderometer reading than a canner; processors require medium-sized red-fleshed strawberries whereas the fresh market does not; consumers in some countries demand green apples, produce markets and wholesalers usually want small white mushrooms which are tight - while flour millers require wheat with a higher protein content than do animal feed compounders.

NEEDS OF THE CONSUMER

Primarily, the consumer requires value for money, with factors such as range-of-choice, product identity, good grading and presentation also being important. The term quality always has a 'sense of value' about it.

In fresh produce, there is flexibility between price and level of quality as far as the consumer is concerned; for example, small apples with blemishes may be acceptable to the consumer if they are sold at a low price, but the same consumer may also be prepared to pay a premium for apples of high quality There is less price/quality flexibility in processed products, presumably because there is a narrower range in quality compared to fresh products. In addition, many processed foods cannot be seen until the pack is opened and most consumers have 'fairly strict quality ideas' as to what they expect. However, there is still some price/quality flexibility, especially in the "own-brand" area, jams (variable fruit content), and in the composition of frozen mixed vegetables, e.g. the relative proportions of peas/carrots/sweet corn. Sometimes there is no price/quality flexibility, for instance, the consumer will not purchase stale bread or sloughed bottled carrots whatever the price.

INTEGRATION NEEDS FROM GROWER TO CONSUMER

Integration of needs can only be brought about through good communication between those in the chain. Obviously, R and D, effective trouble shoot-ing, and marketing capability, are also important. The role of quality assurance is of paramount importance. In the past, quality control has been thought of as a strictly in-factory situation; however, the much broader concept of quality assurance could span the whole food chain and has

application right back to research level [3], for
example, the plant breeder must ensure that the high
yielding fruit cultivar being selected will also
give fruit with good sensory quality. If quality
assurance principles are applied throughout the
whole food chain then the dual requirements of high
yield - whether during production or processing - and
good sensory quality can be achieved.

   Some examples of integration, or the lack of it,
between growers, middle-men and consumers are outlined below with reference to specific crops.

Peas

This is a crop where good integration of needs has
been possible. Level of quality and payment is based
on tenderometer readings and this procedure is well
accepted by growers. Both the growers and processor
have requirements in terms of yield and the rate of
maturation of different pea cultivars [4, 5] which
are critically important in relation to the textural
properties of the product. The needs of the
consumer are also well catered for as most consumers
know what to expect in terms of quality in frozen,
canned or dehydrated peas and the processor normally
supplies them with this level of quality.

Mushrooms

There is often conflict between the grower and
processor as the premium price is for small canned
mushrooms which means a low yield and more expensive
picking costs for the grower. Large mushrooms are
normally canned as 'stems and pieces' [6] and command
a poor price. It has been shown [7] that harvesting
mushrooms as buttons gave a yield of $7 \cdot 4$ kg/m^2
compared with $9 \cdot 3$ kg/m^2 at the medium stage (partially
stretched veil) and $9 \cdot 7$ kg/m^2 at the near-mature
stage (tightly stretched veil). It is frequently
felt that price compensation for the low yield is
insufficient.

   Processors require less shrinkage in canned
mushrooms; likewise in blanched frozen mushrooms.
This must be achieved while preserving good sensory
quality in the product. Vacuum soaking [8] or the
use of the so called 3S process, i.e. soak/store/soak
[9], reduces shrinkage but recent research at
Kinsealy Research Centre suggests that the 3S process

adversely affects flavour and texture in canned mushrooms (Table 1). Most canned mushrooms are purchased by caterers who demand a bright white/cream coloured product with a tight size grade specification.

Table 1 – Effect of 3S process[1] on the flavour texture of canned mushrooms.

Storage (2°C) in 3S process (h)	Total shrinkage[2] (%)	Firmness[3] (kg)	Flavour
0	39	79	1st
24	31	83	2nd
48	26	82	3rd
72	24	90	4th

[1] Soak/store/soak prior to blanching.
[2] Based on difference between fresh weight and drained weight.
[3] Shear press, 100 g sample.

The sale of unprocessed mushrooms is normally through a produce market and/or agent. A premium is paid for buttons and for whiteness, although it has been shown that more mature mushrooms have a better flavour [10]. Most consumers don't demand small white button mushrooms; these requirements are imposed at the market/wholesaler level presumably because white button mushrooms have a longer shelf-life and therefore allow greater flexibility during distribution and retailing. Whiteness and weight retention are of paramount importance and this has necessitated detailed studies on packaging and chilling [11].

In general, the integration of needs from grower to consumer is good in the case of fresh mushrooms. With processed mushrooms, yield/maturity issues cause most conflict.

Strawberries

The needs of growers and consumers are well integrated in that cultivars for the fresh market such as Cambridge Favourite give high yields of well-flavoured fruit with a good shelf-life. Good

handling and chilling procedures are essential in
order to maintain sensory quality [12]. The practice
of pick-your-own encourages good relations between
grower and consumer.

There are increasing demands for red-fleshed
strawberries by processors. However, high yielding
cultivars/selections often have a poor flesh colour;
a correlation coefficient of -0·59 between yield and
red flesh has been found for 21 cultivars/selections
grown in Ireland [13]. However, breeding programmes
have been reasonably successful; for example, a
selection named Clonderg (Cambridge Vigour x Senga
Sengana) yielded 20·7 tonnes/ha in 1980 [14] and
had a much darker red flesh (Hunter L=44) than
Cambridge Favourite fruit (L=56).

Apples

A major conflict exists between growers, the wholesalers and consumers in Ireland in relation to
Golden Delicious (GD). This cultivar represents
about 60% of apple production in Ireland. The Irish
consumer prefers green apples of uniform size with a
good skin finish and this requirement is ideally
fulfilled by French GD [15]. The consumer is also
prepared to pay more for the French fruit on a kg
basis [15, 16]. Imports of French apples have
increased by 530% during 1970-80 while home
production has fallen by 51%. Evaluation of 20
cultivars/selections [17] has shown no 'ready'
alternative to GD in terms of yield.

Green Irish-grown GD are inferior both in flavour
and appearance to green French-grown GD apples;
however, mature Irish GD apples (green/yellow to
yellow skin) are superior in flavour and texture to
the green French fruit [15] but the Irish consumer
associates the yellow skin with over-ripeness.
Wholesalers prefer to handle French apples because
of the ready supply of fruit of uniform quality and
the French apples are sold as 'firm price sales'
while Irish fruit is sold on a commission basis [18].

A similar situation prevails in Belgium where
home-grown GD apples sell for a much lower price than
those imported from France or South Africa [19]. In
the UK, the position is different because high
quality Cox is an alternative to GD but despite this
French GD apples have made major inroads on the UK

market with over 200 000 tonnes being imported in
1980. The Kingdom Pack Scheme [20], utilising high
quality Cox was introduced in 1980 to counteract
this situation. The Scheme has made good progress
to date [21].

The GD issue illustrates the importance of
marketing in integrating the needs of growers, wholesalers and consumers. French public relations high-
lighting the sensory properties of French GD apples
('crisp, crunchy, etc.') had conditioned the sensory
expectations of consumers and has given the French
product a strong image in sensory terms. The sensory
quality of GD apples is also affected by the
intensity of production and this will be discussed
below.

Tomatoes

Glasshouse growers want high yields while consumers
demand firmness, flavour and value for money in fresh
market tomatoes. There have been complaints
recently from the market place in The Netherlands,
the UK and in Ireland about bruising and premature
softening of tomato fruit, especially during periods
of warm weather. These complaints started with the
introduction of the cultivar Sonato. Tests have
shown [22] that Sonato fruit from trial plots was
not softer than other cultivars either at the time of
picking or after a period of storage, and it is
unlikely that the problem was nutritional as there
was no difference in mineral composition between
bruised and unbruised fruit [23]. However, work in
The Netherlands which suggested a fruit handling
problem [24], was confirmed by tests at Kinsealy
Research Centre [23]. These showed that the
'bumping' of fruit during normal grading or the
position of the fruit in a bulk-bin had a significant
effect on the number of fruit that were cracked or
mouldy (Table 2). The effect of dropping tomatoes
on the incidence of bruising is shown in Table 3;
every effort should be made, therefore, to minimise
fruit falling during picking, grading and packing,
and it helps to line picking trays and bulk-bins
with foam rubber. Improved handling, therefore, is
of special importance in relation to the sensory
quality of tomato fruit.

Table 2 — Effects of handling on the development of cracks/moulds in tomato fruit.

Handling treatment	% Cracked/mouldy fruit after 14days at 15-17°C
Picked into tray (not graded)	3
Graded and packed	10
Fruit from top of bulk-bin	3
Fruit from bottom of bulk-bin	16

Table 3 — Effects of dropping on the development of bruising in tomatoes

Height dropped (cm)	% Fruit bruised 4 h aftor dropping
0	3
50	43
100	70

Potatoes

Irish potato grading standards are the most liberal in the EEC and this has resulted in consumer complaints about potato quality to the disadvantage of potato industry in Ireland. Studies for the National Prices Commission [25] have confirmed that potato quality is poor and that grading standards are not being enforced rigidly. The position in Britain is better with a controlled market situation since 1955; a compulsory grading system for ware potatoes also operates in Germany and in The Netherlands [25]. This results in good quality ware potatoes and gives a stable basis on which to build a processing industry. A survey [26] was carried out in the UK in 1972/73 to investigate consumer buying behaviour and attitudes towards potatoes. It was found that attitudes were very favourable; size, shape and quality were noticed by consumers as the year progressed and there seemed to be certain key appearance criteria that consumers monitor each time they buy. This type of consumer information enables wholesalers and growers to meet consumer requirements.

Other fruits and vegetables

Most consumers have fairly fixed ideas, and know what
to expect, in terms of sensory quality of a given
processed fruit or vegetable. In fresh fruit and
vegetables, improved conditions for storing produce
at wholesale and retail level and also during
transit [27] is a general requirement for maintaining good sensory quality as is date stamping of
certain products. The home production of high
quality fruit and vegetables, out of season, is also
a major requirement in order to compete with imports.

Breadmaking wheat

Most consumers in Ireland and the UK demand white
bread with a soft crumb and a reasonably long shelf-
life. This places restrictions on the miller/baker
in terms of the quality of the wheat used to produce
this product. In Ireland, millers use a grist with
11·5% protein; this is achieved by blending high
protein containing Canadian wheat with native wheat
(usually spring sown) and with wheats imported from
other countries.

However, due to poor harvesting conditions for
spring wheat in 1980 and the higher yields obtainable
with winter wheat (7·5-8·8 tonnes/ha compared to
5-6·3 tonnes/ha for spring wheat) there was a major
swing to growing winter wheat in 1981 and again in
1982 (Table 4). Because of the lower protein content
of winter wheat [28], the Irish flour millers
introduced a minimum purchasing standard of 9·5%
protein (at 15% moisture) in 1981 with a bonus for
> 10·5% protein and an extra supplement for spring
wheat. The protein standard caused a considerable
proportion of the winter wheat submitted for milling
to be rejected. The farmers claim that the supplement for growing spring wheat is too low and that it
is more profitable to grow winter wheat for animal
feed instead of for bread. This example illustrates
how a conflict of needs between farmers and processors
can suddenly arise.

Table 4 — Acreage (ha) under wheat in Ireland 1979/82.

	Winter-sown	Spring-sown
1979	12 146	36 721
1980	12 551	34 777
1981	30 364	8 097
1982	48 583	not available

INTENSIVE PRODUCTION

There is much criticism by consumers of lack of flavour in intensively-grown produce and also an increasing awareness of the use of fertilisers, pesticides and other chemicals.

Tests on five samples of intensively-grown GD apples, have shown negative correlations ranging from -0·72 to -0·97 between taste panel response and yield [29]; in another experiment, involving different orchard locations similar results were found [30]. In the intensive cultivation of winter wheat, a negative correlation has been obtained between yield and gluten quality [31]. These data suggest that it is difficult to combine high yield with top sensory quality.

The sensory quality of intensively produced foods has also been of concern to the EEC. Results from an EEC funded (SCAR Agro-Food) project at Kinsealy Research Centre in 1981 showed that while tomato fruit colour and firmness were satisfactory, the values for purée conductivity, and to a lesser extent soluble solids and acidity, in the fruit were low. In general, fruit flavour was not highly rated by taste panelists.

Tomatoes produced under different growing systems (peat, soil and nutrient film technique) and from the different sources (Kinsealy Research Centre, commercial growers and Dublin market) were similar in composition. No cultivar, growing system or treatment gave fruit of outstanding compositional quality during the season. This result is to be expected as it is unlikely that the increase in yield of glasshouse tomatoes over the last decade, from about 190 to 250 tonnes/ha, took place without loss of sensory quality. It is important to note that the cultivar Ailsa Craig, of reputed good flavour, did not perform any better in these tests than the modern cultivars in terms of fruit composition and flavour; in fact, it was often inferior. Tomato fruit composition values declined in these experiments as the growing season progressed (Table 5); this is a matter of concern and will be studied further.

Table 5 — Change in tomato fruit composition[1] over the growing season.

Time of season	Soluble solids %	Titratable acidity[2]	Conductivity[3] (μmhos)
May	4·4	8·2	701
July	4·2	7·9	653
October	4·3	7·0	630

[1] 60 samples from Dublin market were tested each month.
[2] mequiv./100 g tomato purée.
[3] Based on dilution of 1 part purée + 9 parts distilled water (w/w).

ORGANIC AGRICULTURE

There has been much controversy about the sensory quality and nutritive value of foods grown using organic fertilisers. It is claimed [32] that organic foods are considered safe and good by millions of Americans while regular foods have become suspect due to possible "contamination" with chemicals.

Retail sales of organic foods have risen in the US from about $ 500 million in 1972 to a predicted $ 3 billion in 1980 [33]; a recent study in the USA shows that 'back to nature' farming makes sense [34] and that organically grown products are being increasingly sought by consumers. In the UK, there has also been a steady increase both in demand, and in the number of "organic" growers - at present though supply is far short of demand [35]. It seems, therefore, that more consumers will demand organic foods since they consider them (rightly or wrongly) safer, more nutritious and of higher sensory quality; growers must respond to this need.

ENERGY SAVING AND SENSORY QUALITY OF FOOD

Energy saving is essential throughout the food chain
particularly for the processor and those involved
in the long-term storage of frozen products. Some
of the steps being taken to reduce energy costs (see
below) could influence the sensory quality of the
product with subsequent consumer reaction.

Reduced or zero blanching

Until recently all vegetables and many fruits were
blanched on a routine basis prior to processing [36].
However, rising energy costs have forced a
reappraisal of this practice and an investigation
into the energy requirements of different blanching
techniques. A meeting held in Paris in 1981 under
the auspices of the EEC COST 91 programme discussed
the effect of thermal processing on the quality and
nutritive value of food. Papers were presented on
the physical and chemical changes during freezer
storage of non-blanched vegetables and fruits, on
thermal requirements for blanching fruits and
vegetables to be frozen, and on blanching methods
in relation to equipment, BOD status and energy.
It was suggested that Bell peppers, cucumbers, green
leeks, some herbs, onions, swedes and artichokes
do not require blanching prior to freezing. Research
at Long Ashton Research Station has shown that in the
domestic situation unblanched frozen carrots, spinach
and peas can be stored for 12 months without
significant loss of quality.

There is a major requirement for low energy
consuming alternatives to blanching such as the use
of gases like carbon monoxide [37] and combinations
of non-blanching/partial blanching with vacuum
packing of the product.

Storage temperatures for frozen foods

Pressure for higher storage temperatures for frozen
foods is coming from processors, commercial cold
storage companies, retailers and those involved in
transporting frozen foods; this could have serious
implications for the sensory quality of the product
especially if combined with non-blanching. Such a
change in practice would demand more intensive time/
temperature/tolerance studies on frozen foods. This
was discussed at a meeting held in Karlsruhe in 1981
under the auspices of the COST 91 programme.

Alternative processing methods

The term 'alternative' is used in a broad sense to describe processes other than the straightforward thermal food processing techniques.

There is renewed interest in food irradiation which it is claimed requires far less energy and is 70-80 % less costly than canning or freezing [38]. Recent advances in the irradiation process have meant that spoilage bacteria are killed without producing any major changes in sensory or nutritional quality [38]. However, approval of the Federal Drugs Administration on irradiated foods in the USA will not produce an overnight takeover of the frozen and canned food markets by irradiated foods as consumer resistance is likely to be great. However, informative marketing coupled with 'product value for money on the shelf' may quickly dispel the fears of most consumers.

Processes employing modified atmospheres coupled to correct packaging such as 'Gaspak' [37] may also give significant energy saving compared with conventional processing techniques while still maintaining high sensory quality in the product.

FAST FOODS, CONVENIENCE FOODS AND NEW PRODUCTS

The demand by consumers and caterers for fast foods, convenience foods and new products has increased dramatically in recent years, and the survival of some food processors has depended on their ability to meet this need [39]. Pressure has also been created through good advertising and marketing by the food industry. The McDonald hamburger story is a prime example where a combination of good marketing together with a consistent sensory quality has resulted in satisfied consumers, especially among the younger generation.

Much progress, largely due to fast foods and convenience foods, has been made in the area of institutional catering in recent years [40]. Large scale institutional catering has always had problems of consumer satisfaction but modern catering systems coupled with good integration between caterers and food processors has raised the sensory quality of these products and has given the consumer variety and good portion sizes.

Convenience foods now form a major part of food
consumed in most homes as exemplified by breakfast
cereals, bread mixes, oven ready chips, instant
coffee, canned rice, frozen and canned sauces, frozen
pizzas and many other items.

A product development programme is also an
essential dimension for most food processors and is
usually linked to the areas of fast and convenience
foods. Consumer demand for variety in foods has
stimulated new products but development can only
proceed in association with careful market intell-
igence, embracing consumer attitudes, and also their
requirements in terms of the sensory quality of the
product. Modern technology has generated many new
and exciting products and product concepts none more
so than in the area of extrusion cooking [41].

MARKETING, CO-OPERATIVES AND PICK-YOUR-OWN

Good marketing is essential in integrating needs
from grower to consumer. However, consistent quality
in the product together with continuity of supply are
also essential if good sales are to be realised.
Grower co-operatives, sometimes with a facility for
processing, have done much to integrate grower-
processor activities.

Pick-your-own marketing of fruit and vegetables
[42] and farm shop operations help to integrate grower
and consumer needs. Perishable produce such as soft
fruit and green broccoli are especially suited to
pick-your-own operations as the grower does not have
the worry of packing and transporting a short-shelf
life product to the market; the consumer in turn
obtains produce of high sensory quality.

CONCLUSIONS

Integrating needs from grower to consumer is a complex
problem in view of the many factors which influence
the production, processing, distribution and marketing
of food. Even when all seems well a food may fail at
point of sale because the consumer may not purchase
it for a variety of unforeseen reasons.

REFERENCES

1. Kramer, A.   An analytical and integrative approach
     to sensory evaluation of foods.   J. Sci. Fd
     Agric. 1973, 24, 1407-1418.

2. Gormley, T.R.; McKenna, B.; Maguire, A.   Research
     and development requirements in an expanded
     fruit and vegetable processing industry.
     Proc. NBST Seminar on Technology for the
     Food Industry, Wexford, 1980, 105-111.

3. Gormley, T.R.   Food quality assurance at research
     level. Fm and Fd Res. 1977, 3, 67-69.

4. Murphy, R.F.   Screening pea cultivars for dehy-
     dration. Ir. J.agric. Res. 1973, 12, 293-
     325.

5. Murphy, R.F.   Plant population requirements of
     green peas. Ir. J.agric. Res. 1975, 14,
     357-368.

6. Gormley, T.R.; MacCanna, C.   Canning tests on
     mushroom strains. Ir. J.Fd Sci. Technol.
     1980, 4, 57-64.

7. Kneebone, L.R.; Mason, E.C.   Mushroom yields as
     influenced by degree of maturity at time of
     harvest. Mushroom Sci. V, 1962, 448-453.

8. McArdle, F.J.; Kuhn, G.D.; Beelman, R.B.
     Influence of vacuum soaking on yield and
     quality of canned mushrooms. J. Fd Sci.
     1974, 39, 1026-1028.

9. Beelman, R.B.; McArdle, F.J.   Influence of post
     harvest storage temperatures and soaking on
     yield and quality of canned mushrooms. J.Fd
     Sci. 1975, 40, 669-671.

10. Gormley, T.R.   Flavour of mushrooms. Horticulture
     Research Report, An Foras Taluntais, Dublin,
     1976, 106.

11. Gormley, T.R.   Chill storage of mushrooms. J.Sci.
     Fd Agric. 1975, 26, 401-411.

12. Kenny, T.A.   Studies on precooling of soft fruit.
     1. Strawberries. Ir. J.Fd Sci.Technol. 1979,
     3, 19-31.

13. MacLachlan, J.B.; Gormley, T.R.   Field and
    quality assessment of strawberry cultivars.
    J.Sci.Fd Agric. 1974, 25, 165-177.

14. MacLachlan, J.B.   Strawberry breeding.   Proc.
    Seminar for Instructors in Horticulture,
    An Foras Taluntais, Dublin, 1981, 105-107.

15. Gormley, T.R.; Egan, J.P.   Comparison of the
    quality of Irish and French grown Golden
    Delicious apples. Ir. J.Fd Sci.Technol. 1977,
    1, 23-32.

16. Cowan, C.   Apple prices at Dublin retail outlets.
    Fm and Fd Res. 1974, 5, 47-48.

17. Gormley, T.R.; O'Kennedy, N.D.   Quality evaluation
    of fruit of a range of apple cultivars/clones
    grown in Ireland.   Ir. J.Fd Sci.Technol.
    1980, 4, 133-142.

18. Bowbrick, P.   Commission sales or firm price
    sales - a conflict of interest.   Ir. J.agric.
    Econ. Rur.Sociol. 1974-75, 5, 229-258.

19. Monin, A.   Relationship between quality and price
    of Golden Delicious apples.   Acta Hort. 1974,
    40, 467-469.

20. Anon.   Kingdom pack all set for October 6 start.
    Grower 1980, 94, 2-3.

21. Neuteboom, D.   English apples: the way ahead.
    Grower, 1981, 95, 6-7.

22. Gormley, T.R.; Egan, S.   Firmness and colour of
    the fruit of some tomato fruit cultivars
    from various sources during storage.   J.
    Sci. Fd Agric. 1978, 29, 534-538.

23. Egan, S.   Handling of tomato fruit - an Irish/
    Dutch experience.   Fm and Fd Res. 1982,
    In press.

24. Buitelaar, K.   Zorg rond bewaarkwaliteit wordt-
    beloond.   Tuinderij 1977, 17, 64-67.

25. Cowan, C.A.; McStay, T.P.   Potato grading stan-
    dards in three European countries.   National
    Prices Commission,Dublin, 1977, Report No.62,
    21-53.

26. Potatoes - Consumer buying behaviour and
    attitudes during 1972-73. A report of a
    survey conducted for the Potato Marketing
    Board (UK) by Research Bureau Limited, 1974,
    pp. 47.

27. Goldenberg, N. Post-harvest handling of fresh
    fruit and vegetables. South African Fd Rev.
    1975, 2, 93-105.

28. Dwyer, E.; Walshe, T.; Gormley, T.R. Wheat
    quality 1. Mean values for wheat quality
    parameters 1974-1980. Fm and Fd Res. 1981,
    12, 17-19.

29. Gormley, R.; Robinson, D.; O'Kennedy, N. The
    effects of soil management systems on the
    chemical composition and quality of apples
    1. Golden Delicious apples. J. Sci.Fd
    Agric. 1973, 24, 227-239.

30. Gormley, T.R.; Harrington, D.; McDonnell, P.F.
    Quality of Golden Delicious apples grown in
    seven different orchard locations. Ir. J.
    Fd. Sci.Technol. 1981, 5, 165-169.

31. Primost, E. Effects of intensive cultivation on
    yield and quality of winter wheat. Muhle +
    Mischfuttertechnik. 1980, 117, 66-68.

32. Fryer, L.; Simmons, D. "Earth Foods", Follet
    Publishing Company, Chicago, 1st edn, 1972,
    pp.180.

33. Knorr, D. Quality of ecologically grown fruit.
    Lebensm.-Wiss.u.-Technol. 1979, 12, 350-356.

34. Anon. US study shows that 'back to nature'
    farming makes sense. New Sci. 1981. 89,740.

35. Larkcom, J. Marketing organic produce. Hort.
    Ind. 1980, April, 22-23.

36. Foley, J.; Buckley, J. Pasteurisation and therm-
    isation of milk and blanching of fruit and
    vegetables. In "Food Quality and Nutrition
    Research, Priorities for Thermal Processing"
    (Downey, W.K. Ed.), Applied Science
    Publishers, 1977, 191-216.

37. Kramer, A. Qualities we aim to maintain. In
    "Quality in Stored and Processed Vegetables
    and Fruit"(Goodenough, P.W.; Atkin, R.K.
    Eds), Academic Press, 1981, 1-13.

38. Unger, H.G. Return to irradiation? Fd
    Processing Ind. 1981, November, 17.

39. Mills, J. Thoughts on fast food innovation from
    the manufacturers viewpoint. Quick Frozen
    Foods International 1980, 21, 156-157.

40. O'Connor, J.; Youngs, A. Food storage equipment
    and methods in catering. Proc. IFST, 1978,
    11, 162-173.

41. Olkku, J. Extrusion processing - a study in
    basic phenomena and application of systems
    analysis. In "Developments in Food
    Preservation - 1" (Thorne, S. Ed.), Applied
    Science Publishers, 1981, 177-214.

42. Bowbrick, P.; Twohig, D. Pick-Your-Own Fruit
    Marketing, An Foras Taluntais, Dublin, 1977,
    pp. 27.

Chapter 1.3

Industrial approaches to defining quality

J.L. Sidel, H. Stone and J. Bloomquist
Tragon Corporation, Palo Alto, California, USA

SUMMARY

Traditionally the food and beverage industry has defined product quality primarily in terms of degree of excellence and deviation from a standard. As the industry evolved from one of processing simple commodities and agricultural products to one of manufacturing complex finished goods, the traditional definition and methods for measuring quality required modification.

Sensory acceptability, consumer testing, and complex statistical procedures for relating product attributes to consumer preferences represent important changes to the traditional approaches for defining and identifying desirable product attributes. Approaches to monitoring and maintaining the sensory quality of existing products also have been modified to be more consistent with the current methods used to define product quality.

In the final analysis, industrial approaches to defining and maintaining quality now treat quality more in terms of the operations related to or used to measure consumer acceptance rather than those related to expert opinion.

INTRODUCTION

The food industry recognises the potential marketing
and sales benefits from claims about product quality.
Manufacturers readily advertise and promote attributes of their products which, in their opinion, make
those products superior in quality. However, all
too frequently there is a large discrepancy between
what the manufacturer and consumer consider to be a
quality product. If a manufacturer is convinced
that a product of superior quality is being provided,
and the consumer either does not perceive that
quality or does not respond to it as anticipated,
that manufacturer may have a serious problem surviv-
ing in the marketplace. Therefore, it is critical
that manufacturers recognise, understand, and resolve
any discrepancies between their concept of quality
and the consumer's response to their products.

Resolution of this discrepancy necessitates
an assessment of the term "quality" as it is now
used in the food industry, and consideration of the
problems associated with those uses. Currently,
quality as used in the food industry has multiple
meanings and uses. It is used to refer to 1) a
degree of excellence, 2) a deviation from a standard,
or 3) as a synonym for the terms "attribute" or
"characteristic".

In the discussion that follows, particular
emphasis is given to the first two issues: measuring degree of excellence, and deviation from a
standard. The former is primarily consumer-related,
while the latter is more typically a trained panel
responsibility. In our experience these two issues
have had the greatest impact on sensory evaluation
and are important in the development and formulation
of those products that best meet consumer expectations.

DEGREE OF EXCELLENCE

The most frequent use of "sensory quality" is in the
context of degree of excellence. Adjectives such as
"excellent" or "poor" often are used in conjuction
with "quality" to express the notion of different
levels of quality [1].

The early literature related to the sensory
evaluation of food products is devoted primarily to

describing procedures for establishing and grading
product quality in terms of degree of excellence.
Examples of such assessments can be found for numerous products, including dairy products [2], fermented beverages [3], fruit [4] and edible oil [5].
Technical associations and trade groups have also
been actively involved in the establishment of procedures for measuring product quality. Association-
approved grading systems have been developed and
used for many years by the American Dairy Association, the American Oil Chemists Society, and others.
Typically a summary grade or score is assigned to
the product. That grade may be the result of scoring
a single scale (e.g., edible oil) or it may be a
summation of individual attribute scores (e.g., wine
and most dairy products). In either situation the
panelist is trained to associate specific product
characteristics with a specific rating or score.

In the early industrialization of the food
industry and as part of an overall need to provide
a common basis for comparison of raw materials and
finished products, such industry-wide efforts represented a logical and needed resource. However,
the process of grading quality has remained essentially unchanged while numerous improvements have
occurred in measuring the sensory properties of
products and the consumer's reactions to those properties. Therefore, a problem for sensory evaluation in the industrial setting is the difficulty
associated with measuring quality according to
"traditional" approaches. In a recent publication
[6] dealing with the operational aspects of quality
grading systems, the inherent errors in scaling,
data handling, and subject selection associated with
these types of quality tests are described. Criticisms of quality evaluation practices are found in
the sensory evaluation literature published from
1949 [7] to the present [8] [9]. These researchers
have been very critical of adding and averaging of
scores from different descriptive scales to arrive
at a single, total, quality score for a product.
They are also critical of composite scales which use
different descriptive terms along a single continuum
to measure product quality.

Our present emphasis is somewhat different.
It is concerned with the problems and issues created
by not properly distinguishing between sensory
quality and sensory acceptance. Quality as degree
of excellence, implies an objective, absolute,

context-free set of criteria for establishing and
judging excellence. Acceptance implies none of these.
It is subjective, variable, and context-determined.
If the relationship between quality and acceptance
was always constant one could be used to predict
the other, and the difference between the two would
be trivial. What keeps this from being a trivial
matter is the evidence to the contrary, with consequences which can be costly to the food manufacturer.
McBride [10], for example, found "no correlation
between consumer preference and dairy graders'
scores".

        In the early development of sensory evaluation
as a scientific discipline, quality as a degree of
excellence, and quality grading as a measure of that
excellence, offered a systematic, less private (i.e.,
more externalized) and "scientific" approach to
product assessment. Products usually were basic
agricultural commodities; e.g., canned fruits and
vegetables, beer and wine, etc. It was reasonable
to assume that impurities, bruises, etc. which low-
ered product quality also would lower product acceptance. Technical experts were used to establish the
sensory profile for products and then develop an
evaluation system for distinguishing between products
of different quality. However, as the end product
of the food industry became more complex, through a
greater degree of processing and formulation, prediction of comsumer acceptance has become more a
matter of consumer research than one of technical
expertise. Sensory evaluation panels and consumer
research studies are increasingly replacing the
expert in establishing the appropriate sensory
profile for products. This development is in part a
reaction to the large potential difference between
consumer opinion and expert opinion regarding
sensory quality.

        An example of this is the brewmaster brewing a
beer using, in his judgement, the best quality
ingredients. While the finished product may have
strong appeal to a specific market segment (especially brewmasters), this segment may be too small
to support the brand and from a marketing point of
view, the product would be considered as having poor
sensory quality. This does not mean that one or the
other view is at fault; however, as emphasis is
placed on reactions in the marketplace, sensory
quality becomes more synonymous with sensory accept-

ance and the impact of the expert opinion and of quality grading systems is lessened.

By moving away from a technical determination of sensory quality one approaches a more consumer-related measure, one which may change with shifts in consumer behaviour but still one that can be measured. Preliminary studies by Schutz et al [11] suggested it was possible to develop models to predict product acceptance based on specific sensory properties.

Schutz's approach has been further developed by providing precise product sensory descriptions through the use of Quantitative Descriptive Analysis - QDA [12] [13] [14] [15]. This approach, referred to as Product Optimization (PROP), involves evaluation of a large array of products (as many as 25 or more). The evaluation includes sensory, chemical and physical analyses. The final sensory input is consumer acceptance rating (e.g., hedonic scale data) of the test products. Factor analysis, multiple correlation and regression analyses are then used to determine the contribution of the perceived sensory attributes to the consumer acceptance ratings. Optimal product acceptance also is predicted. The prediction is based on optimal combinations of the sensory and/or instrumentally measured attributes determined from statistical analysis of the data. Once the equation for optimization has been derived it can be used to predict consumer acceptance ratings for variations of the product as a result of ingredient, formulation, or process changes. Using these data eliminates the need for trained panelists to directly assess product acceptance, either in deriving the initial prediction equation or evaluating reformulated product.

Test systems such as the one described above focus on sensory acceptance without reference to sensory quality. The discrepancy between sensory acceptance by consumers and sensory quality judgements (degree of excellence) by experts, should it arise, becomes less important as manufacturers can more accurately anticipate how acceptance will be influenced by various ingredient, formulation, and process combinations.

We anticipate that the food industry will come to rely more on consumer testing and less on expert

opinion in establishing the sensory target for
products. As this occurs the concept of excellence
or degree of excellence will become more consistent
with consumer acceptance judgements.

DEVIATION FROM A STANDARD

In the previous section we discussed sensory quality
as it is used in the development or selection of a
product for use as a production target or reference
standard. Now we discuss sensory quality as it is
used in activities related to monitoring and maintaining a target product (often referred to as monitoring and maintaining product quality). Responsibility for these activities usually is that of
quality assurance (QA) and quality control (QC)
groups.

One important task of QA is to prepare written
specifications identifying, in quantitative terms if
possible, the sensory description for ingredients
and the finished product. In some companies QA will
also test products and monitor plant compliance with
prescribed testing procedures.

QC refers to monitoring product quality on a
day-to-day basis, for each production lot in each
plant. Operationally this means maintaining production within specified limits. Establishing these
limits for a product can be as difficult as developing the original target product itself. Essentially
it is a multi-dimensional problem; i.e., one must
take into account the precision and reliability of
both processing and measuring systems, and the
economics of too loose or too narrow limits. Use
of procedures incorporating consumer testing to
establish a target is on the increase; however,
their use in establishing QC limits is still novel.
This situation will change as manufacturers make
more use of optimization techniques that relate
specific sensory attribute changes to increases or
decreases in a product's sensory acceptance. Such
precision allows a manufacturer to more accurately
estimate consumer acceptance for production variations from a specified target. It also provides a
better assessment of the risk of selling a product
which does not conform to specification. In the
absence of such precise information (i.e., knowing
how a specific sensory difference will affect acceptance), a manufacturer may focus on minimal deviations

from the reference product. However, the less
deviation allowed, the more costly it is to manufacture (the product), and there is an optimal range
between these two before increased production costs
significantly reduce profits. Optimization procedures are sensory techniques that assist one in
identifying that optimal range.

Once a product standard and its tolerance
limits have been identified the manufacturer's task
is to develop test procedures to monitor production.
In most companies, those test procedures will include
sensory evaluation. Here the object is to maintain
sensory quality rather than develop it. How a
company defines what is meant by "maintaining sensory
quality" will have a direct influence on the methods
or procedures it employs to satisfy that objective.
For example, if a company has defined a single product as its target, and chooses to reject samples that
are discriminably different from that target, the
discrimination test method with a single reference
(e.g., paired comparison, duo-trio, triangle test)
would be an appropriate model. However, using this
approach might be counter-productive; i.e., too
much product is rejected. The alternative accepts
the concept of tolerance limits and views the production target not as a single sample, but rather as
a range of products that can be discriminably different, yet are more similar to one another than they
are different. In this case, a multiple standards
discrimination procedure might be more appropriate.
It allows multiple references and rapid analysis of
data, a critical requirement if the method is to
have application on production lines.

The multiple reference discrimination model
provides the tester with a set of reference samples
representing the range of product difference which
is acceptable. The respondent then samples actual
production samples and judges whether the test
samples are within the limits represented by the
set of reference samples. This may be accomplished
by direct matching with members of the reference set
or by training individuals to recognize samples
exceeding the established tolerance limits even in
the absence of a reference.

The multiple standard discrimination model
described above, with or without a reference available, is a sorting task in which the subject rejects
products exceeding the range represented by those

references.   The procedure may be used on ingredients, products during processing, or finished
product.

The discrimination procedure should be supplemented on a regular basis by descriptive analysis.
However, most quantitative descriptive procedures
are not intended for in-plant use because of the
complexity of the data collection, analysis and
interpretation. Descriptive techniques, e.g., QDA
[13] [14] allow the manufacturer to identify attribute differences between production and reference
samples. They also provide the manufacturer with
a sensory record which can be used to identify and
track subtle product changes which will not be detected with the discrimination model. This does not
mean that one test model is better than the other;
each has its strengths and weaknesses. Used together they provide a useful tool for monitoring and
maintaining sensory quality.

The procedures described above clearly indicate
that defining quality in terms of deviation from a
reference need not imply anything about the inherent
goodness of that reference, beyond its proven acceptability to consumers.

CONCLUSION

The term "Sensory Quality" has multiple meanings and
uses in the food industry. This multiplicity often
results in unclear communication and misdirected
development and testing activity. Evolution of the
food industry from processors of basic commodities
to formulators of complex finished goods is changing
the methods manufacturers use to establish target
products, specify the tolerance limits for those
products, and test to determine whether production
samples comply with those tolerance specifications.
The primary change involves greater reliance on
consumer acceptance and sensory analysis, and the
mathematical models used to relate the one to the
other.

The success of these new approaches will depend
ultimately on their continued refinement in terms of
accuracy and utility. Equally important, is the
requirement that researchers and manufacturers continue to remind themselves of the distinction between
sensory quality and sensory acceptance and recognize
the increasing role the consumer now has in deter-

mining what he likes, will purchase, and will consume.

REFERENCES

1. Ramsbottom, J.M. Freezer storage effect on fresh meat quality. Refrig. Eng. 1947, 53, 19-23.
2. Downs, P.A.; Anderson, E.O.; Babcock, C.T.; Herzer, F.H.; Trout, G.M. Evaluation of collegiate student dairy products judging since World War II. J. Dairy Sci. 1954, 34, 1021-1026.
3. Amerine, M.A.; Roessler, E.B.; Filipello, F. Modern sensory methods of evaluating wine. Hilgardia, 1959, 28, 477-567.
4. Baten, W.D. Organoleptic tests pertaining to apples and pears. 1946, Food Res. 11, 84-94.
5. Mosher, H.A.; Dutton, H.J.; Evens, C.D.; Cowan, J.C. Conducting a taste panel for the evaluation of edible oils. Food Technol. 1950, 4, 105-109.
6. Sidel, J.L.; Stone, H.; Bloomquist, J. Use and misuse of sensory evaluation in research and quality control. J. Dairy Sci. 1981, 64, 2296-2302.
7. Boggs, M.M.; Hanson, H.L. Analysis of foods by sensory difference tests. 1949. Advances in Food Research, 2, 219-258.
8. Pangborn, R.M.; Dunkley, W.L. Laboratory procedures for evaluating the sensory properties of milk. Dairy Sci. Abstracts. 1964, 26, 55-62.
9. O'Mahony, M. Psychophysical aspects of sensory analysis of dairy products: a critique. J. Dairy Sci. 1979, 62, 1954-1962.
10. McBride, R.L. Cheese grading versus consumer acceptability: an inevitable discrepancy. Aust. J. Dairy Technol. 1979, 34, 66-68.
11. Schutz, H.G.; Damrell, J.K.; Locke, B.H. Predicting hedonic ratings of raw carrot texture by sensory analysis. J.Text. Studies, 1972, 3, 227.232.
12. Sidel, J.L.; Stone, H. Principles of sensory evaluation of new foods. Presented at: "New Foods and Ingredients Workshop". Agric. and Food Chem. Div., ACS. San Francisco CA. 1976. Unpublished.

13. Stone, H.; Sidel, J.; Oliver, S.; Woolsey, A.;
    Singleton, R.C. Sensory evaluation by quan-
    titative descriptive analysis. Food Technol.
    1974, 8, 24-34.
14. Stone, H.; Sidel, J.L.; Bloomquist, J. Quanti-
    tative descriptive analysis. Cereal Foods
    World, 1980, 25, 642-644.
15. Stone, H.; Sidel, J.L. Quantitative descriptive
    analysis in optimization of consumer accept-
    tance. Presented at: Eastern Food Science
    and Technology Conference on "Strategies of
    Food Product Development". IFT, Lancaster,
    PA. 1981. Unpublished.

Chapter 1.4

Understanding and interpreting consumer answers in the laboratory

Nicole Daget
Nestle Products Technical Assistance Co. Ltd. Research Department, CH-1814 La Tour-de-Peilz, Switzerland.

SUMMARY

Developing and launching a product is costly and risky. To ensure the maximum chance of success it is therefore necessary to match the product to the consumer's needs and preferences. Such information is obtained from the consumer through the marketing services and is used in the development laboratory to formulate the right product. The pathway by which this information reaches the laboratory is complex and can involve several routes. The communicating language has to be clarified in order to avoid loss of information and bias along the chain.

A good deal can be done in the laboratory to understand the response of consumers to foods.

INTRODUCTION: THE PARTNERS

In the traditional family situation, food is consumed within the family circle. It has usually been prepared by one of the participants who receives information about the quality of his/her cooking from the conversation made around the table. In restaurants too, chefs maintain contact with the consumer, by circulating amongst the clients and questioning them on how they have enjoyed their meal. Such feedback is also a necessary input to laboratories in the food industry where new recipes or new formulae for old recipes are developed.

PRESENT SITUATION

In the past, experts served as a personal link between
the consumer and the laboratory, and were able to
perceive the consumer's attitude towards changes in
product specifications. Today, attitudes to food are
changing all over the world[1] [2]. Travel abroad has
mixed populations and cultures creating even more
complex markets and all sorts of opinions are expressed due to an interest in dietetics, health, tradition,
etc. The exchange of raw food materials between
countries has also contributed to a change in
traditional diets [3]. Food producers on the other
hand are becoming multi-national and are directing
their field of distribution to a great diversity of
consumers. The traditional market no longer exists
and consequently the value of experts as predictors
of market trends has diminished.

Food technologists need to know what makes a
product acceptable, what it is which motivates the
consumer. The consumer's attitude to foods is
related to the sensory factors: appearance, odour,
taste and texture of the product and each of these
interacts differently with the consumer according to
the situation. The consumer is also influenced by
non-sensory factors, including those related to
physiology, health, culture, geography and climate,
as well as other variables such as availability,
convenience and other competing products.

MARKETING: A LINK BETWEEN RESEARCH AND THE CONSUMER

Faced with such a complex situation, the approach
that is adopted to determine why certain foods are
consumed is therefore empirical. Food acceptance is
determined in the field by asking appropriate
questions to the representatives of the consumers.
Specific techniques are used to gather information
about the different factors affecting acceptability.
This needs an adequate communication language [4] [5]
so that questions can be asked and answers interpreted.

The task of obtaining information is undertaken
by members of the marketing department which already

has a great deal of data about products and the
consumer from the market sales.

The information they acquire must be used by
research staff in another department. These two
groups make up important elements in the data
collection pathway along which information must be
passed and also interpreted. An outline of the pathway by which information is passed from the consumer
to the laboratories is shown in Figure 1.

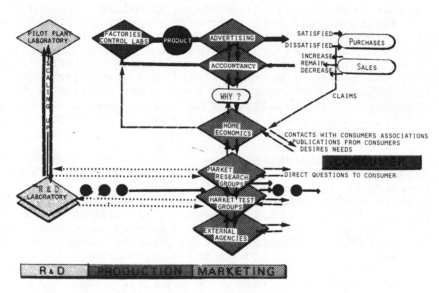

Fig. 1 — Centres and pathways of information between consumer and
laboratories.

Marketing departments make contact with the
consumer in several ways:

- The accounting department is linked with
  production in that it knows which products'
  have been bought and which have not. It
  therefore provides information on the
  behaviour of the consumer and also detects
  changes in consumer attitudes.

- Home economics or consumer services departments are also linked with production as

as they deal with consumer correspondence and
claims. They also have contacts with consumer
associations and with the press. They are thus
able to keep informed about consumer needs and
desires and also supply suggestions for future
developments.

- The market research team examines the
  structure of the market. Thus it may use the
  information provided through the consumer
  affairs department to establish, for example,
  how many people use taste as their principle
  criterion when purchasing and consuming foods;
  and the extent to which overweight, health
  and social status influences the purchasing
  and eating behaviour of consumers.

- The market test group tests new products that
  are about to be launched.

- Occasionally independent agencies are employed
  to identify socio-economic reasons for
  consumer behaviour.

All these groups rely on qualitative studies,
such as individual interviews,"day dreaming", and
group discussions which produce information on the
factors motivating the public when they buy and the
concepts they may have about a product. More
quantitative studies may also be undertaken involving either a sample of shops or using consumer panels
of 200 to 2000 people. Participants may also be
invited to complete questionnaires. These questionnaires "explore the problem comprehensively from many
angles to find out reasons for acceptability and the
factors influencing it" [6]. The questions should be
structured and worded in everyday language and not
take the interpretation for granted [4].

The services at the end of the data collection
pathway are the Research and Development pilot plant
laboratories where the new ideas are developed into
products. The sensory analysis laboratory is
associated with the first of these. This team uses
both small panels of experts and people trained in
the laboratory. They describe what the product is
like at each step of its development. They use
comparative descriptive or quantitative tests to
check if the product matches the image defined in
cooperation with the marketing people. The
technologist is also involved at each step until the

product is ready for a market test.

TRANSMISSION OF INFORMATION

Information is generally transmitted via reports,
meetings or personal contacts [7] [8], and care
must be taken to avoid losses or bias of interpretation through decoding and other treatments of
the basic information. In this information pathway
there are two areas where erroneous results can be
generated. The first of these occurs at the consumer/
marketing personnel interface and can result from
improper sampling of the market, assessing the wrong
product, and using wrongly worded questionnaires [4].
The second of these areas is situated between the ·
marketing and the research department and can be the
result of invalid statistical methods, incomplete
reports, inadequately supported conclusions, and the
inaccurate interpretation of data by both marketing
and technical personnel [9] .

    Lacking adequate information the research worker
is tempted to rely on his own resources, and may put
the question of acceptability to his specialised
laboratory panel or rely on one expert opinion. This
is a dangerous practice [10] and could be very waste-
ful of precious research resources. To avoid this
situation developing it is necessary to reinforce
the various links that exist between the two
services by organising joint meetings at which each
team can express its points of view. In this and
other ways contacts are fostered and the best use is
made of the available information [11].

    Large organisations need to develop methodology
which can give quick information, without the
necessity of elaborate market surveys. Small
consumer acceptance tests tied in with sensory profile techniques are one such approach [12][13][14].
At the early stages in the development of a project
it may be appropriate to use a panel of employees
and an external panel attached to the laboratory
[15][16]. However, such panels cannot replace the
market test, though they do provide general information quickly.

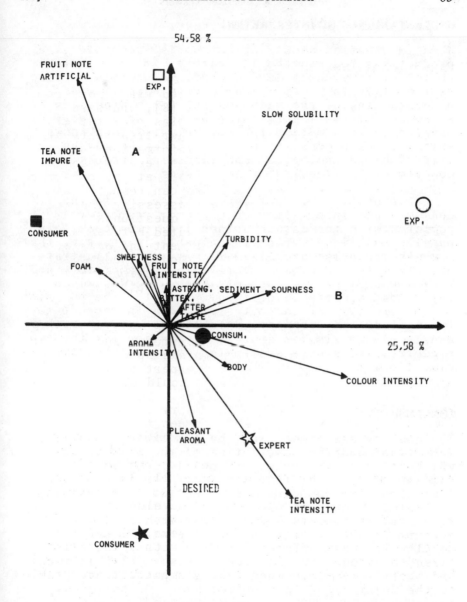

Fig.2 — Positioning of the products A (squares) and B (circles) together with their ideals (stars) as profiled by a panel of consumers and experts, as obtained on the first two canonical axes.

UNDERSTANDING AND INTERPRETING

When information about the consumers' response to a product has reached the laboratory, it is used to guide future product development. Such data is also kept on file to provide a base from which a wider understanding of the main reasons for a product's acceptability in a particular market can be derived. Using such information the technologist then knows what sort of product to make, although he may be limited by technological and financial factors. A compromise has inevitably to be found.

A prototype product can be presented to the consumer and information on consumer responses is compared with the data obtained from the laboratory panel. Such information is valuable in checking that any discrepancies are minimal. Figure 2 illustrates data from two beverages profiled by a laboratory and by a consumer panel, each of which also described their most acceptable or ideal product. The position of the profiles of these two products in respect to their first two canonical axes[17] is given. Both panels give a similar spacial separation for the two products, but show a systematic shift in the same direction.

CONCLUSIONS

The quality assessment made by a marketing services department and the description of the food product which interests research and development are complementary. The integration of the information from these two sources gives a better understanding of what a product should be. Financial and technical restraints however must also be taken into account in the interpretation of what the product finally is, when offered for sale. Care must also be taken to reduce the difference between what is ideal and what is feasible when making a product acceptable to the majority of the public.

REFERENCES

1. Pao, E.M. Changes in American food consumption and their nutritional significance. Fd Technol. 1981, 35 (2), 43-53.

2. Brewster, L.; Jacobson, M.F. The changing American diet. Center for Science in the Public Interest, Washington, 1978.

3. Morgan, D. Merchants of Grain. The Viking Press, New York, 1979.

4. Payne, S.L. The art of asking questions. Princeton University Press, Princeton, 1971.

5. Blair, J.R. Interface of marketing and sensory evaluation in product development. Fd Technol. 1978, 32 (11), 61-62.

6. Katz, D. Survey techniques and polling procedures as methods in social science. J.Soc. Issues 1946, 2(4), 62-66.

7. Elrod, J. Bridging the gap between laboratory and consumer tests. Fd Technol. 1978, 32 (11), 57-66.

8. Erhardt, J.P. The role of the sensory analyst in product development. Fd Technol. 1978, 32 (11), 57-66.

9. Hirsh, N.L. Getting fullest value from sensory testing - Part I: Use and misuse of testing methods. Food Prod. Dev. 1974, 8 (10), 33-34.

10. Gatchalian, H.M. Sensory evaluation methods with statistical analysis. College of Home Economics, University of the Philippines Pub., Diliman Quezon City, Philippines, 1981.

11. Tauber, E. Translating consumer food values into solid R & D and marketing ideas. Fd Prod. Dev. 1980, 14 (7), 26-27.

12.   Szczesniak, A.S.; Loew, B.J.; Skinner, E.Z.
      Consumer texture profile technique.
      J. Fd Sci. 1975, 40, 1253-1256.

13.   Civille, G.V. Case studies demonstrating the
      role of sensory evaluation in product
      development. Fd Technol. 1978, 32 (11),
      59-60.

14.   Moskowitz, H.R.; Stanley, D.W.; Chandler, J.W.
      The eclipse method: optimizing product
      formulation through consumer generated
      ideal sensory profile. Can. Inst. Fd Sci.
      Technol. 1977, 10 (3), 161-168.

15.   Hirsh, N.L. Getting the fullest value from
      sensory testing, Part III: use and misuse
      of test panels. Fd Prod. Dev. 1975, 9
      (2), 78-80-83.

16.   Pearce, J. Sensory evaluation in marketing.
      Fd. Technol. 1980, 34 (11), 60-62.

17.   Vuataz, L.; Sotek, J.; Rahim, H.M. Profile
      analysis and classification. Proc. IV Int.
      Congress Fd Sci. and Technol. 1974, 1,
      68-78.

Section 2

MEASUREMENT OF SENSORY QUALITY: SENSORY METHODS, STATE OF THE ART

Chapter 2.1

Adapting short cut signal detection measures to the problem of multiple difference testing: the R-Index

M.A.P.D. O'Mahony
Department of Food Science and Technology, University of California, Davis,
California 95616, USA

SUMMARY

A short cut Signal Detection R-index procedure is
described for sensory multiple difference testing.
Using simple ranking or rating procedures probability measures of degree of flavour difference
between several products can be obtained.

INTRODUCTION

Signal Detection Theory [1] has had a considerable
impact on psychophysical measurement, providing an
alternative approach to sensitivity measurement
which circumvents some of the problems involved in
threshold determination [2,3]. It treats the
sensory systems as communications systems, providing
various indices of sensitivity (d' P(A) etc) for
distinguishing incoming sensory signals from mere
noise in the system. However, traditional signal
detection measures of sensitivity require a large
number of replicate trials (c. 200), making them
unsuitable for the chemical senses or for the
general measurement of flavour. However, Brown [4]
introduced a variation in signal detection measurement, the R-index, whereby signal detection measures
could be obtained after only a few trials (c. 20);
such a short cut procedure is readily adaptable to

sensitivity measurement in the chemical senses [5,6].

PAIRED DIFFERENCE TESTING

It is not the intention here to discuss Signal
Detection Theory or its use in psychophysics as an
alternative to threshold measurement; nor to discuss
the relationship between the short cut R-index
procedures and the older signal detection measures
(the R-index is equivalent to P(A) or P(C)). Merely
let it be said that the R-index as a measure of
sensory sensitivity is an estimated probability
value; it is the probability that a judge can distinguish an incoming sensory signal from mere background noise.

Methodologically, a procedure for measuring
sensory sensitivity is really a difference test; it
measures the ability of a judge to distinguish
between one experimental condition (the presence of
a small sensory signal) and another (the absence of
that signal, mere background 'noise'). Thus, the
general methods available for sensory sensitivity
measurement should be adaptable to sensory difference testing for foods. Such is the case for the
R-index which becomes a measure of the degree of
difference between two products, the probability of
a judge distinguishing between two products by
flavour.

To measure whether differences in flavour
occur between two foods, the commonly used difference tests, paired-comparison, triangle and duo-
trio, are suitable [7]. Whether any observed
differences are significant or merely due to chance
is tested statistically using the nonparametric
binomial test. Should differences occur, it is
sometimes useful to determine the degree of difference. For instance, should several products be
tested against a standard product, it might be useful to know the degree of difference between these
products and the standard. An example would be the
testing of several reformulations against an established food product or the testing of several
imitation formulations against a rival company's
market leader. The traditional method for measuring
such degrees of difference is by using some sort of
scaling procedure: a 9-point category scale, magnitude estimation, placing a mark on a 10 cm line etc.
However, scaling procedures involve judges having to

generate numbers, or their equivalent, in some way. Judges perform this task with a high degree of error so that the numbers generated are generally only approximate. This may not be so important when the differences between the items to be scaled are large. However, when the differences are barely perceptible, as would be the case should difference testing be necessary, the judges' estimation error might well obscure the small differences between the products. In this case, the use of a scaling technique would seem inadvisable; what is needed is a form of difference testing, which generates measures of degree of difference directly, without requiring the judges to perform subsequent scaling.

Such a procedure is the R-index procedure for difference testing [8,9]. As already mentioned, this yields estimated probabilities of distinguishing between pairs of products by flavour. The higher the probability, the greater the degree of difference; it thus becomes a useful measure of degree of difference. Here, the use of the R-index procedure will first be examined as a simple measure of the degree of difference between two products only. Its extension to multiple difference testing, measuring the relative degree of difference between several products will then be considered; this will then be extended to see how R-indices can be obtained by different behavioural procedures.

To examine the R-index in its simplest form, consider the following example. Let us assume that a judge is required to distinguish by flavour between two products 'S' and 'N'. 'N' could be a regular product while 'S' could be a reformulated version of this product (In signal detection terminology, 'S' is a 'signal' and 'N' the 'noise'. The task is to distinguish any flavour change 'signal', due to reformulation, from the 'background noise' of the flavour of the regularly formulated product.) We give the judge a given number of S-samples and N-samples in random order and require him to say whether each sample is 'S' or 'N'. He could make these judgements based on a session of practice at distinguishing between the two; he could make the judgements on the basis of 'same as N', 'different from N', with a standard N-sample provided. He could even make the judgements in terms of 'same as S', 'different from S'. Should there be a predictable specific difference in flavour between S and N, this could be used as the basis for judgement. For example, should S have added sugar, the judge might be required to distinguish the samples in terms of 'sweet' versus 'not sweet'.

Thus, the judge is required to distinguish which of randomly presented samples are 'S' and which are 'N'. He is also required to say whether he is sure of his judgement or not. Often it may not be clear whether the product is, in fact, 'S' or 'N'; should the judge not be sure of his judgement, he is required to say so. Thus, each sample can be responded to as 'definitely S' (S), 'perhaps S but not sure' (S?), 'definitely N' (N), 'perhaps N but not sure' (N?). This procedure whereby the judge gives graded category responses is called the rating procedure.

Let us assume that the judge is presented with ten N-samples and ten S-samples in random order. The exact number of samples is a matter of convenience for the specific task at hand; ten is chosen here merely to simplify the mathematics. Let us assume that the judge rates six of the S-samples as 'S', two as 'S?' and two as 'N?'. Let us assume that he rates seven of the N-samples as 'N', two as 'N?' and one as 'S?'. His performance can be summarised by the matrix shown in Figure 1.

Judge's Response

		S	S?	N?	N	
Sample presented	S	6	2	2		$n_S = 10$
	N		1	2	7	$n_N = 10$

Number correct: $6 \times (1 + 2 + 7) = 60$

$$2 \times (2 + 7) \quad = 18$$

$$2 \times 7 \quad = 14$$

Don't know $\quad 2 \times 1 \quad = 2$

$$2 \times 2 \quad = 4$$

$$R = 60 + 18 + 14 + \tfrac{1}{2}(2 + 4) = 95$$

Fig. 1 — Response matrix for a judge distinguishing between two products 'S' and 'N'.

The question now becomes: Can we estimate
from this performance matrix, the probability of the
judge distinguishing between an S-sample and an N-
sample? The answer is 'yes'; it can be done in the
following manner.

Let us imagine that each S-sample was presented
in paired-comparison with every possible N-sample;
this would result in a total of 100 (n_S x n_T = 10 x
10) possible paired comparisons. The question
becomes one of predicting from the response matrix,
the number of these 100 possible theoretical paired-
comparisons, in which the S- and the N-samples would
be correctly identified. This percentage of correct
paired-comparisons is a good estimate of the probability of correctly distinguishing between 'S' and
'N'; 73% correct paired-comparisons would mean that
there is a 73% chance ($\underline{P}$ = 0.73) of distinguishing
between the two. This estimated probability value
is the R-index. The chance level for correctly
distinguishing between the two is 50% while a probability of 100% would indicate perfect discrimination.
Thus, the R-index ranges from 50% (chance) to 100%
(perfect discrimination). We now proceed to our
example, summarised in Figure 1, and predict the
percentage of pair comparisons which would be correct.

Examining the response matrix in Figure 1, let
us consider the 6 S-samples identified as 'definitely
S' (S). When paired with any of the 7 N-samples
identified as 'N', the 2 identified as 'N?' and the
one identified as 'S?', they would be correctly
identified as S-samples. Even the N-samples rated
as 'S?' would not be chosen as 'S', because faced
with a choice between a sample with a flavour rated
'S' and one rated 'S?', the judge should sensibly
choose the one rated 'S' as the S-sample. So this
gives 6 x (1 + 2 + 7) = 60 correct identifications,
so far. In the same way, the 2 S-samples rated
'S?' would be identified correctly in pair comparison with the 2 N-samples rated 'N?' or the 7 N-
samples rated 'N'. This gives a further 2 x (2 + 7)
= 18 correct identifications. However, when these
2 S-samples are compared to the N sample rated 'S?',
the judge would not know which to choose as the S-
sample because they were both rated as exactly the
same (S?); so these two comparisons are scored as
"don't know". The 2 S-samples rated N? would be
identified correctly when compared to the 7 N-samples
rated N because forced to choose whether a sample

rated 'N?' or 'N' was an S-sample, the one that was only doubtfully N (N?) would be the most likely to be 'S' (score a further 2 x 7 = 14 correct). Comparison of these 2 N?-rated S-samples with the 2 N-samples rated 'N?' would, on the other hand leave the judge undecided (score another 2 x 2 = 4 don't knows). Thus, the predicted final tally of paired-comparisons is 92 (60 + 18 + 14) correct identifications of S and 6(2 + 4) 'don't knows'. Incidentally, the two S-samples rated N? would be identified incorrectly (as N-samples) when compared with the N-samples rated S? (score 2 x 1 incorrect responses so that the total tally comes, as it should, to 100: 92 correct + 6 'don't knows' + 2 incorrect).

The judge, however, is not allowed a 'don't know' response; he is forced to choose. It is assumed that when the judge is undecided, he must guess; half of these guesses on average will be correct and half incorrect. Thus, 6/2 = 3 of the 'don't knows' can be added to the 'correct' scores giving a total of 92 + 3 = 95. From the matrix, it would be predicted that the judge would correctly distinguish between S and N on 95 out of 100 paired-comparisons; the estimated probability of distinguishing S and N is thus 95% or 0.95. This estimated probability is called the R-index and, as such, is a useful measure of the degree of difference between S and N for this judge.

In the example, there were 10 replications given for both S- and N-samples; any convenient number of samples may be chosen, bearing in mind that the larger the number chosen the more representative the sample will be of the judge's behaviour. In general, the argument may be summarised by the following formula. For the response matrix given in

Judge's Response

		S	S?	N?	N	
Sample presented	S	a	b	c	d	n_S = a+b+c+d
	N	e	f	g	h	n_N = e+f+g+h

Fig.2 — Response matrix for a judge distinguishing between two products 'S' and 'N'. General case.

Figure 2 the R-index is given by:-

$$R = \frac{a(f+g+h) + b(g+h) + ch + \frac{1}{2}(ae+bf+cg+dh)}{n_S \; n_N}$$

This gives a fractional R. Often a percentage is conceptually easier (multiply by 100).

Of course, there is no reason why there need be only four response categories (S, S?, N?, N). More (not less) can be used to obtain greater resolution (e.g., S, S?, S??, N??, N?, N) although it is always better to have an even number. A middle "don't know" category is inadvisable because it does not force the judge to choose; i.e., it would allow less confident judges not to try to distinguish. For most purposes, however, four categories are usually satisfactory.

This procedure for measuring a degree of difference between two foods (probability of distinguishing between the two) may require more time and samples than the simpler paired-comparison, duo-trio and triangle tests; this is a disadvantage. However, it does allow a more powerful parametric statistical analysis (analysis of variance), over a group of judges, should this degree of difference be compared to other degrees of difference; this is because the R-index is a numerical score allowing parametric analysis. The regular sensory difference tests (triangle, duo-trio, pair comparison), using category data (correct versus incorrect choice) are only amenable to nonparametric analysis. As far as traditional measures of degree of difference are concerned, there are serious doubts about data obtained by scaling degrees of difference, with regard to the assumptions concerned for parametric statistical analysis. End effects on a category or line scale would distort distributions seriously, challenging assumptions about normality and homo-scedasticity, while favoured number effects for magnitude estimation [10] would also break assumptions of normality.

The chance value for an R-index is 50%, although, in practice, it is likely to be exceeded because of the small numbers of readings taken for this procedure. A control experiment in which the

S-samples and N-samples are identical would give an experimental estimation of chance probability (the chance value of the R-index), for a given judge. If this could not be done, an alternative, more vigourous statistical approach, to determine whether there was an above chance discrimination, would be to use the statistical test sometimes called the Wilcoxon Rank Sums Test or the Mann-Whitney Test [11].

MULTIPLE DIFFERENCE TESTING

The R-index procedure may have some advantages for sensory difference testing of two foods, but, in general, the more traditional sensory difference tests will be quite adequate, having the advantage of brevity. Where the R-index procedure does show its advantage is in the realm of multiple difference testing, where several items are to be compared to determine the degrees of difference among them or to determine the degrees of difference between them and a given standard. This would generally involve difference testing between all pairs of items followed by a procedure for scaling the degree of difference between them. For instance, following our example, instead of merely distinguishing between two samples S and N, the degree of difference might be required between N and several S-samples: S_1, S_2 and S_3. N might be a regular food product and S_1, S_2 and S_3 three alternative reformulations which are being tested to determine the degree of flavour difference between them and the regular product. Such data could be used to determine which reformulations should be used for further research. Instead of following the usual procedure of difference testing between these products followed by scaling procedure to determine the degree of difference, the shorter R-index procedure could be used.

The application of the R—Index: an example

For multiple difference testing, 10 samples (10 is chosen once again for simplicity) of each product (N, S_1, S_2, S_3: 40 total) would be presented in random order, while the judge would be required to categorise them as before. We can represent the results on a response matrix as before, except this time the matrix would not have two rows (S and N) but four rows (S_1, S_2, S_3, N); such a matrix is shown in Figure 3..

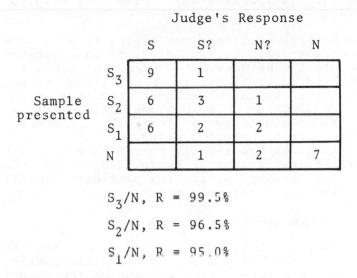

Fig.3 — Response matrix for a judge distinguishing between several products
S_1, S_2, S_3, and N.

R-index values can be calculated for the probability of distinguishing S_1 from N, S_2 from N, and
S_3 from N, in the same way as before (in fact,
comparisons could also be made between any pairs of
S_1, S_2 and S_3, if required). For S_1 (6,2,2) and
N (1,2,7) the R-index is 95% (these are the same
values as in the two sample example). For S_2 and N,
R = 96.5% and for S_3 and N, R = 99.5%.

Thus, in this example, the judge could distinguish between the reformulations and the regular
product nearly all the time; the reformulations were
fairly distinct from the original product. S_3 was
the most different from N; S_1 the least different.
Whether any of these R-indices are above chance can
be tested as outlined before (statistically or
arranging that S_1 was identical to N, to get an
experimental chance level). Whether the R-indices
are significantly different from each other can also
be tested, as previously outlined. Further non-
parametric tests are available for testing ranking
trends. The Page Test [12] is a useful test for
examining whether there is a significant ranked trend
(S_3 > S_2 > S_1) in the degrees of difference from N,
over a sample of judges; the Jonckheere Test [11]

can be applied in the same way to the matrix for a
single judge.

The R-index procedure now begins to show some
distinct advantages. Degrees of difference between
food products can be determined using one sensory
test, requiring only simple judgements, with no need
for 'high error' rating procedures to determine the
degrees of difference. The mathematical values are
obtained from manipulation performed by the experimenter rather than numbers provided by the judge.
The R-index values are readily susceptible to parametric statistical analysis, there being doubts about
how well data obtained by scaling procedures fulfill
the assumptions for parametric analysis.

The application of the R—Index to ranking procedures

The R-index approach to multiple difference testing
has been described using a rating or categorisation
procedure, with a random presentation of the samples.
However, it can also be used when the judge is
required to rank the samples to be compared. Such
a procedure would involve the presentation to the
judge of four samples, one each of: S_1, S_2, S_3 and
N. He would be required to rank them in order of
difference (or similarity) from the standard. Alternatively, they could be ranked in order of amount of
off-flavour, rancid odour or any simple single
dimension; here let us choose degree of difference
from the standard sample, N. First place is given
to the sample that is most different from the
standard and 4th place to the sample most like the
standard; if the judge can distinguish at all, the
N-sample should come 4th. The four samples are
presented to the judge (in random order) and ranked
accordingly. Then there are replications and a
response matrix can be constructed just as before,
giving the number of occasions that a given product
was given a particular rank. Such a response matrix
is shown in Figure 4.

Here the matrix is constructed using ranking
responses, rather than rating responses. As can be
seen S_3 came first 10 times, so 10 is inserted in
the 1-column for S_3. S_2 came second 6 times, third
3 times and fourth once, so the appropriate columns
are filled by 6, 3 and 1 for S_2. The same is done
for S_1 and N. This data, in the martix, now summarises the judge's performance. R-indices are calcu-

	1	2	3	4
Rankings	S_3	S_2	S_1	N
	S_3	S_1	S_2	N
	S_3	N	S_2	S_1
	S_3	S_2	S_1	N
	S_3	S_1	S_2	N
	S_3	S_2	N	S_1
	S_3	S_2	S_1	N
	S_3	S_2	S_1	N
	S_3	S_1	N	S_2
	S_3	S_2	N	S_1

Judge's Total Ranked Response

		1	2	3	4
	S_3	10			
Sample presented	S_2		6	3	1
	S_1		3	4	3
	N		1	3	6

$$S_3/N, \quad R = 100\%$$

$$S_2/N, \quad R = 82.5\%$$

$$S_1/N, \quad R = 67.5\%$$

Fig.4 — Response matrix for a judge distinguishing between several products S_1, S_2, S_3, and N using a ranking procedure.

lated in exactly the same way; here they represent
the degree of difference in terms of the dimension
along which the judge was ranking. All the statistical analyses conducted with the previous matrix
(Fig. 3) can be used here.

It is worth noting a behavioural point. With
this ranking procedure, judges are forced to spread
their responses across the response matrix. Each
set of four samples to be ranked must have one
response placed in each column of the matrix. In
the rating procedure, this forced spreading across
the matrix is not imposed on the judge; in theory,
all samples could be rated identically. This
tendency for ranked responses to be spread across
the response matrix would cause there to be less ties
(due to less identical ratings); this would give
higher R-index values because ties only contribute
by half to the R-index. When R-indices were obtained
both by rating and by ranking, the values obtained
by ranking were indeed higher [13] although the
relative perceived relationship between the food
samples was not altered.

It has already been stated that when the
rating procedure is used, it is important to use an
even number of response categories ('S, S?, N?, N'
or 'S, S?, S??, N??, N?, N'). This forces the judge
to distinguish between S- and N-samples. Ranking,
on the other hand, involves forced choices anyway,
so the worry about an uneven number of categories
does not apply. The number of categories will simply
be equal to the number of samples to be ranked. The
number of samples that may be ranked during any one
trial will depend on the task at hand. For visual
ranking, many samples may be used. For taste and
smell judgements three, four or five samples are
generally possible. It depends on the judges ability
to remember the flavours and the procedures adopted
to avoid fatigue due to the adaption effects [14].

CONCLUSION

The R-index procedure provides a useful, simple and
economical approach to multiple difference testing,
susceptible to parametric statistical analysis. It
has the advantage of being obtained by more than one
behavioural technique, rating or ranking.

1. Green, D.M.; Swets, J.A.. Signal Detection
        Theory and Psychophysics, 1966, Wiley, New
        York.
2. O'Mahony, M.; Hobson,; A; Garvey, J.; Davies, M.;
        Birt, C.. How many tastes are there for low
        concentrations 'sweet' and 'sour' stimuli? -
        threshold implications, Perception, 1976,
        5, 147-154.
3. O'Mahony, M.; Kingsley, L.; Harji, A.; Davies, M.
        What sensation signals the salt taste thresh-
        old?, Chemical Senses and Flavor, 1976, 2,
        177-188.
4. Brown, J.. Recognition assessed by rating and
        ranking, Br. J. Psychol., 1974, 65, 13-22.
5. O'Mahony, M.; Gardner, L.; Long, D.; Heintz, C.;
        Thompson, B.; Davies, M.. Salt taste detect-
        ion: an R-index approach to signal-detection
        measurements, Perception, 1979 , 8, 497-506.
6. O'Mahony, M.; Klapman-Baker, K.; Wong, J.;
        Atassi, S.. Salt taste sensitivity and
        stimulus volume: Effect of stimulus resid-
        uals, Perception. (In press).
7. Amerine, M.A.; Pangborn, R.M.; Roessler, E.B..
        Principles of Sensory Evaluations of Foods,
        1965, Academic Press, New York, 1st edn.,
        321-348.
8. O'Mahony, M.. Short-cut signal detection measure-
        ments for sensory analysis, J. Fd Sci., 1979,
        44, 302-303.
9. O'Mahony, M.; Kulp, J.; Wheeler, L.. Sensory
        detection of off-flavours in milk incorpor-
        ating short-cut signal detection measures,
        J. Dairy Sci., 1979, 62, 1857-1864.
10. O'Mahony, M. and Heintz, C.. Direct magnitude
        estimation of salt taste intensity with
        continuous correction for salivary adaption,
        Chemical Senses, 1981, 6, 101-112.
11. Leach, C.. Introduction to Statistics, 1979,
        Wiley, Chichester, 1st edn., 49-85, 170-187.
12. Hollander, M.; Wolfe, D.A.. Non-parametric
        Statistical Methods, 1973, Wiley, New York,
        1st edn., 147-150.
13. O'Mahony, M.; Garske, S.; Klapman, K.. Rating
        and ranking procedures for short-cut signal
        detection multiple difference tests, J. Fd
        Sci., 1980, 45, 392-393.
14. O'Mahony, M.. Salt taste adaptation: the psycho-
        physical effects of adapting solutions and
        residual stimuli from prior tastings on the
        taste of sodium chloride, Perception, 1979,
        8, 441-476.

Chapter 2.2

Flavour description and flavour classification

J.F. Clapperton Pedigree Petfoods, Melton Mowbray, Leicestershire, UK
J.B. Harwood Target Training Associates, Scalford Hall, Scalford, Leicestershire, UK

SUMMARY

The role of descriptive sensory analysis in quality
assurance and in flavour research is discussed, and
procedures for the collection and analysis of
descriptive data are described.

INTRODUCTION

Descriptive sensory testing was introduced initially
to overcome the problem of carry-over of persistent
flavours from one sample to the next in multiple-
sample tests. The first formal method to be
developed was the Arthur D. Little Flavour Profile
Test [1] which remains in use today together with a
number of developments of it [2,3]. Descriptive
tests are used to identify the single sensory
components of complex flavours. Each component is
scored for intensity. Thus, the tests provide
records of flavours for comparison with other
information, for example, on recipe changes, processing treatments or with results of instrumental
analyses. Descriptive testing, possibly more than
other sensory testing procedures, benefits from experimental design and planning, larger panel sizes
and replication of tests so allowing real effects
to be separated from artefacts. Many factors influence the flavour of food products and beverages.
These include the quality of raw materials, formula-

tion, treatments during processing and packaging and, not least, the physiological and psychological states of the subjects who perceive the flavours.

Where, as in one of the original applications of the technique [4], descriptive tests are used to identify flavour differences directly or where they complement results of difference tests, the sensitivity of the test should be tuned to the maximum. This is achieved by panel training and by setting the descriptive terminology of the test form and the scoring scale to detect the finest possible differences.

In classification studies on the other hand [5,6], the task is to sort the products into flavour groups rather than identify fine differences between individual products. The aim of such studies is to provide new knowledge about the flavours from the underlying basis of the classification. In a study of beer flavour [7], malt quality, hop bitterness and alcohol strength were identified as the three most important factors accounting for differences in flavour of beers from different countries of origin. The descriptive terminology used focused on the product set as a whole rather than on individual beers. It would have been possible to direct a different form of terminology to each of the 30 beers in the trial and to have come up with 30 unique flavour profiles. The latter would have been interesting to the quality assurance departments of the breweries concerned. The results of the classification study are much more interesting to researchers. Why are there differences in malt quality? Why should these differences have such marked effects on flavour? How should beer bitterness and strength be adjusted for different markets? With answers to these questions, products could be developed and flavour-quality 'controlled' from a position of understanding.

DATA HANDLING AND ANALYSIS

The disadvantage of experimental designs, larger panel sizes, replication of tests and the use of multi-term test forms is the large amount of data produced. Each scale on the test-form must be measured and the scores transferred to a master file.

There are several ways of solving the data handling problem, including the use of direct keyboard entry into computers, punched cards and marked-form

readers. The system best suited to our needs is the
one developed for the Swedish Food Preservation
Research Institute (SIK) and which allows direct
entry of data <u>via</u> a graphics tablet into a desk-top
computer. The system for data-entry from the tablet
has been linked to analysis programmes that we had
already developed for data entered from the keyboard
into the computer. The combined system offers three
programmes:

   (i)   General Block Analysis

   (ii)   Sensory Panel

   (iii) Form Preparation

The first analyses any data arranged in com-
plete-, incomplete- or chain-block designs [8]. Results can be analysed at intermediate stages using
existing data to estimate missing data. If there is
insufficient data for these estimates the average
scores for the test products or treatments are ranked.
The Sensory Panel programme collects and files data
from the graphics tablet. Although out of sequence,
the third programme is used to draw up details of the
test form and simultaneously prepares a data tape for
whole trial taking account of the number of samples,
number of panelists and the experimental design. The
test form is displayed on a screen for editing. A
hard copy is taken for photocopying the required number of forms for the trial.

There is a choice of either a graphic scale or
a category scale. If the former is selected each
scale is measured to the nearest 0.1 cm. If the category scale is selected the measurements are rounded
to 1, 2, 3, 4 or 5 as indicated (Table 1). Data are
entered by touching the entry points on each of the
scales with a stylus which transmits a signal to the
graphics tablet. When all the data points have been
entered the complete entry is displayed for checking
prior to being filed (Table 2).

If the entry is OK, key Y is pressed to file
the data. If the data according to the Panelist,
Block No. and Treatment No. files have already been
entered there is the option either to overwrite the
data or to ignore the new data. If the entry is not
OK, key N is pressed to return the programme to the
point of entry to allow the correct data to be entered.

Table 1 — Definition of test-form.

Panelist No. _____   Date _____   Sample code _____

5-point category scale	Slight 1	2	Moderate 3	4	Strong 5

Overall Intensity* |___|___|___|___|___|

Oily |___|___|___|___|___|

Fatty |___|___|___|___|___|

Meaty |___|___|___|___|___|

Fishy |___|___|___|___|___|

Sweet |___|___|___|___|___|

Sour |___|___|___|___|___|

Rancid |___|___|___|___|___|

Stale |___|___|___|___|___|

Any other comments?

*You must score this term.

Table 2 — Data entry display.

Panelist No. _____   Block No. _____   Treatment No. _____

Overall intensity	4	7.8
Fatty	2	2.4
Meaty	1	0.8
Rancid	3	5.3
Stale	2	3.8
	(5-point category scale)	(10 cm graphic scale)
Is this OK?	Enter Yes (Y) or No (N)	

Results are analysed term by term. Treatment means and standard errors for each panelist are listed. Scores by individual panelists are correlated with the panel scores. Panelists whose scores are negatively correlated with the panel score are rejected. The treatment means are then recalculated and the reliability and significance of the figures are printed. The decision to reject panelists on the basis of negative correlation with the panel result is a first option which is still being tested. Other bases for accepting or rejecting data from individual panelists could easily be written into the analysis programme. By way of illustration, scores for the odour terms "fishy" and "meaty" from a recent trial are shown in Table 3. The trial comprised

Table 3 — Data analysis.

Odour Term - Fishy

Panelist Number	1	2	3	4	5	6	7	8	9	10	11	12	13	Std Error	Correlation*
1	0.5	1.5	3.0			3.0						0.3	3.3	0.78	0.902
2	*		4.5			4.0	*	*	*				5.0	0.41	0.733
3	1.0	0.5	2.8		0.8	2.0	0.3		0.5			0.3	3.5	0.55	0.870
4			3.8			3.3							3.5	0.47	0.365
5	1.3	1.3	0.5	0.8		1.5	0.5	0.8	0.5			0.8	0.5	1.12	0.246
6			1.3					0.8	0.8				1.5	0.87	0.355
7			3.3			3.3							3.5	0.34	0.739
8	0.5	0.3	0.5			1.5	0.3			0.8	0.3	1.0	1.8	1.02	0.785
9	3.0	2.0	5.0	0.3	1.0	3.8	1.0	1.5	2.7	1.3	3.0	1.8	5.0	1.49	0.790
10		0.3	2.0	0.8	0.8	1.8	0.5	0.3	0.5	0.5	0.5	0.8	2.0	0.76	0.425
11	0.3	0.8	1.0	0.5		0.5		0.3				0.3	1.5	0.68	0.694
12			2.0			2.8					0.3	0.3	2.8	0.73	0.771
13	0.3	0.5	3.0	0.5	0.5	2.5	0.8		0.5	2.5		1.3	2.5	1.21	0.604
14			4.8		1.3	4.3						0.5	4.3	0.64	0.729
15	1.0		4.0		0.5	2.8							1.8	0.91	0.775
16	1.3		3.0	0.3		2.8						0.3	3.0	0.58	0.864
Panel Mean Score (N = 16)	0.6	0.44	2.77	0.15	0.29	2.47	0.19	0.23	0.31	0.38	0.23	0.45	2.84	Reliability = 0.98) Significance Level, P = 9.7 x 10^{-36}	

* Spearman's rank correlation coefficient.

Odour Term - Meaty

Panelist Number	1	2	3	4	5	6	7	8	9	10	11	12	13	Std Error	Correlation*
1				1.8	0.5		1.3	1.0	1.0		0.3			0.58	0.617
2	*	1.0			1.0		*	*	*			3.0		0.82	0.504
3				0.5	0.5		0.3	1.8	0.5		0.3	1.5		0.51	0.850
4		1.5		1.0	2.3		1.5	1.3	0.8		0.3	1.0		0.92	0.847
5	0.5	0.5	0.3	0.5	1.0		0.5	0.3	1.0		1.0		0.5	0.85	0.188
6				0.8			1.3					0.5		0.65	0.525
7		0.8		0.8	0.5		0.5							0.63	0.422
8	0.5	0.3	1.5	1.0	1.3	0.8	1.3	1.0	2.0	0.8	1.8	1.3	1.0	0.92	0.420
9	0.5	0.5		2.0	2.3		3.3	3.3	1.3	0.5	1.0	2.8	0.0	1.11	0.898
10										0.3	0.8			0.44	-0.36
11				0.8			0.3	0.5						0.37	0.539
12						0.5								0.28	0.271
13				1.3	1.0		0.5	0.5			0.3	0.5		0.65	0.816
14		0.5		0.3	0.3	0.3	1.8	0.5	0.8	0.5	1.8	1.3	0.5	0.98	0.676
15	0.3	0.5	0.3	1.5	1.5	0.5	1.8	2.0	1.3		0.8	2.0		0.69	0.926
16				0.2	0.2		0.8				0.9			0.39	0.464
Panel Mean Score N = 14	0.11	0.32	0.12	0.59	0.86	0.09	0.78	0.75	0.68	0.13	0.43	0.81	0.11	Reliability = 0.86) Significance Level, P = 1.4 x 10^{-5}	

* = Missing data   Means = 0.0 are omitted

* Spearman's rank order correlation coefficient.

13 products, three of which contained fish! Scores listed under Treatments 1-13 are means of four separate analyses. The P value is the probability of the result occurring by chance.

When all the data have been analysed and the results printed, the operator is asked to enter a value for P. Panel scores against treatment number are then plotted for terms that differ between treatments at or beyond that level of significance.

Finally, profiles of reach of the treatments (products) are printed as bar diagrams as shown in Table 4. All terms included in the test form are listed. Panel scores are entered for terms that differ significantly from zero.

Table 4 — Treatment (product) profiles.

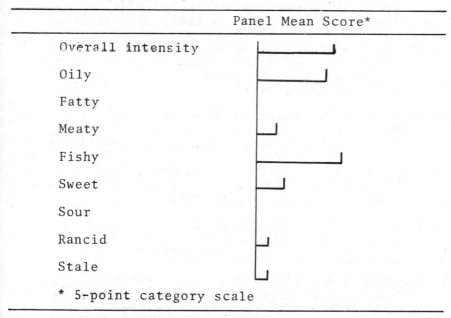

	Panel Mean Score*
Overall intensity	
Oily	
Fatty	
Meaty	
Fishy	
Sweet	
Sour	
Rancid	
Stale	

* 5-point category scale

The data tapes may be stored or the data transferred to other tapes or disks for mass storage. Further programmes are available for multivariate statistical analyses of either the whole data or the refined data using the same desk-top computer.

CONCLUSION

Descriptive sensory analysis can provide much information on factors affecting the flavour quality of
foods and beverages. New procedures for the collection, analysis, refinement and storage of data should
considerably increase the value and scope of the analysis method. However, successful sensory analysis
does not depend on methods, experimental designs and
computers; it depends on people. Without the support
of top management and the commitment of the panel
leaders and panelists to the type of work involved,
sensory analysis will not succeed.

REFERENCES

1. Caul, J.F. The profile method of flavour analysis.
   Adv. in Fd Res., 1957, 7, 1-40.

2. Harper, R.; Land, D.G.; Griffiths, N.M.; Bate-
   Smith, E.C. Odour qualities: A glossary of
   usage. Br. J. Psychol. 1968, 59, 231-252.

3. Stone, H.; Sidel, J.; Oliver, S.; Woolsey, A.;
   Singleton, R.C. Sensory evaluation by quantitative descriptive analysis. Fd Technol.
   1974, 28 (11), 24-32.

4. Amerine, M.A.; Pangborn, R.M.; Roessler, E.B.
   Principles of Sensory Evaluation of Food.
   Academic Press, New York, 1965, 377-378.

5. Harper, R.; Bate-Smith, E.C.; Land, D.G. Odour
   Description and Odour Classification. J. & A.
   Churchill Ltd., London, 1968.

6. Brown, D.G.W.; Clapperton, J.F. Analysis of
   sensory and instrumental data on beer.
   J. Inst. Brew., 1978, 84, 318-323.

7. Brown, D.G.W.; Clapperton, J.F.; Dalgliesh, C.E.
   The language of flavour and its use in product
   specification. Proc. Am. Soc. Brew. Chem.
   1974, 32, 1-4.

8. Cochran, W.G.; Cox, G.M. Experimental Designs.
   John Wiley & Sons, New York, 2nd edition.

Chapter 2.3

The application of Procrustes statistics to sensory profiling

S.P. Langron
Food and Beverages Division, Long Ashton Research Station, University of Bristol,
Long Ashton, Bristol BS18 9AF, UK

SUMMARY

Data from sensory profile experiments are usually
summarized by the panel mean. An alternative
summary is the consensus configuration from a
generalized Procrustes analysis. The Procrustes
approach, however, does not require each judge to
have the same interpretation of the adjectives in
the profile vocabulary. Furthermore, inspection of
the transformations applied during the analysis
illustrates how the judges vary in their interpretation of the profile vocabulary.

INTRODUCTION

Procrustes analysis is the name given [1] to the
technique of matching two configurations of points
under translation, rotation/reflection and possibly
an isotropic scale change. The Procrustes statistic
is the residual distance between the two configurations after the Procrustes analysis. The technique
was originally developed for use in factor analysis,
but more recently it has been applied in multidimensional scaling [2,3,4,5].

In sensory profile analysis the K adjectives
scored by M judges on N samples can be visualized as

M configurations of N points in K-dimensional space.
An M configuration extension of Procrustes analysis,
known as generalized Procrustes analysis [6,7,8,9],
allows the simultaneous matching of M such configurations to their common average or consensus
configuration.

The translation, rotation/reflection and isotropic scale change transformations can be inspected
to identify discrepancies in the interpretation of
the vocabulary used by each judge. The consensus
summarizes sample information independently of any
discrepancies in adjective interpretation and scale
use by the judges.

GENERALISED PROCRUSTES ANALYSIS

Translation

The configuration of scores for each judge is
centre-at-origin standardized. This is equivalent
to removing judge effects in the usual linear model
and adjusts for the effect of judges scoring at
different levels of the scale.

Rotation/Reflection

The judges use K adjectives to describe a sample
which consists of a combination of unknown stimuli.
Each judge will associate a particular linear combination of the stimuli with each adjective. The
linear combinations will differ for different judges,
as judges interpret adjectives differently. For
example, 'bitter' and 'acid' are often confused.

The combination of stimuli which correspond to
the direction of maximum variation among the samples
will correspond to a linear combination of adjectives; different for each judge. Similar samples
should be given similar scores by a particular judge,
but, because different judges may use different
combinations of adjectives to describe the same
combination of stimuli, the scores given by two
judges to the same sample may vary widely. This is
equivalent to assuming that the judges' scores
represent configurations which have different
orientations. This type of judge inconsistency is
eliminated by the rotation/reflection stage in a
Procrustes analysis.

Inspection of the rotation/reflection matrices will identify the adjectives upon whose interpretation the judges disagree.

Isotropic scale change

Scaling accounts for judges using different ranges of the adjectives scales. Some judges prefer to use a narrow band within the scale while others will range over the whole scale.

Residuals

If the judges are all in agreement on the position of the samples after a generalized Procrustes analysis, then the residual sums of squares for each judge should all be of a similar size. The residual sum of squares for a particular judge is the squared distance between the judge configuration and the consensus configuration. A large residual sum of squares denotes a lack of fit by that judge.

This could be due to:-

(a) Physiological differences between the judges.

(b) Varying sensitivity to certain attributes by the judges.

(c) An inability of a judge to perform the required task.

Replicated experiments will identify judges who cannot perform the task, as their results will not be reproducible. When the results are reproducible then a judge who has a different sensitivity will have a large residual in one dimension only; the judge who is perceiving something different will have a more even spread of his residual across the dimension. If varying judge sensitivity is suspected, then INDSCAL [10] may prove to be informative.

EXPERIMENTAL

The data to be analysed is a four judge subset of the external aroma of Cox's Orange Pippin (Williams, A.A. *et al.*, unpublished).

The data consists of twenty-seven batches of apples (which vary by virtue of the time spent in three storage regimes) scored on fourteen adjectives.

STATISTICAL ANALYSIS

Tables 1-3 summarise the Procustes transformations which were required to match the four configurations.

Table 1 — Translation terms

Adjective	Judge			
	1	2	3	4
Alcoholic	0.11	0.93	0.30	1.00
Green	0.74	0.63	0.30	1.18
Sharp	0.15	0.15	1.07	0.11
Scented	0.59	0.30	0.74	0.37
Cox	1.56	1.59	2.15	2.37
Banana	0.00	0.18	0.37	1.11
Fruity	0.07	0.00	0.22	0.26
Estery (Synthetic)	0.07	0.30	1.41	0.18
Estery (Waxy)	0.48	0.70	0.48	0.41
Sugary	0.00	0.26	0.44	1.30
Spicy	0.00	0.85	0.70	0.41
Dried leaves	0.67	1.85	1.52	0.52
Fatty	0.04	0.37	0.00	0.52
Rancid	0.00	0.04	0.00	0.22

Table 2 – Rotation/reflection relative to the first consensus principal axis

Adjective	Judge			
	1	2	3	4
Alcoholic	.11	.17	.07	-.09
Green	-.79	-.48	-.31	-.68
Sharp	.10	.04	.25	.11
Scented	.10	.15	.06	-.06
Cox	-.25	.30	.13	.41
Banana	-.09	.27	.34	.50
Fruity	-.08	.01	.16	.00
Estery (Synthetic)	.17	.07	.13	.11
Estery (Waxy)	-.37	-.07	.20	-.07
Sugary	.12	-.03	.33	.19
Spicy	-.01	.02	.09	.04
Dried leaves	.13	-.69	-.70	.08
Fatty	.27	.07	-.07	-.12
Rancid	.00	-.26	-.03	-.12
% variance	*18.23*	*18.13*	*20.60*	*15.00*

Table 3 – Judge scaling factors

Judge	Scaling factor	Residual
1	1.38	85.76
2	0.84	83.94
3	0.98	82.49
4	0.75	83.40

CONCLUSION

The residual sums of squares (Table 3) are all
approximately equal, an indication that the judges
are all in basic agreement. Cox character is
present in all the samples and is consistently given
a high score (Table 1) which is not surprising as
the apples under investigation are all Cox's Orange
Pippin.

The first principal axis is known to correspond to time spent by the apples at 17°C [11]. This
axis can be seen (Table 2) as a loss of the fresh
characteristics (green and dried leaves) and a
corresponding rise in the mature characterstics
(banana, Cox, sugary). Each judge, however, applies
different weights to the adjectives; notice in
particular judge one who scores fatty and not banana,
this judge is most likely interpreting banana as
fatty minus estery (waxy).

The scaling factors (Table 3) show judge one to
have a condensed configuration while judge four
scores over a larger range of the scales.

The average of the judge scores after the
Procrustes transformations, which is known as the
consensus configuration, summarizes sample information. This configuration does not have a unique
orientation and is consequently usually reported
relative to its principal axes.

The Procrustes transformations have shown
interesting differences in judge responses which are
due to their interpretation of the sensory profile
language and scoring procedure. These differences
are not due to differences in judge perception of
the stimuli and are ignored in a more conventional
analysis such as principal components.

REFERENCES

1. Hurley,J.R.; Cattell,R.B. The Procrustes
     Program: producing direct rotation to test a
     hypothesized factor structure. Behav. Sci.
     1962, 7, 258-262.
2. Schönemann,P.H.; Carroll,R.M. Fitting one matrix
     to another under choice of a central dilation
     and a rigid motion. Psychometrika 1970, 35(2),
     245-255.

3.   Gower, J.C. Statistical methods of comparing
     different multivariate analysis of the
     same data. In"Mathematics in the Archaeol-
     ogical and Historical Sciences", 1970.
     University Press, Edinburgh.

4.   Sibson, R. Studies in the robustness of multi-
     dimensional scaling: Procrustes statistics.
     J.Roy.Statist. Soc. (Series B) 1978, 40
     (2), 234-238.

5.   Sibson, R. Studies in the robustness of multi-
     dimensional scaling: perturbational
     analysis of classical scaling. J. Roy.
     Statist. Soc. (Series B)1979, 41(2),
     217-229.

6.   Kristof, W.; Wingersky, B. Generalization of
     the orthogonal Procrustes rotation
     proceduro to moro than two matricos.
     Proceedings of the 79th Annual Convention,
     American Psychological Association, 1971,
     89-90.

7.   Gower, J.C. Generalized Procrustes analysis.
     Psychometrika, 1975, 40(1), 33-50.

8.   Ten Berge, J.M.F. Orthogonal Procrustes
     rotation for two or more matrices.
     Psychometrika, 1977, 42(2), 267-276.

9.   Williams, A.A.; Baines, C.B.; Langron, S.P.;
     Collins, A.J. Evaluating tasters' perform-
     ance in the profiling of foods and
     beverages. (Schreier, P., Ed). In "Flavour
     '81". Walter de Gruyter, Berlin, New York.

10. Carroll, J.D.; Chang, J.J. Analysis of individ-
     ual differences in multi-dimensional
     scaling via an N-way generalization of
     'Eckart-young' decomposition. Psychometrika,
     1970, 35 (3), 283-319.

11. Langron, S.P. The statistical treatment of
     sensory analysis data. Ph.D. Thesis,
     University of Bath, 1981.

Chapter 2.4

Is there an alternative to descriptive sensory assessment?

D.M.H. Thompson and H.J.H. McFie
ARC Meat Research Institute, Langford, Nr Bristol, UK

SUMMARY

The use of numerical scores of pairwise judged differences among samples to replace descriptive profiles is discussed. It is suggested that the technique is of particular use in quantifying the primary perceptual dimensions of a food. The Individual Differences Scaling approach (INDSCAL) also gives a more coherent model of inter-judge variation. Examples are given using electrocutaneous stimuli and beef homogenates.

INTRODUCTION

Contemporary methods for qualitative sensory evaluation of foods are characteristically descriptive. In practice this usually means that sensory assessors must identify and describe the intrinsic qualities of a perceived phenomenon (for example, flavour) and then quantify the intensity of the sensation associated with each descriptor. The resulting expression of what was perceived, in words and numbers, is usually called a word profile. Descriptive sensory assessment has seen considerable application in recent years, particularly in the field of food and beverage flavour research (see Table 1).

Table 1 — Some examples of specialised application of descriptive sensory
         assessment.

Application	No. of descriptive terms			Reference
	Aroma	Taste	Flavour	
Bilberry juice	36	-	-	von Sydow et al. [1]
Blackcurrants	31	-	-	von Sydow and Karlsson [2]
Canned meat	27	-	-	Persson et al. [3]
Cooked beef	41	-	-	MacLeod and Coppock [4]
Beer	-	-	43	Clapperton [5]
Beer	-	-	12	Mecredy et al.
Apples	22	10	-	von Sydow et al. [7]
Apples	21	24	-	Williams and Carter [8]
Cider	51	-	-	Williams [9]
Tea	-	-	11	Palmer [10]

Frequent usage and apparent success in application
pay tribute to the general utility of descriptive sensory
assessment, but this should not be allowed to obscure certain
fundamental shortcomings. A principal criticism of descriptive sensory methodology is that perceived phenomena are
usually compared qualitatively by comparing respective word
profiles [11] without giving due consideration to the overall
impression created by the associated qualities in combination.
Reference to the well known Gestalt aphorism "the whole is
more than the sum of the parts", surely validates such
criticism.

The second possible drawback to descriptive sensory
techniques is that they presuppose that all perceived phenomena can be meaningfully and adequately expressed in words;

the mere existence of the word "indescribable", and its frequency of usage in every day language, should instantly dispel this notion. Thus, the utility of any form of descriptive sensory assessment, must be limited by our ability to find words that express precisely the sensations that we perceive. Additionally the same word may be used to describe different components by different assessors. This difficulty is to some extent overcome by use of the Procrustes methods described by Langron, at this Symposium but the problem of obtaining a coherent model of differences among assessors remains.

To appreciate what is meant when we suggest an alternative to descriptive sensory assessment, it is helpful to consider the process of qualitative sensory evaluation as having two distinct phases:

(i)   The first phase is the process of elucidating and discovering the qualitative sensory components of a perceived phenomenon; we call this the Discovery Phase.

(ii)   The second phase is the process of actually interpreting, communicating and otherwise utilising this qualitative characterisation, once the qualitative components have been discovered; we call this the Utilisation Phase.

It is the use of descriptive terms for unravelling and discovering the qualitative characteristics of a perceived phenomenon (i.e. in the Discovery Phase) for which an alternative is proposed.

The alternative procedure may be stated simply thus: a number of samples of a particular food are selected. This may be done by systematically varying physical components of the food or by selecting randomly from a heterogeneous population. Assessors are then presented with all possible pairs of the samples and asked to score each pair for difference. In the extreme case no further instructions are given, but more normally the assessors may be asked to score difference along a particular sensory dimension (flavour, texture, odour etc.,). The results thus obtained are input to a multidimensional scaling program. The resulting dimensions and configurations provide information about the important perceptual dimension of the samples and individual differences among assessors.

These concepts are illustrated using data on the perception of nine electrocutaneous stimuli. The choice of

such stimuli may seem unusual but was prompted by the fact
that the sensations were unfamiliar to most subjects and
hence difficult to describe. In addition the stimuli were
highly reproducible.

       Finally, to prove that the method is applicable to food
stimuli we report very briefly a pilot study testing the
perceptual significance of two possible components of
variation in the flavour of homogenized meat samples.

EXPERIMENTAL

Electrocutaneous stimuli

The variable components of the stimuli were voltage and
frequency. Three levels each of voltage (6, 8, 10 volts)
and frequency (9, 27, 81 Hz) were selected by preliminary
experimentation [12] to give perceptual intervals of the same
order. By combining all levels of both components nine
different stimuli were produced and numbered 1 to 9 as
shown in Figure 1.

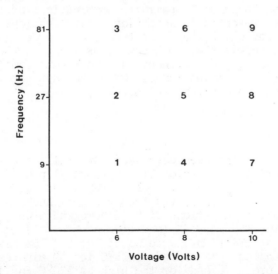

Fig. 1 — Numbering of nine electric shocks derived from all possible binary
       combinations of three levels of voltage (6, 8, 10 volt) and three levels
       of frequency are plotted after transformation by log to the base 3.
       (From *Perception and Psychophysics* (1981), by courtesy of the
       Psychonomic Society).

Nine assessors were recruited from among the staff at the Meat Research Institute. All had participated in pre-liminary experiments of this type, but it must be emphasised that no formal training or direction was given. The assessors were deliberately kept unaware of the precise nature of the stimuli and objective of the experiment.

The apparatus has been described in detail elsewhere [13]. The stimuli were applied across the first and second fingers of the assessor's left hand by means of two separate electrodes, which simply comprised plastic tubes fitted with an electrical terminal and containing 0.001 N salt (NaCl) solution. In practice none of the stimuli were considered to be uncomfortable by the assessors.

The procedure was as follows: once the assessors were familiar with the range of stimuli, the stimulus was initiated by the assessor and terminated by the experimenter after 3 seconds. The interval between the two stimuli in each pair and between successive pairs was 10 and 30 seconds respectively. The assessors were required to give a number reflecting the overall perceived difference within each pair of stimuli. No constraints on magnitude or direction were imposed. The 36 possible pairwise combinations of the nine stimuli were presented in a session. Five sessions were carried out, of which the first two were regarded as pre-liminary, to permit them to become consistent in the use of numbers for scoring differences, and to ensure familiarity with the entire stimulus range. Only the last three sessions were analyzed and are reported here.

Beef homogenates

This experiments has been described more fully elsewhere [12], so a brief description of experimental procedure will suffice here. Water soluble solids (WSS) and water insoluble residue (WIR) were recovered from raw comminuted beef muscle. Three separate formulations of beef homogenate were prepared by recombining WSS and WIR in different proportions. Two different heat treatments were used; for the low heat treat-ment, homogenates were cooked at 75°C for 30 minutes at atmospheric pressure and for the high at 120°C for 40 minutes at a pressure of 1 bar in excess of atmospheric. The three formulations and two heat treatments gave six different treatment combinations, numbered 1-6 as shown in Figure 2.

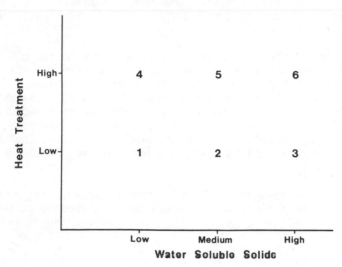

Fig.2 – Numbering of six beef homogenates derived by combining two levels of heat treatment and three levels of water soluble solids.

Twelve assessors were selected after preliminary training and asked to score for perceived difference in flavour between the 15 pairings of the 6 samples. There were five sessions, each consisting of a reference pair (samples 1 and 6) given at the start and then three experimental pairs. Each assessor participated in three replicate experiments of which the first was regarded as preliminary and therefore is not reported further.

Individual differences scaling

INDSCAL [14] postulates an underlying configuration of points (in this case, six points representing the six samples) which is 'modified' by the individual assessors, in that they may weight the underlying dimensions differently in perceptual scaling. Assuming a Euclidean metric, INDSCAL derives the coordinates of the stimuli relative to a number of dimensions (specified by the experimenter) for the "group" space which has equal weights on each of the specified dimensions. At the same time, the assessor weightings are estimated to enable each "private" space to be calculated. The normalised squared score (i, j) given by the assessor k to the distance between stimuli i and j is modelled as:

$$d(i,j) = \sum_{m=1}^{a} Wkm\ (Xim - Xjm)^2$$

where Wkm is the weight given by assessor k to the mth dimension of the INDSCAL solution and Xim, Xjm are the co-ordinates of the stimuli relative to this dimension. In this form it constitutes the normal three-way INDSCAL analysis (assessors and the object data presented as rows and columns). As replicate sessions were available for each assessor, it was possible to extend to a four-way analysis, estimating an extra set of weights, one for each session and each dimension of the group space.

The version of INDSCAL used to analyze the electrocutaneous and beef homogenate stimuli was implemented as part of the MDS (X) suite of multidimensional scaling programs [15].

RESULTS

Electrocutaneous stimuli

Figure 3 illustrates the configuration of electrocutaneous stimuli in the group space obtained by four-way INDSCAL run, (nine assessors on each of three sessions). The internal structure of this configuration closely resembles that of Figure 1 although the interdistances indicate interation between the two dimensions [13]. Differences in voltage and frequency are associated with variation along the horizontal and vertical axes respectively. The 'goodness of fit' of the solution may be judged from the correlations of the computed private configuration of each assessor. These are shown in Table 2 and appear satisfactory.

The two ancillary plots of session and assessor weights appear in Fig. 4. The three points A, B, and C, which refer to the three sessions, are clustered at the top right corner, indicating good recovery by INDSCAL and equal weighting on both dimensions. The distance of the assessor points from the origin are all of the same order, suggesting that Fig. 3 is reasonably representative of all assessors. Three categories of behaviour emerge: Assessors 1, 2, 3, 6 and 9 weight heavily on the horizontal dimension associated with voltage. Assessors 4 and 5 weight the horizontal dimension slightly more than the vertical, and assessors 7 and 8 weight the vertical more than the horizontal. It is interesting to note that these last two assessors were both physicists and there-fore very familiar with the concept of frequency in electric impulses.

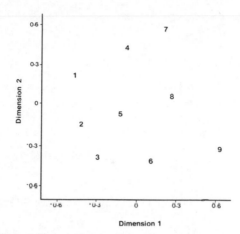

Fig.3 – Two-dimensional configuration of nine electric shocks in the group space given by a four-way INDSCAL. Numbering of electric shocks is as in Fig.1.
(From *Perception and Psychophysics* (1981), by courtesy of Psychonomic Society).

Table 2 – Correlations between INDSCAL solution and original data for each session of each subject

Subject	Session 1	Session 2	Session 3
1	.83	.83	.84
2	.81	.94	.85
3	.76	.81	.90
4	.82	.87	.85
5	.79	.82	.77
6	.87	.91	.83
7	.71	.84	.79
8	.81	.87	.88
9	.85	.89	.90

NOTE.   Correlations greater than 0.52 are statistically significant P <.001) on 34 degree s of freedom (36 distances at each session).

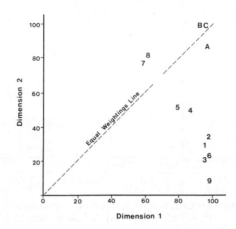

Fig.4 — Two-dimensional configuration of Replicates 3, 4 and 5 (denoted by
A, B and C respectively) and subjects (denoted by digits 1 to 9), as
defined by their relative weightings on the dimensions of the group space.
(From *Perception and Psychophysics* (1981) by courtesy of the
Psychonomic Society).

Beef homogenates

The group space obtained by a four-way INDSCAL of the
assessors scores for differences in flavour appears in Figure
5. It is again possible to interpret the dimensions of this
group space in terms of the experimental treatments applied
to the samples. Furthermore, it is also clear that assessors
were able to distinguish simultaneous variation in heat
treatment and content of water soluble material.

The relative weightings of the 12 assessors and the two
replicates on the dimensions of the space appear in Figure 6
As before the two replicates, denoted by A and B in the
Figure, fall close to the line of equal weighting and are
in the top right corner of the graph. Only assessor 3
weighted dimension 2, associated with the heat treatment,
more than dimension 1, associated with the level of water
soluble material. We conclude that for most assessors the
level of water soluble material was perceived as the
dominant cause of variation in these samples.

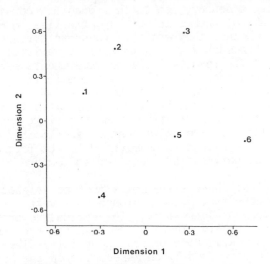

Fig.5 – Two-dimensional configuration of six beef homogenates in the group
space for flavour (all assessors and replicates in combinations), given
by a four-way INDSCAL.

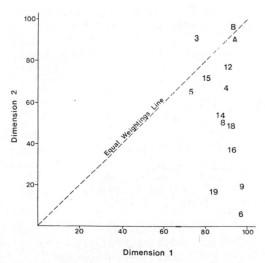

Fig.6 – Two-dimensional configuration of replicates 2 and 3 (denoted by A and B
respectively) and assessors (denoted by digits), as defined by their relative
weightings on the dimensions of the flavour group space (Fig.5).

DISCUSSION

In proposing a sensory method that does not constrain the assessors use of number in any way, the first question to resolve is whether they are able to score differences reproducibly and in such a way as to reflect variation in more than one factor. The results for both experiments were very encouraging with respect to the close similarity in weights for the replicates. Nevertheless the price paid to achieve this has been to discard the first two replicates in the case of the electrocutaneous stimuli and the first replicate for the beef samples. The extra cost of this method relative to the descriptive method is compounded by the fact than $n(n-1)/2$ difference comparisons are required to compare n samples.

Against these extra costs must be weighed the advantage of the non-descriptive approach in investigating the perception of component dimensions. The evaluative procedure is essentially Gestalt. There is no need for the experimenter to 'guide' the assessors towards particular dimensions. If they are not perceived by an assessor then the best INDSCAL solution will not contain them. The main advantage of INDSCAL is that it provides a mathematically coherent model within which assessors may weight the component dimensions differently in their overall rating.

The results from these pilot scale studies suggest that inter-sample dissimilarity estimation in conjunction with multidimensional scaling may, with further development, offer a worthwhile alternative to contemporary descriptive sensory assessment.

REFERENCES

1.   Sydow, E. von.; Andersson, J.; Anjou, K.; Karlsson, G.; Land, D.G.; Griffiths, N.M. The aroma of bilberries (Vaccinium myrtillus L.). 2. Evaluation of the press juice by sensory methods and by gas chromatography and by mass spectrometry. Lebensm. Wiss. Technol. 1970, 3, 11-17.

2.   Sydow, E. von.; Karlsson, G. The aroma of blackcurrants. 5. The influence of heat measured by odour quality assessment techniques. Lebensm-Wiss. Technol. 1971, 4, 152-157.

3.   Persson, T.; Sydow, E.von.; Akesson, C. Aroma of canned beef: sensory properties. J. Fd.Sci. 1973, 38, 386-392.

4. MacLeod, G.; Coppock, B.M. Sensory properties of the
    aroma of beef cooked conventionally and microwave
    radiation. J. Fd Sci. 1978, 4, 145-151.

5. Clapperton, J.F. Derivation of a profile method for the
    sensory evaluation of beer flavour. J. Inst. Brew.
    1973, 79, 495-508.

6. Mecredy, J.M.; Sonnemann, J.C.; Lehmann, S.J. Sensory
    profiling of beer. Brewers Digest, 1975, 50, 42-46.

7. Sydow, E.von.; Moskowitz, H.R.; Jacobs, H.; Meiselman,
    H. Odor-taste interaction in fruit juices. Lebensm-
    Wiss. Technol. 1974, 7, 18-24.

8. Williams, A.A.; Carter, C.S. A language and procedure
    for the sensory assessment of Cox's Orange Pippin
    apples. J. Sci. Fd Agric. 1977, 28, 1090-1104.

9. Williams, A.A. The development of a vocabulary and
    profile assessment method for evaluating the flavour
    contribution of cider and perry aroma constituents.
    J. Sci. Fd Agric. 1975, 26, 567-582.

10. Palmer, D.H. Multivariate analysis of flavour terms
    used by experts and non-experts for describing teas.
    J. Sci. Fd Agric. 1974, 25, 153-164.

11. Clapperton, J.F. In "Progress in Flavour Research" (Land,
    D.G., Nursten, H.E. Eds.). 1979, Applied Science
    Publishers Ltd., London, 1-14.

12. Thomson, D.M.H. An investigation of non-verbal methods
    for evaluating meat flavour. Doctoral thesis,
    University of Bristol, 1981.

13. MacFie, H.J.H.; Thomson, D.M.H. Perception of two-
    component electrocutaneous stimuli. Perception and
    Psychophysics, 1981, 30, 473-482.

14. Carroll, J.D.; Chang, J.J. Analysis of individual
    differences in multidimensional scaling via a N-way
    generalization of "Eckart-Young" decomposition.
    Psychometrika, 1970, 35, 288-319.

15. Coxon, A.P.M.; Jones, C.L.; Muxworthy, D.T.; Prentice,
    M.J. The MDS(X) series of multidimensional scaling
    programs (Report No.37, Inter-University/Research
    Councils Series). Program Library Unit, Edinburgh,
    1977.

Posters

Chapter 2.5

A tasting procedure for assessing bitterness and astringency

G.M. Arnold
University of Bristol, Long Ashton Research Station, Bristol BS18 9AF, England

INTRODUCTION

Investigations have been carried out recently at Long Ashton Research Station into qualities of bitterness and astringency in ciders [1]. It was desired to make a quantitative assessment of these characters in bittersweet ciders and isolated procyanadin fractions. Two main problems were encountered in the sensory assessment of such samples due to their intense astringency. This created a strong cumulative effect on the palate leading quickly to taster fatigue. It also meant that the assessment of a second or subsequent sample was highly influenced by the first sample tasted.

This carry-over effect appeared to increase the perceived bitterness and astringency of the latter sample. In order to overcome these problems a paired comparison tasting procedure was devised based on a model suggested by Scheffé [2]. This enabled any carry-over effect to be evaluated and eliminated, giving more precise estimates of parameters for comparison.

METHOD OF ASSESSMENT

In a given session, in order to minimise taster fatigue, each person had only one pair of samples

to assess. To compare a set of m samples, it was
necessary to have m(m-1)/2 sessions to give a
complete replication of all possible pairs, as
within a session the same pair of samples was
assessed by all tasters, half in each order. The
assessors were asked to taste in a given order and
then decide whether one sample was more or less
bitter and astringent than the other sample. This
was initially scored on a five point scale but
later extended to the seven point scale shown below,
with the numerical allocation of the scores given
on the right.

	Much more bitter/astringent		+3
	More bitter/astringent		+2
Sample	Slightly more bitter/astringent	than	+1
y	Equal in bitterness/astringency	Sample	0
is	Slightly less bitter/astringent	z	-1
	Less bitter/astringent		-2
	Much less bitter/astringent		-3

Another possible extension is to use a continuous
line scale.

MODEL

Using similar notation to Scheffé, the model of
response can be written as

$$x_{ijk} = \alpha_i - \alpha_j + \gamma_{ij} + \delta + (\delta_{ij} - \delta) + \varepsilon_{ijk} \quad i,j = 1\ldots m; \quad k = 1\ldots r$$

for r tasters comparing a complete replicate of m
samples. x_{ijk} is the score for taster k comparing
samples i, j. α_i, α_j are the characteristic parameters for samples i, j. δ_{ij} is the effect of tasting
the sample pair in the order (i, j) which can be
rewritten as $\delta + (\delta_{ij} - \delta)$ if the assumption is made
that δ_{ij} is the same for all i, j (δ), and the terms
$(\delta_{ij} - \delta)$ can·be used to test this. γ_{ij} is a term
included to test deviations from the hypothesis of
subtractivity, that the difference in characteristic
can be expressed as a difference in characteristic

parameters, and ε_{ijk} is a term for error. As it is only differences between characteristic parameters that are of interest, the constraint is made that

$$\sum_{i=1}^{m} \alpha_i = 0.$$

Underlying the model is the assumption that for a given pair of samples i, j in the order (i, j), all the x_{ijk} (k=1...r) have the same mean, and the same variance σ^2 not dependent on (i, j). For the purposes of analysis the mean difference in characteristic of sample i to sample j when presented in the order (i, j) is denoted by μ_{ij} and in the reverse order by $-\mu_{ji}$. The average of these two means $\Pi_{ij} = (\mu_{ij} - \mu_{ji})/2$ can be thought of as the average difference of i compared to j ($\Pi_{ji} = -\Pi_{ij}$) and the order effect can be given by $\delta_{ij} = (\mu_{ij} + \mu_{ji})/2$ ($\delta_{ji} = \delta_{ij}$).

ANALYSIS

The parameters of the model are estimated by the following equations:-

$$\hat{\mu}_{ij} = \sum_{k=1}^{r} x_{ijk}/r \qquad (\hat{\mu}_{ii}=0)$$

$$\hat{\Pi}_{ij} = (\hat{\mu}_{ij} - \hat{\mu}_{ji})/2$$

$$\hat{\delta}_{ij} = (\hat{\mu}_{ij} + \hat{\mu}_{ji})/2$$

$$\hat{\delta} = \sum_{i<j} 2\delta_{ij}/m(m-1) \qquad (i, j=1...m)$$

$$\hat{\alpha}_i = \sum_{j=1}^{m} \hat{\Pi}_{ij}/m \qquad (\hat{\Pi}_{ii}=0)$$

The total sum of squares can then be partitioned as follows:-

Source	df	SS
Samples	$(m-1)$	$2rm \sum\limits_{i=1}^{m} \hat{\alpha}_i^{\,2}$
Deviations from subtractivity	$(m-1)(m-2)/2$	by subtraction
Average differences	$m(m-1)/2$	$2r \sum\limits_{i<j} \hat{\pi}_{ij}^{\,2}$
Average order effect	1	$rm(m-1)\,\hat{\bar{\delta}}^{\,2}$
Differences in order effect	$(m+1)(m-2)/2$	by subtraction
Means	$m(m-1)$	$r \sum\limits_{i=1}^{m} \sum\limits_{j=1}^{m} \hat{\mu}_{ij}^{\,2}$
Error	$(r-1)m(m-1)$	by subtraction
Total	$rm(m-1)$	$\sum\limits_{i=1}^{m} \sum\limits_{j=1}^{m} \sum\limits_{k=1}^{r} x_{ijk}^2$

The estimate of variance $\hat{\sigma}^2$ is the error mean square. An F test can be used to test the signif-icance of the various effects in the usual way. If there is no evidence of deviations from subtract-ivity, it is suggested that comparisons of the samples using the estimates of the characteristic parameters $\hat{\alpha}_i$ should be carried out using the 'yard-stick'

$$Y_\varepsilon = q_{1-\varepsilon}\sqrt{(\hat{\sigma}^2/2rm)}$$

where $1-\varepsilon$ is the confidence coefficient and $q_{1-\varepsilon}$ is the upper point of the studentised range for m variates and $(r-1)m(m-1)$ degrees of freedom. Any two samples for which the difference $(\hat{\alpha}_i-\hat{\alpha}_j)$ is at least Y_ε are then deemed to be significantly different for that characteristic.

A SIMPLE EXAMPLE

The following data have been extracted from an experiment to compare ciders made from fruit from three single cultivars. They are the results from eight tasters per group comparing bitterness on a five point scale.

$$\text{Samples:- } 1 - \text{Tremlett's Bitter}$$
$$2 - \text{Dabinett}$$
$$3 - \text{Vilberie}$$

Sample Pair	DATA						ESTIMATES		
	Nos. in each score category					Total Score	$\hat{\mu}_{ij}$	$\hat{\Pi}_{ij}$	$\hat{\delta}_{ij}$
	-2	-1	0	+1	+2				
1,2	0	0	1	4	3	+10	+1.25	+1.50	-0.25
2,1	6	2	0	0	0	-14	-1.75		
1,3	0	1	1	3	3	+ 8	+1.00	+1.13	-0.13
3,1	3	4	1	0	0	-10	-1.25		
2,3	3	3	1	1	0	- 8	-1.00	-0.50	-0.50
3,2	1	2	2	2	1	0	0		
	13	12	6	10	7				

Source	df	SS	MS	F
Cultivar	2	60.17	30.08	
Deviations from subtractivity	1	0.08	0.08	<1
Average differences	3	60.25		
Average order effect	1	4.08	4.08	4.70*
Differences in order effect	2	1.17	0.58	<1
Means	6	65.50		
Error	42	36.50	0.87	
Total	48	102.00		

$$\hat{\alpha}_1 = +0.88 \qquad \hat{\delta} = -0.29$$

$$\hat{\alpha}_2 = -0.67 \qquad Y_{.05} = 0.46$$

$$\hat{\alpha}_3 = -0.21 \qquad Y_{.01} = 0.59$$

From the estimates $\hat{\alpha}_i$ of the bitterness characteristic parameters α_i it can be seen that cider made
from Tremletts Bitter fruit is rather more bitter
than from the other two cultivars (significant at
1% level) and also that from Vilberie is more bitter
than that from Dabinett (significant at 5% level).
The order effective is significant and negative,
indicating a cumulative effect of bitterness on the
palate as expected. The deviations from subtract-
ivity are not significant, so the parameter
estimates $\hat{\alpha}_i$ adequately summarise the relative
bitterness of the samples.

REFERENCES

1. Lea, Andrew G.H. and Arnold, Gillian M. <u>J. Sci.
Fd Agric</u>. (1978), 29, 478-483. •
2. Scheffé, H. <u>J. Am. Statist. Ass</u>. (1952), 47,
381-400.

Chapter 2.6

Use of micro-computer with card reader system for flavour profile data handling and storage

A.M. Duffield and J.J. Stagg
General Foods Ltd, Banbury, Oxon, England

THE COMPUTER/CARD READER SYSTEM

The 'mark sense' card reader provides a means of using a micro-computer system for profile data handling without essentially changing the established profile method and session procedure. Panelists' results are marked on cards and the information is processed immediately, presenting calculated composite data on screens for panel discussion. Benefits of this system include the ability to retrieve information easily and flexibly from data stored on disk, reduction of session duration, mathematically consistent averaging and automatic comparison with previous results.

The micro-computer/card reader system is in daily use for coffee flavour profiles. Panels usually consist of 6-8 people, evaluating 3-4 samples per session.

The equipment comprises:
        micro-computer + VDU
        dual floppy disk drive
        'mark sense' card reader
        printer
        two additional monitor screens

Table 1 compares the 'manual' and computer/card reader systems for handling sensory profile data and storage.

Table 1 — Session procedure: comparison between the manual and computer/card reader systems.

'Manual System'		Computer/Card Reader System
On printed form	1. Panelists' record results	On 'mark sense' cards (1 per sample)
Results listed on blackboard. Estimation of averages by panel leader	2. Preliminary composite visible to panel	Cards fed directly into card reader. Composite appears on screens, (programmed to calculate averages based on same principles as used in 'manual' system). Print out of individuals' results.
Composite modified if necessary as a result of discussion	3. Discussion and agreement of final composite	Composite can be adjusted if necessary using data modifica-tion options, by keyboard entry.
	4. Samples' identities revealed. Further discussion. End of session.	Print-out of agreed composite. Immediate comparison with any previous evaluations of same samples
Agreed composite written on profile form, filed with individual's results. Copy of recorded composite used as report.	5. Report composite. Storage of all results	Data stored on disk and on print-out. Copy of print-out used as report.

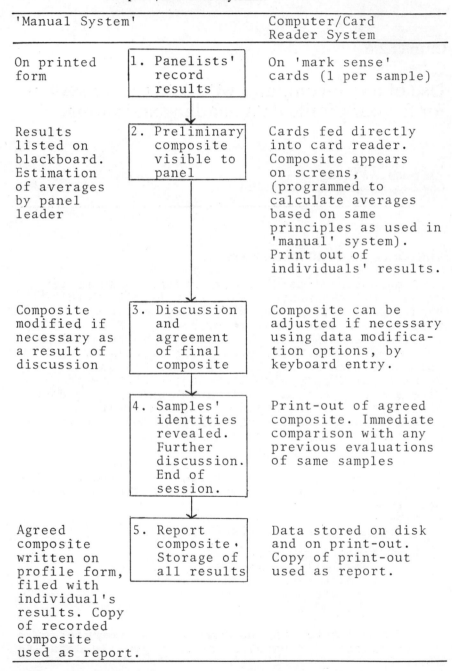

ADVANTAGES OF THE COMPUTER SYSTEM

Where these advantages are related to a particular stage in the session procedure, this is indicated by the numbers in brackets which relate to the numbers shown in the boxes in Table 1.

Methodology is the same, so 'manual' and computer system results are comparable.

The change to the computer system involves a minimum of change for panelists - the same rating scales and terminology are used and there is scope for additional terms (1).

The computer's ordered tabulation is more easily assessed than blackboard presentation (2).

The composite is mathematically more consistent (2).

The data modification capability maintains flexibility and comparability with the 'manual' system (3).

There is an automatic print-out of previous composite-of-composites, where applicable (4).

Session time is reduced because data collection and compositing is much quicker (4).

Less space is required for data storage (5).

Information retrieval is quick, easy and flexible (5).

Assessment of panelist performance versus composite is possible (5).

MEASUREMENT OF SENSORY QUALITY: INSTRUMENTAL METHODS AND THEIR VALIDATION

Chapter 3.1

Instrumental assessment of the appearance of foods

D.B. MacDougall
ARC Meat Research Institute, Langford, Bristol, England

SUMMARY

The appearance of an object is a combination of the visually perceived information contained in the light reflected, transmitted and scattered, and its colour. Colour is a psychological phenomenon but it can be specified in visually uniform terms in the CIE system, and translucency and opacity can be assessed by the Kubelka-Munk analysis of reflectance. The interaction of light scatter and pigmentation on colour appearance is demonstrated for orange juice dilutions. The effects of chilling and handling meat on its colour are related to variation in opacity and the state of the muscle pigment myoglobin.

INTRODUCTION

The first quality judgement made by a consumer on a food at point of sale is on its appearance, either on its colour alone or in conjunction with other attributes such as the wetness or dryness of the surface, its structural uniformity, the product's consistency or the abundance and arrangement of its sub-components. An understanding of the different attributes of food appearance, both in the sense of physical cause and subjective response, is essential for effective grading and quality control. Foods exhibit an almost infinite variety of appearance characteristics ranging from the matte opaque whiteness of flour, to the irregular

granularity of breakfast cereals, to the wet glistening
semi-translucency of red meat, to the translucency of fruit
juice and jam whose appearance varies with the direction of
incident light as well as the concentration of the
ingredients. Undoubtedly the most important appearance
attribute is colour because abnormal colours, especially
those associated with deterioration in eating quality or with
spoilage, cause the product to be rejected by the consumer.
Surface structure and internal transmittance can be as
important as colour in some commodities, for example, the
bloom on chocolate or the problem of the dark cutting
appearance in fresh meat. Probably more foods are
translucent or semi-translucent than opaque and the main
purpose of this paper is to illustrate the interaction of the
light transmitting properties of food with its measured
colour and visual appearance. In the author's experience
those involved with visual or instrumental assessment of food
appearance, although cognizant of the relationship of product
colour to acceptance, are often insufficiently aware of the
consequences that relatively small changes in translucency
have on food appearance.

THE COMPONENTS OF APPEARANCE

The appearance of an object is a combination of the visually
perceived information contained in the light reflected from
its surface, the light transmitted through or scattered by
the internal structure and its colour. Foods are seldom
viewed in isolation but as part of complex scenes, for
example, as the focus of attention in a retail display, often
with a bright background, illuminated by lamps with
distorting or enhancing colour rendering properties and
surrounded by advertising material of contrasting colours.
An object's appearance is generated by several independent
but interacting variables, some physical in nature and hence
readily measurable and others that are psychological and vary
with presentation and the individual observer's vision. The
physical factors include size, shape, uniformity and location
in the scene. The major psychological variable is colour.
The sensory response to the colour producing stimuli detected
by the retina and interpreted by the brain is such that the
scene perceived is a synthesis of the psychological
superimposed on the observer's recognition of the location of
the physical objects [1]. As has been known from the time of
Isaac Newton, an object has no colour; colour exists only in
the mind of the observer and is the sensation generated by
the spectral composition of the light leaving the object.
Modification of the object's spectrum, for example, by
changing the illuminant will induce a visual colour shift

[2,3,4]. Similarly, circumstances that alter the brain's interpretation of the stimuli will induce a visual colour shift, for example, if the object is in juxtaposition to a contrasting colour, or a reference colour such as white is removed from the field of view. Of the many factors which influence the appreciation of colour, those of particular importance in defining limits for the construction of colour assessment and measurement systems are the intensity of the illuminant and chromatic adaptation.   In luminance levels $<10^{-3}$ cd m^{-2}, objects appear white, grey or black because detection is exclusively by the rods in the retina.   This scotoptic vision undergoes transition through a mesoptic stage to true photoptic colour vision by detection via the retinal cones at luminance levels >125 cd m^{-2}.   When the illuminant is changed, for example in moving from daylight to tungsten, there is an immediate and often large colour shift.   However, when the visual mechanism becomes accustomed to the quality of the new light and adapts, the object regains much but not necessarily all of the colour sensation it originally appeared to possess [5,6,7]. For visual assessment the illumination must be standardised both in intensity and quality, preferably by the use of either tungsten or artificial daylight at photoptic levels [8].

THE PSYCHOPHYSICS OF COLOUR MEASUREMENT

By strictly defining viewing conditions and constraining those factors which vary colour perception it was possible to define a standard observer with normal colour vision as the basis for colour measurement.   The initial viewing condition was a 2° field which was supplemented in 1964 with a 10° field.   It is worthy of note that the Golden Jubilee of the Food Group of the SCI which led to this meeting on sensory quality coincided with that of the 1931 CIE (Commission Internationale de l'Eclairage) standard observer whose colour matching functions are the first human sensations to be incorporated into an agreed and proven measurement system [9]. The system relies on the fact that any colour can be matched by mixing appropriate amounts of monochromatic red, green and blue primary lights, although negative quantities are required to match precisely every monochromatic colour. The red, green and blue primaries were linearly transformed into the tristimulus values $\bar{x}(\lambda)$, $\bar{y}(\lambda)$, $\bar{z}(\lambda)$ for the imaginary primaries X, Y, Z in such a way that addition of the transformed primaries to match any colour is positive for all values and, most important, the primary Y contains the entire lightness stimuli.   Y for object colours is referred to as its luminous transmittance or reflectance.   The familiar 1931 (x, y) chromaticity diagram is a plot of the locus of the visible spectrum from 380 to 770 nm in which x =

X/(X + Y + Z) and y = Y/(X + Y + Z). Every colour can be located uniquely in the chromaticity diagram along with it Y value relative to the spectral energy distribution of standard illuminants A(tungsten), B(sun-light), C(north-sky) or D65. The last is the spectral distribution of daylight at the correlated colour temperature of 6500°K. Details of the development and use of the 1931 CIE system are fully described in several text-books and have been summarised recently with respect to food colourimetry [3,10-16].

The 1931 system suffers from one serious fault; although colours are uniquely defined they are not spaced uniformly with respect to visual discrimination. If the visually uniformly spaced colours in the Mumsell Color Atlas are located in the 1931 diagram the distance between greens is much larger than between blues. Many attempts have been made to improve the spacing of the system. The Hunter 1948 L, a, b space is of particular interest in food colour measurement because it is incorporated into photoelectric colour difference meters which are instruments frequently used by the food industry [17]. The more recent 1976 CIELUV L*, u*, v* and CIELAB L*, a*, b* transformations are attempts to reduce and standardise the many scales to two [18,19].CIELUV is recommended in cases where coloured lights are mixed additively and CIELAB is favoured by those concerned with colourant mixtures because of its high correlation with visual data. L* for both formulae is identical but there is no simple relationship between u*, v* and a*, b* [15].

Because of the paucity of words to describe colour sensations the perceptual terms, lightness, hue, chroma etc have been defined in psychometric terms relative to CIELUV and CIELAB [15,18,20].For CIELAB they are:

metric lightness, L*;
metric hue angle, H° = $\tan^{-1}(b*/a*)$;
metric chroma, C* = $\sqrt{(a*^2 + b*^2)}$;
colour difference, $\Delta E* = \sqrt{[(\Delta L*)^2 + (\Delta a*)^2 + (\Delta b*)^2]}$;
metric hue difference, $\Delta H* = \sqrt{[(\Delta E*)^2 - (\Delta L*)^2 - (\Delta C*)^2]}$.

SURFACE REFLECTANCE AND INTERNAL TRANSMITTANCE

The reflectance of a translucent or opaque object depends on attenuation by pigment absorption, scatter by internal structural elements in the material and external and internal reflection at the air/object surface. Few foods are sufficiently flat to be amenable to measurement of their surface characteristics, but gloss or the irregular specular components of surface reflectance have to be accounted for in measuring colour, and should be, but not always are in measuring absorption and scatter [21]. Colour measuring instruments are of three classes; visual matching instruments for example the Lovibond Tintometer which uses coloured filters; tristimulus meters, for example Hunter or Gardner Colour Difference Meters, which use filter x photocell combinations to match the standard observer's colour matching functions, usually to source C; spectrophotometers whose output is converted to CIE or uniform colour space, now with the use of on-line computers to more than one illuminant and both 2° and 10° observer.   Spectrophotometers are the only means of computing colour of mixtures, whereas colour difference meters are more precise and rapid for use in colour grading or "pass-fail" assessments.   The optics of most colour instruments are designed to eliminate the effect of the surface specular component; geometry is usually 45° illumination/0° viewing, or near 0° illumination/diffuse.

The relationship of absorption and scatter to reflectance is best described by the two variable turbid media theory of Kubelka and Munk in which reflectivity (R_∞) is related to an absorption coefficient (K) and a scatter coefficient (S) by $K/S = (1-R_\infty)^2/2R_\infty$ [22]. K and S are determined from measurement of R_∞, which is the reflectance of an infinitely thick layer, and the reflectance of thin layers of the material on black and white backgrounds.   The technique is fully illustrated by Judd and Wyszecki [3].

Measurement of the colour and directional distribution of surface reflectance is usually adequate to describe the appearance of paper, paint and ceramic tiles because all the reflected light returns from the thin surface layer, that is infinite thickness may be 1 mm or less as is the case for complete opacity in paint films.   However, colour specification alone is insufficient to describe the visual appearance of translucent foods. Orange juice and fresh meat are examples of foods typical of the situation where, in addition to colour measurement, an indication of the magnitude of the interaction of scatter and absorption on the internal transmittance (T_i) is required for appearance specification.

ORANGE JUICE TRANSLUCENCY

Orange juice colour is difficult to measure because the incident light is dispersed throughout the sample causing the particulate suspension to glow.   Instrumental colour values vary with presentation geometry so much so that a specially designed citrus colorimeter, which takes account of light scatter, is used for grading orange juice [23]. It has been shown that best results for such translucent materials are obtained if the instrument has a large sample port and photoreceptor relative to the incident beam illumination area and if the receptor is close to the sample, or a sphere collector is used [24].The validity of using the Kubelka Munk analysis has been questioned because diluted orange juice is not a perfect diffuser [25].However measurements of dilute samples of pigmented milk (MacDougall, D.B.; Jones, S.J., unpublished) have shown that the scatter coefficient, S mm^{-1} (1 mm defined as unit thickness) determined in a pair of 2 mm thick cells, one with black and the other with white backing, gives values that are related to concentration in the same scattering range as orange juice. A series of orange juice samples were therefore prepared with the object of illustrating the relationship of measured colour values, and K, S and T_i to the visual estimate of the colour differences throughout the series.

Four-fold concentrated Florida orange juice was diluted with distilled water to give a series of concentrations 0.25, 0.33, 0.5, 0.66, 1.0, 1.33, 2.0, 4.0 relative to reconstituted juice at normal concentration of 1.0. These dilutions were chosen to give visual steps that would be approximately equally spaced on the basis that observer response might be a power function of concentration. The dilutions presented to the panel were unfiltered but for short path length measurements on the spectrophotometer dilutions <2.0 were filtered through muslin to remove large pieces of debris.

Specially constructed pairs of cells with 4 cm and 2 mm path lengths and backed with black and white plastic adhered to the inside of the rear face of the cells were used for reflectance masurements relative to BaSO$_4$ on a Pye Unicam SP8-100 spectrophotometer interfaced with a Hewlett Packard 9815A calculator and a colour measurement software package. Colour was measured as X, Y, Z relative to source C and the 2° observer to be comparable with the colour difference meters, and the colour space used for all instruments was Hunter L, a, b converted to psychometric lightness, hue angle and chroma. The cells were wide enough to cover completely the 5 cm^2 port of the sphere and the illuminated area was one-third of the port. Reflectance of the most dilute suspension (0.25) did not distinguish between black and white backing at 4 cm and hence were truly infinite for all samples. (3 cm thickness was found to be infinite on the colour difference meters). Concentrated orange juice is orange which on dilution becomes yellow. At infinite thickness (Figure 1B) every sample absorbed strongly at <500 nm (R$_\infty$ = <5%), that is ,the light reflected is a varying

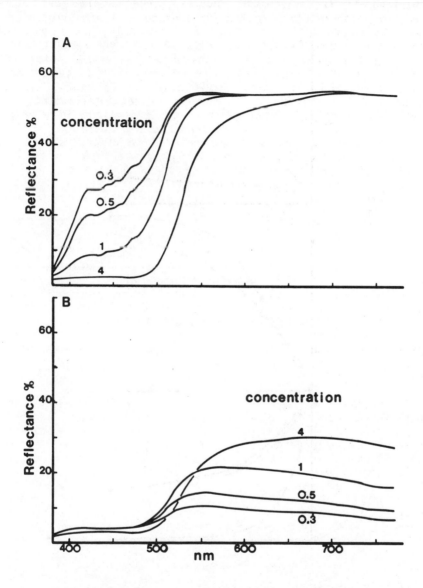

Fig. 1 — Reflectance spectra of concentrated and diluted orange juice.

Reconstituted juice at normal concentration = 1.0.
A.   2 mm path length on white background.
B.   4 cm path length equal to infinite thickness.

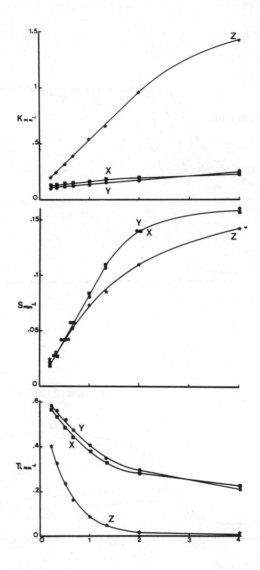

Fig.2 — Kubelka-Munk analysis of absorbance (K), scatter (S) and internal transmittance (T$_i$) for concentrated and diluted orange juice.

Reconstituted juice at normal concentration = 1.0.
Tristimulus values ■X, ●Y, ★Z.

mixture of predominantly green and red stimuli. On dilution reflectance at >500nm decreased because of loss of scattering power and therefore the more concentrated juice is instrumentally the lightest. Reflectance spectra of the white backed 2 mm cell (Figure 1A) shows the opposite effect to the infinite spectra. Absorption at >600 nm is of little consequence except for the most concentrated juice (4.0), but on dilution there is progressive increase in transmittance at <500 nm. K, S and T_i mm^{-1} for the tristimulus values X, Y and Z (Figure 2) determined by the Kubelka-Munk analysis are interpretive of the cause of the differences in the colour parameters. K is virtually constant on dilution for X and Y (red and green and lightness) but is linear with concentration for Z (blue) at concentrations <2.0. S for X and Y is also linear with concentration for the more dilute samples. The combined effect of K and S on T_1 is such that comparatively small changes in transmittance occur at concentrations >2.0 but there are large changes at concentrations <1.0, especially for the tristimulus value Z. This explains the change in hue from orange to yellow on dilution. The effect of the different rates in transmittance change relative to concentrations <1.0 is to produce large changes in measured lightness, hue and chroma. The smaller change in transmittance at concentrations >2.0 explain the fall-off in lightness and chroma at higher concentrations (Figures 3 and 4).

The effect of presentation geometry on measured colour is illustrated (Figure 3) for orange dilutions measured in four modes:

a)   45° twin beam 1 cm diameter small spot illumination on a Gardner XL10 colour difference meter with 0° 2 cm diameter detection port.

b)   as a) but with 5 cm diameter detection port.

c)   45° incident illumination from multiple circumferentially arranged mirrors on a 4 cm diameter port on the M optic sensor of a Hunter D25 colour difference meter with 0° detection from the same area.

d)   SP8-100 spectrophotometer with near 0°/diffuse sphere collection with 1.5 cm^2 illumination in a 5 cm^2 port.

The colour difference meters were calibrated with their respective white tiles and the spectrophotometer with BaSO$_4$. Samples were presented to the colour difference meters in a 5 cm diameter container with optical glass base and filled to a

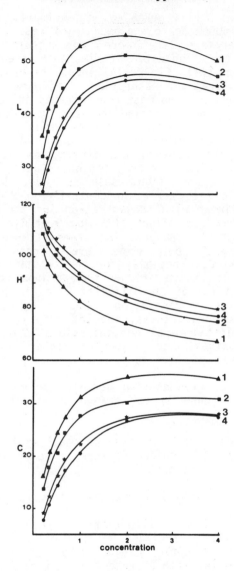

Fig.3 – Effect of presentation geometry on Hunter lightness (L), hue angle (H°) and chroma (C) for concentrated and diluted orange juice.

Reconstituted juice at normal concentration = 1.0.
1 ▲ small spot, 45° / 5 cm diameter, 0°.
2 ■ 4 cm diameter, 45° / 4 cm diameter, 0°.
3 ★ 1.5 cm², near 0° / 5 cm² port, sphere.
4 ● small spot, 45° / 2 cm diameter, 0°.

depth of 3 cm. Measurement was carried out in dim ambient illumination to exclude possible light transmission from external sources. Reflected lightness was related to detection port area, the 1 cm / 5 cm condition giving largest values of L and the 1 cm / 2 cm the least with the 4 cm / 4 cm intermediate. Colour values from the spectrophotometer were similar to that from the 1 cm / 2 cm colour difference meter mode although the geometry of the system was different. The displacement of the colour values illustrates the care that is required in interpreting data from different instruments, but the relative differences within the orange juice series were similar for each mode.

A set of 7 juice dilutions was presented to a 10 member panel with normal colour vision and experience in estimating colour differences. The dilutions were displayed in 100 ml 4.5 cm diameter glass beakers filled to a depth of 4 cm. The beakers were placed in order of concentration on numbered 8 cm white filter paper discs in line in a neutral grey viewing booth. Illumination was by 700 lux of fluorescent artificial daylight from a combination of over-head and over-the-shoulder luminaires, that is the samples were viewed by essentially reflected light. Panelists were free to use their own scale values to estimate the magnitude of the colour differences between adjacent samples. They were viewed on 4 occasions and on alternate sessions their left to right order was reversed. Panelists were unaware that the same freshly made dilutions were presented at each session. Seven panelists attended every session and their scores were adjusted to give a cumulative total colour difference of 1.0 between the most dilute and most concentrated suspensions; the results were analysed by analysis of variance. The cumulative panel mean score was found to be linear with the logarithm of concentration (Figure 4). The plot shows that although the standard errors increase with addition of successive means, the variance was still so small that the linearity of the plot was unaffected. Comparison of the panel's spacing with the psychometric colour values from the spectrophotometer shows that lightness, L, approaches linearity only for the most dilute suspensions and the cumulative calculated colour difference, ΔE, is curvilinear. The change in hue angle, $H°$, as the juice progresses from yellow to orange is linear with the logarithm of concentration and in association with change in chroma, C, may have more effect on the panelist's judgement of colour differences than L. A most important incongruity between the panel's spacing and the instrument's specification is the reversal of the order of visual lightness to L. In addition to assessing the differences between samples, the panelists were asked to state which samples in the set were the

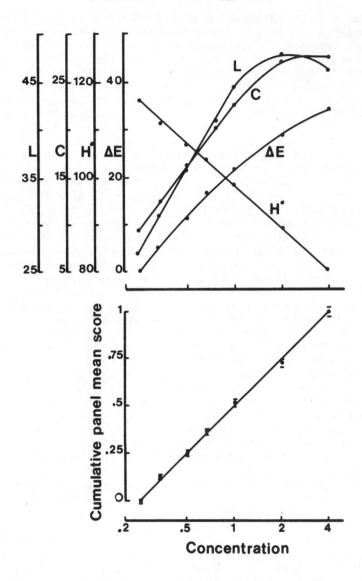

Fig.4 — Relationship of calculated cumulative colour difference (ΔE), lightness (L), hue angle (H°) and cumulative panel mean score (±s.e.) of visual differences between adjacent samples to the logarithm of the concentration of concentrated and diluted orange juice.

Reconstituted juice at normal concentration = 1.0.

lightest and the darkest. The most dilute was stated unanimously as being the lightest which is exactly opposite to that determined instrumentally. Such an anomalous situation is known to occur in orangeade where brightness measurements are nowhere near the brightness one would expect considering the appearance of a glass of orangeade [25]. It might be construed therefore that the instrumental measurement of colour is misleading. For scattering materials in dilute suspension, especially if they are strongly coloured, the instrumental measurement is inadequate rather than wrong because it does not measure what human vision perceives as appearance, that is the synthesis of colour and translucence. Whereas the instrument measures intensity of back scattered light over a limited solid angle, the human visual appreciation of lightness, or probably in this case more correctly brightness, is stimulated by the internally scattered light which emerges multidirectionally from the suspension as well as that which is reflected directly.

FRESH MEAT COLOUR AND OPACITY

In the foregoing example of orange juice, scatter and absorption were codependent on dilution. A more complex situation obtains in fresh meat where the pigment exists in more than one form and scatter is independent of pigment concentration [26]. The variables which control the colour appearance of fresh meat are:

a) concentration of the haem pigment myoglobin which ranges from <1 mg g^{-1} for pork and veal to 3-5 mg g^{-1} for young beef to >6 mg g^{-1} for old cows

b) degree of desiccation and state of the pigment on the exposed cut surface and for several mm underneath; either deoxygenated ferrous myoglobin which is purple, oxygenated ferrous oxymyoglobin which is bright red or oxidised ferric metmyoglobin which is brown to greenish-brown.

c) light scattering properties of the muscle proteins.

Muscle cut immediately after slaughter is translucent and dark but during rigor mortis it acidifies from pH 7.0 to 5.5 as residual muscle glycogen is converted to lactic acid [27]. Below pH 5.9 the appearance changes, becoming progressively paler and brighter in colour, and opaque. Increased opacity results from increased light scatter from the muscle proteins as they approach their isoelectric point. Pre-rigor meat with pH >6.0 has a scatter coefficient S mm^{-1} for Y of <0.1 and looks dark in colour because light penetrates several mm into the gel-like structure and is absorbed by myoglobin. Meat from animals whose glycogen reserves are so depleted from pre-slaughter stress or exhaustion that muscle pH will not fall below 6.0 has a similar appearance to pre-rigor mortis muscle and is described as dark cutting or dark, firm and dry [28]. Normal bright red meat with pH 5.5 - 5.7 has S mm^{-1} for Y of 0.15 to 0.25, the range attributable to events during handling, chilling and storage of the carcass. Slow cooling produces higher values of S and extremely slow cooling, for example,in muscles adjacent to the femur in beef carcasses chilled conventionally, S mm^{-1} may be >0.3 or even >0.4 [29]. The structural changes which take place as meat is aged to improve its tenderness also increase S.

Very rapid acidification after slaughter in carcasses from stress susceptible pigs result in a pH fall to <5.9 in <45 minutes; combination of high temperature (>35°C) and acid produces meat that is extremely pale, soft and exudative [27,30]. Thus the scattering power of fresh meat doubles from pre-rigor muscle to normal fresh meat (<0.1 to 0.15 to 0.25) and doubles again (0.25 to 0.4) if acid conditions prevail at high temperature.

Because of the wide range of scatter, it is impossible to estimate pigment concentration with any accuracy from reflectance or colour values. Typical colour values for oxygenated bovine muscle at the scattering power found in normally chilled meat (Table 1A) illustrate the contracting decrease in colour difference with increasing concentration; the difference in L between 1 and 2 mg g^{-1} is four times that between 3 and 4 mg g^{-1}. Thus, in veal, very small changes in pigment concentration can produce changes in colour that have considerable consequences commercially, whereas similar pigment changes in mature beef might not be noticed [26,31]. Decrease in L is accompanied by a change in H° and C from pale orange red to more intense purple red. The effect of variation in light scatter on the colour of beef at typical myoglobin concentration (Table 1B) can be compared to that produced by increasing the pigment concentration; the 5 unit difference in L between chilling rates is equivalent to that produced by a 2 mg g^{-1} change in concentration. The low scattering dark cutting meat is 7 L units darker with a reduction in C of 10 units. The differences in L between dark, firm and dry pork, normal pork and pale, soft, exudative pork are larger than the same conditions in beef (Table 1C).

Table 1 — Factors contributing to the colour of fresh meat, lightness, (L), hue
angle ($H°$), and chroma (C).
Values are typical for those at each condition.

A. Effect of pigment concentration in veal and beef

pH 5.5
S mm^{-1} 0.2

myoglobin mg g^{-1}	L	H°	C
1	50	48	15
2	43	39	16
3	39	34	18
4	36	31	20
5	35	29	21
6	34	28	22

B. Effect of light scatter in beef

myoglobin
5 mg g^{-1}

pH	S mm^{-1}	L	H°	C
5.5	0.15	31	27	20
5.5*	0.25	37	30	21
6.0	0.1	23	22	12

* slow chilled

C. Effect of light scatter in pork

myoglobin
0.7 mg g^{-1}

	S mm^{-1}	L	H°	C
Normal	0.2	50	50	13
Dark, firm, dry	<0.1	34	30	12
Pale, soft, exudative	>0.3	57	51	14

D. Oxidation to metmyoglobin in beef

myoglobin
5 mg g^{-1}

	metmyoglobin percent	L	H°	C
Reduced	0	32	32	15
Oxygenated	0	34	28	<24
	10	34	30	21
	20	34	33	18
	45	35	39	14
Oxidised	75	34	46	11

Oxidation of oxymyoglobin to metmyoglobin is the major reason for rejection of pre-packaged meat in the supermarket [32,33].Change in chromaticness, H° and C, has been specified adequately relative to the progress of oxidation (Table 1D) [26,34].For beef, C >20 is red and <12 is greenish brown. In side by side display, beef is rejected at the 20 per cent level of metmyoglobin with C <18 [35].

INSTRUMENT ASSESSMENT AND THE ILLUMINANT

One advantage that instrumental measurement has over visual judgement is that human memory is eliminated as a variable. Degree of colour change with time, temperature or other environmental factors such as illumination level or composition of the atmosphere, can be measured without recourse to a product reference standard, which may be difficult to prepare or have limited stability. Until recently, instruments were calibrated to only one illuminant approximating that used for critical visual appraisal, but not for conditions used in commerce. Some spectrophotometers are now made with the built-in facility of calculating uniform colour spaces to several illuminants. However, when estimating colour differences produced between illuminants for any food whose appearance is used as an index of quality or depends on its attractiveness for sale, great care must be exercised in interpreting the magnitude and importance of the colour shift because corrections for adaptation are not incorporated easily into the calculation procedure [36]. Experiments with beef and bacon viewed under different fluorescent tubes have shown that on switching from tubes with poor colour rendering to those with red enhancing spectra the perceived colour shift was equal in magnitude to about half of the difference between attractive pink and red, and unsightly brown [37]. Hence calculated colour differences or loci of colour changes from either change in illuminant or product deterioration must not be used in a qualitative manner unless confirmed by visual appraisal.

ACKNOWLEDGEMENTS

The author wishes to thank the meat viewing panel of the MRI for assessing the orange juice, and Mrs   S.J. Jones for assistance in measuring meat colour.

References

1.   Wright, W.D. The Rays Are Not Coloured. Adam Hilger
     Ltd, London, 1967, pp.17-31.

2.   Halstead, M.B. Colour rendering: past, present and
     future. In: AIC Color 77. Adam Hilger Ltd, London,
     1977, pp.97-127.

3.   Judd, D.B.; Wyszecki, G. Color in Business, Science and
     Industry. John Wiley and Sons, New York, 3rd edn, 1975.

4.   Ohta, N.; Wyszecki, G. Color changes caused by
     specified changes in the illuminant. Color Res. Appl.
     1976, 1, 17-21.

5.   Bartleson, C.J. Changes in color appearance with
     variation in chromatic adaptation. Color Res. Appl.
     1979, 4, 119-137.

6.   Hunt, R.W.G. Specification of colour appearance. 1.
     Concepts and terms. Color Res. Appl. 1977, 2, 55-68.

7.   Hunt, R.W.G. Specification of colour appearance. 11.
     Effects of changes in viewing conditions. Color Res.
     Appl. 1977, 2, 109-120.

8.   British Standard 950. Specification for artificial
     daylight for assessment of colour. British Standards
     Institution, London, 1967.

9.   Wright, W.D. The golden jubilee of colour in the CIE
     1931-1981. Color Res. Appl. 1982, 7, 12-15.

10. Billmeyer, F.W.; Saltzman, M. Principles of Color
     Technology. John Wiley and Sons, New York, 2nd edn.
     1981.

11. Francis, F.J.; Clydesdale, F.M. Food Colorimetry:
     Theory and Applications. AVI Publishing Company, Inc.,
     Westport, Connecticut, 1975.

12. Wright, W.D. The Measurement of Colour. Adam Hilger,
     London, 5th edn, 1980.

13. Wyszecki, G.; Stiles, W.S. Color Science: Concepts and
     Methods, Quantitative Data and Formulas. John Wiley and
     Sons, New York, 1967.

14. Francis, F.J. Colour and appearance as dominating
     sensory properties of foods. In: Sensory Properties of
     Foods. (Birch, G.G.; Brennan, J.G.; Parker, K.J. Eds),
     Applied Science Publishers Ltd, London, 1977, pp.27-43.

15. McLaren, K. Food colorimetry. In: Developments in Food
     Colours. Vol. 1 (Walford, J. Ed), Applied Science
     Publishers Ltd, London, 1980, pp.27-45.

16. Tarrant, A.W.S. The nature of colour - a physicist's
     viewpoint. In: Natural Colours for Food and Other
     Uses. (Counsell, J.N. Ed), Applied Science Publishers
     Ltd, London, 1981, pp.1-25.

17. Hunter, R.S. Photoelectric color difference meter. J.
     Opt. Soc. Am. 1958, 48, 985-995.

18. Commission Internationale de l'Eclairage.
     Recommendations on uniform color spaces - color
     difference equations, psychometric color terms.
     Supplement No. 2 to CIE Publication No. 15 (E-1.3.1)
     1971/(TC-1.3). Paris, 1978.

19. Robertson, A.R. The CIE 1976 color-difference
     formulae. Color Res. Appl. 1977, 2, 7-11.

20. Hunt, R.W.G. Colour terminology. Color Res. Appl.
     1978, 3, 79-87.

21. Saunderson, J.L. Calculation of the color of pigmented
     plastics. J. Opt. Soc. Am. 1942, 32, 727-736.

22. Kubelka, P. New contributions to the optics of
     intensely light scattering materials. J. Opt. Soc. Am.
     1948, 38, 448-457.

23. Huggart, R.L.; Barron, R.W.; Wenzel, F.W. Evaluation of
     Hunter citrus colorimeter for measuring the color of
     orange juices. Food Technol. 1966, 20, 677-679.

24. Eagerman, B.A. Orange juice color measurement using
     general purpose tristimulus colorimeters. J. Food Sci.
     1978, 43, 428-430.

25. Rummens, F.H.A. Color measurement of strongly
     scattering media, with particular reference to
     orange-juice beverages. J. Agr. Food Chem. 1970, 18,
     371-376.

26. MacDougall, D.B. Colour in meat. In: Sensory
     Properties of Foods. (Birch, G.G.; Brennan, J.G.;
     Parker, K.J. Eds), Applied Science Publishers Ltd,
     London, 1977, pp.59-69.

27. Bendall, J.R. Postmortem changes in muscle. In:
     Structure and Function of Muscle. Vol. 2 (Bourne, G.H.
     Ed), Academic Press, Inc., 2nd edn, 1973, pp. 204-309.

28. MacDougall, D.B.; Jones, S.J. Translucency and colour
     defects of dark-cutting meat and their detection. In:
     The Problem of Dark-Cutting in Beef. (Hood, D.E.;
     Tarrant, P.V. Eds), Martinus Nijhoff, The Hague, 1981,
     pp.328-339.

29. Taylor, A.A.; Shaw, B.G.; MacDougall, D.B. Hot deboning
     beef with and without electrical stimulation. Meat
     Sci. 1980-81, 5, 109-123.

30. Cheah, K.S.; Cheah, A.M. The trigger for PSE condition
     in stress-susceptible pigs. J. Sci. Fd Agric., 1976,
     27, 1137-1144.

31. MacDougall, D.B.; Bremner, I.; Dalgarno, A.C. Effect of
     dietary iron on the colour and pigment concentration of
     veal. J. Sci. Fd Agric. 1973, 24, 1255-1263.

32. Giddings, G.C. The basis of color in muscle foods.
     Crit. Rev. Food Sci. Nutr., 1977, 9, 81-114.

33. Livingston, D.J.; Brown, W.D. The chemistry of
     myoglobin and its reactions. Fd Technol., 1981, 35,
     244-52.

34. Taylor, A.A.; MacDougall, D.B. Fresh beef packed in
     mixtures of oxygen and carbon dioxide. J. Fd Technol.,
     1973, 8, 453-461.

35. Hood, D.E.; Riordan, E.B. Discolouration in
     pre-packaged beef: measurement by reflectance spectro-
     photometry and shopper discrimination. J. Fd Technol.,
     1973, 8, 333-343.

36. Bartleson, C.J. Comparison of chromatic adaptation
     transforms. Color Res. Appl. 1978, 3, 129-136.

37. MacDougall, D.B. Visual estimate of colour changes in
     meat under different illuminants. Proc. 4th Congress of
     the Association Internationale de la Couleur, AIC Color
     81, Deutsche Farbwissenschaftliche Gesellschaft, Berlin,
     1981, Po7.

Chapter 3.2

Colour in beverages

C.F. Timberlake and P. Bridle
Long Ashton Research Station, University of Bristol, Long Ashton, Bristol BS18 9AF, UK

SUMMARY

After reference to colour in beverages, attention is focused on beverages containing anthocyanin pigments. Factors affecting colour and the difficulties attending colour interpretation are illustrated by work on pure anthocyanins, red wines and fruit juices. Depending upon conditions, anthocyanins can display both negative and positive deviations from the Beer-Lambert Law. The findings imply that colour in anthocyanic beverages is arbitrary in the sense that it is the net result of conflicting effects and pertains only under the actual conditions and concentrations in the product itself. Application of tristimulus colour measurements is described and brief reference made to the subjective effect of colour on other quality attributes.

INTRODUCTION

In studies of colour measurements in foods and beverages, much use has been made of Hunter L, a, b measurements [1-5]. Plots of these parameters versus pigment concentration give curves but Francis and Clydesdale and others have sought to modify the original relationships to produce straight line graphs, usually using computer programming to produce lines of best fit.

Our approach differs in that we are seeking to
understand the chemistry of colour and the factors
which determine colour rather than trying to transform non-linear relationships between colour and pigment concentration into linear relationships; we have
tried to explain the reasons for the observed non-
linearity.

The colour of beverages may be due to many different types of pigments: oxidised phenolics in white
wines, cider, beer and tea; carotenoids in citrus
juices, apricots, peaches and tomatoes; and anthocyanins in red wines, berry juices and strawberries.

Some pigments are added to beverages and these
can be classified thus:

Synthetic (organic) - coal tar-derived colours,
e.g. Tartrazine, Sunset
Yellow FCF, Yellow 2G,
Quinoline Yellow, Choco-
late Brown HT, Orange 2G,
Amaranth, Carmoisine, Pon-
ceau 4R, Green S, Indigo,
Carmine and Brilliant Blue
FCF.

Synthetic (nature   - carotenoid derivatives,
identical)   e.g. Canthaxanthin used in
tomato products and soft
drinks.

Natural, Flavonoids - anthocyanin extracts (e.g.
from grape or cranberry).

Carotenoids- orange or citrus peel
extracts, tomato extracts
(lycophene).

Melanoidin - caramels (soft drinks,
beer, vinegar, spirits).

Betalaines - beetroot extracts.

Quinoid   - cochineal, cochineal carmine, alkannet.

EXPERIMENTAL STUDIES OF ANTHOCYANINS

This paper concentrates on one group of natural colours, the anthocyanins, the basic structure of which

is shown in Figure 1. Their chemistry and properties have been described elsewhere [6].

Anthocyanins are not simple compounds, but can exist in four pH-dependent equilibrium forms[6], each having different colour characteristics (Fig. 2). However, in acidic solution all forms are converted to the red cationic form, which can be used as an estimate of the total amount of anthocyanin, by measurement at the absorption maximum (around 520 nm). In this way, it is possible to express colour at beverage pH (3-4) as a percentage (α) of the total available colour.

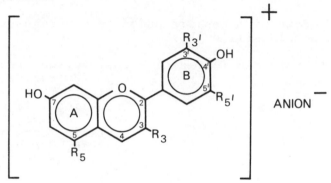

Fig. 1 —The common anthocyanidins and anthocyanins.

Anthocyanidins: R_3 = OH , R_5 = OH

		$R_3{}'$	$R_5{}'$
Pelargonidin	(Pg)	H	H
Cyanidin	(Cy)	OH	H
Peonidiñ	(Pn)	OCH_3	H
Dephinidin	(Dp)	OH	OH
Petunidin	(Pt)	OCH_3	OH
Malvidin	(Mv)	OCH_3	OCH_3

Anthocyanins Pg, Cy, Pn, Dp, Pt, Mv with

R_3 = O-sugar or O-acylated sugar

R_5 = OH or O-glucose

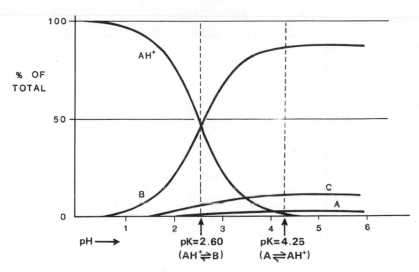

Fig.2 — Distribution of anthocyanin structures with pH: malvidin-3-glucoside, 25°C.

AH^+ = red cation;
   B   = colourless carbinol base;
   C   = colourless chalcone;
   D   = blue quinoidal base.

The foregoing was derived from studies involving weak solutions of anthocyanins (i.e. <5 x 10^{-5}M or 20 mg 1^{-1}). However, natural beverages contain larger amounts of pigment, so it is necessary to discover how colour varies with increasing concentration.

Effects of pH, including self association and co-pigmentation

The first phenomenon, not described previously, concerns the negative deviation from Beer's Law of solutions of pure anthocyanins, wines and fruit juices in N HCl i.e. at pH O. Figure 3 (Graph A) illustrates that it is necessary to dilute the sample to give a low absorbance (e.g. 0.100 using a 10 mm cell) for an accurate measurement of total pigment. This procedure was used in subsequent work.

A second phenomenon concerns measurements at higher pHs (2.6 - 4.0). In contrast to the effect above, increases in pigment levels at these pHs caused an augmentation of the colour, or produced

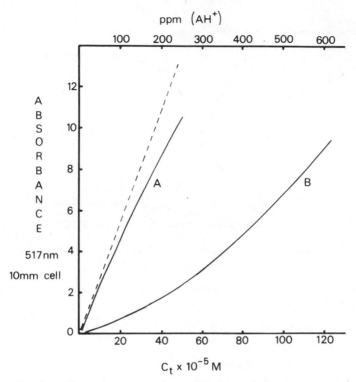

Fig.3 – Effect of concentration of malvidin-3-glucoside on absorbance
(measured at 517 nm and 10 nm cell)

A – in N HCl (pH 0);　B – at pH 3.5.

more colour per unit weight in terms of α. This
effect is shown in Figure 3 (Graph B) and illustrates
a positive deviation from Beer's Law. Hence, dilution
of a strong anthocyanin solution from 600 to 60 mg 1^{-1}
reduces the absorbance by a factor of 20 rather than
10. This effect, which still awaits an adequate
explanation is known as "self association" or "ion
association". It follows that there must be a cross-
over point from negative to positive deviation from
Beer's Law, as the pH is raised. This was confirmed,
again using pure anthocyanin (Fig. 4).

In this experiment, the absorbance of a very weak
solution (curve B) was compared with that of a very
strong solution (curve A), at four pH values. In
practice this could only be achieved by correcting
for the dilution of B; thus, B x 100 gives curve C,

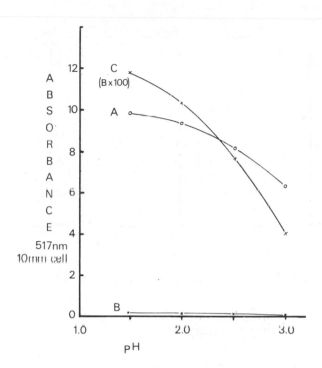

Fig.4 – Effect of concentration of malvidin-3-glucose on absorbance at various
pH values.

Curve A. C_t = 46 x 10^{-5} M   (230 mg l^{-1});
Curve B. C_t = 0.46 x 10^{-5} M   (2.3 mg l^{-1});
Curve C. C_t = 0.46 x 10^{-5} M   corrected for dilution (i.e. B x 100).

which crosses curve A at about pH 2.5, illustrating
that negative deviation occurs up to pH 2.5 and positive deviation above this pH. Similar results were
obtained using red wines and fruit juices. In natural
systems, anthocyanins do not occur in isolation and
the presence of other organic components gives rise
to another phenomenon known as co-pigmentation - a
third physical effect, causing colour augmentation.
Co-pigments are natural components of fruit juices
and the colour increase due to co-pigmentation is more
pronounced at high pH values. However, co-pigmented
solutions are not only darker; they are more saturated
and are more violet coloured than simple anthocyanin
solutions. These differences are shown well by tristimulus measurements (Fig.5).

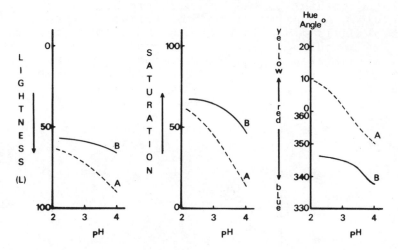

Fig.5 — Malvidin-3-glucose: effect of co-pigmentation.

Curve A alone (- - - - - -):
Curve B + copigments (————).

So far, we have considered only variation of α (i.e. percentage of anthocyanin in the coloured form) with pH.   Graphical treatment of these data usually produces curves.   A straight-line relationship may be obtained by introducing the concept of a coloration index (I), derived as follows:-

$$I = \frac{\text{colourless anthocyanin species}}{\text{coloured anthocyanin species}} \times H^+$$

since total anthocyanin = coloured + colourless species.

$$I = \frac{(\text{total - coloured})}{\text{coloured}} \times H^+$$

$$\text{but } \alpha = \frac{\text{coloured}}{\text{total}}$$

$$\text{Hence } I = (\frac{1}{\alpha} - 1) \times H^+$$

$$\text{and } pI = -\log_{10} I$$

Thus, for a given pH value, the larger the value of
pI the greater is the coloured proportion of anthocyanin. A typical plot of pI versus pH for a model
solution is given in Figure 6 and illustrates the
value of this concept as a diagnostic feature.   Line
B, illustrating "self association" has a very small
slope, whereas line C representing co-pigmentation
has a much larger slope.   Thus, the magnitude of the
slope may be used as a diagnostic feature to indicate
self association only (small slopes); or in this
strong anthocyanin solution, the maximum extent of
co-pigmentation (slope 0.5); or with varying slopes
between these extremes, showing the extent of super-
imposition of co-pigmentation on self association.

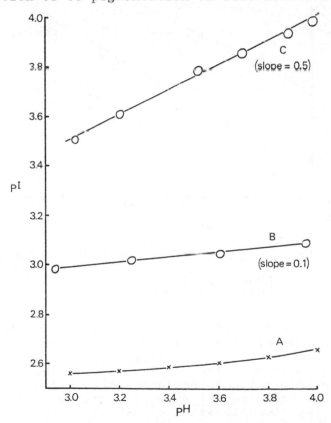

Fig.6 —Malvidin-3-glucose: effects of concentration and co-pigmentation.

Curve A   25 mg l^{-1}
Curve B   122 mg l^{-1}
Curve C   122 mg l^{-1} + co-pigmentation

In natural systems, such as fruit juices and wines, the full implications of this treatment become evident (Fig. 7).

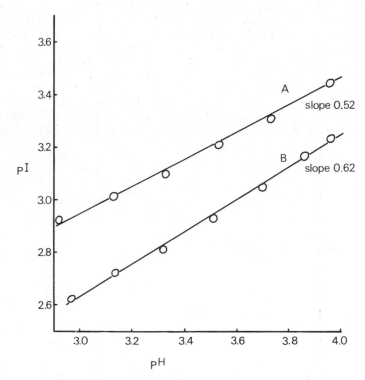

Fig. 7 — Red grape juice (Tinta Santarem): Effect of dilution.

Curve A. undilated:
Curve B. diluted 1 → 10.

From the linearity and slope of the undiluted juice (A), we might anticipate a large degree of co-pigmentation of the juice anthocyanins. The diluted sample (B) has the expected lower pI values, but the slope is still linear indicating that although the colour has been reduced by more than the dilution factor, the pigments still remain appreciably co-pigmented. In fact, the slope has actually increased in the diluted sample.

This result may be explained as follows. The phenomena of self-association and co-pigmentation act in opposition, i.e. anthocyanin molecules which are

co-pigmented are not available for self-association
and <u>vice versa</u>. Both mechanisms can occur in the
same solution to different relative extents according
to pH. Self-association is likely to predominate at
lower pHs where the concentration of flavylium cations
is high and co-pigmentation is more dominant at higher
pH values, as co-pigments tend to combine with the
quinoidal base form of anthocyanins. An increased
slope therefore, may be due to dilution having a
relatively greater effect on self association (pH 3)
than on co-pigmentation (pH 4).

A similar increase of slope with dilution occurs
in fresh strawberry juice which indicates that strawberry juice also contains some strong co-pigments.
In blackcurrant juice and some red wines, the diluted
sample does not produce a linear pI v pH relationship,
showing that in these instances co-pigmentation is
partly diluted out, especially at lower pHs (2.9 -
3.5).

To summarise then, anthocyanins in red wines and
fruit juices show several effects:

(i)   In acid solution, there is negative
         deviation from Beer's Law.

(ii)   At higher pHs, there is positive
         deviation from Beer's Law. This
         augmentation of colour with increas-
         ing concentration is a result of
         two effects which can occur simult-
         aneously: (a) "self-association" -
         which operates particularly at low
         pHs, and (b) co-pigmentation - which
         is more prominent at higher pHs.

On dilution of the product, the colour is proportionally less than the dilution factor. The implications
are that colour is arbitrary in the sense that it is
the net result of several conflicting effects and
pertains only under the actual conditions and concentrations in the product itself. The results also
emphasise how important it is not to lose anthocyanins
either by dilution or degradation during processing,
since these will produce a proportionally greater
loss of colour. By the same token, if a manufacturer
deems it necessary to replace lost colour with artificial colour, then a correspondingly larger amount
will be required.

ANTHOCYANINS AND WINE QUALITY ATTRIBUTES

Effect of co-pigmentation and self-association on red wine quality

Some effects of these observations were measured in red wines, using tristimulus and absorbance measurements.

Firstly we measured the effect of dilution at constant pH using the same cell path length (Table 1). As pigment concentration increases, the wine becomes darker (L), more saturated and browner (hue angle increases). The browning effect is a result of the constant ratio of co-pigment to anthocyanin. With an increase in total concentration, the equilibrium between self-association and co-pigmentation shifts towards self-association, decreasing the co-pigmentation and making the solution less violet (i.e. browner).

Table 1 — Effect of diluting red wine on tristimulus measurements

Dilution	L	Saturation	Hue angle
None	56.9	52.6	1.3
1 + 1	78.2	28.4	357.6
1 + 4	90.9	11.8	356.4
1 + 9	95.3	6.0	354.3
1 + 19	97.7	2.8	346.1
1 + 39	98.9	1.4	328.8

Secondly, the effect of variation in path length on colour quality was investigated. This experiment mimics the situation of a red wine in a glass, with a gradation in liquid depth from the centre of the glass to the meniscus at the rim (Table 2).

As the path length decreases the wine becomes lighter in colour, less saturated and more violet (hue angle decreases). The hue angle shows this latter effect more clearly than the conventional method of absorbance ratios of E_{420} (brown) to E_{520} (red). Thus, young wines look bluer at the rim

Table 2 – Effect of depth of red wine on tristimulus measurement.

Cell path length (mm)	L	Saturation	Hue angle	Tint E_{420}/E_{520}
40	54.1	61.5	27.6	0.62
20	67.7	39.6	9.0	0.61
10	81.4	23.7	4.3	0.61
5	90.3	13.5	0.6	0.57
2	95.9	5.3	353.2	0.58
1	97.7	3.1	347.4	0.59

of the glass and browner towards the centre. In older wines, where monomeric anthocyanins have condensed to polymeric pigments, the colour becomes amber towards the rim of the glass. In old wines, self-association and co-pigmentation effects probably do not operate.

Table 3 – Effect of diluting wine, with compensating cell size, on tristimulus measurements.

Dilution	Cell path length (mm)	L	Hue angle	Saturation
0	1	74.2	356.8	34.4
x 2	2	78.2	357.6	28.4
x 5	5	80.5	2.8	25.4
x 10	10	81.1	5.0	23.8
x 20	20	81.7	6.4	23.0
x 40	40	81.7	7.6	22.6

Lastly, wine was diluted and the colour measured in a cell of path length which compensated for the dilution factor (Table 3). This experiment did not produce constant measurements for colour and so it is clear that the same path length cell must be used throughout any set of measurements.

Effect of colour on the flavour of wines

Turning to sensory aspects, we studied the effects of colour on flavour using white wines. Two wines were made at Long Ashton, one avoiding oxidation by the use of SO_2 at crushing and pressing, under a CO_2 blanket, and a second in which no attempt was made to restrict oxidation. Thus, the unoxidised wine was very pale in colour, while the oxidised wine had undergone some browning. In tasting trials, the colour of the oxidised wine was significantly pre-ferred to the unoxidised wine, but the flavour of the unoxidised wine was liked better. The result is inter-esting, but chemically paradoxical, since browning (preferred colour) cannot occur without initial oxid-ation (poorer flavour).

Table 4 — Subjective effect of colour on other quality attributes of Bordeaux Rouge (75 mg l^{-1} total SO_2, increased to 115 mg l^{-1}).

Wine	Glass	Colour	Aroma	Flavour
Normal	Clear	6.95	5.67	5.81
Normal	Dark	-	5.35	6.17
Difference		-	0.32	-0.36
Normal	Clear	6.95	5.67	5.81
+ SO_2	Clear	6.31	5.17	5.83
Difference		0.64**	0.50	-0.02
+ SO_2	Clear	6.31	5.17	5.83
+ SO_2	Dark	-	4.69	5.63
Difference		-	0.48	0.20

** $\underline{P}$ < 0.01.

Using a red wine, we again examined the psychological effect of colour on flavour. This was done in two stages:

(i)   a red wine was tasted from clear glasses then from dark glasses (obscuring the wine's colour).

(ii)   The colour was bleached significantly by the addition of SO_2, and this wine again tasted using clear and dark glasses.

The results (Table 4) show that there appears to be no subjective effect of colour on other quality attributes of this red wine.

However, Tromp and van Wyk [7] have obtained different results in tests to discover whether a panel of tasters would predict wine quality from its colour, or predict colour from assessment of aroma and flavour. The results showed that tasters could guess the quality of the wine from its colour ($r = 0.97$), but could not guess the colour from the aroma and flavour ($r = 0.86$). Indeed, quality was predicted more easily using a spectrophotometer ($r = 0.94$). These authors[7] conclude that provided a red wine has only minor defects and the aroma and taste do not vary too much from preconceived expectations aroused by colour, the colour of red wine appears to be the most important single factor for determining its quality. However, more work should be done to determine the significance of the subjective effect of colour on other quality attributes.

REFERENCES

1.   Francis, F.J. and Clydesdale, F.M. Food Colorimetry - Theory and Applications, AVI Publishing Co. Westpoint, Conn. USA.
2.   Francis, F.J. Colour and appearance as dominating sensory properties of foods. *In* "Sensory Properties of Foods" (Birch, G.G.; Brennan, J.G.; Parker, K.J.Eds), Applied Science, 1977.
3.   Clydesdale, F.M. Colorimetry - Methodology and Applications CRC Crit. Rev. in Food Science and Nutrition 1978, 10, 243-301.

4.   Kostyla, A.S.; Clydesdale, F.M. The Psycho-
        physical relationships between colour and
        flavour, CRC Crit. Rev. in Food Science and
        Nutrition, 1978, 10, 303-321.
5.   Food Colour and Appearance - Extended abstracts
        of a Symposium of the Colour Group (Great
        Britain) at the University of Surrey, 1978.
6.   Timberlake, C.F.; Bridle, P. Developments in
        Food Colours - 1. (Walford, J. Ed.), 1980,
        Applied Science, London, 115-149.
7.   Tromp, A.; van Wyk, C.J. The influence of
        colour on the assessment of red wine quality,
        Proc. South African Soc. Enol. Vitic. 1977,
        107-118.

Chapter 3.3

Correlating instrumental measurements with sensory evaluation of texture

M.C. Bourne
New York State Agricultural Experiment Station and Institute of Food Science,
Cornell University, Geneva, New York 14456, USA

SUMMARY

Literature values for correlations between instrumental
measurements and sensory evaluation of texture range from
excellent to awful. Any one of a number of deficiencies in
experimental procedure can lead to low correlations including: using the wrong test principle, improper use of
the instrument, inadequately trained panel, and deficiencies
in selecting and preparing the test samples. Some foods
give better correlations than others even when the best
experimental procedures are used. A system is outlined that
enables one to move expeditiously to the type of instrument
that has a high probability of yielding good correlations
with sensory evaluations.

INTRODUCTION

A large number of instruments are avilable for measuring
textural properties of foods. These have been classified as
fundamental, empirical and imitative [1, 2]. Most of the
instruments used by the food industry are empirical or
imitative, and fundamental tests are rarely used because
they generally give poor correlations with sensory evaluations
of textural quality [3]. A list of the better known texture
instruments is given in Table 1. They range from simple to
complex, from low cost to high cost and use various principles.

Table 1 — Commercially available texture measuring instruments.

Principle of Measurement	Instruments
Puncture (force)	Ballauf, Chatillon, Effi-Gi, U.C. Fruit Firmness Tester, Bloom Gelometer, Stevens LFRA Texture Analyser, Marine Colloids Gel Tester, Maturometer, Armour Tenderometer
Compression-Extrusion (force)	FMC Pea Tenderometer, F.T.C. Texture Press (Kramer Shear Press), Ottawa Pea Tenderometer, Vettori Manghi Tenderometro
Shear (force)	Warner-Bratzler Shear
Torsion (force)	Farinograph, Mixograph, Plint Cheese Curd Torsiometer
Bending (force)	Structograph
Tensile (force)	Extensograph, Instron, F.T.C. Texture Test System fitted with tension test cell accessory
Distance (length)	Bostwick Consistometer, Ridgelimeter, Penetrometer, Adams Consistometer, USDA Consistometer
Volume ($length^3$)	Loaf Volumeter, Succulometer
Time	BBIRA Biscuit Texture Meter
Multiple Measuring (force, work, distance, time)	GF Texturometer, F.T.C. Texture Test System, Instron, Ottawa Texture Measuring System

Each one successfully predicts sensory texture quality for some foods but none of them have been successful for all foods. The universal testing machines have a high success rate because of the wide range of test cells and test conditions they employ. However, even these will not be successful if an inappropriate test principle or incorrect test conditions are used. Also, we have to concede that some texture measurement problems have not yet been resolved even with the use of universal testing machines.

It is well recognised that sensory evaluation of textural properties of foods is important because this is the primary way consumers judge quality. There is no point in measuring physical properties that are not perceived by the human senses or that are judged unimportant. If the consumer considers the texture is poor, then the texture is poor no matter what readings an instrument gives or how well it has been calibrated in fundamental units.

Nevertheless, most food scientists prefer to use instruments because they are objective, have a constant standard, require much less labour, and yield results more quickly than sensory methods. Also, there seems to be a greater implicit trust in the numbers generated by an instrument than in those generated by sensory techniques.

Over the last decade there has been a pronounced trend to abandon the calibration of texture-measuring instruments by arbitrary standards [4] and to calibrate in fundamental internationally recognised standards based on units of mass, length, and time. For example, the unit of force is the Newton which is defined as one metre. kilogram. second^{-2}. The next major trend in texture measurement should be the calibration of instruments against the human senses. The concept that sensory evaluation of textural quality should be the ultimate calibration of instrumental methods is steadily gaining wider acceptance.

This trend has already been identified by Brennan [5] who stated: "Texture is a sensory attribute, perceived by the senses of touch, sight and hearing. Thus the only direct method of measuring texture is by means of one or more of the senses. Non-sensory techniques can never be more accurate than sensory methods. The accuracy of the former can only be judged by their ability to predict the sensory quality being studied".

The question is, how do we correlate instrumental results with the consumer's perception of quality and what problems need to be resolved to improve these correlations? This paper is restricted to a discussion of correlations between instrumental tests and sensory intensity scaling (i.e amount of a texture property). It should not be confused with another branch of sensory testing methodology, acceptability or hedonic scaling (i.e. degree of liking of a textural property).

A GOOD EXAMPLE

The most thorough piece of work correlating instrumental measurements with sensory assessment was performed by the texture group at the General Foods Corporation approximately 20 years ago. The GF Texturometer is a multiple measuring instrument that compresses a bite-size piece of food two times in a manner that imitates the action of the human jaw. The force-time curve is analyzed to yield five different textural parameters [6]. Each of these textural parameters correlated highly with sensory evaluation of those parameters [7]. Figure 1 shows the correlation between hardness as measured by the GF Texturometer and by a trained panel. Although no correlation coefficient was given it is obvious from this graph that an excellent correlation was obtained. Similar excellent correlations were obtained for the textural parameters of fracturability (originally called brittleness), chewiness, gumminess, and adhesiveness.

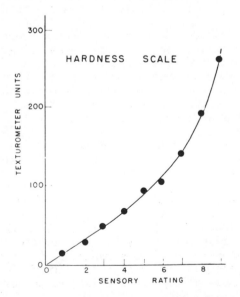

Fig. 1 — Correlation between sensory panel and GF Texturometer for hardness of cream cheese, cooked egg white, frankfurter, pasteurized process cheese, stuffed olives, peanuts, raw carrot, peanut brittle and rock candy (from [17]).

It is worth examining the GF texture profiling technique
to identify those features that were responsible for the
excellent correlations that were obtained. The important
features are:

(i)   Each textural property was carefully defined
        and well understood by the trained panel.

(ii)   The standard samples that were selected encompassed
        the entire range of intensity of the textural
        parameter that they represented.

(iii)   A wide range of foods were used for the
        reference standards. These were very carefully
        selected according to the following criteria:

> (a)   Each item possessed the desired
>   intensity of the textural character-
>   istic.
>
> (b)   The textural characteristic was an
>   outstanding property of the food,
>   easy to perceive sensorially and not
>   overshadowed by other textural para-
>   meters.
>
> (c)   The textural characteristic of each
>   food was reasonably constant from
>   sample to sample.

Other criteria for inclusion in the standard scales were availability, constant quality, familiarity, minimum handling to prepare the product for evaluation, and a relatively small temperature effect.

In commenting on the high correlations that were obtained,
the authors said" It should be kept in mind, however, that
the standards on the scales were carefully selected for the
absence of overshadowing characteristics, which facilitated
their sensory evaluation and undoubtedly contributed to the
good correlation" [7].

The great care given to all interrelated aspects of the
problem - instrument,panel,commodities - was essential to the
success of this project. It provides an elegant example
of "how to do it right". The GF texture profiling technique
is an excellent case study to emulate, even for those of us
who work with a limited range of foods that pose difficult
problems.

A DEFECTIVE EXAMPLE

The instrument most widely used for measuring the tenderness of meat is the Warner-Bratzler Shear [8, 9]. In an extensive review of tenderness of meat, Szczesniak and Torgeson [10] summarised 38 studies on beef, 4 on pork, and 9 on poultry where researchers had listed correlation coefficients between the Warner-Bratzler Shear and some method of sensory testing and found correlations ranging from r = -0.001 to r = -0942. Most of the correlation coefficients were fairly evenly distributed between about r = -0.2 and r = -0.9. Reports published subsequent to this review article continue to show very wide correlation coefficients between the Warner-Bratzler Shear and sensory measurements of meat texture. Why is this very wide range of correlation coefficients found? Are there differences in techniques used by researchers who report widely different correlation coefficients or are the differences related to samples tested, or panel selection?

The following questions should be asked when low correlations are obtained from an instrument that generally gives high correlations:

(i)   Instrument problems. Is the instrument working properly? Are the working parts bent or blunt? Has it been calibrated recently? Did the operator use it correctly?

(ii)   Panel problems. Was the panel trained properly? Did the panel use the correct procedure? Was the definition of the measured textural property clear to the panel? Did the panel have standard samples to serve as anchor points? Is the parameter of interest (e.g. tenderness-toughness of meat) a combination of characteristics that is not amenable to description by a single sensory score? Did other parameters (such as juiciness or appearance) sway the panel's judgement?

(iii)   Commodity problems. Was the sample representative of the lot from which it was taken? Was the sample size large enough and were a sufficient number of replicates used? Was the sample uniform? Was it free from tough connective tissue and soft fatty tissue? (Meat is notorious for lack of uniformity.) Was the sample prepared correctly? Degree of cooking affects WB Shear readings. Were all samples tested at the same temperature?

Caporaso et al., [11] reported WB Shear values on
cooked beef of 6.3 lb at 50°C and 7.2 lb at 22°C.
Were the dimensions of the test samples uniform?
Kastner and Henrickson [12] showed that mounting
the cutting tool in a drill press gave samples that
were more uniform in diameter, closer to the diameter of the boring tool, slightly larger than
the hand cut samples, and gave higher WB readings.
Was a suitable range of textural qualities studied?
Narrowing the range usually lowers the correlation
coefficient (Fig.2).

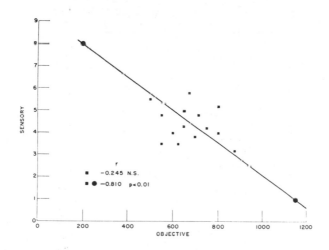

Fig.2 — Effect of texture range on correlation coefficient between objective and
sensory measurements. Notice how adding two points at the extreme
ends raises the correlation coefficient from r = 0.245 to r = 0.810
(from [13]).

THE FLOATING STANDARD

A frequent problem in correlating instrument tests with
sensory scoring is poor definition of the property to be
measured. People often use the same adjective to describe
different physical properties. For example, Szczesniak and
Bourne [14] studied how a consumer might test foods for
firmness without involving the mouth. Nine different pairs
of foods were presented to 131 people who were asked to
determine by non-oral methods which sample in the pair was
more firm. The technique used to determine firmness of each
type of food was noted (Fig. 3). With very soft foods,
firmness was generally determined by means of a viscosity

test (e.g. resistance to stirring with a spoon). A deformation test was used on foods of intermediate firmness. Foods with high firmness were tested by a puncture technique, and elongated foods of very high firmness were tested by bending (flexure). Deformability was usually the first test attempted. When it failed to differentiate between a pair of samples the subject worked down or up the scale until a method that differentiated between the samples was found.

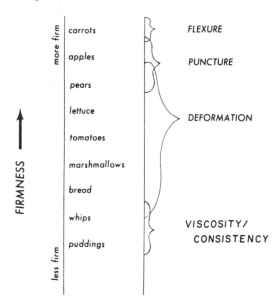

Fig.3 — Schematic representation showing how the sensory method used to measure firmness depends upon the firmness of that food (from [14]).

This study leads to two conclusions:

(i)   the type of sensory test used to judge differences in firmness of foods depends on the level of firmness in the test sample. It may be viscosity, deformability, puncture, or flexure depending on whether the food is soft, firm, or very firm.

(ii)   the test principle used in an instrumental measurement should be the same as that used in the sensory test. The respondents in the firmness study readily switched from one principle to another while continuing to use the descriptive adjective "firmness".

Boyd and Sherman [15] found a similar effect in oral evaluation of hardness. Soft products such as mousse were evaluated by compressing the food between the tongue and hard palate while hard products such as chocolate were evaluated by biting between the incisors. With foods of intermediate hardness such as madeira cake, some respondents used compression while others used the biting test (Fig.4). The researcher who fails to realize that people will float from one principle to another may find he is measuring an irrelevant property.

One can expect to have poor correlations if the wrong objective test is used. Bourne [16] measured the firmness of apples by both deformation and puncture and found very poor correlation between these two methods (Fig. 5). It is impossible for both puncture and deformation to give a high correlation with sensory evaluation of apple firmness.

PROCEDURE FOR SELECTING A SUITABLE OBJECTIVE TEST

Table 1 shows that a number of different principles are used for objectively measuring texture of foods. Although each instrument has its field of success, none of them are suitable for all foods. The procedure described below is designed to lead a researcher to a physical test that is most likely to give good correlation with sensory tests [17].

STEP 1   Eliminate unsuitable test principles

Test principles that are obviously unsuited for the commodity should be eliminated from consideration at the outset. or example, a snapping test is unsuited for flexible or fluid foods, the extrusion test is unsuited for products such as potato chips that do not flow, and the cone penetrometer test is unsuitable for fibrous materials. There is always the temptation to use a certain instrument "just because it is there" without considering whether it is suitable for the purpose. The rejection of unsuitable test principles can be done quickly and often saves considerable time.

STEP 2   Preliminary selection

In this step the field should be narrowed to the most promising 2 or 3 test principles. These can usually be selected by observing what kind of test principle people use in the sensory evaluation of textural quality. For example, if people judge textural quality by jabbing their thumb into the food, consideration should be given to the puncture test;

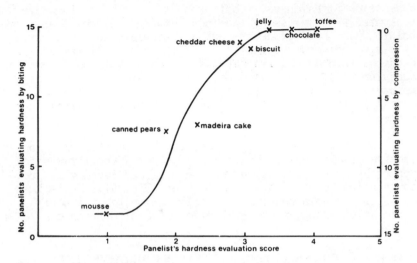

Fig.4 —Mechanism for panelists' oral evaluation of hardness (from [15]).

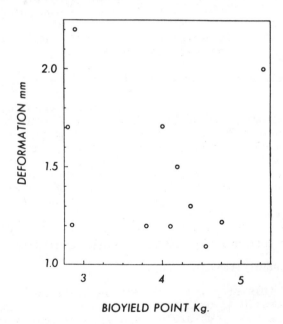

Fig.5 —Firmness of 11 apple varieties as measured by deformation plotted
against firmness of the same varieties as measured by a puncture test
(from [16]).

if they bite the product between the incisors, the
cutting-shear principle should be considered; and if
the people squeeze the product gently in their hand,
the deformation principle should be considered.

The test principles that should be considered are:

> puncture
> deformation
> extrusion
> penetration
> cutting-shear
> snapping-bending
> viscosity-consistency
> crushing
> tensile
> texture profile analysis
> indirect methods.

If any instrument fails to give satisfaction after
adequate testing, its use should be abandoned and
one should look for another instrument that uses a
different test principle. For example, if the Magness-
Taylor puncture test gives low correlations after a
fair trial, then other instruments that work on the
puncture principle will probably be unsatisfactory also. Consideration should then be given to other test
principles such as extrusion, deformation or cutting-
shear. One can easily spend more than the cost of
another instrument in labour costs by persevering
with a test that uses the wrong principle for that
particular application.

STEP 3   Final selection

The test principles that still show promise after this
preliminary selection should now be used over the full
range of textures that will normally be encountered
with the food. This can usually be done rather quickly.
For example, the author was once faced with measuring
the firmness of whole potatoes. Having gone through
the preliminary selection it was agreed that the most
suitable test would be either a puncture test or a deformation test. Three groups of potatoes were selected by hand (soft, medium, hard) with about 10
potatoes in each group. Each of these potatoes was
then tested in the Instron using first a deformation
test and then a puncture test. The mean values were
calculated and are shown in Figure 6. This simple test
clearly shows that the puncture principle is unsuitable
for measuring the kind of firmness that was being

sensed in the hand, but that the deformation test
showed promise. Therefore, we concentrated on re-
fining the deformation test and spent no more time
trying to perfect the puncture test principle for
this particular application. [18].

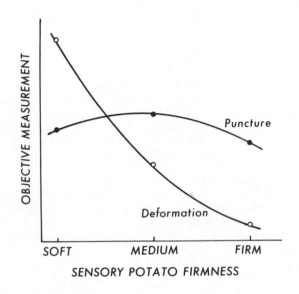

Fig.6 — Two objective methods for measuring firmness of whole potatoes versus
sensory evaluation of firmness of the same potatoes (from [18]).

STEP 4   Refine test conditions

A systematic study of the effect of various test
conditions on the correlation should be performed
after the most promising test principle has been
identified. Variables such as sample size, test
cell dimensions, speed of travel of the moving parts,
chart speed, degree of compression and sample temperature should be studied to find which gives the
best resolution between similar samples. For example, Bourne [19] showed in the deformation test
that a small force usually gives a better resolution
than a large force (Table 2).

Table 2 — Deformation of marshmallows.

Deforming force (g)	Deformation (mm)		Deformation ratio (A/B)
	A. Soft	B. Firm	
20	0.80	0.022	3.64
100	2.37	0.92	2.52
1000	10.7	6.9	1.55
5000	18.7	14.9	1.25

(Data from [19]).

Shama and Sherman [20] showed that the speed of compression had a far-reaching effect on firmness measurements of cheese. A panel rated Gouda cheese as harder than White Stilton cheese. When these cheeses were compressed at 5 cm/min in the Instron, the force at all degrees of compression was higher for the White Stilton than for the Gouda, i.e. the instrument reading indicated that White Stilton was harder than Gouda cheese. At a compression speed of 20 cm/min the force curve for White Stilton was above that for Gouda cheese between 0-38% compression and 62-80% compression, and below that of Gouda between 38-62% compression, i.e. at 20 cm/min compression speed the objective test would have agreed with the panel score only between 38-62% compression. At 50 cm/min compression speed the objective test would have agreed with the panel score only between 35-68% compression and at 100 cm/min between 24-73% compression. Shama and Sherman [20]constructed a three-dimensional plot of force-degree of compression-rate of compression that established a three-dimensional judgement zone that defined the test conditions to be employed if the mechanical test was to give results that agreed with the sensory scores (see shaded zone in Fig. 7). In contrast, the speed of testing has little effect on the puncture test force on apples [21].

The test conditions that are shown to give the best resolution should then be standardized and recorded for future use.

Occasionally, none of the established procedures give satisfactory results. In these cases the researcher should have the confidence to develop a new test procedure that is suitable for the purpose.

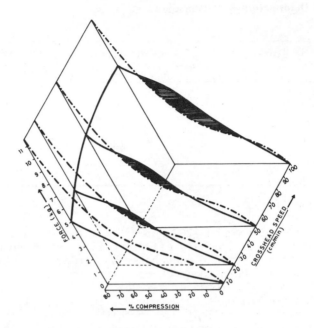

Fig. 7 — Three-dimensional plot of force-degree of compression-rate of loading data for White Stilton cheese (—.——.——.) and Gouda cheese (——). The shaded areas define the test conditions in which the Instron test will rank the samples in the same order as the sensory panel (from [20]).

SCATTER DIAGRAMS

It is useful to make a scatter diagram of the subjective scores (intensity scaling) and objective measurements obtained in the preliminary tests before calculating the correlation coefficient because this enables one to see certain aspects of the correlation that may otherwise be overlooked. For example, a good fit to a curved line will give a poor apparent correlation because the correlation coefficient is calculated for a straight line fit. The simple correlation coefficient for a curvilinear relationship does not adequately reflect the goodness of fit of the experimental points to the line. Under these conditions it is advisable to transform the data in some way to straighten the curve for example, by taking logarithms on one or both axes before calculating the correlation coefficient. A line with a steep slope and close fit of the data points to the line is needed for a good correlation between subjective and objective measurements. The line may have a positive or negative slope and may be rectilinear or curvilinear.

The use of these scatter diagrams does not replace
statistical analysis of the data but it does enable one to
have a better understanding of the relationship before
embarking on statistical analysis. Scatter diagrams can
also save unnecessary effort in computation. If there is
considerable scatter or shallow slope, it is preferable to
continue to explore other test procedures rather than put
a lot of effort into sophisticated statistical analysis of
data that is obviously unsatisfactory.

Kramer [22] makes the following recommendations about the
suitability of correlation coefficients for quality control
purposes provided that representative samples and adequate
sample size are used. When the simple correlation coefficient
between the instrument test and sensory score is $\pm$ 0.9 to $\pm$ 1.0
(r^2 = 0.81 to 1.00), the instrument test can be used with
confidence as a predictor of sensory score. When the correlation coefficient lies between $\pm$ 0.8 and $\pm$ 0.9 (r^2 = 0.64
to 0.81), the test can be used as a predictor but with less
confidence. Extending Kramer's concept further, when the
correlation coefficient lies between $\pm$ 0.7 and $\pm$ 0.8 (r^2 =
0.49 to 0.64) the test is of marginal use as a predictor and
when it is less than $\pm$ 0.7 (r^2 0.49) it is practically worth-
less for predictive purposes.

A statistically significant relationship between an
instrument test and sensory score may be found with a low
correlation coefficient if the sample size is large enough.
Szczesniak [13] pointed out that when only five samples are
tested, a correlation coefficient of r = 0.86 is not significant
at the 5% level, whereas if the number of samples is increased
to 28 a correlation coefficient of 0.38 is significant at the
5% level. A low correlation coefficient, even though
statistically significant, is not adequate for predictive
purposes. One needs to distinguish between statistical
significance and predictive reliability.

EASY FOODS VERSUS DIFFICULT FOODS

The textural properties of some foods change in unison and in
the same direction during maturation, processing and storage;
in these cases, several types of texture measurement will
correlate well with other texture test principles and with
a panel using intensity scaling. An example of this is fruit
that softens greatly as it ripens (e.g. pear, peaches, bananas).
Measuring the changes in firmness of these commodities is fairly
straightforward because any one of several different tests
will give satisfactory results. Figure 8 shows the changes in

textural parameters of pears as they ripen. Notice how all the textural parameters change in the same direction and at approximately the same rate. In this situation one can even measure the wrong parameter and still get the right answer because of the parallel nature of the interrelationships between the different parameters. Such foods give a high correlation between instrument readings and sensory intensity scores fairly easily.

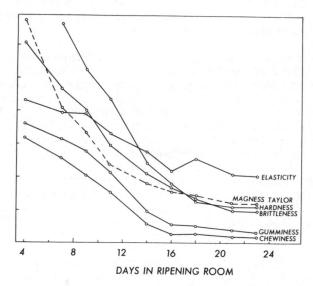

Fig.8 —Changes in Texture Profile parameters and Magness Taylor puncture test on pears as a function of time in ripening room (from [23]).

In contrast, the textural properties of some foods change in different directions and at different rates. With these foods one must be careful to select an instrument that uses a test principle that corresponds closely with the description of the property that is to be rated by the sensory panel. These foods are vexing. It is frequently very difficult to achieve satisfactory correlations with this kind of food.

Multicomponent foods that contain more than one textural element must have each component tested separately. It is usually necessary to use a different test principle on each component. For example, a viscosity test is obviously needed for the broth of chicken noodle soup, but this test will be unsuited for the solids in the soup. Since the chicken pieces are fibrous and the noodles are nonfibrous, it will be necessary to use one kind of test on the chicken

pieces and another on the noodles. Hence, at least three
different test principles will be needed to specify the
texture and viscosity of chicken noodle soup. It is futile
to expect a single overall test to successfully specify the
textures of a composite food that is comprised of more than
one textural element.

REFERENCES

1.   Scott Blair, G.W. Rheology in food research. Adv.Fd Res.
     1958, 8, 1-61.

2.   Szczesniak, A.S. Objective measurements of food texture.
     J.Fd Sci. 1963, 28, 410-420.

3.   Bourne, M.C. Texture measurements in vegetables. In
     "Theory, Determination and Control of Physical
     Properties of Food Materials" (C.Rha, Ed.) 1975,
     Reidel Pub. Co. Dordrecht, Holland, 131-162.

4.   Bourne, M.C. Standardization of texture measuring
     instruments. J. Texture Stud. 1972, 3, 379-384.

5.   Brennan, J.G. Food texture measurement. In "Develop-
     ments in Food Analysis Techniques". Vol.2.
     (R.D.King, Ed.).Applied Science Publishers Ltd.,
     Essex, England, 1-78.

6.   Friedman, H.H., Whitney, J.E. and Szczesniak, A.S.
     The Texturometer-a new instrument for objective
     texture measurement. J.Fd Sci.1963, 28, 390-396.

7.   Szczesniak, A.S., Brandt, M.A. and Friedman, H.H.
     Development of standard rating scales for
     mechanical parameters of texture and correlation
     between the objective and sensory methods of
     texture evaluation. J. Fd Sci. 1963, 28, 397-403.

8.   Bratzler, L.J. Measuring the tenderness of meat by means
     of a mechanical shear. M.S.Thesis, Kansas State
     College, 1932.

9.   Warner, K.F. Progress report of the mechanical test
     for tenderness of meat. Proc. Am. Soc. Animal Prod.
     1928, 114-116.

10. Szczesniak, A.S. and Torgeson, K. Methods of meat
     texture measurement viewed from the background of
     factors affecting tenderness. Adv. Fd Res. 1965,
     14, 33-165.

11.   Caporaso, F., Cortavarria, A.L. and Mandigo, R.W.
      Effects of post-cooking sample temperature on
      sensory and shear analyses of beef steaks.
      J. Fd Sci. 1978, 43, 839-841.

12.   Kastner, C.L. and Henrickson, R.L. Providing uniform
      meat cores for mechanical shear force measurement.
      J. Fd Sci. 1969, 34, 603-605.

13.   Szczesniak, A.S. Correlations between objective and
      sensory texture measurements. Fd Technol. 1968.
      22, 981-986.

14.   Szczesniak, A.S. and Bourne, M.C. Sensory evaluation of
      food firmness. J. Texture Stud. 1969, 1, 52-64.

15.   Boyd, J.V. and Sherman, P. A study of force-compression
      conditions associated with hardness evaluation in
      several foods. J. Texture Stud. 1975, 6, 507-522.

16.   Bourne, M.C. Two kinds of firmness in apples. Fd Technol.
      1969, 23, 333-334.

17.   Bourne, M.C. Food Texture and Viscosity: Concept and
      Measurement, Academic Press, New York, 1982.

18.   Bourne, M.C. and Mondy, N. Measurement of whole potato
      firmness with a universal testing machine. Fd
      Technol. 1967, 21, 1387-1406.

19.   Bourne, M.C. Deformation testing of foods. 1. A precise
      technique for performing the deformation test.
      J. Fd Sci. 32, 601-605.

20.   Shama, F. and Sherman, P. Evaluation of some textural
      properties of foods with the Instron Universal
      Testing Machine. J. Texture Stud. 1973, 4,
      344-353.

21.   Bourne, M.C. Studies on punch testing of apples. Fd
      Technol. 1965, 19, 113-115.

22.   Kramer, A. Objective testing of vegetable quality. Fd
      Technol. 1951, 5, 265-269.

23.   Bourne, M.C. Texture profile of ripening pears. J. Fd
      Sci. 1968, 33, 223-226.

Chapter 3.4

Measurement of particular textural characteristics of some fruits and vegetables

J.G. Brennan
National College of Food Technology, University of Reading, Weybridge, Surrey, UK

SUMMARY

Brief reports on two studies are presented. A constant loading rate instrument was used to test samples of apples and the sound produced during the collapse of the samples was recorded. Highly significant relationships were established between sensory crispness and some of the instrumental results. The importance of sound as an index of crispness was confirmed.

Samples of asparagus and rhubarb were tested by two instrumental methods with a view to measuring fibrousness. Again, significant relationships were established between some of the instrumental results and sensory fibrousness and a more complete definition of this textural characteristic is proposed.

INTRODUCTION

Texture is an important quality attribute of both raw and processed fruits and vegetables and it is often used as a major criterion in selecting such foods for processing. Most instrumental methods (e.g. fruit pressure tester, pea tenderometer and the Kramer Shear cell) used commercially for texture evaluations are of an empirical nature and give results which provide a crude indication of the hardness, firmness or toughness of the material.

The texture of a fruit or vegetable results
from a combination of its physical properties which
in turn reflect its structure, i.e. the size, shape,
number, nature and conformation of its constituent
structural elements [1]. Although all fruits and
vegetables are basically cellular in structure,
there are major differences between different plants
in the size, shape and arrangement of the parenchyma
cells, and the amount and composition of the substances holding the cells together. Differences also
occur in the conductive, supportive and protective
cells of plants. Each fruit or vegetable will there-
fore have its own particular textural character-
istics. A textural feature which is considered to be
desirable in one fruit or vegetable may be regarded
as undesirable in another. Thus, it is necessary to
identify and define the important textural
characteristics of each one before decisions are made
as to how to 'measure' its texture. This can be done
by sensory means using the texture profile technique.
Less progress has been made in measuring specific
textural characteristics by instrumental means.

This paper presents brief reports of two
studies of particular textural features of some
fruits and vegetables.

CRISPNESS

This term is frequently used in the description of
the texture of some fruits, such as apples. The
term is normally associated with a cellular structure
which may be broadly defined as being composed of
cells or cavities having a structured phase and a
filler phase [2]. Crisp, dry foods such as biscuits,
break into many pieces when masticated and their
eating quality is affected by the size of the air
cells and the thickness of the cell walls [3,4].
Fruit and vegetables do not react to stress in a
purely elastic manner but also exhibit some viscous
behaviour, i.e. are viscoelastic [5,6]. The breakage
of these cells is accentuated by the sudden release
of fluid rather than the brittle fracture of the
cells [7]. Iles and Elson [8] concluded that when
fruits and vegetables were subjected to stress, shear
breakdown occurred rather than compressional collapse
of the tissue. In dry, friable food breakdown
occurred along lines of weakness. However, since
both dry and wet crisp foods collapse suddenly under
stress it has been suggested that the application of

a load, increasing at a constant rate, and monitoring the deformation as the structure collapses might characterise the textural property of crispness better than the more usual procedure of deforming the sample at a constant rate, controlled entirely by the testing machine [9]. Many authors have stated that sound is an important contributor to the evaluation of crispness by sensory means [2,10]. One objective of the study, briefly reported here, was to investigate the validity of these statements. A more complete report will be found elsewhere [11,12].

Five varieties of apple were used in this study. Some apples of each variety were stored at $4^{\circ}C$, the remainder at $27^{\circ}C$ for eight days. Cylindrical samples, diameter 20 mm, height 12 mm, from the ten different lots of apples were tested by the instrumental methods outlined below. Slices from the same ten lots of apples were assessed by a trained panel using the technique of magnitude estimation. Crispness and hardness were the two characteristics studied. A constant loading rate (CLR) instrument was used to deform the samples [9]. Both a punch and a 'biting' test probe were used (Fig. 1). The force-time and deformation-time curves (Fig. 2) were recorded on a fast response, transient-signal recorder. Tests were carried out in an anechoic chamber and the sounds produced during each test were recorded. These were analysed as described by Mohamed *et al.* [13] and a quantity known as the equivalent continuous sound level (Leq) was calculated. This represents the level of sound which, if it persisted, would result in the same total of sound energy reaching the microphone.

Fig. 1 — Principles of the (a) Puncture and (b) 'Bite' tests.

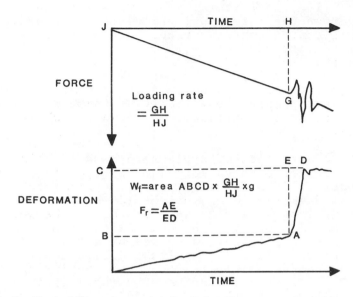

Fig. 2 — Typical force-time and deformation-time traces obtained using the constant loading rate (CLR) instrument.

Sensory crispness correlated significantly (0.1% level) with sensory hardness. Both sensory properties correlated significantly with several measurements taken from the curves obtained with the CLR instrument, including some taken before and during breakdown. In all cases the results from the 'biting' test correlated better (high values of r^2) with the sensory results than did those from the puncture test.

Good correlations were also found between the sensory results and the Leq values calculated from the sound recordings.

With crispness, the sensory results correlated best with the work done during fracture, Wf in Nm x 10^3, and the fracture rate, Fr in ms^{-1}, and the Leq values in dB. The regression lines for these relationships are shown in Figures 3, 4 and 5. When these instrumental results were combined together by multiple regression, a number of equally well fitting equations were derived for the prediction of sensory crispness. The most significant relationships were:

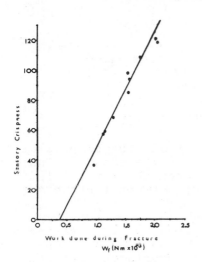

Fig.3 — Relationship between sensory
crispness and the work done
during fracture using the 'bite'
probe on the Constant Loading
Rate (CLR) instrument.

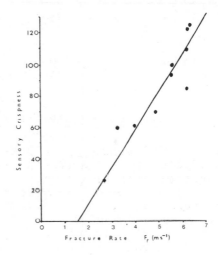

Fig.4 — Relationship between sensory
crispness and the fracture rate
using the 'bite' probe on the
Constant Loading Rate (CLR)
instrument.

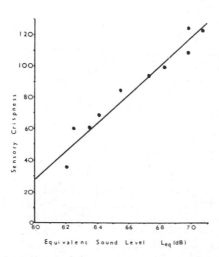

Fig.5 — Relationship between sensory crispness and the
equivalent sound level using the 'bite' probe on
the Constant Loading Rate (CLR) instrument.

Crispness   =   - 153.2 + 2.45 (Leq)
                + 52.4 (Wf) - 0.5 (Fr)   .... (1)
                r = 0.994***

    and

Crispness   =   - 505.3 + 338.5 log (Leq)
                + 240.5 log (Wf)
                - 83.6 log (Fr)   .... (2)
                r = 0.996***

(Level of significance: * = 5%, ** = 1%, *** = 0.1%)

Values for sensory crispness of all the samples were predicted using equation (1) and are shown in Table 1 together with those obtained from the panel. There is a good measure of agreement between the two sets of results.

The high correlation between sensory crispness and hardness and between these two sensory properties and several instrumental measurements confirm the difficulties encountered by many others in distinguishing between these two sensory characteristics by instrumental means [14]. A crisp but soft apple has yet to be found. The results agree with the views of Vickers and Bourne [2] and Voisey and Stanley [15] that the more usual instrumental measurements, i.e. slopes and forces, do not measure actual brittleness or crispness but other characteristics that change similarly as conditions alter.

Attempts to cause sudden breakdown of the apple tissue by compression, a technique successful with dry, crisp foods [13], failed. However, the puncture and 'bite' tests achieved this. In these tests, shear played an important part, confirming that the modes of breakdown of dry and wet crisp foods are different [8]. However, the sounds produced during the breakdown of the apple tissues were similar to those produced by dry crisp foods as they collapsed [13]. A number of tones occur simultaneously and there are no dominant overtones or harmonics. In general, less sound was produced by samples from apples stored at 27°C as compared with those stored at 4°C. This may be due to a higher rate of deterioration of the substances holding the cells together at the higher temperature. There is a greater tendency for cells to separate rather than rupture, producing less noise [16]. The high correlation between sensory crispness and the Leq values underlines the importance of sound as an

index of crispness. The highly significant relationship that emerged from the multiple regression
analysis further confirms this. Recording the
behaviour of samples during breakdown together with
analysis of the sounds produced during such breakdown seem to be useful techniques for studying crispness in apples.

Table 1 — Observed and predicted values of sensory crispness of different
varieties of apples stored at 4°C and 27°C.

Variety	Sensory crispness			
	4°C		27°C	
	Observed	Predicted	Observed	Predicted
Worcester Pearmain	124.4	124.0	86.3	88.1
Miller's Seedling	123.3	126.0	68.7	69.9
Victoria	109.3	109.4	60.3	57.1
Epicure	100.0	97.2	58.9	54.4
Discovery	95.3	95.0	36.7	42.4

FIBROUSNESS

This is a textural feature of many vegetables
(asparagus, French beans, celery and spinach) and
fruits (rhubarb, dates, mango and sugar-cane, which
is considered a fruit in some countries). In such
foods, the perception of fibrousness is expected and
tolerated to a certain level. In other vegetables
and fruits (avocado, courgettes, watermelon, strawberries, papaw and cantaloup) fibrousness is regarded
as an undesirable characteristic. There are
relatively few reports of fibrousness in the literature. In some, fibrousness has been assumed to be a
reflection of the toughness or resistance to cutting
of the fibres. In others, the amount of fibre
present has been taken as an index of fibrousness.
This may be valid for foods in which fibres are not
normally present and are considered undesirable, but
is unlikely to apply to foods which normally contain
fibres.

Instrumental techniques which have been used to measure fibrousness include wire cutting devices [17, 18] and blade cutting instruments [19]. The Kramer Shear Cell and extrusion cells have also been applied to the study of the texture of fibrous foods but have not yielded much information about the particular characteristic of fibrousness.

In this study, sensory and instrumental techniques were used to study the textural characteristics of asparagus and rhubarb [20]. Numerous panel sessions and discussions with panelists, individually and collectively, established a more complete definition of sensory fibrousness comprising four components:

(i)   Detection of fibres in the mouth.
(ii)   Resistance to fibres of biting.
(iii)   Behaviour of the fibres during mastication
        (mouth feel).
(iv)   Residual sensation after swallowing.

In addition to fibrousness, firmness was identified as an important textural characteristic of these foods. Creaminess in the case of asparagus and smoothness in the case of rhubarb were also identified as important textural features. Early work with a trained panel indicated that interval scaling was not suited to the sensory evaluation of these characteristics and the technique of magnitude estimation was used in the main experiments. A pictorial, hedonic scale was used with an untrained panel to determine the acceptability of the samples.

Several instruments were evaluated and two, the Volodkevitch Bite Tenderometer (VBT) and a Back Extrusion Cell (BEC), were selected for this study. Diagrams of these cells and typical curves obtained from them are shown in Figures 6 and 7. Both were mounted on an Instron Universal Test Machine.

Several varieties of asparagus and rhubarb, both cooked and uncooked, were tested on these instruments and the cooked samples were assessed by both trained and untrained panels.

Sensory firmness showed an inverse relationship with the hedonic rating for both foods. Creaminess in the case of asparagus and smoothness of rhubarb showed no significant relationship to the acceptability of these foods. At low values of fibrousness,

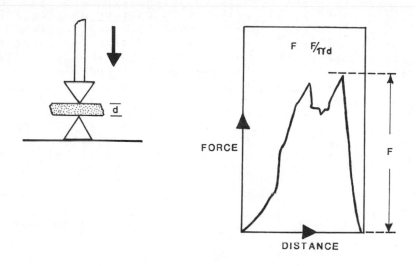

Fig. 6 — Typical force-distance trace obtained from the Volodkevitch Bite
        Tenderometer (VBT) instrument.

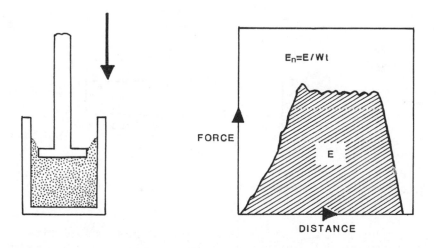

Fig. 7 — Typical force-distance trace obtained from the Back Extrusion Cell
        (BEC).

the hedonic rating of asparagus remained almost
constant. After a certain increase in fibrousness,
the hedonic rating fell suddenly and then remained
constant again at higher values of fibrousness. A
similar pattern was observed with rhubarb but could
not be confirmed as this food did not have low
values of fibrousness comparable with asparagus.
This suggests that there is a threshold value of
objectionable fibrousness (at around 60 on the
scoring system used). Samples of other foods were
assessed for fibrousness and acceptability and the
results (Fig. 8), seem to confirm the threshold
theory.

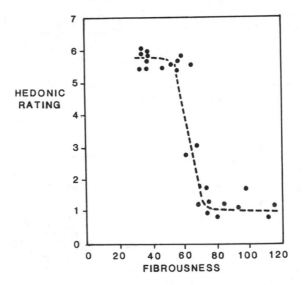

Fig.8 — Relationship between the hedonic rating and sensory fibrousness for a
range of foods.

The relationships between the results obtained
by sensory and instrumental means were investigated
by regression analysis. Equations were obtained for
both asparagus and rhubarb. The difference between
the two sets of equations was mainly in the value of
the ordinates and the slopes were in the same range.
The results were pooled to increase the power of the
equations. The most interesting relationships found
were as follows:

Sensory fibrousness and firmness were highly correlated, the best relationship being:

$$\text{Fibrousness} = 0.571 \, (\text{Firmness})^{1.097} \qquad \dots (3)$$
$$r = 0.785**$$

This might indicate that there is an important component of fibrousness due to the resistance of the food to deformation. Neither creaminess nor smoothness correlated significantly with fibrousness or firmness.

Several well-fitting equations were derived relating the results from the VBT instrument on the cooked and uncooked samples to sensory fibrousness and firmness. The best fit equations were:

$$\text{Fibrousness} = 88.47 \, (M_f)_c^{0.586} \qquad \dots (4)$$
$$r = 0.750*$$

$$\text{Fibrousness} = 38.13 \, (M_f)_u^{0.714} \qquad \dots (5)$$
$$r = 0.860**$$

$$\text{Firmness} = 83.60 \, (M_f)_c^{0.281} \qquad \dots (6)$$
$$r = 0.500*$$

$$\text{Firmness} = 52.07 \, (M_f)_u^{0.454} \qquad \dots (7)$$
$$r = 0.767**$$

where M_f is the maximum force registered divided by the perimeter of the samples ($kN \, m^{-1}$) and the suffixes c and u indicate cooked and uncooked samples respectively. The results for sensory firmness are less significantly related to the instrumental results from the cooked samples as compared with those from the uncooked material. The considerable change in structure which occurs during cooking makes it difficult to distinguish between the cooked samples by instrumental testing.

The best relationships derived from the BEC results were:

$$\text{Fibrousness} = 8.48 + 0.76 \, (E_n)_c \qquad \dots (8)$$
$$r = 0.960**$$

$$\text{Fibrousness} = 13.64 + 0.134 \, (E_n)_u \qquad \dots (9)$$
$$r = 0.936**$$

$$\text{Firmness} = 9.34 \, (E_n)_c^{0.474} \qquad \ldots (10)$$
$$r = 0.620^*$$

$$\text{Firmness} = 5.26 \, (E_n)_u^{0.442} \qquad \ldots (11)$$
$$r = 0.704^*$$

where E_n is the energy required for extrusion per unit weight of sample ($J \, kg^{-1}$). This instrument seems to provide results which are equally good indices of fibrousness and firmness.

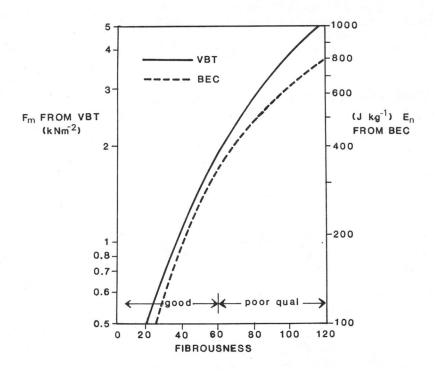

Fig.9 — Relationships between sensory fibrousness and results obtained from the VBT and BEC instruments.

The equations for fibrousness involving the instrumental results from the uncooked samples are presented graphically in Figure 9. Using this curve, sensory crispness of the cooked samples of asparagus and rhubarb, used in this study, were predicted from

the results obtained on the uncooked samples using
both the VBT and BEC instruments. These results
together with the results obtained from the panel
(Table 2) show a good measure of agreement for both
foods.

Table 2 – Observed and predicted values of sensory crispness of different
varieties of asparagus and rhubarb.

| | Sensory fibrousness | | |
Sample	Observed	Predicted from VBT results	Predicted from BEC results
Asparagus			
Var. Anetto	55.0	53.8	44.4
Var. Minerva	71.4	80.1	73.6
Var. No. 54	43.0	44.5	44.8
Var. Giant Mammoth I	29.0	37.0	37.4
Var. Giant Mammoth II	32.0	37.4	39.6
Var. Kidner	53.0	51.0	48.0
Rhubarb			
Variety A	103.0	82.5	96.8
Variety B	114.0	90.1	113.8
Variety C	92.0	91.7	87.8

VBT = Voldkevitch Bite Tenderometer
BEC = Back Extrusion Cell

Fibrousness is a complex property not just
related to the strength and amount of fibres present,
but also to their perception during and after
mastication. Sensory fibrousness of the cooked
asparagus and rhubarb can be measured instrumentally
using the VBT and BEC instruments. When the results
from these instruments are combined by multiple
regression analysis an even more significant (0.1%
level) relationship emerges.

$$\text{Fibrousness} = 9.198 = 18.025 \ (M_f)_c$$
$$+ 6.606 \ (E_n)_c \qquad \ldots (12)$$

Thus the results from the two instruments appear to complement each other.

Sensory fibrousness of the cooked product can be predicted from the results of tests on the uncooked material with these same instruments. In this case combining the results from the two instruments does not improve the accuracy of the prediction signifi- cantly. Similar predictions of sensory firmness can be made using the appropriate equations. None of the instrumental results related to the sensory properties of creaminess and smoothness at the 5% level of significance or better.

REFERENCES

1. Anon. Glossary of terms relating to the sensory analysis of foods, 1975. B.S.5098, British Standards Institution, London.
2. Vickers, Z.; Bourne, M.C. A psycho-accoustical theory of crispness. J.Fd Sci. 1976, 41, 1158-1164.
3. Coppock, J.B.M.; Carnford, S.J. Texture in foods, SCI Monograph No. 7, 1960, 64.
4. Matz, S.A. Food Texture. AVI Publishing Co., Westport, Connecticut, USA, 1962.
5. Schmidt, T.R.; Ahmed, E.M. Textural and elastic properties of Irish potatoes; I. Textural properties. J.Texture Stud. 1971, 2, 460-474.
6. Kapsalis, J.G.; Segars, A.R.; Krizik, J.G. An instrument for measuring rheological properties by bending - applications to food materials of plant origin. J.Texture Stud. 1972, 3, 31-50.
7. Jowitt, R. An engineering approach to some aspects of food texture. In 'Food Texture and Rheology' (Sherman, P., Ed.) Academic Press, London, 1979, 143-155.
8. Iles, B.C.; Elson, C.R. Crispness. BFMIRA Research Report No. 190, London, 1972.
9. Jowitt, R.; Mohamed, A.A.A. An improved instru- ment for studying crispness in foods. In 'Food Process Engineering, Vol.1' (Linko, P., Malkki, Y., Olkku, J. and Larinkari, J., Eds), Applied Science Publishers Ltd, London, 1980, 292-300.

10. Sherman, P.; Deghaidy, F.S. Force-deformation conditions associated with the evaluation of brittleness and crispness in selected foods. J.Texture Stud. 1978, 9, 437-459.

11. Mohamed, A.A.A. Sensory and instrumental measurement of food texture, with particular reference to crispness. Ph.D. Thesis (unpublished), University of Reading, Engand, 1981.

12. Mohamed, A.A.A.; Jowitt, R.; Brennan, J.G. Sensory and instrumental measurement of food crispness. II. In a high moisture food. J.Fd Engng 1982, 1 (in press).

13. Mohamed, A.A.A.; Jowitt, R.; Brennan, J.G. Instrumental and sensory evaluation of crispness. I. In friable foods. J.Fd.Engng 1982, 1 (in press).

14. Brennan, J.G.; Jowitt, R.; Mohamed, A.A.A. Instrumental measurement of fruit texture: a study on apples. Ann.appl.Biol. 1977, 87, 121-127.

15. Voisey, P.W.; Stanley, D.W. Interpretation of instrumental results in measuring bacon crispness and brittleness. Can.Inst.Fd Sci. Technol.J. 1979, 12, 7-15.

16. Reeve, R.M. Relationship of histological structure to texture of fresh and processed fruits and vegetables. J.Texture Stud. 1970, 1, 247-284.

17. Townsend, C.T.; Somers, I.R.; Lamb, F.C.; Olson, N.A. A Laboratory Manual for the Canning Industry, 1956. National Consumers' Assoc. Res. Lab., Washington, USA.

18. Bernell, A.M.; Calvo, C.; Duran, L.; Primo, E. Revista de Agroquimica y Tecnologia de Alimentos 1973, 13, 463.

19. Kramer, A.; Haut, I.C.; Scott, L.E.; Ide, L.L. Quick recorders of fibrousness in asparagus. Fd Industry 1949, 21, 1075.

20. Anzaldua-Morales, A. The texture of fibrous fruits and vegetables. Ph.D. Thesis (unpublished), University of Reading, 1982.

Chapter 3.5

Measuring of sensory quality: assessing aroma by gas chromatography

P. Dürr
Eidg. Forschungsanstalt für Obst–, Wein– und Gartenbau, CH–8820 Wädenswil, Switzerland

SUMMARY

Gas chromatography (GC) is often used for the assessment of flavour quality of food products. This paper describes all associated techniques from sample preparation, injection, separation, detection, identification of components and finally to the interpretation of the results. The advantages of high resolution GC on glass capillaries for quantitative analysis, detection of adulterations, alterations, character impact compounds and taints are reviewed. Relevant examples from the extensive literature are cited.

INTRODUCTION

Most of our food odour impressions are stimulated by complex mixtures of volatile odourous chemicals, belonging to different chemical classes and occuring at variable concentrations. Any technique, therefore, for investigating this complex of odours is of interest. During the last decade, gas chromatography-mass spectrometry (GC-MS) became popular due to its efficiency in separation and identification of volatiles. This development is largely based on the use of glass capillary columns [1,2,3,4].

Strictly speaking, GC is a separation technique, but in its broader context it includes all associated techniques such as sample preparation, injection, separation, detection, identification and interpretation. This paper deals with the most common approaches to each step and discusses their value in the evaluation of food aroma in terms of quantitative analysis, detection of adulterations, alteration, character impact compounds, taints and correlations to sensory characteristics. Selected references are given as examples.

ANALYTICAL TECHNIQUES

Sample preparation

Obviously, direct sampling by injecting the liquid food or headspace vapour would be the ideal way of sample examination. Aroma volatiles, however. occur in extremely low concentrations at different concentrations and they vary in their functional groups. Non-volatile components also can prevent good separations. Therefore, food aromas have to bo extracted, concentrated and pre-separated. In a few cases only can the volatiles be separated on a capillary column by direct injection of a liquid food. By directly injecting distillates like brandy, higher alcohols, and some esters and acids can be detected. More common is the direct injection of the odourous headspace as we smell it [5,6]. The limiting factor here is the low concentration of volatiles in the headspace vapour. The usual way of overcoming this problem is to concentrate the volatiles on cold traps or absorbent material like charcoal, Chromosorb or Tenax GC. Nitrogen or carbon dioxide gas is used to transport volatiles from the food sample. Subsequently the volatiles are desorbed by heat or a solvent [7,8,9].

In most cases, however, food aromas have to be extracted from the sample using a suitable solvent. There are many solvents with different characteristics [10]. To avoid problems caused by emulsions, foods are often distilled or steam distilled and the distillate extracted. The Likens-Nickerson technique [11] of which many modifications have been made combines distillation and extraction [12,13]. Solvent extracts can be injected directly or are further concentrated by solvent evaporation. It may also be necessary to pre-separate the complex aroma extract by liquid chromatography on silica gel [14,15].

Every manipulation of a food aroma changes its composition and complicates any quantitative analysis. A sample preparation technique should therefore be as simple as possible.

Injection

The liquid or gaseous sample with an optimal concentration of volatiles has to be transferred on to the
capillary column in the best way to give a narrow
starting band for the chromatographic process [16].
Common procedures used are split injection [17], split
injection with cold trapping and split-less injection
with solvent effect [18]. By using the solvent effect, a relatively large sample of 0.5 - 2 µl, which
allows the detection of trace components, is introduced into the column. A newer development is direct
on-column injection of a liquid extract [19,20].

Separation

Capillary columns, including both glass and fused
silica, probably represent the greatest advance in
aroma research [21]. Variables are the column diameter and length, the type of liquid phase and the
thickness of the liquid film [22]. A wide range of
liquid phase materials are normally used and for a
particular application, the important criteria are
polarity, temperature range for routine use and application characteristics. Most common phases for
complex food aromas are the Ucon oils and the more
polar Carbowaxs. Suitable carrier gases, in order of
decreasing velocity, are hydrogen, helium and nitrogen, the purity of the carrier gas and the nature of
pressure reducing valves also being critical.

Detection

The thermal conductivity detector (TCD) is non-destructive but due to its low sensitivity is inadequate
for many purposes. The flame ionisation detector
(FID) is non-selective, reasonably sensitive, destructive, stable and simple to use and therefore finds
wide favour in aroma separation. The photo-ionisation
detector (PID) is more sensitive, non-destructive and
selective for components with a high ionisation potential. The electron capture detector (ECD) is very
sensitive, selective to halogen-containing components
and is therefore of particular interest in pesticide
research. The flame photometric detector (FPD) is
destructive and detects sulphur- and phosphorus-
containing components. Figure 1 compares the sensitivity of various detectors. The detectors are connected to recorders and computing integrators for

signal analysis.

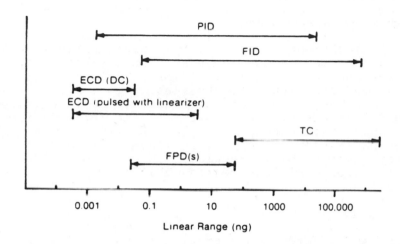

Fig.1 — Linear dynamic ranges of various GC detectors (from Driscoll, J.N.,
      Amer. Lab., 1976, 9,71).

An important detector in aroma research is the
human nose - the most sensitive detector to many aroma
components. It is also a selective detector. The
sniffing person can describe the intensity and the
quality of the odour, and can locate the components
of sensory value in a chromatogram.

Identification

There is no single technique which clearly identifies
all components of a complex aroma. The experienced
analyst, by examining the size and shape of a peak
and absolute and relative retention times to standard
peaks, can obtain an indication of the identity of a
component. Examination of the expected compound under
different chromatographic conditions (temperature,
liquid phase) augments this data. Much information
can also be derived by sniff detection.

Spectroscopic techniques, such as mass spectrometry (MS), nuclear magnetic resonance (NMR) and
infra-red spectroscopy (IR) are more reliable and
more costly. Most powerful in flavour research is the

coupled high resolution gas chromatograph-mass specto-
meter, where the MS can also be used as a detector for
specific components.

APPLICATION IN THE ANALYSIS OF FOOD AROMA

Quantitative analysis of volatiles

The GC techniques provide a reliable quantitative analysis of a food aroma; because such analyses are
costly and only a small fraction of all identified
volatiles contribute to the sensory quality, they are
not done routinely. Computerized lists of volatiles
found in foods are available [23] and for many foods
the quantitative composition of the volatiles has
been published. The creative flavourist needs such
information as basic knowledge for his work. Under
controlled conditions reproducibility of ±10% can be
expected.

Sniff evaluation

Using sniff detection operating in parallel with FID
and signal integration, the sensory value of a peak can
be evaluated. Nevertheless, the possibility of flavour
enhancing or supressing effects between components
should be kept in mind. Some so-called character impact compounds [24] or taints [25] can readily be
detected by sniffing, but occasionally a distinct odour
is detected in a region where the FID gives no signal.
Such events illustrate the limits of the FID for aroma
research. For many odourous components, the human
nose is more sensitive and selective than any other
GC-detector.

Food adulterations and alterations

The aroma of a food is often characteristic of that
food, and so specific and complex that it can be used
as a fingerprint. Adulterations, contaminations and
alterations can often be detected by quantitative analysis of some typical volatiles. Volatiles, unfortunately, can be added or lost during the processing
of a product. However, the lack of volatiles can not
be interpreted as food adulteration, rather as an
alteration. On the other hand, the detection of an
unusual proportion of volatiles or unidentified peaks,
may suggest adulteration or contamination. The identification of the GC peaks enables one to understand
what may have happened. Any treatment or processing

of a food product affects its aroma. Such alterations
can be followed using GC providing a better understanding of the process and consequently leading to
its improvement. The addition of flavours to food
plays an important role in today's food technology;
GC is a tool to control such additions.

Correlations to sensory characteristics

Many researchers use both GC and sensory methods to
evaluate food aromas. An important question is:
"Why is an aroma good or bad?" Both approaches
usually produce much raw data from which correlation
are derived. Techniques applied to the problem range
from simple graphical plots (two- or multi-dimensional)
to statistical methods employing multivariate analysis
[26,27]. The success of such statistical approaches
relies on effective cooperation between instrumental
analysis, computer programmers and statisticians.

CONCLUSIONS

GC and sensory data are complementary, and both approaches are important in the evaluation of food aromas. Large amounts of data are usually obtained, so
it is usually necessary to refine the data to abstract
the required information. Furthermore, a food aroma,
whether in its natural state or extracted should be
regarded as unstable, since the components contain
various reactive functional groups. Many important
sensory constituents occur at very low concentrations
(ppb range) and investigators have to be very careful to avoid contamination from laboratory air,
glassware, solvents or carrier gas. GC alone
enables the identity of a complex food aroma to be
checked, but for quality evaluation it needs to be
connected to sensory measurements.

REFERENCES

1. Schomburg, G.; Dielmann, R.; Husmann, H.; Weeks,
   F. Gas chromatography analyses with glass
   capillary columns. J. Chromatogr. 1976, 122,
   55-72.
2. Schreier, P. Aromastoff-Analytik in Lebensmitteln.
   Deutsche Lebensmittel-Rundschau, 1978, 74,
   321-329.
3. Tressl, R. Probleme bei der Beurteilung von
   natürlichen Aromen. Lebensmittelchem. gerichtl.
   Chem. 1980, 34, 47-53.

4. Teranishi, R.; Flath, R.A.; Sugisawa, H.(Eds).
    Flavor Research. Marcel Dekker, New York and
    Basel, 1981.
5. Charalambous, G. (Ed.) Analysis of Foods and
    Beverages, Headspace Techniques. Academic
    Press, New York, 1978.
6. Green, J.D. Direct sampling method for gas
    chromatographic headspace analysis on glass
    capillary columns. J. Chromatogr. 1981, 210,
    25-32.
7. Williams, A.A.; May, H.V.; Tucknott, O.G. Obser-
    vations on the use of porous polymers for
    collecting volatiles from synthetic mixtures
    reminiscent of fermented ciders. J. Sci. Fd
    Agric. 1978, 29, 1041-1054.
8. Cole, R.A. The use of porous polymers for the
    collection of plant volatiles. J. Sci. Fd
    Agric. 1980, 31, 1242-1249.
9. Parliment, T.H. Concentration and fractionation
    of aromas on reverse-phase absorbents.
    J. Agric. Fd Chem. 1981, 29, 836-841.
10. Weurman, C. Isolation and concentration of vol-
    atiles in food odour research. J. Agric. Fd
    Chem. 1969, 17, 370-384.
11. Likens, S.T.; Nickerson, G.B. Detection of cer-
    tain hop oil constituents in brewing products
    Am. Soc. Brewing Chemists Proc. Annual Meeting
    1964, 5-13.
12. Römer, G.; Renner, E. Einfache Methode zur
    Isolierung und Anreicherung von Aromastoffen
    aus Lebensmitteln, Z. Lebensm. Unters. Forsch.
    1974, 156, 329-355.
13. Au-Yeung, Ch.Y.; MacLeod, J. A comparison of the
    efficiency of the Likens and Nickerson ex-
    tractor for aqueous, lipid/aqueous and lipid
    samples. J. Agric. Fd Chem. 1981, 29, 502-
    505.
14. Schreier, P.; Drawert, F. Quantitative Bestim-
    mung flüchtiger Spurenkomponenten in Lebens-
    mitteln mit der Adsorptions-Chromatographie
    und Gas-Chromatographie-Massen-spektrometrie.
    Z. Anal. Chem. 1976, 279, 141-142.
15. Murray, K.E.; Stanley, G. Class separation of
    flavour volatiles by liquid chromatagraphy on
    silica gel at 1°C. Chromatogr. 1968, 34, 174.
16. Schomburg, G.; Behlau, H.; Dielmann, R.; Weeke,
    E.; Husmann, H. Sampling techniques in cap-
    illary gas chromatography. J. Chromatogr.
    1977, 142, 87-102.

17. Jennings, W.G. Glass inlet splitter for gas
     chromatography. J. Chromatogr. Sci. 1975,
     13, 185.
18. Grob, K.; Grob, K. Splitless injection and the
     solvent effect. J. High Resolution Chromatogr.
     Communications 1978, 1, 57-64.
19. Schomburg, G.; Husmann, H.; Weeke, F. New devel-
     opments and experiences with glass capillary
     column production and sampling techniques.
     Chromatographia 1977, 10, 580.
20. Grob, K.; Neukom, H.P. Factors affecting the
     accuracy and precision of cold on-column in-
     jections in capillary gas chromatography.
     J. Chromatogr. 1980, 189, 109-117.
21. Jennings, W.; Shibamoto, T. Qualitative Analysis
     of Flavor and Fragrance Volatiles by Glass
     Capillary Gas Chromatography. Academic Press,
     New York, 1980.
22. Grob, K.; Grob, K. Are we using the full range
     of film thickness in capillary-GLC? Chromato-
     graphia, 1977, 10, 250-255.
23. van Straten, S. (Ed). Volatile Compounds in
     Food. TNO, Zeist, the Netherlands, 1977 and
     complements.
24. Jennings, W.G. Chemistry of flavor. Lebensm.-
     Wiss. Technol. 1969, 2, 75.
25. Tanner, R.; Zanier, C.; Buser, H.R. 2,4,6-Trich-
     loranisol: Eine dominierende Komponente des
     Korkgeschmacks. Schweiz. Z. Obst Weinbau
     1981, 117, 97-103.
26. Fienberg, S.E. Graphical methods in statistics.
     Amer. Statistician, 1979, 33, 165-179.
27. Morrison, D.F. Multivariate Statistical Methods.
     McGraw-Hill Books, New York, 1976.

Chapter 3.6

Headspace gas-chromatography as a means of assessing the effect of non-volatile food components on volatile flavour compounds

Bonnie M. King* and J. Solms
Department of Food Science, Swiss Federal Institute of Technology, 8029 Zurich, Switzerland

SUMMARY

Reliable information concerning the effects of non-volatile food components on volatile flavour compounds has been obtained by examining the headspace of model systems using gas-chromatography. For many systems, changes in concentration of headspace components can be correlated directly to the amount of the non-volatile component present. Sensory methods corroborate headspace-gas chromatographic (HS-GS) measurements by confirming a decrease in odour intensity for those systems in which the headspace concentration decreased. Data for model systems containing purines such as caffeine, theobromine and 1,3,7, 9 - tetramethyluric and phenols, such as chlorogenic acid, naringin and propyl gallate show that these components decrease the headspace concentration of many volatile flavour compounds.

INTRODUCTION

It has been said that the only reliable measurement of sensory quality is actually smelling or tasting the food in question. While it is true that instruments cannot make absolute value judgements for us, they can be used effectively for quality control once criteria for food acceptability have been established in terms of measurable parameters. The use of headspace gas chromatography (HS-GC) instead of "sniffing" is one example of an efficient routine application of instrumental analysis to measure sensory quality.

**Present address:* Van Der Pers Developments, Skarpskyttevagen 22 A, 222 42 Lund, Sweden.

A food might be rejected because it does not have the odour normally considered desirable or characteristic of that food. Perhaps some contaminant is present creating an "off-flavour", or the relative concentrations of volatiles are disturbed so that the aroma becomes unbalanced. Both of these problems could be detected by comparing headspace chromatograms from the food under consideration to those obtained from samples judged acceptable.

Flavour imbalance or decreased flavour intensity can be the result of interactions between volatile flavour compounds and other food components. Blandness in foods that can be attributed to insufficient volatiles present is measured by making use of quantitative as well as qualitative HS- GC analysis. The same methods make it possible to study interactions of flavour compounds, especially interactions with non-volatile food components. A knowledge of these interactions is of considerable importance in reconstructing specific aromas from chemical flavour analyses.

Many workers have shown that certain classes of non-volatile food components have predictable effects on volatile flavour compounds. Salts, for example, usually increase the headspace concentrations of aldehydes, esters and alcohols [1]. Decreases in headspace concentrations of volatiles have been caused by oils [2], emulsifiers [3], and proteins [4,5].

THE EFFECT OF PURINES AND PHENOLS ON HEADSPACE CONCENTRATION OF VOLATILE FLAVOUR COMPONENTS

We have used the HS-GC technique to examine the effect of non-volatile purines and phenols on volatile flavour compounds. In a closed system consisting of a flavour compound in aqueous solution, the amount of flavour compound present in the system, C, is given by equation (1) where C_{HS} and C_S are the concentrations in the headspace and solution respectively, and V_{HS} and V_S are the corresponding volumes of each phase. As long as C is not sufficient to saturate the aqueous solution, C_{HS} will be directly proportional to C_S as shown in equation (2), where K is the air/water partition coefficient determined for the particular system.

$$C = V_{HS}C_{HS} + V_S C_S \qquad \ldots\ldots\ldots (1)$$

$$C_{HS} = K C_S \qquad \ldots\ldots\ldots (2)$$

A non-volatile substance dissolved in the system may interact with the volatile flavour compound and modify the value of K. Fig. 1 shows that K decreases when the purine caffeine is added to aqueous solutions of ethyl benzoate. Linear relationships, as shown in Fig. 1, have been obtained for many systems containing other volatile flavour compounds, as well as other purines.

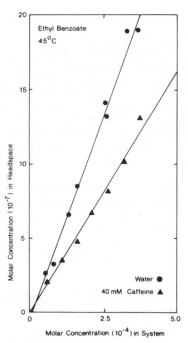

Fig. 1 — Effect of caffeine on the headspace of ethyl benzoate.

Caffeine, theobromine and 1,3,7,9-tetramethyluric acid (TMUA) are three purines which occur in tea, coffee, cola, cocoa and maté. Any one of these purines dissolved in an aqueous solution containing a volatile flavour compound decreases the headspace concentration of that volatile. Increasing the concentration of purine in solution decreases the headspace concentration of the volatile in a non-linear way: there is levelling off as the solution becomes saturated in the purine [6]. The non-linear decreases in headspace concentration with increasing purine concentration obtained for caffeine, theobromine and TMUA were found to be similar. By comparing decreases in systems containing equimolar solutions of these purines, it was shown that TMUA caused the largest decreases in volatile headspace concentration followed by caffeine and theobromine respectively [7].

The beverages mentioned above also contain non-volatile phenols, like chlorogenic acid. Figure 2 shows that the presence of chlorogenic acid decreases the headspace concentration of 2, 3-diethyl pyrazine. Other phenols which had the same effect on the headspaces of volatile flavour compounds were naringin and the common antioxidant propyl gallate.

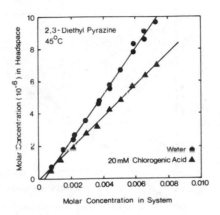

Fig.2 — Effect of chlorogenic acid on the headspace of 2,3-diethyl pyrazine.

CHLOROGENIC ACID

NARINGIN

PROPYL GALLATE

Figure 3 shows the decrease in headspace concentration for anisole in the presence of propyl gallate. The values of K for these and other systems have been determined [8]. The data indicate that in systems containing aqueous solutions of purines, phenols or combinations of the two, the headspace concentrations of volatile flavour compounds are decreased, and therefore the perceived odour intensity should be reduced.

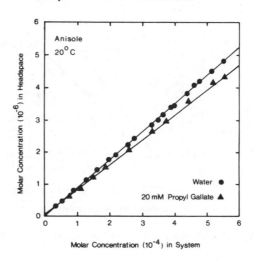

Fig.3 — Effect of propyl gallate on the headspace of anisole.

This was tested in the system containing ethyl benzoate (6.6×10^{-6}M) in water containing various concentrations of caffeine. The ethyl benzoate solution was of moderate intensity to a panel of 18 assessors. At each panel, assessors selected the sample perceived to be stronger from each of a number of random pairs of samples, one of which was ethyl benzoate solution and the other, the same solution also containing varying amounts of added caffeine (Table 1). The results clearly demonstrate significant decreases in odour intensity in the presence of 40 mM caffeine and thus confirm the sensory consequence of the decrease in headspace concentration.

Table 1 – The effect of added caffeine on the odour intensity of 6.6×10^{-6} M ethyl benzoate in aqueous solution at 20°C using the paired comparison test.

Added caffeine (mM)	Responses of 18 assessors [a] Panel sessions			
	1	2	3	4
5	–	10.5	12	12
10	8.5	10	13	13
20	14^b	10	13	13
40	15^c	14^b	14^b	14^b
80	15^c	–	–	–

[a] Number perceiving ethyl benzoate alone as stronger plus half "No Difference" responses.

[b] Significantly different at $\underline{P}=0.05$.

[c] Significantly different at $\underline{P}=0.01$.

CONCLUSIONS

The HS-GC is a helpful and valid technique for measuring sensory quality. Aroma deficiency can be detected both quantitatively and qualitatively. Often the cause of the deficiency can be traced to interactions between volatiles and non-volatile food components. These interactions can be studied in model systems by the same HS-GC techniques.

ACKNOWLEDGEMENTS

This work was carried out as part of a study by A. Tunaley and N. Griffiths at the ARC Food Research Institute, Norwich, UK.

REFERENCES

1. Nelson, P.E. and Hoff, J.E. J.Fd Sci. 1968 33, 479.

2.   Grab, W., Beck, E. and Bernegger, T. <u>Int. Flavours</u>
      <u>Fd Addit</u>. 1977,8 (2), 63-66.

3.   Franzen, K.L. and Kinsella, J.E. <u>J. Agr. Fd Chem</u>.1974.
      22(4), 675-678.

4.   Gremli, H.A. <u>J. Am. Oil Chemists' Soc</u>. 1974,51, 95A
      -97A.

5.   Land, D.G. and Reynolds, J. Proc. 3rd Weurman Symposium,
      Walter de Gruyter, Berlin, 1981, 701-705.

6.   King, B.M. and Solms, J. Proc. 3rd Weurman Symposium,
      Walter de Gruyter, Berlin, 1981,707-716.

7.   King, B.M. and Solms, J. Proc. 7th Int. Symposium on
      Olfaction and Taste, Information Retrieval Ltd.,
      London, 1980,23-26.

Chapter 3.7

Bitterness, astringency and the chemical composition of ciders

A.G.H. Lea and G.M. Arnold
Long Ashton Research Station, University of Bristol, Long Ashton, Bristol BS18 9AF, UK

SUMMARY

Bitterness and astringency in ciders (tannin) is due to phenolic procyanidins ranging in size from the dimeric to the heptameric. The Scheffé method of reversed-pair tasting has been used to assess the relative bitterness and astringency of these procyanidins in relation to their molecular weight. Bitterness predominates in the lower members of the series (oligomeric) and astringency predominates at higher molecular weight (polymeric). Chromatographic analysis of two cider apple cultivars whose tannin is traditionally described as 'hard' and 'soft' has confirmed that the ratio of oligomeric to polymeric procyanidins is greater for the 'hard' cultivar than it is for the 'soft' one, providing a chemical basis for this traditional description.

INTRODUCTION

The work described here was carried out some five or six years ago, when we were particularly interested in the bitterness and astringency of English ciders [1]. These characteristics have traditionally been regarded as typical of good quality ciders and they are certainly a most distinctive feature of the bittersweet cider apples which are grown specifically in the south-west of Britain for cider making. Even to-day, our large (and small) cider manufacturers still take considerable trouble to include

such apples in most of their blends, although much
of the juice used nowadays comes from other sources
and this is reflected in an increasing blandness
compared to the traditional product.

For many years this bitterness and astringency
has been attributed to 'tannin', a word of
notoriously imprecise definition. Even in the early
1800s, however, Thomas Andrew Knight, a famous
Herefordshire cider-maker, was able to show by the
reaction with iron salts that the tannin of cider
apples was chemically different from the tannin of
oak bark then commonly used to tan leather. Without
dwelling on this in too much detail, it is worth
pointing out exactly which compounds constitute the
tannins of apples and ciders (Fig. 1).

All are phenols but not all of them are tannins
in the sense of forming complexes with protein and
being astringent to the taste. Indeed, only the
latter class of compounds, the procyanidins, have
this tanning action. These compounds are pre-formed
in the fruit and are *not* produced by enzymic action
during cell disruption. All these compounds (Fig. 1)
are colourless, and their oxidation, a whole subject
in itself, is not discussed here.

ISOLATION OF PROCYANIDINS

Our isolation procedures have been described elsewhere [2] but, briefly, they consist of continuously
adsorbing the procyanidin fraction from a large
volume of cider on to Sephadex LH-20, washing away
the phenolic acids and then desorbing the procyanidins by the use of 60% acetone. After drying
to a solid, the procyanidin fraction is subjected to
counter-current distribution between ethyl acetate
and water, a little-used but nevertheless powerful
technique which will produce gram **quantities of**
partly purified procyanidins suitable for tasting
purposes. Figure 2 gives the partition distribution
of cider procyanidins; the more polymeric procyanidins have the lower partition coefficient into
the ethyl acetate and hence are more hydrophilic.
Our detailed monitoring system at the time was by
various techniques of thin-layer chromatography.
Figure 3, for instance, shows the range of cider
procyanidins related to partition coefficient and
degree of polymerisation. It seems in ciders that
we can detect a range of procyanidin polymers up to

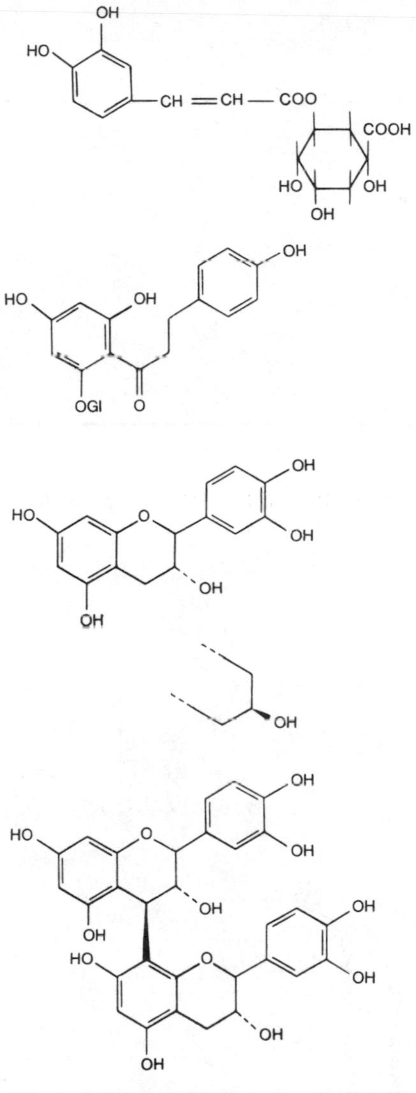

Chlorogenic acid

Phloridzin

(–) Epicatechin

(+) Catechin

Procyanidin B2

Fig. 1 – Classes of phenolics found in ciders.

the heptameric. Within each molecular-weight class there will be a number of stereo-isomers which can also be resolved by different chromatographic means. If we were repeating this work to-day, we would make much greater use of high-performance liquid chromatography which has revolutionised our approach to the study of phenolics in beverages, but at the time the equipment and techniques were not available [3,4].

Major component	$K \dfrac{EtOAc}{H_2O}$ (approx.)	Approx. content g/l in bittersweet cider	Taste
Polymeric procyanidins (ethyl acetate insoluble).........	0	1.15	Most astringent.
Pentameric procyanidins......	0.18	0.50	
Tetrameric procyanidins......	0.26	0.45	Most bitter.
Trimeric procyanidin C1.....	0.58	0.45	
Dimeric procyanidin B2......	0.91	0.65	
Epicatechin................	4.0	0.45	

Fig. 2 — Counter-current distribution of cider procyanidins.

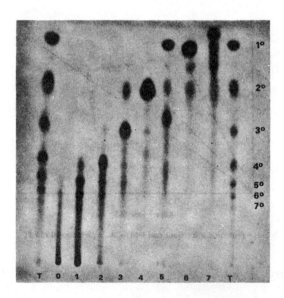

Fig. 3 — Silica h.p.t.l.c. of cider procyanidins.

T　　　　= total tannin extract.
0–7　　　= counter-current fractions.
1°–7°　　= degree of polymerisation.

SENSORY ASSESSMENT OF PROCYANIDINS

Having isolated procyanidins from ciders it was
necessary to devise a protocol for tasting them and
ranking them in order of taste sensation. The major
problem is that the procyanidins can be so intense
in their physical tanning action on the tongue that
the second sample in a set is always judged more
astringent than the first because of the intense
carry-over. To overcome this, a reversed-order pair
comparison test has been devised at Long Ashton,
based on a method of Scheffé. By dividing the panel
into two groups and having them taste their pair of
samples in reverse order, it was possible to assess:
(i) the differences in main effects between samples,
i.e. whether 'A' really *was* more bitter and astringent than 'B', and (ii) the magnitude of the order
effect itself, which in nearly all cases was significant even when there was no difference in the main
effects themselves.

The type of scoring sheet used is shown in
Figure 4, using a 5 or 7 point centre-zero scale.
Bitterness and astringency are assessed in the same
sample. The training for this involved the use of
a dilute caffeine or quinine sample to demonstrate
bitterness and a sample of high tannin perry to
demonstrate astringency. It is difficult to find a
liquid vegetable extract with a pure astringency and
no accompanying bitterness - but the differences here
were sufficiently marked that the panel was confident
in distinguishing the two standards at any rate.

After tasting all possible pairs of procyanidins
against each other at equal concentrations in water
containing 5% ethanol, we could rank the procyanidins
in order of their bitterness and astringency. Rather
surprisingly, the polymeric procyanidins came out top
for astringency but the oligomeric procyanidins
(peaking with the tetramer) came out top for bitterness. Figure 5 represents this diagrammatically.
We also found that the effect of ethanol was to
increase the perceived bitterness but to *decrease*
the perceived astringency.

EXPLANATION OF PERCEIVED EFFECTS

Although we are not physiologists, we found it
possible to explain these results by the following
hypothesis. Astringency is due to non-specific

PHENOLIC TASTING

NAME ....   DATE.............................

SESSION NO. ....   GROUP...........................

Please taste Sample ....first

	BITTERNESS	ASTRINGENCY
Much more	☐	☐
Moderately more	☐	☐
Slightly more	☐	☐
The same	☐	☐
Slightly less	☐	☐
Moderately less	☐	☐
Much less	☐	☐

Sample ...... has   than Sample ......

Please state if you find any other major taste differences:

Fig.4 — Tasting sheet for bitterness and astringency.

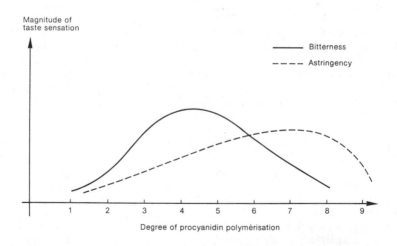

Fig.5 — Representation of bitterness and astringency with relation to procyanidin polymerisation.

hydrogen bonding between the procyanidin and any proteins in the mouth [5] - generally, the total amount of this hydrogen bonding will be greater the larger is the procyanidin. Hence, on average, a large procyanidin will be held closer to the protein

for longer than will a small one - so large procyanidins are more astringent than small ones up to
the point, presumably, where they are too large to
be soluble.

The sensation of bitterness, however, demands
the interaction of a procyanidin with a specific
bitter taste receptor at the back of the tongue [6].
To interact with the receptor the molecule has first
to cross a lipid membrane, so it must have some
solubility in a non-polar phase. This would explain
why the oligomeric procyanidins which are slightly
lipid-soluble taste bitter whereas the polymeric
procyanidins, with a partition coefficient of zero,
do not (cf. Fig. 2).

This hypothesis also accounts for the enhance-
ment of tannin bitterness by alcohol with a simultaneous decrease in astringency. By a co-solubility
effect, the procyanidins will pass more easily into
the lipid membrane and increase the perceived bitterness, whereas the effect of the alcohol in supressing
hydrogen-bonding will prevent the phenolic-protein
interaction and diminish the perceived astringency.

To summarise, there are a range of procyanidins
in cider from monomeric to heptameric. Each of them
is both bitter and astringent, but the sensation of
bitterness predominates in the oligomeric members of
the series and the sensation of astringency predominates with the polymers.

INTERPRETATION OF 'HARD' AND 'SOFT' CIDERS

The tannin of bittersweet cider varieties is often
described as 'hard' or 'soft', which seems to
correspond largely with what we would call 'bitter'
or 'astringent' respectively. Even cider apples
whose total tannin content is quite similar (around
0.3%) and which would both be described as bittersweet, can show this effect, so it is not due to a
change in concentration. Two such apples traditionally described in this way are the cultivars
'Vilberie' (soft) and 'Tremlett's Bitter' (hard).
We established by means of our tasting procedure
that Vilberie was regarded by our panel as
predominantly astringent, but Tremlett's Bitter was
predominantly bitter. By quantitative measurement
of the oligomeric to polymeric ratio, whether gravi-
metrically from counter-current isolation or by

quantitative chromatographic means, we obtained the
data in Table 1. The ratio of oligomeric:polymeric
procyanidins for Vilberie is 1.85:1, and for
Tremlett's is 2.50:1. Hence, Tremlett's has
relatively more oligomeric procyanidins and in terms
of our hypothesis might be expected to be more
bitter than Vilberie, which indeed it is.

Table 1 — Comparison of Vilberie and Tremlett's ciders.

Variety	Oligomers (g litre^{-1})	Polymers (g litre^{-1})	Ratio	Total procyanidins (g litre^{-1})
Vilberie	2.29	1.23	1.85	3.52
Tremlett's	2.65	1.06	2.50	3.71

CONCLUSIONS

Our work has shown not only that bitterness and
astringency are distinguishable taste sensations in
ciders, but that they are quantifiable in both
chemical and organoleptic terms. Work at the
University of California at Davis with grape-seed
extracts has given similar conclusions [7,8].
Researchers at Davis have further shown that an
increasing absolute concentration of procyanidins
increases the perceived intensity of astringency to
a greater extent than the perceived intensity of
bitterness.

REFERENCES

1. Lea,A.G.H.; Arnold,G.M. The phenolics of ciders:
      bitterness and astringency. J.Sci.Fd Agric.
      1978, 29, 478-483.
2. Lea,A.G.H. The phenolics of ciders: oligomeric
      and polymeric procyanidins. J.Sci.Fd Agric.
      1978, 29, 471-477.
3. Lea,A.G.H. Reversed-phase gradient h.p.l.c. of
      procyanidins in ciders and wines. J. Chromatog.
      1980, 194, 62-68.
4. Lea.A.G.H. Reversed-phase h.p.l.c. of pro-
      cyanidins in fresh and oxidising apple juice.
      J. Chromatog. 1982, 238, 253-257.

5. Joslyn,M.A.; Goldstein,J.L. Astringency of fruits and fruit products. Adv.Fd Res. 1964, 13, 179-217.
6. Koyama,N.; Kurihara,K. Mechanism of bitter taste reception. Biochim.biophys.Acta 1972, 288, 22-28.
7. Rossi,J.A.; Singleton,V.L. Flavor effects of grape seed phenols. Am.J.Enol.Vitic. 1966, 17, 240-246.
8. Arnold,R.A.; Noble,A.C.; Singleton,V.L. Bitterness and astringency of phenolic fractions in wine. Ag.Fd Chem. 1980, 28, 675-678.

Poster

Chapter 3.8

Two instruments designed to measure texture or related properties in food products

G. Lambert
Laboratory Division, C. Stevens and Son (Weighing Machines) Ltd. Holywell Hill,
St. Albans, Herts.

Both the Stevens LFRA Texture Analyser and the
Stevens CR Analyser have been designed to compare the
reaction of food products to a probe being pressed
either on to, or in to a surface(see Figs 1 and 2).

The Texture Analyser is available in two capac-
ities of either 100 g with a sensativity of 0.1 g or
1000 g with a sensitivity of 1 g. The method of
operation is for the distance of penetration to be
selected on the thumbwheel switch, in older models
the maximum was 29 mm, in later models this has been
increased to 50 mm, and the speed of penetration
selected, this can be either 0.2, 0.5, 1 or 2 mm/sec.

The instrument can also be pre-set to operate in
3 modes:

Normal. The sample is placed beneath the probe
and the start button pressed. The probe
will descend at a speed of approximately
4.5 mm/sec. until the surface of the
product is reached. When a resistance of
5 g is detected by the probe the instrument drops into its pre-selected speed
and travels its pre-selected distance.
When this distance is reached the display
locks and the probe returns to its start
position.

Fig.1 – Stevens LFRA Texture Analyser

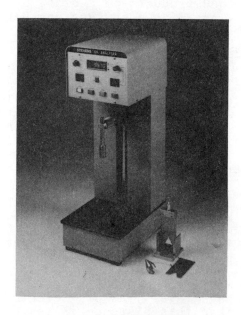

Fig.2 – Stevens Compression Response Analyser

Cycle. The sample is placed beneath the probe and
the mode switch moved to cycle. The probe
will descend at the pre-selected speed
until the surface of the product is reached
and a resistance of 5 g detected when it
will travel its pre-selected distance and
retract at its pre-selected speed.

Hold.   This is similar to the normal mode until
the distance of travel is reached when the
probe will lock but the display will stay
live and show any variation of force being
exerted on the probe.

Approximately 20 different probes are currently available ranging from cylinders, cones, needles, balls or
wires which are available for use on different products.

The Texture Analyser has an analogue output socket
to which a chart recorder can be connected to record
load against time.

The Stevens Compression Response Analyser is
available with 5 interchangeable load cells with cap-
acities of 5 kg x 2 g, 10 kg x 5 g, 20 kg x 10 g, and
50 kg x 20 g. The instrument can recognise which cell
is in use and the display will adjust the sensitivity
accordingly.

Speeds of penetration can be pre-set from 5 to
999 mm/min in 1 mm steps by means of a thumbwheel
switch. Another switch enables this distance of penetration or a selected load to be pre-set.

A knob above this switch will determine whether
distance or load is being pre-set and the display will
show grams if distance is selected or millimetres (to
0.1 mm) if load is selected. The same knob will also
select whether the peak load in grams or the load
achieved at the end of the distance of travel will be
displayed. If load is pre-selected the distance of
travel will be displayed. A further option with this
knob is to select "Track Load". This selection over-
rides all of the modes of test selected and enables
a pre-selected load to be continuously applied to a
product while the distance at which this load penetrates is displayed. With this option it is possible
to alter the pre-selected load during the test.

The second control knob enables one of the four modes to be selected:

Single/Return. The sample is placed below the probe and the start button pressed. The probe descends at an approach speed of 200 mm/min until a resistance equal to 5 times the smallest increment of the load cell in use is reached. (This being 10 g with the 10 kg cell, 50 g with the 20 kg cell or 100 g with the 50 kg cell.) The probe will then drop into either its pre-selected speed and travel its pre-selected distance, displaying either peak load or load at the end of the distance of travel OR drop into its pre-selected load and measure the distance travelled. At the end of the test the display will lock and the probe return to its start position.

Single/Hold. As above, but the probe does not return and the display will not lock.

Cycle/Stop. The probe will continuously cycle at the pre-selected load or distance.

Cycle/Contact. The probe will continuously cycle at the pre-selected load or distance from the point when initial contact with the product was made.

The Stevens CR Analyser is fitted with a rapid up/down switch and a button to select the position from which it is convenient to set the initial start position of the probe. An analogue output is provided for use with either a chart recorder or an XY recorder. Output is available of both distance and load. As an optional extra a BCD output can be provided. The response time is better than 0.035 sec.

SENSORY AND INSTRUMENTAL METHODS AND THEIR APPLICATION TO SPECIFIC PRODUCTS

(a)   Vegetables

Chapter 4.1

Quality appraisal of processed fruits and vegetables

D.H. Lyon
The Campden Food Preservation Research Association, Chipping Campden, Glos. UK

SUMMARY

For many years, the Campden Food Preservation Research Association has been widely recognized for its quality appraisal systems for the assessment of canned fruits and vegetables. Known as the Campden QC6, these systems are used throughout the food processing industry to measure and compare the different quality characteristics of canned fruits and vegetables and to monitor consistency of production.

Although the QC6 system is well suited for this purpose, there are certain drawbacks when used to compare fruit and vegetable varieties for processing. The QAV method (Quality Appraisal of Varieties) has therefore been developed to record the differences in quality and to enable identification of true distinctions between varieties. The QC6 has provided the basis for the new method, with colour, flavour and texture being assessed, but in the QAV, each is divided into its component parameters. The results of these tests, together with relevant agronomic data, enable processors to select varieties with the quality characteristics most suitable to their requirements.

INTRODUCTION

Although the products assessed at Campden during 1981 ranged from chicken to soft drinks including fruit juices and beer, the Campden Food Preservation Research Association has become best known for the methods it has developed for the quality appraisal of processed fruits and vegetables.

Systems for the quality appraisal of canned fruits and vegetables were developed soon after the last war and were intended to replace the old National Mark Scheme by classifying samples into two or more grades. The National Mark Scheme which came into operation in 1930 as part of the Agricultural Produce (Grading and Marketing) Act 1928, sought to define national standards for the rapidly developing canning industry. Canners who packed to certain standards were allowed to display the National Mark design on their packs. Its presence on canned produce meant, amongst other things, that the cans contained only suitable cultivars of each kind of fruit and vegetable and that the product conformed to the statutory definitions of quality.

The National Mark Scheme was discontinued on the outbreak of war in 1939 and **was never reintro**duced. A tentative scheme for examining the quality of canned fruits and vegetables was put forward in 1946 whereby samples could be assessed for quality on a voluntary basis. The standards were unofficial in that there was no guarantee on the label such as an official grade mark or other designation of quality. But developed with the backing of the industry they carried with them some degree of general acceptance and recognition and were intended in part to replace the old National Mark Scheme. Subsequent revisions approved by the Heat Preserved Foods Technical Advisory Committee of the Campden Research Association **has resulted in** the present Standards of Quality, the Campden QC6.

THE QC6 SYSTEM

In the new Standards of Quality it was suggested that packs should be grouped into two grades: Grade A - equivalent to a strict interpretation of the old National Mark Scheme, and Grade B - a reasonably good standard for cheaper packs. Samples not meeting the requirements of either grade were considered sub-

standard and unfit for sale through normal channels;
cans of exceptional quality were classified as Grade
A*.

The idea of having a minimum total score and a
minimum score for each quality characteristic was
examined, and a method which was used in the
National Mark Scheme was retained, with all minima
prescribed on a simple system of percentages.

The agreed minima were:

Grade	Minimum for total score	Minimum for each item (Quality Characteristic) score
A*	90%	80%
A	80%	70%
B	70%	60%

In the QC6 system, all products are scored out
of a total of 100 points. Five quality characteristics of colour, flavour, texture, absence of defects and size grading are judged individually, and
the scores allotted to each item are weighed according to their importance for the particular product
being assessed.

The maximum scores for individual items and
the minimum score for Grade A*, Grade A and Grade B
for fruits and vegetables are given in Tables 1 and 2.

Table 1 – QC6 Score card – fruit

Item	Maximum Score	Minimum Score		
		Grade A*	Grade A	Grade B
Colour	20	16	14	12
Texture	20	16	14	12
Absence of Defects	30	24	21	18
Size Grading	10	–	–	–
Flavour	20	16	14	12

Table 2 — QC6 Score card — vegetables

Item	Maximum Score	Minimum Score		
		Grade A*	Grade A	Grade B
Group A				
Colour	20	16	14	12
Texture	30	24	21	18
Absence of Defects	20	16	14	12
Size Grading	10	8	7	6
Flavour	20	16	14	12
Group B				
Colour	20	16	14	12
Texture	40	32	28	24
Absence of Defects	20	16	14	12
Flavour	20	16	14	12

In fruit therefore, there are no restrictive minima for size grading whilst in vegetables, the packs are divided into those in which size grading is, and is not, of some importance. The most important quality item in canned fruit is absence of defects, while in canned vegetables it is texture. The assessment and scoring of each characteristic is now considered in turn.

Colour

In scoring each type of fruit or vegetable there should be an ideal colour to aim for. Theoretically this could be defined on a colour scale and the appropriate range of colours prescribed for each product. In practice, this is difficult to operate as the colour varies over the surface of each fruit or vegetable or from one sample to the next. It is best therefore to assess colour on the general impression given, against an ideal standard and to analyse the impression of colour into the four constituents of hue, tints, uniformity and brightness. Hue is the actual colour itself and the first point is to ascertain whether the colour is of the correct hue. A bluish colour in red fruit, perhaps due to the action of tin on the natural colour, is a case where points have to be deducted for the wrong hue. Tint is the strength or the degree of dilution of the colour and distinguishes, for example, deep red from pale red of the same hue. Brightness and uniformity are both desirable features of canned fruit and vegetables and the samples are scored accordingly, with points being deducted for variations in colour between individual fruits and vegetables in the sample.

A typical example of a colour assessment is given in Table 3.

Table 3 — QC6 Assessment of canned peas — colour (20)

		Score
Excellent	Uniform, bright natural green comparable with colour of the best home-cooked or frozen peas	20
Very good	Very slightly short of perfection	18-19
Good	Slight lack of uniformity with faint brown or olive green hues; fairly bright; attractive	16-17
Fairly good	Slight lack of uniformity with slight blue, grey, olive-green or yellow hues; slightly dull	14-15
Moderate	Rather uneven; rather noticeable blue, grey, olive-yellow or brown hues; somewhat dull but not unattractive. Rather deep or unnatural colour in the liquid	12-13
Poor	Uneven, patchy or unattractive colour	6-11
Very poor	Very unpleasant or unnatural colour	0-5

Nearly all samples show obvious minor defects of colour so that a good average sample with no major defects is normally awarded 16 points out of 20. Samples with below good average colour and more obvious faults of hue or tint and noticeable dullness or lack of uniformity, score 14 or 15 points. If the faults are more severe but insufficient to justify a customer's complaint, the sample is awarded 12-13 points. All samples with faults sufficient to justify complaints by a reasonably critical consumer are scored less than 12 points.

Texture

The texture of processed products is of great significance since the consumer is often purchasing a commodity which is ready to eat. There are two methods used for the assessment of texture by the QC6 system - the mouthfeel test and finger feel test.

Most vegetables are assessed by the mouthfeel test to assess the degree of maturity of the product. With canned peas (Table 4), the maturity rating depends on a separate estimate of the firmness of the skins, the firmness of flesh and the degree of mealiness of the flesh; cloudiness of the liquor is also allowed for.

Most fruit and root vegetables are normally assessed by the finger feel test to gain some impression of the texture. With carrots, for instance, tenderness is estimated by penetrating the root with the edge of a spoon. A good quality carrot sample should be firm yet tender and free from any fibrous

Table 4 — QC6 Assessment of canned peas — texture (30)

1. Firmness of Skins (10)		Deduction
Very tender	Skins hardly detectable	0
Tender	Skins just noticeable but offering very little resistance	1
Firm	Distinctly firm, but not objectionably so. Very slightly uneven	2-3
Rather tough	Just sufficiently tough to be considered very noticeable, or rather objectionable. Slightly uneven	4-5
Tough	Distinctly tough; skins tend to stick between the teeth or remain in the mouth. Uneven	6-10

2. Firmness of Flesh (10)		Deduction
Very tender	Uniform plump peas easily crushed by the tongue	0
Tender	Uniform texture; peas offer distinct resistance to crushing by the tongue	1
Firm	Peas noticeably firm; difficult to crush with the tongue. Slightly uneven	2-3
Rather tough	Distinctly firm, but not objectionably so. Peas require to be chewed. Uneven texture	4-5
Tough	Objectionably firm. Flesh of peas with compact, "under-cooked" texture; very uneven	6-10

Table 4 — QC6 Assessment of canned peas — texture (30) (continued)

		Deductions
3. Mealiness (15)		
Very good	Immature, plump peas, virtually free from any trace of mealiness	0–1
Good	Mealiness just detectable	2–3
Moderate	Slight general mealiness but not objectionable. About 5 per cent of the peas at this stage have generally skins burst due to swelling of starch, and in about half the peas the radicles are clearly visible	4–5
Rather poor	Distinctly mealy, but easily distinguishable from processed peas. About 10 per cent of the peas at this stage have generally skins burst due to swelling of starch and in about 75 per cent of peas the radicles are clearly visible	6–9
Poor	Peas of very mealy or grainy texture difficult to distinguish from processed peas	10–15
4. Cloudiness of Liquid (5)		Deductions
Very slight	Very slight opalescence. No suspended solid matter or sludge	1
Slight	Slightly cloudy; slight deposit of pea solids	2
Moderate	Rather cloudy; noticeable sludge	3
Severe	Cloudy; rather heavy sludge	4
Very severe	Very cloudy; thick; very heavy sludge	5

cores; points are deducted for each piece which shows slight, moderate or bad deviation from this ideal. With fruit (Table 5), the wholeness and tenderness are examined; wholeness is considered as the freedom from any type of rupture or disintegration and the retention of its natural size and shape. The tenderness is taken to be freedom from woody texture, seeds, hard cores or tough skins. Evidence of breakdown shown by the presence of pieces of suspended or disintegrated solid matter in the syrup is also taken into consideration.

Flavour

Flavour is more difficult to define than either colour or texture. The assessment of flavour by the

Table 5 — QC6 Assessment of canned golden plums — texture (20)

The following points to be deducted for faults in the fruit indicated below:-

(a) <u>Slight</u> - Slightly shrivelled; slight loss of shape (not broken); slightly too firm.

(b) <u>Moderate</u> - Moderately shrivelled; too soft or rather too firm; breakdown of portion of plum, but not complete disintegration.

(c) <u>Bad</u> - Badly shrivelled; very tough; complete collapse or breakdown.

Additional points to be deducted for faults in the syrup indicated below:

(a)	Virtually clear	- deduct	0 points	
(b)	Slightly opalescent	- "	1	"
(c)	Distinctly cloudy	- "	2-3	"
(d)	Cloudy	- "	4-5	"
(e)	Very cloudy	- "	6-8	"

No. of Plums Affected	Up to 20 in can			21-35 in can			Over 35 in can		
	Slight	Mod.	Bad	Slight	Mod.	Bad	Slight	Mod.	Bad
1	1	2	2	1	2	2	1	1	2
2	2	3	4	1	2	3	1	2	3
3	2	4	6	2	3	4	2	2	3
4-5	3	5	8	2	4	6	2	3	4
6-7	4	7	10	3	5	8	2	4	6
8-9	5	8	12	3	6	9	3	5	8
10-12	6	9	16	4	7	11	3	6	9
13-15	7	10	20	5	8	15	4	8	12
16-20	7	12	20	6	10	20	5	9	15
21-35	-	-	-	7	12	20	6	10	20
Over 35	-	-	-	-	-	-	7	12	20

QC6 method depends solely on personal judgement, even with the help of the descriptors used to describe the flavours of each type of fruit or vegetable. For this reason it is recommended that more than one judge makes the assessment, and that samples are judged in batches of four or five in order to have the benefit of direct comparison of flavours. In all sample measurements done at Campden, a team of at least three judges is used. A typical example of a flavour score card is shown in Table 6.

Absence of defects

Products are rarely perfect and a decision must be made on how much departure from perfection can be tolerated before the product is downgraded from top quality. More important is the point at which the product passes from being acceptable to one which is

Table 6 — QC6 Assessment of canned dwarf beans — flavour (20)

		Score
Excellent	Full characteristic flavour	20
Very good	Fine characteristic flavour (above the average)	18–19
Good	Good natural flavour (normal)	16–17
Fairly good	Slightly weak natural flavour, or very slightly harsh or bitter	14–15
Moderate	Rather weak natural flavour or slightly harsh, or bitter	12–13
Poor	Distinct foreign flavour	6–11
Very poor	Strong objectionable foreign flavour	0–5

rejected. Defects can be important in determining the acceptance or rejection of a sample because products highly rated for all other aspects of quality can be rejected on this one item alone.

Most defects can be classified as either physiological (e.g. structural malformation), pest, pathological or mechanical (e.g. bruising) defects. In applying the QC6 method for the assessment of absence of defects, blemishes are classed as either slight, moderate or bad. Slight blemishes are only obvious to the critical eye and are important only when present in a large proportion of the fruit; for example, small corky patches on the surface of gooseberries. Moderate blemishes should be obvious to the reasonably critical consumer but not bad enough to justify a complaint. Bad blemishes are ones which might make the fruit or vegetable inedible.

As with the finger feel assessment of texture, points are deducted for each piece which shows slight, moderate or bad deviation from the ideal. A typical Absence of Defects score chart is shown in Table 7.

Size grading

Size grading is considered to be the least important of the five quality characteristics scored by the QC6 system, but even so, 10 points are allocated to this item because uniformity of size gives an added

Table 7 – QC6 Assessment of canned golden plums – absence of defects (30)

The following points to be deducted for faults indicated below:-

(a) <u>Slight</u> - Blemishes only visible on close inspection. Slight general speckling; not more than two spots 2-3 mm in diameter.

(b) <u>Moderate</u> - Blemishes easily noticeable, but not serious. Rather severe speckling; less than $\frac{1}{4}$ surface bruised or covered with scab or other continuous blemish; slight stone-gum.

(c) <u>Bad</u> - Blemishes which are unsightly. Very severe speckling; over $\frac{1}{4}$ surface area covered with continuous blemish; severe stone-gum.

(d) <u>Defects</u> - Maximum deductions for extraneous matter.

Leaves and stalks	–	deduct 3 points each
Stones, wood, paper etc.	–	" 10 " "
Small insects	–	" 15 " "
Obnoxious insects	–	" 30 " "

Dirt - according to quantity and nature.

No. of Plums Affected	Up to 20 in can			21-35 in can			Over 35 in can		
	Slight	Mod.	Bad	Slight	Mod.	Bad	Slight	Mod.	Bad
1	1	1	2	1	1	2	1	1	2
2	1	2	5	1	1	3	1	1	3
3	2	3	8	1	2	5	1	2	5
4-5	3	4	12	2	3	8	2	3	8
6-7	4	7	15	3	4	10	3	4	10
8-9	5	9	20	4	6	12	3	5	12
10-12	6	12	24	5	8	15	4	6	14
13-15	7	15	30	6	12	20	5	8	18
16-20	9	20	30	7	15	24	6	10	23
21-35	–	–	–	9	20	30	8	15	29
Over 35	–	–	–	–	–	–	9	20	30

attraction to the overall appearance of the pack. Ten points are awarded only where all the pieces are of virtually the same size and their shape is perfect. Nine points are awarded where there is slight variation in size or imperfection of shape, and 8 points where the sample is graded according to the standard laid down but without tolerance. If the full tolerance is used, the sample is given 6 points. An example of size grading is given in Table 8.

THE QAV METHOD

When judged in isolation the Campden QC6 has some fundamental faults, but none-the-less has been widely

Table 8 — QC6 Assessment of canned whole carrots — size grading (10)

	Size–Grading (10)	Score
Excellent	All carrots of virtually the same size	10
Very good	Very slight divergence from perfection	9
Good	Carrots with transverse diameters at widest point not greater than $1\frac{1}{4}$" (32mm) or less than $\frac{1}{2}$" (13mm) and ratio of diameters of smallest and largest carrots not greater than $1:1\frac{1}{2}$)))))	8
Fairly good	Up to 10 per cent outside $1:1\frac{1}{2}$ ratio of diameters))	7
Moderate	10–20 per cent outside $1:1\frac{1}{2}$ ratio of diameters))	6
Poor	20–35 per cent outside the standards for "Good"))	3–5
Very poor	Worse than for "Poor"	0–2

accepted by the food canning industry. It works reasonably well, but it has certain drawbacks when used for the assessment of experimentally produced samples. For instance, in assessing the suitability of new varieties of fruits and vegetables for processing, two varieties might be down-graded for colour because one is too pale and the other too dark. Clearly both could receive the same score for colour. Therefore, a more detailed description of each variety was needed so that the causes of down-grading the samples could be ascertained.

Some differences in quality characteristics of varietal samples are caused by environmental factors which can change from site to site and year to year; others are the result of true differences between varieties. A more detailed assessment and a statistical analysis of the results enables distinctions to be drawn between these two sources of variation within a variety, and for this reason the QAV method for the quality appraisal of varieties was designed.

The QAV method is based on the established assessment of colour, flavour and texture but each factor is further divided into its component parameters. For instance, four components of colour are considered; the tint of the primary colour, the amounts of the secondary colours, uniformity and brightness.   Table 9 shows a typical score card.

Table 9 — QAC Colour assessment of frozen cauliflower

Rating	White/ Cream	AMOUNTS OF OTHER COLOURS				Brightness	Uniformity
		Green in Stems	Grey	Pink	Brown		
1	White	Very slight	Very slight	Very slight	Very slight	Dull	Extremely non-uniform
2	Off white	Slight	Slight	Slight	Slight	Slightly dull	Very non-uniform
3	Cream	Moderate	Moderate	Moderate	Moderate	Moderately bright	Moderately non-uniform
4	Cream/ Yellow	Considerable	Considerable	Considerable	Considerable	Bright	Slightly non-uniform
5	Yellow	Very large	Very large	Very large	Very large	Very bright	Very uniform

Most fruits and vegetables exhibit secondary colours, such as grey in cauliflowers or yellow in peas.   Some vegetables however, such as shredded cabbage or leeks, have no primary colour and here all the colours are assessed as the amounts of colours present.   Uniformity of colour is again a desirable quality in most products but the presence of different tints is normally desirable in those products which have no primary colour.   An example is given in Table 10

Table 10 — QAV Colour assessment of frozen cabbage

Rating	AMOUNTS OF COLOURS					Brightness
	Pale Green	Medium Green	Dark Green	Cream	Yellow	
1	Very slight	Very slight	Very slight	Very slight	Very slight	Dull
2	Slight	Slight	Slight	Slight	Slight	Slightly dull
3	Moderate	Moderate	Moderate	Moderate	Moderate	Moderately bright
4	Considerable	Considerable	Considerable	Considerable	Considerable	Bright
5	Very large	Very large	Very large	Very large	Very large	Very large

Each panel member makes an assessment of the colour attributed in a sample and using the relevant standard decides which description most closely fits the sample.   Each factor is scored on a 1-5 scale. Texture and flavour are similarly divided into their component characteristics (see Table 11).

Table 11 – QAV Texture and flavour assessment of canned or frozen broad beans

	TEXTURE				FLAVOUR		
Rating	Skins	Flesh	Mealy	Brine (Canned Samples)	Sweet	Bitter	Strength of bean
1	Not at all tough	Not at all firm	Not at all	Not at all cloudy	Not at all	Not at all	Moderately weak
2	Slightly tough	Slightly firm	Slightly	Slightly cloudy	Slightly	Slightly	Fairly weak
3	Moderately tough	Moderately firm	Moderately	Moderately cloudy	Moderately	Moderately	Slightly weak
4	Very tough	Very firm	Very	Very cloudy	Very	Very	Slightly strong
5	Extremely tough	Extremely firm	Extremely	Extremely cloudy and thick	Extremely	Extremely	Moderately strong

The results of the QAV assessments may be used
in several ways. The scores for each character can
be analysed statistically so that differences between varieties can be detected. Alternatively, the
overall performance of a variety in the tests can be
determined and variety selections made; for instance,
when selecting a variety of carrot for processing
whole, a deep orange tint is usually preferred. The
scores can also be used to build a description of
each variety. For example, a vining pea variety
scoring 2 for green, 1 for yellow, 2 for grey, 2 for
brightness and 3 for uniformity is slightly pale
green with very slight yellow and slight grey tints,
and is slightly dull and moderately non-uniform in
colour. Flavour and texture can be described similarly.

Descriptions based on information from the full
trial period of three years, enables commercial firms
and research workers to judge the performance of the
new varieties and their suitability for processing.

GENERAL REMARKS

It is important to recognize that both the QC6 and
the QAV systems can only be employed by a fully
trained and experienced panel and that proper care
should be given to the selection of panel members
responsible for the sensory evaluation. At the
Campden Food Preservation Research Association,
11 members of staff are employed full-time on the
quality appraisal of processed and fresh foods, which
involves examining some 10,000 samples of processed
fruits and vegetables each year by these methods. A

screening procedure eliminates at interview persons
with abnormal colour or tasting abilities. Persons
who are shy, domineering or unable to communicate
well with others are not considered suitable for
training.

Under an experienced team leader, an individual
develops the ability to discriminate between samples
showing small differences, and normally it is six
months before sufficient samples have been examined
to enable the panelist to correctly judge the quality of samples according to the QAV and QC6 standards.

Care has been taken in the design and decor-
ation of the new, purpose built, quality appraisal
facilities at the Campden Food Preservation
Research Association so that all tests are done under
conditions which are conducive to sensory evaluation.
All the rooms, for instance, are lit by artificial
daylight tubes which give a constant light intensity
at the bench level, and minimum shadow or reflection
on samples - this is an important factor when assessing uniformity and brightness. All the benches,
walls, floors and ceilings are grey, the colour considered most relaxing to the eye and least distract-
ing when samples are assessed for colour.

To summarize, therefore, the QC6 and QAV
systems for the quality appraisal of processed
fruits and vegetables were designed as practical
systems to be used by the food processing industry
and the Research Association with the ultimate aim
of using the information gained from such assessments
as a basis on which to improve the quality of products offered to the consumer.

Chapter 4.2

Relationships between sensory and chemical quality criteria for carrots studied by multivariate data analysis

M. Martens, B. Fjeldsenden,* H. Russwurm Jr and H. Martens
Norwegian Food Research Institute, P.O.Box 50, N–1432 Aas–NLH, Norway.
* *Present address:* Bamble PP-kontor, N–3960 Stathelle, Norway.

SUMMARY

Fresh carrots (*Daucus carota* L.) from three seasons have been analysed by sensory and simple chemical methods. Juiciness, crispness, sweet, bitter and fruity taste were confirmed as important sensory criteria, and the chemical analyses described about the same amount of variation in the material as these sensory variables (Principal Component Analysis studies). However, the covariation between the sensory and chemical quality criteria was rather low: about 23% of the sensory variables could be explained by the chemical variables (Partial Least Squares regression studies). Dry matter, soluble solids, sugars (mainly sucrose) and total titratable acids were found to be relevant for prediction of the sensory quality. Sensory analysis was an important method for characterising the texture and flavour of carrots, and cannot be readily replaced by simple chemical analyses.

INTRODUCTION

The eating quality of vegetables may be measured directly by sensory methods or indirectly by chemical and physical measurements. In both cases there is a need for precise methods to measure the most important quality criteria. For practical reasons these

criteria should be easily measurable. It would
therefore be desirable to replace sensory evaluations
by faster or simpler instrumental analyses, but it is
not easy to find chemical or physical measurements
that give a true prediction of the sensory quality.
Studies of relationships between the two types of
measurements may reveal appropriate quality criteria,
which may be related on one hand to agronomic data
and, on the other, to consumer tests with a view to
developing better vegetables for the market. Quality
criteria might also be used to classify vegetables.

There are few reports relating the sensory
quality of carrots to chemical measurements. Kuusi
et al. [1] conclude that sensory evaluation is best
for characterizing the intrinsic quality of lettuce,
tomatoes and carrots, but other methods are less
suitable as they are influenced by too many factors.
Simon et al. [2] have reported that sugars and individual and total volatile terpene compounds are important in determining raw carrot flavour.

Relating sensory data to chemical or instrumental
data usually involves large and complex data matrices
which are difficult to interpret. Multivariate data
analysis takes care of the complexity and aids the
interpretation of large data tables. Powers [3]
reviews various methods for relating sensory and
instrumental data. It is important to be aware of
the level of validity (ad hoc, predictive, causal)
of the different models for relating two sets of
data, as stressed by von Sydow et al. [4].

This paper gives the final results from sensory
profiling and simple chemical analyses of raw carrots
over three seasons (1978, 1979 and 1980). Earlier
reports discussed the establishment of sensory and
chemical quality criteria for the same carrots in
1978 and the main quality factors in carrot samples
for each of the three seasons [6]. The terms crispness, juiciness, bitter, sweet and fruity taste were
found to be important for characterizing the sensory
quality of carrots.

The present study aims to determine whether any
of the chemical methods can be used to predict the
sensory quality of carrots. A recently developed
multivariate regression method [7,8] is used for
relating several chemical variables to several
sensory variables and is compared with other standard
multivariate analyses.

EXPERIMENTAL

Material

Fresh carrots (*Daucus carota* L.) were collected
during 1978, 1979 and 1980, the number of batches
being 20, 37 and 24 respectively. The samples,
obtained from all over Norway, were representative
of the Norwegian market with respect to the varieties
and cultural conditions, details of which were
supplied by the producers. The carrots were stored
at $1^{\circ}C$ and 90-95% relative humidity before sensory
analysis.

Sensory analysis

The carrots were washed, peeled and served as whole,
raw samples to a trained profile panel. Each batch
of carrots was evaluated 28 times in 1978 (7 judges
x 4 replicates), 32 times in 1979 (8 judges x 4 replicates) and 36 times in 1980 (12 judges x 3 replicates). Five of the judges participated in all three
years. At each session, 9-12 samples of carrots were
served in a statistically balanced order within and
between each replicate. During training a qualitative and quantitative understanding of the sensory
terms were established. A signal-noise-analysis [9]
was used to check the performance of individual
judges. In 1978, a list of sensory terms was collected from the literature [10,11] and from the growers, agriculturists, and the judges themselves. In
1979 and 1980 this list was shortened on the basis
of results from the previous year [6]. These terms
are given in Table 1. The preference terms "Total
impression of colour and appearance", "Total impression of texture" and "Total impression of flavour"
were evaluated from 0 (= very bad) to 9 (= very good),
while the other terms were judged along intensity
scales (0 = none, 9 = very strong intensity). The
term "Fruity taste" was defined as the characteristic
aromatic, rich flavour of carrots that may exist in
addition to, but independent of, sweet taste.

Chemical analyses

Samples used for sensory assessment were also analysed chemically: Soluble solids (water soluble,
"Brix number") were measured at $20^{\circ}C$ with a Hilger
and Watts refractometer; dry matter, after drying
under vacuum at $70^{\circ}C$ overnight; total titratable
acids by potentiometric titration with 0.1 N NaOH to

pH 8.1 [12]; and pH was measured in expressed juice.
Reducing sugars were determined with alkaline ferricyanide [13] in 1978, but was replaced in 1979 and
1980 by a high-pressure liquid chromatography method
(HPLC) [14] to determine fructose, glucose and sucrose.

Statistical analyses

The error in each variable was checked by factorial
analysis of variance (ANOVA) for each year. To describe the main tendencies of variation in the material and to find variables characteristic for these,
both chemical and sensory variables (a total of 19
variables) were submitted to joint Principal Component Analysis (PCA). In this method, a few linear
combinations of the variables (PCA factors) describing most of the variation in the data, are estimated.

To describe how well the chemical variables
could predict the systematic variation in the sensory
variables, the block of 12 sensory variables was
related to the block of 7 chemical variables by the
method of Partial Least Squares regression on latent
variables, version 2 (PLS2) [7,8]. The method extracts a few linear combinations of the chemical data
(PLS2-factors) that together predict as much of the
variation in the sensory data as possible. The
method has recently been applied to sensory data of
cauliflower [15].

In both PCA and PLS2, the factors are characterized in terms of factor loadings for all the variables and factor scores for all the batches. The
method of cross validation was used to determine the
maximum number of significant factors, to ensure the
predictive validity and to avoid over-fitting of the
data. Each variable was standardized prior to the
statistical analyses. PCA and PLS2 were applied for
each individual year and for all three years together
(total, 81 batches). Sugar analyses for 1978 were
treated as missing values in the latter instance.

In 1978, the problem of relating sensory and
chemical variables was first tackled by canonical
correlation (CC) [5]. An advantage of the PLS2
method, in contrast to CC, is that PLS2 may be used
in situations where the number of samples is less
than the number of variables. Stepwise multiple
linear regression (SMLR) analysis was done for
individual sensory variables on the data for each

year. However, since PLS2 was found to be superior to CC and SMLR, only the PLS2 results are given here.

All the statistical analyses were done on a NORD-10S minicomputer. The PCA and PLS2 calculations used microcomputer programmes CPRIN and CPLS2 with small modifications (SIMCA-programme [16]) in BASIC language.

RESULTS AND DISCUSSION

Input data

Table I shows the means and standard deviations and minimum/maximum values for each of the sensory variables, and the means for each chemical variable in 1978, 1979 and 1980.

Table 1 — Sensory and chemical variables included in the study of relationships between the two blocks of data. Means (x) and standard deviations (sd) for the sensory data and minimum (min)/maximum (max) values and the means for the chemical data are shown.

Sensory variables (0-9 point scales)	Symbol	1978 x̄ (sd) n=20	1979 x̄ (sd) n=37	1980 x̄ (sd) n=24
Even colour (xylem/phloem)	co	4.98 (0.63)	5.29 (0.67)	5.40 (0.53)
Total impression of colour and appearance	tca	5.93 (0.33)	5.67 (0.41)	5.6 (0.39)
Crispness	cr	5.45 (0.47)	6.46 (0.52)	6.33 (0.43)
Chewing resistance	ch	4.92 (0.45)	4.33 (0.47)	4.16 (0.46)
Juiciness	ju	5.29 (0.62)	5.51 (0.45)	5.85 (0.51)
Total impression of texture	tt	5.41 (0.61)	6.03 (0.60)	5.99 (0.55)
Total flavour strength	fl	5.05 (0.34)	-	5.71 (0.32)
Sweet taste	sw	4.19 (0.75)	5.33 (0.40)	5.11 (0.52)
Bitter taste	bi	1.89 (0.69)	2.22 (0.82)	1.35 (0.63)
Fruity taste	fr	1.40 (0.30)	2.07 (0.53)	3.96 (0.57)
Earthy taste	ea	1.42 (0.39)	1.76 (0.49)	1.43 (0.98)
Total impression of flavour	tf	4.93 (0.70)	5.40 (0.62)	5.46 (0.62)

Table 1 — (contd.)

		1978	1979	1980
Chemical variables		x̄ (min-max)	x̄ (min-max)	x̄ (min-max)
Soluble solids (%)	SS	8.9 (7.7-9.8)	8.9 (7.5-9.7)	8.3 (7.6-8.9)
Dry matter (%)	DM	11.2 (10.0-12.4)	11.0 (9.9-11.8)	10.8 (9.6-11.5)
Total titratable acids (%)	TA	5.2 (2.0-9.0)	5.9 (3.3-8.6)	5.5 (3.0-7.7)
pH	pH	6.7 (6.5-7.0)	6.6 (6.3-6.9)	6.8 (6.6-6.9)
Reducing sugars* (mg/100 g)	RS	60.6 (46.0-68.5)	-	-
Glucose (mg/100 g)	GU	-	1.3 (0.8-1.6)	1.1 (0.8-1.7)
Fructose (mg/100 g)	FU	-	1.1 (0.7-1.4)	0.9 (0.6-1.4)
Sucrose (mg/100 g)	SU	-	2.5 (1.3-3.6)	2.3 (1.3-3.3)

* not included in the multivariate analyses (n=81)

The signal/noise analysis of individual judges showed them to conform with one another each year. The univariate ANOVA showed highly significant between-batch variation for every variable; judge x batch interactions were not significant or very low. The values for each sensory and chemical variable for each batch, averaged over judges and/ or replicates provided data for the multivariate analyses.

PCA—studies: between and within block variations

A summary of the total variation in both the sensory and chemical variable blocks for all three years together is presented by the PCA factor loadings from factor 1 and 2 in Figure 1.

Three significant factors were found and the explained variances after each factor and the rest variances are shown in Table 2. Factor 1, accounting for 35.3% of the total covariance, is mainly a "sensory factor" dominated by the texture terms juiciness, crispness (both positively loaded) and chewing resistance (negatively loaded).

The taste terms sweet, fruity (both positively loaded) and bitter (negatively loaded) also contribute to the variance described by this factor. Factor 2, accounting for 16.0% of the total covariance, is

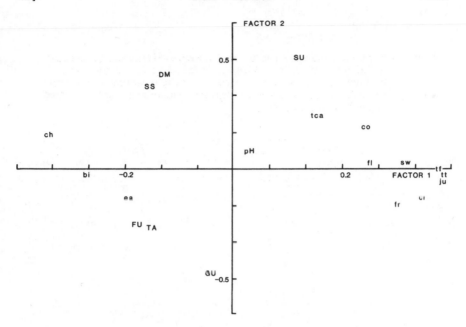

Fig.1 – PCA loadings for factor 1 and 2. n = 81.
Full names of each variable are in Table 1.

mainly a "chemical factor" with sucrose content, dry matter and soluble solids as the main contributors. The reducing sugars (especially glucose) is negatively related to this factor. Factor 3 accounts for 12.3% of the total covariance and is dominated by pH. This PCA-study shows that both sensory and chemical variables are useful for describing the variation in quality of the carrots. VARIMAX rotation of the PCA-solution gave essentially the same interpretation. However, the PCA-studies do not focus on the relationships between the two types of measurements although the PCA-solutions indicate that little or no such relation exists.

PLS2–studies: between-block variations

The essential relationships between the block of sensory variables and the block of chemical variables from all the three years were extracted by PLS2, using the former as regressands and the latter as regressors. Three factors were statistically significant, and factor loadings of the different variables from factor 1 and factor 2 are plotted against each

Table 2 — Explained variances for and rest variances after three statistically significant factors from PCA—studies and PLS2—regression. Full names of each sensory (sens.) and chemical (chem.) variable are in Table 1. Least squares criteria being minimized by the two algorithms are underlined.

Variables	% Explained by factor 1		% Explained by factor 2		% Explained by factor 3		% Rest after three factors	
	PCA	PLS2	PCA	PLS2	PCA	PLS2	PCA	PLS2
co	31	9	13	16	2	0	54	76
tca	12	7	21	21	0	0	68	72
cr	66	6	3	8	18	16	13	70
ch	73	22	6	1	2	13	19	64
ju	81	25	0	3	0	6	20	66
tt	82	10	0	12	9	10	9	68
fl	43	18	0	0	0	0	59	85
sw	53	0	0	10	15	1	32	89
bi	38	11	0	2	23	0	40	88
fr	50	36	5	6	16	0	29	58
ea	18	1	3	0	17	0	62	99
tf	78	6	0	4	0	2	22	88
mean sens.	52.1	12.6	4.1	6.9	8.2	3.7	35.6	$\underline{77.1}$
SS	11	43	47	23	16	21	26	13
DM	7	28	59	8	1	43	33	21
TA	11	23	18	21	1	0	70	56
pH	0	23	2	14	67	32	31	33
GU	0	7	44	14	2	39	54	40
FU	11	54	13	0	44	30	32	16
SU	6	0	70	74	4	10	20	16
mean chem.	6.4	25.4	36.3	21.7	19.3	25.0	38.0	27.8
mean all	35.3	17.3	16.0	12.4	12.3	11.5	$\underline{36.5}$	59.0

other in Figure 2. The explained variances after each factor and the rest variances are shown in Table 2.

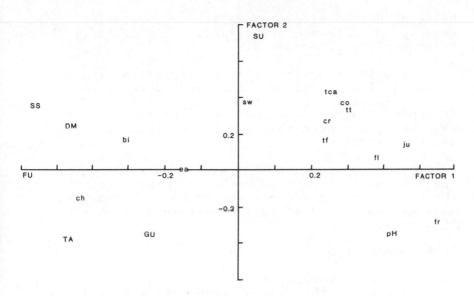

Fig.2 – PLS2 loadings for factor 1 and 2, n = 81.
Full names of each variable are found in Table 1.

In the first PLS2 factor, the chemical analyses
of soluble solids, dry matter and fructose are related negatively to the sensory criteria, juiciness
and fruit taste, and positively to chewing resistance
and bitterness. This means that a high dry matter
content indicates dry carrots with high chewing
resistance and low fruitiness. The second PLS2
factor is dominated by sucrose which relates positively to sweet taste. Total titratable acids is
related negatively to sweet taste although less so
than sucrose. The third PLS2 factor (Table 2) again
emphasises the relationship between soluble solids,
dry matter (and in addition pH), and the texture
variables including crispness.

Only about 23% (77.1% rest variance) of the
total variation in the 12 sensory variables can be
predicted by the chemical criteria after three
factors (Table 2). Juiciness and fruity taste are
best explained (34% and 42% respectively).

Comparing the PLS2 results with the PCA results,
we see that while PLS2 shows limited, but clear,
relations between chemical and sensory variables,
the PCA-studies indicates little or no relation

between the two blocks of variables, probably because the within-block covariances overshadow the between-block covariances.

By using stepwise multiple regression for exploring the relationships between each of the sensory variables (regressand) for all the chemical variables (regressors) much less information was extracted, although this was not contradictory with the PLS2 results.

The CC approach to the same problem used for the 1978 data [5](PCA on each block and CC on the two blocks of PCA scores) was found to be more cumbersome and more difficult to interpret than the PLS2 analysis.

Yearly variations

The PCA and PLS2 solutions from each individual year gave in general the same patterns (Figs I and 2). Although some yearly variations were observed with respect to which relationships were dominating each year, this variation could not be explained by artifacts as changes in judges, missing values, etc. The cross validation ensures the predictive ability of the model. Further confidence can be obtained by interpretation of the raw data and the factor scores.

The PLS2-scores (Fig. 3) show clear differences between the three years. Factor 1, which relates, for example, dry matter and bitterness against fruitiness and juiciness, in separate 1979 batches from 1980 batches, while batches from 1978 are spread along this factor. Carrots from 1979 were generally more bitter, less fruity and less juicy than carrots from 1980, and this corresponds to a high dry matter content in 1979. In 1978, the bitter taste was positively related to total reducing sugars, but in other years was not clearly explained by fructose and glucose content. On the other hand, the sucrose-sweet taste factor (factor 2) was demonstrated in the 1979 batches. However, the batches extremely low in sweet taste from 1980 had a low content of sucrose (factor 2) *and* a high content of total titratable acids (factor 1 and factor 2).

The yearly variations discussed from the factor scores in Figure 3 correspond well to our knowledge of the growing conditions each year: 1980 was considered by producers to be a better year than 1979,

while in 1978, conditions varied from a very dry
summer in northern Norway to very high rainfall in
the western areas. However, many other factors influence the sensory quality [17] including agronomic
factors which will be discussed elsewhere.

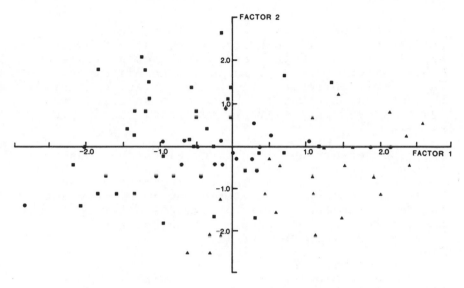

Fig.3 — PLS2 scores for factor 1 and 2 for each year (● = 1978, ■ = 1979,
▲ = 1980).

CONCLUSIONS

Our results confirm that juiciness, crispness, sweet,
bitter and fruity taste are important for characterizing the quality of carrots. These sensory criteria described about 70% of the variation in the
material. The chemical criteria soluble solids, dry
matter and sucrose were described to the about same
degree. No important covariance between sensory and
chemical quality criteria was found by the PCA-
studies.

However, 23% of the variation in the sensory
variables could be explained by the chemical analyses
in a study of the covariance between two types of
measurements (PLS2-studies). Juiciness and fruity
taste, and also crispness were related negatively to

dry matter, soluble solids and fructose (factor 1 and 3). Bitter taste was to some degree positively related to the same chemical variables, and to reducing sugars (espcially in 1978). Sweet taste could be predicted to a certain extent (about 10%) by sucrose (factor 2) and total titratable acids also contributed.

A good carrot with respect to texture and flavour was characterized by the judges as possessing high crispness and juiciness (low chewing resistance), a high sweet and fruity taste and no bitterness. This should correspond to low dry matter content, high sucrose content (or high ratio sucrose : monosaccharides) and preferably low total titratable acids.

The sensory quality of the 81 batches was predicted to some degree by the analyses of dry matter, soluble solids, sucrose and total titratable acids. Whilst these chemical criteria should be relevant for measuring the quality of carrots, they could not however replace the sensory variables, probably because they were not specific enough.

The combination of PCA and PLS2 regression was useful for exploring the relationships within and between sensory and chemical variables.

ACKNOWLEDGEMENTS

We thank S. Hurv and T. Bergersen for their assistance with sensory and chemical analyses, H.J. Rosenfeld for agronomic assistance and P. Lea for statistical help.

REFERENCES

1. Kuusi, T.; Vitanen, T.; Kleemola, K. Studies on the intrinsic quality of lettuce, tomatoes and carrots during marketing. J. Sci. Agric. Soc. of Finland, 1980, 52, 339-356.
2. Simon, P.W.; Peterson, C.E.; Lindsay, R.C. Correlations between sensory and objective parameters of carrot flavour. Agric. Fd Chem. 1980, 28, 559-562.
3. Powers, J.J. Perception and analysis: A perspective view of attempts to find causal relations between sensory and objective data

sets. In Flavour '81 (Schreier, P., Ed.),
Walter de Gruyter and Co. Berlin, New York,
1981, 103-131.

4. von Sydow, E.; Åkesson, C. Correlating instru-
mental and sensory flavour data. In Sensory
Properties of Foods (Birch, G.G.; Brennan,
J.G.; Parker, K.J., Eds), Applied Science
Publishers, London, 1977, 113-127.

5. Martens, M.; Fjeldsenden, B.; Russwurm, H. jr.
Evaluation of sensory and chemical quality
criteria of carrots and swedes. Acta Hortic.
1979, 93, 21-25.

6. Fjeldsenden, B.; Martens, M.; Russwurm, H. jr.
Sensory quality criteria of carrots, swedes
and cauliflower. Lebensm.-Wiss.u.-Technol.
1981, 14, 237-241.

7. Wold, H. Soft modelling: the basic design and
some extensions. In Systems Under Indirect
Observation (Joreskog, K.G., Wold, H. Eds),
North-Holland, Amsterdam, 1981.

8. Wold, S.; Wold, H.; Dunn III,·W.J.; Ruhe, A.
The collinearity problem in linear regression.
The partial least squares (PLS) approach to
generalized inverses. (Submitted to J.
Statist. Comput. 1982).

9. Fjeldsenden, B.; Martens, M.; Russwurm, H. jr.
Criteria for characterization of a panel and
panelists in sensory evaluation of food. In
Olfaction and Taste VII, IRL Press Ltd.,
London, 1980, 445-446.

10. Harper, R.; Bate Smith, E.C.; Land, D.G.;
Griffiths, N.M. A glossary of odour stimuli
and their qualities. Perfum. Essent.Oil
Rec. 1968, 59, 22-37.

11. Szczesniak, A.S. Classification of textural
characteristics. J. Fd Sci. 1963, 28, 385-
389.

12. AOAC. Official Methods of Analysis. Washington,
1975, 12th edition.

13. Hulme, A.C.; Narain, R. Ferricyanide method
for determination of reducing sugars. Bioch-
em.J. 1931, 25, 1051-1061.

14. Conrad, E.C.; Palmer, J.K. Rapid analysis of
carbohydrates by high-pressure liquid chromatography. Fd Technol. 1976, 30, 84-92.

15. Martens, H.; Martens, M.; Wold, S. Preference
of cauliflower related to sensory descriptive
variables by Partial Least Squares (PLS)
regression. (Submitted to J. Sci. Fd Agric.
1982).

16.   Wold, S.   SIMCA-3B Manual.   1981.   Umeå Univ.,
        Sweden.
17.   Mengel, K.   Influence of exogenous factors on
        the quality and chemical composition of
        vegetables.   Acta Hortic. 1979, 93, 133-151.

Chapter 4.3

Quality assessment of watercress

R - M.M. Spence and O.G. Tucknott
Long Ashton Research Station, University of Bristol, Long Ashton, Bristol BS18 9AF, UK

SUMMARY

The use of sensory assessment and consumer preference information, related to physico-chemical data, is an important tool in the definition of quality of a product. A sensory profile for evaluating post-harvest quality changes in watercress has been developed. Aroma changes observed during deterioration of watercress were related to compounds identified after headspace collection of volatiles from watercress kept under different storage conditions.

QUALITY ASSESSMENT OF WATERCRESS

Watercress is a freshwater, perennial plant, normally found growing in shallow, slow-running, calcareous water. Like cabbage and mustard, it is a crucifer, but belongs to the tribe Arabidae, which includes bitter-cress, winter cress, rock-cress and yellow cress. It is native in many temperate regions of the world and has been introduced in America, South Africa and Australasia where it is now a serious river weed [1]. The watercress cultivated in this country to-day is *Rorippa nasturtium-aquaticum* (L.) Hayek and the plant is grown as an annual leafy salad crop producing several harvests

throughout the year. Its characteristic flavour is
its hot taste and in addition the consumer benefits
from its high vitamin A and C content - four times
more vitamin C than lettuce and twice the amount of
vitamin A. Thus, as with other cruciferous vegetables it is a highly nutritious and low-calorie
food.

Commercial cultivation dates from the eighteenth
century in Germany and the nineteenth century in
England where the first watercress beds were built
in Kent in 1808. The main areas of production in
England follow the chalk and soft limestone areas in
Dorset, Wiltshire, Hampshire and Surrey [2].
Commercial beds are concrete lined, approximately
30 m wide and 100 m long, with a gravel base and
irrigated by water from adjacent springs or bore
holes. The irrigating water at source has a constant temperature of 9-10°C and this heat protects
the plants against frost damage in winter. To
support a dense crop, 5-11 million litres of flowing
water are needed per hectare per day.

Traditionally the watercress is harvested by
cutting when the stems are 15-20 cm long, but in
winter the crop is too short for cutting and the
plants are pulled and the roots trimmed off. The
leafy portion is made into bunches, packed into
waxed cardboard or corrugated plastic boxes, chilled
by hydrocooling and stored in a cold room at 2°C
until despatched to market. Some growers are now
developing mechanical harvesters which cut off the
top 8 to 10 cm of the plant. These sprigs are
packed in plastic bags for the large retail markets.
The market value of cress is £3.5 million a year.

Once removed from its aqueous environment the
plant has a limited shelf-life, losing its appeal to
the customer because of wilting and yellowing leaves.
Rapid transport from the producer to the market is
essential, particularly in the summer months when
ambient temperatures are high. The short post-
harvest life is a serious market-limiting factor.
In the 1890s growers suggested cooling the cress to
prolong its shelf-life by placing blocks of ice in
the middle of the boxes [3]. More recent research
[4] has suggested that for maximum shelf-life a
temperature just above 0°C to prevent frost damage
and a relative humidity of 95% are required. However, a completely refrigerated distribution chain

is only cost effective in large units and currently
only one such system is operating; in other cases
the cress is hydrocooled to 2°C before despatch in
insulated transport. From producer to wholesaler
the temperature of the cress fluctuates as ambient
temperatures vary and heat input occurs from the
respiring plant material. Internal stressing of the
plant by fluctuating temperatures and physical
damage during packing result in the rapid deterioration of the cress.

A study of post-harvest deterioration is needed
to devise ways of minimising these marketing problems and ensuring that the consumer is presented
with the highest quality product. The work described
in this paper was concerned with the changes during
post-harvest processing, storage and distribution of
watercress which affect the product's acceptability
by the consumer. Quality changes were assessed by
sensory and analytical techniques with the sensory
results and physiological deterioration being linked
with the production of volatiles. These results
will be used to predict optimum storage and transport conditions for maximum shelf-life.

Watercress bed simulation units consisting of a
gravel substrate irrigated with a nutrient solution,
with controlled lighting and temperature, were
initially used to produce the plant material [5].
These were later modified to a nutrient film system
with the plant material anchored in rock-wool cubes,
allowing the production of uniform plants under controlled conditions.

Sensory evaluation of changes in the post-
harvest quality of watercress was thought to be of
equal or greater value than the simple physiological
measurements which could be undertaken during the
transport chain. Therefore, a taste panel was set
up to establish a simple sensory profile using
attributes which described watercress quality [6].
The panel consisted of 10 people, four female and
six male, aged between 22 and 55 from which any
group of six was selected, and they followed the
sequence of sensory assessments given below:

(i)   Collection of terms to describe watercress properties

In two initial assessments panelists
were asked to describe five bunches

of watercress using their own adjectives with only the following head-
ings as guidelines - colour, sheen,
aroma, size of leaves, flavour,
texture, overall appearance.

(ii)   Rationalisation and reduction of descriptive terms

Discussion by panel members resulted
in a reduction in the number of adjectives describing each characteristic,
but still covering a range from good
to bad quality. The reduced number of
terms was tested on seven different
watercress samples and adjectives added
or deleted as thought necessary during
discussion.

(iii) Use of terms on different formats of record sheets

Different assessment sheet designs were
tested and simple scoring introduced
for some of the characteristics. Alterations were made during four assessments
of 10 different bunches of watercress
until the present version was developed.

The characteristics covered in the assessment
are shown below:

Colour	- Munsell scale
Sheen	- very shiny to dry matt
Aroma	- no smell to rotting cress smell
Size of leaves	
Texture to fingers	- very crisp to wilted
Texture to tongue	- fresh and crisp or wilted
Flavour **and hotness**	- 3 point scale: initially, while chewing, after chewing
Overall appearance	- colour of stalks, yellow leaves, damage

EXAMINATION OF AROMA COMPOUNDS OF WATERCRESS

Surprisingly, aroma proved to be an accurate
indicator of watercress quality. From the analysis
of volatiles collected by trapping on the porous

polymer Porapak Q, compounds were identified which contribute to the characteristic aromas observed at the different stages of deterioration. These compounds were used as odour reference samples for the sensory panel and are shown below:

Compound	Concentration ppm (v/w)	Aroma
Cis-3-hexen-1-ol	25	Wet vegetation
β-Ionone	12.5	Primrose
Phenethyl isothiocyanate	325	Watercress
Dimethyl disulphide	25	Seaweed/rotting

Phenethyl isothiocyanate is the compound responsible for the characteristic 'hot' taste and aroma of watercress. When the plant is damaged it is released from its corresponding glucosinolate by the action of the enzyme myrosinase [7]. Glucosinolates are characteristically hydrolysed by this enzyme to yield glucose and a labile aglucone which spontaneously rearranges with the loss of sulphate to give an isothiocyanate (which are known as mustard oils) as the major product [8]. The plants containing these isothiocyanates, for example mustard, horseradish and cress, have long been known for their pungency and used as condiments, potherbs, preservatives and remedies. They have also been recognised as possessing antibacterial and fungistatic properties [9].

Phenethyl isothiocyanate was first identified by Gadamer in 1899 [10] as the major volatile in watercress. Unfortunately, he and other workers used destructive methods to extract the compounds, thus releasing a high concentration of glucosinolate degradation products which then masked other volatiles produced by the plant [11-15]. To alleviate this problem, a headspace apparatus was developed for the collection of volatiles from watercress with the least amount of damage to the plant material [16]. Sensory monitoring during collection and identification showed that flavour and aroma were not significantly modified by the isolation technique.

Figure 1 shows the dual headspace apparatus used for the comparative collection of volatiles

Fig.1 – Dual headspace apparatus.

from two samples of watercress. The cut material,
15-20 cm long, was placed in stainless steel wire
baskets in each glass vessel. Water-saturated air
was passed through the vessels, permitting normal
respiration of the living plant material, and the
volatiles collected from the effluent air stream by
selective adsorption on Porapak Q. Four daylight
fluorescent tubes placed symmetrically around each
vessel provided illumination when required and the
apparatus was temperature controlled.

The equipment was used to monitor changes in
the production of volatiles from watercress stored
at different temperatures, with and without illumination, to determine the optimum conditions of storage
with the minimum reduction in quality [17]. The
identification of the compounds isolated was made by
gas chromatography and coupled gas chromatography-

mass spectrometry and confirmed using chemical standards. Sensory assessment of the watercress was carried out at the end of each experiment according to the standard assessment sheet, omitting terms referring to bunched cress.

CHANGES IN WATERCRESS DURING STORAGE

Watercress stored for seven days at 5°C in both light and dark was still crisp and fresh-looking with less than 5% of the leaves yellow. However, the aroma of both leaves and stalks indicated the presence of undesirable sulphur compounds and this is supported by chromatograms showing changes in the concentration of dimethyl sulphoxide (peak 3) and dimethyl sulphone (peak 6). Although the latter are odourless, dimethyl sulphone is the oxidation product of dimethyl sulphoxide which in turn is formed by the oxidation of dimethyl sulphide. This compound gives rise to the sulphury odour and has been identified in several brassicas [18-20]. The chromatograms (Fig. 2) are of samples after seven days collection at 5°C with one vessel in the dark and the other illuminated. Some of the compounds identified are shown next to the chromatograms.

The sensory results for the 10°C treatment show that the plant material was still crisp, although the majority of leaves were yellow after a week. The aroma of the leaves was quite different after the light and dark treatments; the illuminated leaves smelt of watercress due to the phenethyl isothio-cyanate and other sulphur compounds present, whereas those in the dark smelt of primroses. It can be seen from the chromatogram of the sample of volatiles from the dark treatment (Fig. 3) that β-ionone, which has a floral odour, was present (peak 5). The main disadvantage of the 10°C treatment compared with the 5°C was the high percentage of yellow leaves after seven days (50% in the light and 66% in the dark).

At 15°C yellowing increased further although the leaves were still crisp. The leaves and stalks had an odour associated with rotting plant material, but this was only indicated on the chromatogram (Fig. 4) by an increase in the amount of dimethyl sulphoxide (peak 3). From both sensory assessment and collection of volatiles, it appears that water-cress can be stored at 10°C in a current of moist air

Figs.2−5 − Chromatograms of samples from the dual headspace apparatus
            acter 7 days trapping. Column: 56 m x 0.5 mm glass, SCOT column
            coated with Carbowax 20M. Attenuation: x 10

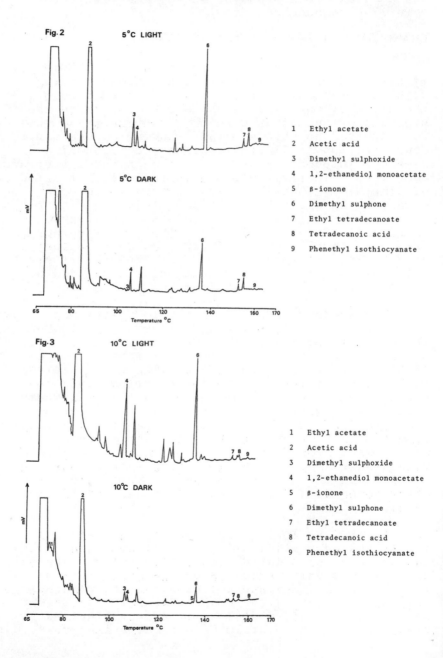

1   Ethyl acetate

2   Acetic acid

3   Dimethyl sulphoxide

4   1,2-ethanediol monoacetate

5   β-ionone

6   Dimethyl sulphone

7   Ethyl tetradecanoate

8   Tetradecanoic acid

9   Phenethyl isothiocyanate

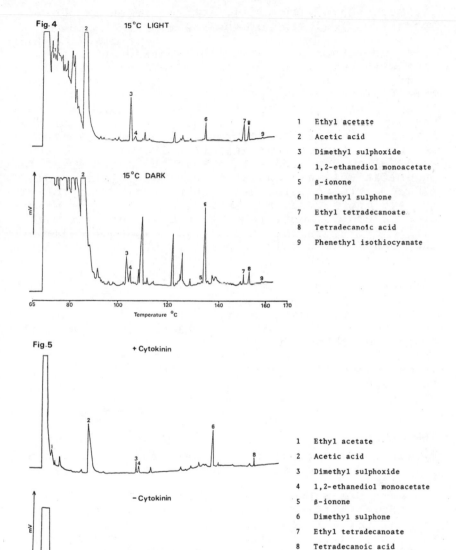

1	Ethyl acetate
2	Acetic acid
3	Dimethyl sulphoxide
4	1,2-ethanediol monoacetate
5	β-ionone
6	Dimethyl sulphone
7	Ethyl tetradecanoate
8	Tetradecanoic acid
9	Phenethyl isothiocyanate

1	Ethyl acetate
2	Acetic acid
3	Dimethyl sulphoxide
4	1,2-ethanediol monoacetate
5	β-ionone
6	Dimethyl sulphone
7	Ethyl tetradecanoate
8	Tetradecanoic acid
9	Phenethyl isothiocyanate

Figs. 2–5 – (continued)

for seven days with little deterioration in quality apart from yellowing of the leaves.

One method of controlling senescence is treatment with cytokinins, which are naturally occurring growth regulators. A preliminary evaluation of the effect of this class of compounds was made on watercress. Before storing at $10^{\circ}C$ in the dark the cress was dipped in a 5 ppm (w/v) aqueous solution of the cytokinin 6-benzylaminopurine. Examination after seven days showed that less than 10% of the leaves were yellow compared with 66% in the control sample. Quantitatively and qualitatively the volatile compounds collected from both the control and cytokinin-treated cress were very similar (Fig. 5). If watercress could be kept fresh at $10^{\circ}C$ in the dark with little deterioration in quality, this would eliminate the need for expensive cooling to $6^{\circ}C$ or lower during storage and transport. However, at present cytokinins have not been passed for use on edible foliage.

An increasing quantity of watercress is being sold packed in plastic bags. Little is known of the effects of these packing materials on the quality and shelf-life of watercress and this is now being investigated in an extension of the work outlined in this paper.

REFERENCES

1. Clapham,A.R.; Tutin,T.G.; Warburg,E.F. Flora of the British Isles. Cambridge University Press, 1962.
2. Howard,H.W.; Lyon,A.G. Biological flora of the British Isles *Nasturtium* R.Br. *Nasturtium officinale* R.Br. (*Rorippa nasturtium-aquaticum* (L.) Hayek). J.Ecol. 1952, 40, 228-245.
3. Glenny,W.W. Watercress, its history and cultivation. J.R.Agric.Soc. 3rd ser. 1897, 8, 607-622.
4. Robinson,J.E.; Browne,K.M.; Burton,W.G. Storage characteristics of some vegetables and soft fruits. Ann.appl.Biol. 1975, 81, 399-408.
5. Spence,R-M.M. A Study of Post-Harvest Changes in Watercress *Rorippa nasturtium-aquaticum* (L.) Hayek. Ph.D. Thesis, University of Bath, 1980.
6. Spence,R-M.M. The development of a vocabulary and sensory profile for the assessment of watercress quality. J. Fd Technol. 1982, 17, 633-639.

7. Fahn,A. Secretory Tissues in Plants. Academic
   Press, London, New York and San Francisco, 1979.
8. Benn,M. Glucosinolates. Pure appl.Chem. 1977,
   49, 197-210.
9. Virtanen,A.I. Some organic sulphur compounds in
   vegetables and fodder plants and their significance in human nutrition. Angcw.Chcm.internat.
   Edn. 1962, 1(6), 299-306.
10.Gadamer,J. Uber ätherischc Kressenole und die
   ihnen zu Grunde liegenden Glukoside. Arch.
   Pharm., Berl. 1899, 237, 507-521.
11.Kjaer,A.; Conti,J.; Larsen,I. Isothiocyanates.
   IV. A systematic investigation of the occurrence
   and chemical nature of volatile isothiocyanates
   in seeds of various plants. Acta Chem.Scand.
   1953, 7, 1276-1283.
12.Anon. Electron capture components in Cruciferae.
   Aerograph Research Notes, Summer Issue 1964.
   Wilkens Instrument and Research.
13.Freeman,G.G.; Mossadeghi,N. Studies on sulphur
   nutrition and flavour production in watercress
   (*Rorippa nasturtium-aquaticum* (L.) Hayek).
   J.hort.Sci. 1972, 47, 375-387.
14.MacLeod,A.J.; Islam.R. Volatile flavour components of watercress. J. Sci. Fd Agric. 1975
   26, 1545-1550.
15.Kaoulla,N.; MacLeod,A.J.; Gil,V. Investigation
   of *Brassica oleracea* and *Nasturtium officinale*
   for the presence of epithiospecifier protein.
   Phytochemistry 1980, 19, 1053-1056.
16.Spence, R-M.M.; Tucknott, O.G. An apparatus for
   the comparative collection of headspace volatiles of watercress. J. Sci. Fd Agric. 1982
   (In press).
17.Spence, R-M.M.; Tucknott, O.G. The effects of
   different storage conditions on the quality
   of watercress (*Rorippa nasturtium-aquaticum*
   (L.) Hayek) and the production of volatiles.
   Submitted to J. Sci. Fd Agric.
18.MacLeod, A.J.; MacLeod, G. Flavour volatiles of
   some cooked vegetables. J. Fd Sci. 1970, 35,
   734-738.
19.MacLeod, A.J.; MacLeod, G. Effects of variations
   in cooking methods on the flavour volatiles of
   cabbage. J. Fd Sci. 1970, 35, 744-750.
20.MacLeod, A.J.; MacLeod, G. The flavour volatiles
   of dehydrated cabbage. J. Fd Sci. 1970, 35,
   739-743.

Posters

Chapter 4.4

Texture profile analysis studies of stored common beans *(Phaseolus vulgaris L.)*

R.dos Santos Garruti and D.dos Santos Garruti
Universidade Estadual de Campinas, Cidade University, Campinas – S.P. Brazil 13100

SUMMARY

Beans *(Phaseolus vulgaris* L.) harvested in both the dry and wet seasons increased in hardness during storage, though beans harvested in the dry season had a better texture ($\underline{P}$ = 0.05) than those harvested in the wet season. Beans cultivated in Red Yellow Podzolic soils had softer skins than those from Red Latossol soil, and differed sensorily and instrumentally from those grown in the Orto Red Yellow Podzolic soil ($\underline{P}$ = 0.05).

MATERIALS AND METHODS

Three common beans *(Phaseolus vulgaris* L.) varieties Carioca, Aroana and Rosinha G2, harvested in the dry and wet seasons, were stored for six months at room temperature ($25 \pm 2^{o}C$) and 65-70% relative humidity. ('Dry season' signifies beans planted in February and harvested in May-June; 'wet season' refers to September and December-January, respectively.)

Eight-gram samples were soaked for 6 hours in 50 ml beakers and cooked in an autoclave at $121^{o}C$ (1.5 atm); cooking time varied and was determined in prior experiments (Table 1). Five-bean samples, held on trays at $\simeq 40^{o}C$ were presented to a panel of seven judges, who assessed their textural properties using the score sheet given in Figure 1 [1]. Scales

were defined using procedures described by Szczesniak
[2] and Breene [3].

**Table 1 — Cooking time (min) for soaked beans from 1978 dry and wet
season harvest*.**

	Type of soil											
	Podzolic Yellow Red				Orto Podzolic Yellow Red				Latossol Red			
Cultivar	dry		wet		dry		wet		dry		wet	
	a	b	a	b	a	b	a	b	a	b	a	b
Carioca	26	42	22	46	28	49	30	50	27	42	25	44
Aroana	24	39	26	34	26	39	36	47	25	35	38	48
Rosinha G2	28	49	36	38	24	45	46	50	38	54	36	46

a = before storage   b = after 6 months storage
* 3 replicates x 25 beans = 75 beans

Skin hardness was measured with an Instron
Universal Machine using a cross-head speed of
10 cm/min [4].

The data from both the sensory and instrumental
examinations were subjected to analysis of variance
(ANOVA), F statistics and the Tuckey test for means.
Principal component analysis (PCA) was also applied
to the panel results.

RESULTS

Sensory texture profile analysis

Typical results of the sensory texture profile
analysis are illustrated in Table 2. Analysis of
variance of the profile data showed there were no
significant differences in unstored beans; following
six months' storage, Carioca and Aroana cultivars
were, however, found to be less hard and differed
from Rosinha G2 at P = 0.05. Geometrical characteristics were, in general, homogeneous with the
exception of Carioca and Aroana cultivars from Red
Latossol soil which were 50:50 homogeneous and non-
homogeneous, respectively. For other characteristics
the degree of humidity was moderate, meaning that
the bean structure was not dry.

Name:_____ Date:_____Product_____

Sample No._____

   I. INITIAL SENSATION (perceived in the first bite)

      (a) Mechanical characteristics   Score

         - Hardness (1-8 scale)
         (skin)   _____

      (b) Geometrical characteristics   _____

      (c) Other characteristics   Harsh   Smooth   Thin   Thick
         (skin nature)

                         ____   ____   ____   ____

  II. MASTIGATORY SENSATION (perceived during mastication)

      (a) Mechanical   Score   No. chews
         - Chewiness (1-6 scale)

                               _____

      (b) Geometrical   Grainy   Creamy   Soft
         (particles size and shape)

                         ____   ____   ___

                     Homogeneous   Non-homogeneous
                     (cellular)
         (particles shape/orientation)

                         _____   _____

      (c) Other characteristics   Slight   Moderate   Strong
         (humidity)

                         ____   ____   ____

III. RESIDUAL SENSATION (before, during, after swallow)

                  None   Slight   Moderate   Strong

       rate of breakdown   ____   _____   _____   _____

Fig. 1 — Sensory texture profile analysis score sheet for common beans.

Table 2 — **Sensory texture profile analysis for Carioca common bean** *(Phaseolus vulgaris L.)* **1978 dry season harvest.**

	Podzolic Yellow Red		Orto Podzolic Yellow Red		Latossol Red	
	a	b	a	b	a	b
I. INITIAL SENSATION						
a. Mechanical Characteristics - skin hardness (1-8 scale)	1.4	1.5	1.1	2.4	1.7	1.9
b. Geometrical Characteristics	Hom.	Hom.	Hom.	Hom.	Mod. Non-hom.	Hom.
c. Other Characteristics (nature of skin)	Smooth-thin	Smooth-thin	Smooth-thin	Smooth-thin	Smooth-thin	Thick
II. MASTICATORY SENSATION						
a. Mechanical Characteristics - chewiness (1-6 scale) - number of chews	1.4 9	1.4 13	1.2 17	2.0 19	1.4 12	1.6 13
b. Geometrical Characteristics (shape and orientation of particles)	-	Normal	Normal	-	Normal	-
c. Other Characteristics - humidity	Mod.	Mod.	Mod.	Mod.	Slight	Mod.-Strong
III. RESIDUAL SENSATION						
- rate of breakdown	Strong	Mod.	Strong	Mod.	Strong	Mod.

a = before storage (initial study).   b = after 6 months storage.

Beans grown in the Podzolic Yellow Red and Orto Podzolic Yellow Red soils differed in chewiness from those from Red Latossol soil (P = 0.05), the last named being harder than the former two. There were no significant differences in the 'number of chews' with respect to cultivars and soils.

The results of cooked beans of the *wet season harvest* gave the following information. Before storage, Carioca beans were softest and differed from Rosinha G2 and Aroana; beans from Podzolic Yellow Red soil were softest, differing from the other two at P = 0.05. Scores for chewiness and number of chews were similar.

After six months' storage, the beans showed no difference in hardness and chewiness. Beans from Podzolic Yellow Red soil, however, had softer texture and differed from those grown in Orto Podzolic Yellow Red and Red Latossol at P = 0.05. The degree of 'humidity' remained between 'moderate-strong', and related to the rate of breakdown.

Table 3 summarises the statistical results obtained from sensory texture parameters for cooked common beans by ANOVA and F statistics [5].

Table 3 — Levels of significance obtained from sensory texture parameters for cooked common beans by ANOVA and F statistics.

PARAMETERS	INITIAL x 6 MONTHS		DRY x WET	
	dry	wet	Initial	6 months
	1978	1978	1978	1978
HARDNESS				
harvest	ʌ(1n)	*(in)	n.s.	*(ds)
soil	n.s.	*(PYR)	*(OPYR)	*(PYR)
cultivar	n.s.	n.s.	n.s.	n.s.
CHEWNESS				
harvest	*(in)	*(in)	n.s.	*(ds)
soil	n.s.	n.s.	n.s.	n.s.
cultivar	n.s.	n.s.	n.s.	n.s.
NO CHEWS				
harvest	n.s.	n.s.	n.s.	n.s.
soil	n.s.	*(PYR)	n.s.	*(PYR)
cultivar	n.s.	n.s.	n.s.	n.s.

n.s. = no significance   PYR = Podzolic Yellow Red
in = initial   OPYR = Orto Podzolic Yellow Red
*   = Significance at 5%

Instron measurement

The results of cooked common beans of the dry and wet season harvests are summarized in Table 4.

For beans harvested in the dry season there was no significant difference among soils, but there was for cultivars: Carioca was softer than Rosinha G2 (0.472 kg) but comparable to Aroana (0.357 kg). After six months' storage there were no differences between any of the parameters studied.

For beans harvested in the wet season, no significant differences were found, but Carioca was generally softer.

Table 4 – **Instron hardness measurement (force in kg/cm) for cooked common beans on 1978 dry and wet season harvest.**

					TYPE OF SOIL						
CULTIVAR	PODZOLIC YELLOW RED				ORTO PODZOLIC YELLOW RED				LATOSSOL RED			
	dry		wet		dry		wet		dry		wet	
	b	a	b	a	b	a	b	a	b	a	b	a
Carioca	0,21	0,45	0,18		0,22	0,35	0,34		0,28	0,50	0,20	
Aroana	0,33	0,36	0,22		0,34	0,56	0,21		0,40	0,41	0,22	
Rosinha G2	0,39	0,35	0,21		0,46	0,34	0,26		0,55	0,40	0,22	

a = after 6 months storage   b = before storage (initial study)

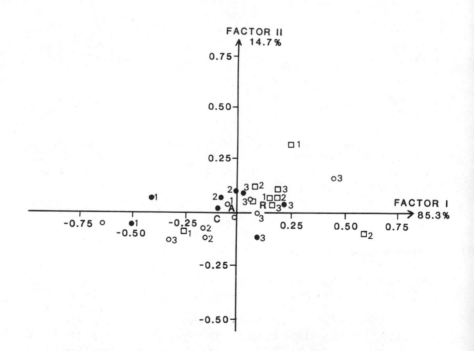

Fig.2 – Principle component analysis (PCA) for sensory parameters of common beans, Carioca (○), Aroana (●) and Rosinha G2 (□) grown on different soils:
Podzolic Yellow Red (1), Orto Podzolic Yellow Red (2), Latossol (3). 1978 dry and wet season harvest.

Principal component analysis

Principal component scores are presented in Figure 2,
85.3% of total variation is represented by the first
axis, and 14.7% by the second axis. The first axis
is related to hardness and chewiness. The second
axis is related to storage time.

    Lower values for beans grown in Podzolic Yellow
Red soil, indicate that their texture was softer
while beans from the Orto Podzolic Yellow Red soil
with higher average values were harder.

    After six months' storage, cooking time showed
correlation with sensory hardness, but did not
correlate with the Instron measurements.

CONCLUSIONS

Common beans of the cultivar Carioca showed a softer
texture by sensory and instrumental measurements,
though the data of the first did not correlate with
the latter. Beans grown in Podzolic Yellow Red
soils also seem softer than those grown in other
soils. Beans were harder and more chewy following
storage at room temperature (25°C) and 65-70% RH.

REFERENCES

1. Bourne, M.C. *et al.* Training a sensory texture
     profile panel and development of standard
     rating scales in Colombia. J. Texture Stud.
     1975, 6 (1), 43-52.
2. Szczesniak, A.A.; Brandt, M.A.; Friedman, H.H.
     Development of standard rating scales for
     mechanical parameters of texture and correla-
     tion between the objective and sensory methods
     of texture evaluation. J. Fd Sci. 1963, 28,
     397.
3. Breene, W.M. Application of texture profile
     analysis to instrumental food texture evalua-
     tion. J. Texture Stud. 1975, 6(1), 53-82.
4. Bourne, M.C.; Moyer, J.C.; Hand, D.B. Measure-
     ment of food texture by a Universal testing
     machine. Fd Technol. 1966, 20(4), 170.
5. Fisher, R.A.; Yates, F. Statistical Tables for
     Biological Agricultural and Medical Research
     3rd edn. Oliver and Boyd, London, 1938. 112.

Chapter 4.5

Relationship between the capsaicoids content and the Scoville Index of Capsicum oleoresins

L.J. van Gemert, L.N. Nijssen, A.T.H.J. de Bie and H. Maarse,
Division for Nutrition and Food Research TNO, Institute CIVO-Analysis, Zeist,
The Netherlands.

SUMMARY

The capsaicinoids content and the Scoville Index were measured in 11 samples of capsicum oleoresins. The capsaicinoids (capsaicin and dihydrocapsaicin) were quantified by a HPLC-method; the Scoville Index was determined by a panel of about 20 assessors, using a certainty rating scale.

Regression analysis showed an equation in which the value of the slope is in good accordance with the Scoville Index of natural capsaicin. The correlation coefficient is close to one. However, the intercept has a relatively high negative value.

INTRODUCTION

The capsaicinoids are responsible for the pungent taste of capsicums and their oleoresins [1]. Since there is no established correlation between the spectrophotometric determination of capsaicin and the Scoville Index [2] a recently published high pressure liquid chromatographic (HPLC)-method [3] has been adopted for the quantitative measurement of these capsaicinoids, of which capsaicin and dihydrocapsaicin are the most important ones. This method should also make it possible to detect adulteration by means of vanillyl nonanylamide (synthetic capsaicin).

A well known sensory measure for the pungency is the Scoville Index. This is based on the determination of the recognition threshold of the pungent sensation after dilution. This Index is expressed as the denominator of the dilution fraction at threshold level. We have used a method developed for ground black pepper [4] to measure the Scoville Index of capsicum oleoresins.

The relation between the capsaicinoids content and the Scoville Index [cf. 1, 5-6]was studied to find out whether it would be possible to replace the sensory measurement by an instrumental method.

MATERIALS AND METHODS

Materials

Samples of capsicum oleoresins were collected from West Germany, India, The Netherlands, the United Kingdom and the United States. Natural capsaicin and vanillyl nonanylamide were obtained commercially.

HPLC analysis

This comprised: an isocratic pump, Varian 5010; sampling valve, Rheodyne 7010; reversed phase column, 125 x 4.6 mm i.d. Hypersyl-ODS 5 µm; recorder, Kipp BD 41; data system, Varian CDS 111. The procedure was as follows:

-   dissolve 0.1 - 1.0 g oleoresin in 100 ml tetrahydrofuran (THF)-methanol (1:1 v/v),

-   dissolve 20 mg capsaicin + 10 mg vanillyl nonanylamide in 100 ml THF-methanol (1:1 v/v); external standard solution,

-   inject in separate runs 10 µl external standard solution,

-   determine the capsaicinoids content by comparing the peak areas of the sample with those of the external standard solution.

The HPLC-solvent was a mixture of methanol and 0.1 M $AgNO_3$ (3:2 v/v) with a flow rate of 2 ml/min. Detection was based on excitation at 280 nm and emission at 360 nm.

Scoville Index

The method is summarized below:

Number of assessors	-	about 20
Response	-	certainty rating scale [4]
Order of stimuli	-	randomized
Number of stimuli	-	5
Concentration step	-	about 1.4
Inter-stimulus duration	-	1.5 min.
Dilution medium	-	2.5% sugar in water
Quantity to be swallowed	-	5 ml
Time between series	-	approx. 10 min.

The Index was calculated by linear regression of mean scores against number of dilutions; and interpolation at a mean score of 3.5.

RESULTS AND DISCUSSION

Figure 1 shows the HPLC-chromatograms of a capsicum oleoresin containing 10% natural capsaicinoids and of the same sample adulterated with 2% vanillyl nonanylamide.

We found that HPLC is suitable for determining the content of capsaicin, dihydrocapsaicin, nordihydrocapsaicin and homocapsaicin of capsicum oleoresins; adulteration by means of vanillyl nonanylamide could be detected.

In our experiments the Scoville Index of natural capsaicin had an average value of about 25.10^6; Indian investigators [1] found a value of 16.10^6. The greater sensitivity of the Dutch panel in comparison with the Indian panel can be explained by the higher consumption of capsicums in India, as it has been shown that frequent users of capsicums are less sentitive than less frequent consumers by a factor of 1.5 [7].

In 11 samples of capsicum oleoresins, the capsaicinoids content (capsaicin and dihydrocapsaicin) ranged from 3 ‑ 30% and the Scoville Index from $0.5.10^6$ - 7.10^6. Regression analysis (see Fig.2)

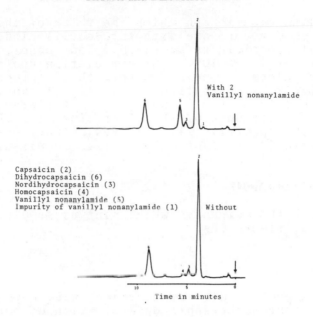

With 2
Vanillyl nonanylamide

Capsaicin (2)
Dihydrocapsaicin (6)
Nordihydrocapsaicin (3)
Homocapsaicin (4)
Vanillyl nonanylamide (5)
Impurity of vanillyl nonanylamide (1)   Without

Time in minutes

Fig. 1 — HPLC-chromatogram of a capsicum oleoresin with and without 2%
vanillyl nonanylamide.

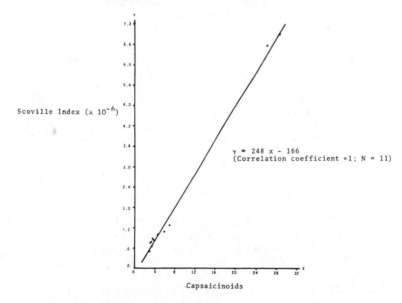

Scoville Index ($\times 10^{-6}$)

$Y = 248 x - 166$
(Correlation coefficient ≈ 1; N = 11)

Capsaicinoids

Fig. 2 — Relation between Scoville Index and capsaicinoids content (capsaicin
and dihydrocapsaicin) of capsicum oleoresins.

showed an equation in which the value of the slope is in good accordance with the Scoville Index of natural capsaicin as measured by our panel, i.e. approximately 25.10^6. The correlation coefficient is very close to one. However, the intercept has a relatively high negative value (significantly different from zero), indicating interference by other constituents of the oleoresins [1]. Further research especially with oleoresins having a capsaicinoids content below 3%, is required.

ACKNOWLEDGEMENT

We thank the Companies which sent us samples of capsicum oleoresins.

REFERENCES

1. Rajpoot, N.C.; Govindarajan, V.S. Paper chromatographic determination of total capsaicinoids in capsicums and their oleoresins with precision, reproducibility, and validation through correlation with pungency in Scoville units. J. Assoc. Off. Anal. Chem. 1981, 64, 311-318.

2. The Oleoresin Handbook, Fritzsche Dodge and Olcott Inc., 3rd edn, 1981, 46-47.

3. Johnson, E.L.; Majors, R.E.; Werum, L.; Reiche, P. "Liquid Chromatographic Analysis of Food and Beverages, Vol.1" (Charalambous, G. Ed.), Academic Press, New York, 1979, 17-29.

4. Gemert, L.J. van.; Nijssen, L.M.; Maarse, H. "Flavour '81" (Schreier, P., Ed.), W. de Gruyter, Berlin, 1981, 211-216.

5. Todd, P.H.; Bensinger, M.G.; Biftu, T. Determination of pungency due to capsicum by gas-liquid chromatography. J. Fd Sci. 1977, 42, 660-665, 680.

6. Woodbury, J.E. Determination of capsicum pungency by high pressure liquid chromatography and spectrofluorometric detection. J. Assoc. Off. Anal. Chem. 1980, 63, 556-558.

7. Rozin, P.; Mark, M.; Schiller, D. The role of
    desensitization to capsaicin in chili pepper
    ingestion and preference. Chem. Senses 1981,
    6, 23-31.

Chapter 4.6

Descriptive sensory analysis of soy sauce

S.M. Tan and J.R. Piggott
Department of Bioscience and Biotechnology, University of Strathclyde, 131 Albion Street, Glasgow G1 1SD, Scotland

SUMMARY

A panel of 12 assessors, from different cultures and with little or no knowledge of soy sauce, used a vocabulary of 22 descriptive terms to examine 36 samples covering the major types of sauce. The assessors were required to score the samples for aroma, flavour-by-mouth and after-flavour for each term using a scale from 0 to 5. A hedonic judgement was also required, using a nine-point scale. The data showed that the assessors could satisfactorily distinguish between the main varieties of sauce. Hedonic judgements showed great inter-individual variation, and the assessors were clearly separated into groups prefering different characteristics.

INTRODUCTION

There is no existing method of sensory analysis for soy sauce usable by inexperienced assessors, traditional tests requiring standards for comparison or expert tasters. Descriptive sensory analysis (the description of flavour by a panel of assessors using a pre-defined vocabulary) has been successfully applied to a number of foods and beverages, especially fermented products with complex flavours. The work described here was carried out to compose a suitable vocabulary and test it on a range of sauces.

EXPERIMENTAL

A panel of 12 assessors was chosen from the members
of the department, from different cultures and of
different ages. The assessors had little or no
knowledge of soy sauce, but two had considerable
experience of descriptive sensory analysis.
Thirty-six samples of soy sauce were obtained,
covering the major types (shown in Table 1).

Table 1 — Samples used.

Code	Brand	Country of origin
1	Delicious soy bean sauce	China
2	Pure soy bean sauce	China
3	Narcissus special grade soy	China
4	Narcissus mushroom sauce	China
5	Pearl River Bridge mushroom soy	China
6	Pearl River Bridge sauce (dark)	China
7	Pearl River Bridge sauce (light)	China
8	Tang soy sauce	Hong Kong
9	Dragon Blue soy sauce	Hong Kong
10	Lotus soy sauce	Hong Kong
11	Amoy soy sauce	Hong Kong
12	Woh Hup soya sauce grade A (light)	Singapore
13	Woh Hup soya sauce grade A (dark)	Singapore
14	Lighthouse brand soy sauce (dark)	Singapore
15	Lighthouse brand soy sauce (light)	Singapore
16	Yeo's soy (special blend) (dark)	Singapore
17	Yeo's soy sauce	Singapore
18	Sharwood's rich soy (Lau Ch'ou)	Singapore
19	Sharwood's light soy (Sheng Ch'ou)	Singapore
20	Kichap Pekat	Malaysia
21	Kichap Ayam Piru Cair	Malaysia
22	Kichap Soya (Cair)	Malaysia
23	Natural soy sauce thick no. 1A	Malaysia
24	Harmony naturally brewed Shoyu	Japan
25	Kikkoman naturally brewed	Japan
26	Yamasa soy sauce	Japan
27	Yamasa soy sauce	Japan
28	Yamasa soy sauce (Sashimi Shoyu)	Japan
29	Yamasa Somen-tsuyu	Japan
30	Seasoning soy sauce (Tsuyu Nomoto)	Japan
31	Kikkoman Teriyaki barbecue sauce	Japan
32	Yamasa Hiyamugi Tsuyu	Japan
33	Soy sauce	U.K.
34	Ketjap	Netherlands
35	Sam Yang	Korea
36	Low salt soy sauce	Japan

A search was made of existing literature [1-5] for descriptive terms previously used for soy sauce. Some of these were for preference assessment, but 10 useful descriptive terms were found: 'heated', sweet and fruity, cooked beef, caramel-like, meat-like, sweet and mellow, rich, meaty, salty. It was thought that these terms could not provide a complete description of the flavour, so informal tasting and discussion sessions were held with the assessors. These sessions provided a total of 106 terms. After the elimination of synonymous and ambiguous terms, a vocabulary of 22 terms (Table 2) was developed. It was ensured that the assessors understood the terms adequately.

Table 2 — Descriptive terms.

Acrid	dry, pungent
Bitter	
Solvent	alcoholic, ketone
Sour	sharp, acid, vinegary
Rancid	lactic, cheesey
Yeasty	yeast extract
Malty	beer-like
Meaty	beefy
Fishy	ammoniacal, manure-like
Caramel	
Buttery	diacetyl, toffee-like
Sweet	
Burnt	
Phenolic	tarry
Fruity	estery
Oily	
Metallic	
Mouldy	musty
Grassy	cut grass
Soapy	
Nutty	
Salty	

The assessors were then required to score the aroma (by sniffing), the flavour (by mouth) and the after-flavour of each sample (in duplicate) for each term using a scale from 0 to 5. An overall hedonic judgement was also required, using a symmetrical nine-point scale [6]. The samples were identified by three-digit random numbers, and no carrier or diluent was used, the samples being nosed and tasted as supplied. Equal amounts of each sample were

provided in tulip-shaped glasses covered by watch-
glasses, similar in shape to wine-tasting glasses
(BS 5586:1978) but of 4 ounces nominal capacity.

RESULTS AND DISCUSSION

Panel mean profiles were calculated for each sample,
and the results subjected to principal components
analyses [7], followed by Varimax rotation [8].
Aroma, flavour and after-flavour data were analysed
separately, aroma and flavour combined, and all data
combined. The first three components accounted for
between 38% (for the combined data) and 53% (for the
aroma data) of the total variance. The components
and sample configurations were generally similar in
all analyses, except for some terms, for example
salty, which were used in different ways in aroma
and flavour data. The samples were clearly separated into groups, depending on their origin and
ingredients. A canonical correlation analysis [7]
was also carried out comparing the aroma and flavour
data. The redundancy in each set of terms, given
the other set, was 57%. As was expected from the
principal components analyses, the first six pairs
of factors (accounting for 52% of variance in the
aroma data and 50% of that in the flavour data) were
generally similar with the exception of terms such
as salty and sweet.

In an attempt to find those terms most useful
in predicting the overall hedonic score, multiple
regression calculations [7] were carried out using
the descriptive terms as predictor variables and the
hedonic score as criterion. Using the raw data from
all assessors, a multiple correlation (R^2) of 0.40
was found for 66 predictors, and 0.28 for the best
ten predictors. To improve the R^2 values, a principal components analysis was carried out on the
preference data. The first three components
accounted for 51% of the variance, and from this the
assessors were classified into three groups. Multiple
regressions using the groups of assessors gave
slightly higher R^2 values, ranging from 0.55 to 0.62
for all variables, and from 0.45 to 0.49 for the best
ten predictors. These rather low values suggested
either that the vocabulary lacked important terms
responsible for a large part of the hedonic judgements (unlikely, since the samples were apparently
well described), or that the individual assessors
were not using the vocabulary consistently.

CONCLUSION

The investigation reported here has shown that a panel of inexperienced assessors could use descriptive sensory analysis to successfully describe and classify a range of soy sauces.

REFERENCES

1. Moris, B. Quality evaluation of shoyu and application of factor analysis. J.Soc. Brewing Japan 1979, 74, 526-531.
2. Aishima, T. Evaluation and discrimination of soy sauce by computer analysis of volatile profiles. Agric.Biol.Chem. 1979, 43, 1711-1718.
3. Aishima, T. Classification of soy sauce by principal components of GC profiles. Agric. Biol.Chem. 1979, 43, 1905-1910.
4. Aishima, T. Objective evaluation of soy sauce by statistical analysis of GC profiles. Agric.Biol.Chem. 1979, 43, 1935-1943.
5. Aishima, T.; Nobuhara, A. Objective specification of food flavour. Analysis of gas chromatographic profiles of soy sauce flavour by stepwise regression analysis. Fd Chem. 1977, 2, 81-93.
6. Peryam, D.R. Sensory testing at the Quartermaster Food and Container Institute. Lab. Pract. 1964, 13, 675-609.
7. Cooley, W.W.; Lohnes, P.R. Multivariate Data Analysis. John Wiley & Sons Inc., New York, 1971.
8. Kaiser, H.F. Computer program for Varimax rotation in factor analysis. Educ.Psychol. Measurement 1959, 19, 413-420.

SENSORY AND INSTRUMENTAL METHODS AND THEIR APPLICATION TO SPECIFIC PRODUCTS

(b)   Fruit and Fruit Products

Chapter 4.7

Enzymes as indices of ripening

P.W. Goodenough
Long Ashton Research Station, University of Bristol, Long Ashton, Bristol BS18 9AF, UK

SUMMARY

The use of enzymes as indices of ripening requires a careful examination of the control mechanisms of protein synthesis to establish that changes in enzyme specific activity are always associated with a certain stage of ripeness. Once this is established then a field test can be devised. Examples of enzyme changes which control non-volatile and volatile compounds contributing to sensory quality are discussed.

INTRODUCTION

When enzymes are going to be used as indices of sensory change in fruit it is necessary to understand what component of quality is changed by the enzyme. As enzymes in biological systems act as organic catalysts and speed up the reaction processes,then all functions of cells depend on enzymes being present most of the time. Apart from the main metabolic pathways, e.g. citric acid cycle, there are also many pathways of secondary metabolism which directly influence the development of flavour volatiles and non-volatile taste components. How these metabolic sequences are connected is important to the overall growth, development and reproduction of the plant. However, the synthesis of these enzymes is itself controlled by the genome of the plant. We must therefore look to the genome for the signals which trigger changes in the type or concentration of

enzyme; these in turn control the substrate concentration giving rise to the sensory characteristic.
There are also carrier proteins which transport
substrates across membranes. The control mechanisms
are made more complicated because both the mitochondria and the chloroplasts have their own genome
(DNA). Furthermore, in chloroplasts the synthesis.
of some proteins is controlled by the chloroplast
DNA, while others (and even sub-units of the same
enzyme, e.g. Fraction I protein) are controlled by
the nuclear DNA.

Thus, changes in enzymes can be the result of
complex control mechanisms affecting synthetic and
transport systems even before activity is expressed
and is measurable. Also, enzyme protein may be
present but an inhibitor can be synthesised and
prevent its activity. To use enzyme activity or
enzyme protein to measure a change in the metabolism,
we must therefore understand how the protein's
formation is controlled. More use might then be
made of biochemical tests to determine quality in
fruit or vegetables.

DNA TO PROTEIN CONTROL POINTS

Figure 1 outlines the way in which genetic information, as retained by the base sequence of the DNA,
is expressed; any one of these steps might be used
as an indicator of incipient change. The essential
features are:(a) transcription of a messenger-RNA
copy of one strand of the DNA using RNA polymerase II
in the nucleus. All the DNA strand is copied
although it is now known that several, perhaps all,
genes have sequences of redundant DNA. RNA polymerase can itself control the transcription of the
DNA and is the first control point in production of
an enzyme; (b) post-transcription processing. Most
nuclear genes are transcribed as sections of linear
RNA of which only certain portions are finally
translated. The sections in between (introns) are
only found in eukaryotes and before the mRNA is
translated these are removed and the mRNA coding for
the enzyme protein is spliced together to form a
linear piece of RNA which is then available for
translation in the cytoplasm. The mRNA may be
stored for a short period or made available for
binding to ribosomes. At this stage, the mRNA may
be further processed by the addition of a 'cap' at
5' end and a tail of poly-adenylic acid at the 3'

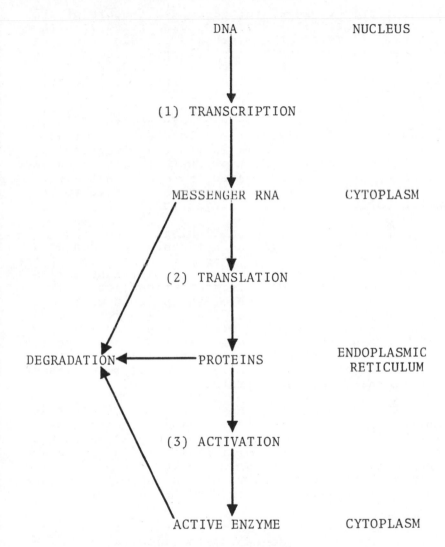

Fig.1 — Gene expression and position in the cell.

end of the molecule. The mRNA is then bound to
ribosomes, and the amino acid-transfer RNA complex
is added. Finally, the amino acids are polymerized
and the resultant protein is released into the cytoplasm to be folded, 'trimmed' and perhaps activated
to form the enzyme.

There is much evidence that developmental
changes are associated with changes in gene

transcription. Regulator genes - a feature of the operator model [1] - have been discovered in higher plants. In maize, the synthesis of zein, a storage protein, is much reduced in 'floury-2' and 'opaque-2' mutants; the genes concerned do not code for zein, but clearly they affect the expression of the zein gene. However, many changes are not controlled at the transcriptional stage and some mRNA molecules are very long lived or enzymes may be stored in the cytoplasm in inactive forms. To use biochemical tests as quality criteria in fruit and vegetables, it will be necessary to know whether certain enzymes are activated or synthesized *de novo*. In the former case, activators of enzyme protein may have to be measured rather than the enzyme itself.

The criteria for establishing whether the appearance of an enzyme or structural protein at a particular developmental stage, is controlled at the transcriptional, translational or post-translational stage are as follows. Transcriptional control means that the appearance of the protein must be preceded by the synthesis of a new species of mRNA. Translational control involves the production of a new protein without the appearance of 'new' species of mRNA. Post-translational control involves the appearance of the protein in an active form without the synthesis of 'new' protein.

If it can be shown by use of radiolabels that an increase in enzyme activity is accompanied by synthesis of the enzyme, it does not necessarily point to *de novo* synthesis; it may reflect a marked change in turnover rates. Turnover rates of enzymes should therefore be determined, along with increases in actual activity. These studies fall into two classes:

(i) Dramatic increases in activity, in the presence of deuterium-labelled water, without incorporation of deuterium into the enzyme; this is post-translational control. If other enzymes do incorporate the label, this indicates that increase in activity is not due to *de novo* synthesis.

(ii) Many enzymes have become labelled with deuterium during their increases in activity, suggesting that this is true *de novo* synthesis. Where turnover rates have been investigated, the increase in activity has been due to increased synthesis (*de novo*) not a decreased rate of degradation.

Thus, changes in enzyme activities are the result of complex control mechanisms which it is desirable to understand if seeking an acceptable enzyme-based test to monitor quality.

FRUIT RIPENING

During ripening of fruit many biochemical reactions convert an unripe, poor tasting organ into a ripe fruit, attractive to the consumer. Some fruits change colour and incipient ripening can be easily detected, but in others there is no easily monitored change. Thus in tomatoes the fruit reddens and softens, loses chlorophyll and starch, and accumulates monosaccharides; changes also occur in the metabolism of citric and malic acid and flavour compounds are synthesised. Several of these changes have been investigated biochemically, and some enzymes can be used as biochemical markers, in particular, the enzyme controlling cell wall softening which reaches a high concentration in ripe fruit [2]. Elegant work at Sutton Bonington, University of Nottingham, has shown that the enzyme has two forms (Fig. 2) and during ripening the one form stays at a fairly low concentration while the other increases greatly in concentration [3]. This increase in activity is due to new synthesis as opposed to activation and therefore the enzyme can reliably be used as an indicator of ripening. This is important in commercial situations where the appearance of this enzyme will lead to loss of a stored crop. However, the appearance of this enzyme can be linked to colour change during storage [4]. Thus, visual appearance would be a better guide to texture loss. This situation does not, however, apply to the non-volatile taste components which change during fruit storage. During even a short period of storage, tomato fruit lose malate and starch and accumulate monosaccharide and citrate [5,6]. When the enzymes controlling these changes are monitored we have established that citrate synthase and malate dehydrogenase rapidly lose 60% of their activity (Goodenough *et al.*, unpublished). We have not yet established the causes for this decreased enzyme activity but it may be that some of the enzyme is bound in the mitochondria and is not lost when synthesis stops whereas 60% is free in glyoxysomes in the cytoplasm and is rapidly turned over. This loss in activity could be used as a measure of storage life or incipient ripeness in stored tomatoes.

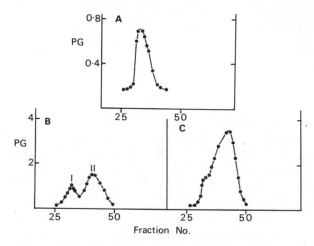

Fig. 2 — Ion exchange chromatography of isoenzymes of polygalacturonase from tomato fruit at different stages of ripeness. A = breaker (just orange fruit), B = turning orange to red, and C = overripe. I is isoenzyme one, and II is isoenzyme two. Column was DEAE—A50 at pH 8.0 (from [3]).

Finally, we have shown that in apples a carboxylic acid esterase increases in activity just before ripening. The substrates of this enzyme include hexyl acetate and butyl acetate - esters produced by the developing fruit. In mature apples the aroma derives from a mixture of these compounds with the corresponding alcohols, hexanal and butanal. We have found that this conversion involves an enzyme which can easily bind and break down hexyl acetate, and also smaller esters, though less readily. Thus, a mixture of esters and alcohol is produced without any one compound predominating. When the apple fruit is immature only a very small amount of the enzyme is present, but with the onset of maturity the specific activity of the enzyme increases rapidly until the enzyme is many fold greater in concentration than previously. This increase seems to occur before the rise in respiration and ethylene evolution. As such, monitoring a rise in esterase would be a good guide, in the absence of a visual change, of when apple fruit is beginning to ripen and is

ready for storage in controlled atmospheres. To
make such a test for reliable field use, it needs to
be linked to a dye such as naphthyl acetate; this is
hydrolysed by the enzyme (if present) to give
naphthol, which is then reacted with a dye such as
Fast Blue to give a red colour (Fig. 3). The
development of a red colour over a certain period of
time could give a rough indication of activity and
therefore of incipient ripening and of storability
of apples.

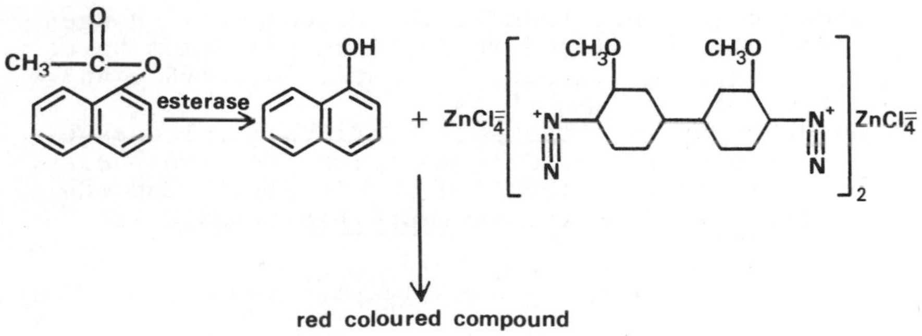

red coloured compound

Fig.3 — Cleavage of α—naphthyl acetate to give α—naphthol which reacts with
Fast Blue B to give a red coloured compound. A rapid test for esterase.

CONCLUSIONS

Enzymes are not as yet used as indices of quality in
fresh produce but investigation of these proteins
will reveal more of the close connection between
them and stages of development. Some results are
already available for adaptation into field scale
chemical tests, but to produce high quality fruit,
more use will have to be made of this technology.

REFERENCES

1. Jacob,F.; Monad,F. Genetic regulatory mechanisms
   in the synthesis of proteins. J.mol.Biol. 1961,
   3, 318-356.

2. Hobson,G. Polygalacturonase in normal and abnormal tomato fruit. <u>Biochem.J.</u> 1964, 92, 324-332.

3. Grierson,D.; Tucker,G.; Robertson,N. The regulation of gene expression during the ripening of tomato fruits. <u>In</u> 'Quality in Stored and Processed Vegetables and Fruit' (Goodenough, P.W.; Atkin,R.K., Eds), 179-191, 1981. Academic Press, London.

4. Goodenough,P.W.; Tucker,G.A.; Grierson,D.; Thomas,T. Changes in colour, polygalacturonase monosaccharides and organic acids during storage of tomatoes. <u>Phytochemistry</u> 1982, 21, 281-284.

5. Goodenough,P.W.; Thomas,T.H. Biochemical changes in tomatoes stored in modified gas atmospheres. I. Sugars and acids. <u>Ann.appl.Biol</u>. 1981, 98, 507-515.

6. Goodenough,P.W.; Thomas,T.H. Biochemical changes in tomatoes stored in modified gas atmospheres. II. Isoenzymes involved in glycolysis and the citric acid cycle. <u>Ann.appl.Biol</u>. 1981, 98, 517-524.

Chapter 4.8

Flavour quality evaluation and specifications for non-alcoholic beverages

R. Dobbs
Assistant Research Manager, Beecham Products, Great West Road, Brentford, Middlesex TW8 9BD

SUMMARY

Consumer acceptability of non-alcoholic beverages, particularly soft drinks, depends very heavily on aroma and flavour performance. Yet these aspects of finished product performance cannot adequately be determined by physical and/or chemical means.

This paper describes the industrial use of a small panel of previously untrained housewives to carry out sensory analysis of a range of blackcurrant drinks. A vocabulary of sensory terms relevant to blackcurrant drinks has been developed and an attempt made to define each term by reference to a chemical odour standard. The potential application of the technique for use in quality control and product development is described.

INTRODUCTION

This paper describes our continuing attempts to apply the technique of sensory profiling as an aid to product development and quality control in a practical industrial situation. I shall refer to our work on blackcurrant drinks but, rather than simply provide detailed results on a specific product, I shall consider mainly the industrial potential of sensory profiling.

CURRENT SITUATION

The term "non-alcoholic beverages" encompasses a wide range of products, from the relatively simple unflavoured, uncarbonated mineral waters, through soft drinks, tea and coffee, to highly textured products such as tomato juice, drinking chocolate and malt food drinks. The product attributes which determine relative consumer acceptability are appearance, aroma, flavour and mouthfeel. Appearance strongly influences acceptability but presents its own unique problems which are not discussed here. As a general rule, within any particular category of beverage, aroma and flavour exert the dominant influence on product acceptability with mouthfeel being somewhat less important. This is specially true of soft drinks where product composition is closely controlled by the Soft Drinks regulations and where often all that distinguishes one product from another is aroma and flavour. With other food products, quality judgements by the consumer are influenced considerably by other factors which are relatively easy to measure chemically or physically.

My own company is heavily involved in the soft drinks business which represents a major segment of the total non-alcoholic beverages market. We have some very successful major brands but we are less than happy about our ability to describe and specify the sensory performance of these products and the raw materials used in their manufacture. Data from some typical finished product flavour specifications illustrate this point:

<blockquote>

Example A.   Clean, characteristic of black-
                      currants.
                      Comparable to standard product.
                      Free of taints and off-flavours.

Example B.   Characteristic of blackcurrant
                      juice plus added flavourings.
                      Comparable to standard product.
                      Free of taints and off-flavours.

</blockquote>

Even this very limited description might be acceptable if the main flavour contributors, say an added commercial flavouring or a processed fruit extract, were adequately specified. However, extracts from some typical specifications show this not to be the case. The raw materials specifications (shown

below) include some fairly elementary physical and
chemical parameters, and sometimes a GLC trace, but
there is no adequate description of the perceived
aroma and flavour of the material:

Example A.   Clean characteristic blackcurrant
                aroma.
                Ethereal blackcurrant flavour with
                faint solvent note.

Example B.   Pungent lime peel aroma with slight
                solvent note.
                Astringent lime peel flavour.

Example C.   Distinct orange peel aroma.
                Clean, orange peel flavour with
                faint solvent note.

General   Appearance, aroma and flavour should
                match the most recently accepted
                sample which was satisfactory
                in use.

                Refractive Index   Trace Metals
                S.G.   Preservative
                Solvent   Emulsifier
                Flammability   Legal
                Anti-oxidant

The lack of an adequate descriptive technique
does not imply a lack of control of sensory performance. No product can be built into a successful
brand unless it delivers consistently the quality
that the consumer knows and expects. We achieve this,
like other manufacturers, by:

(i)   Selecting reliable raw material suppliers
        with technical expertise and facili-
        ties.

(ii) Internal "experts" in R & D, QC and
        Production who are working with the
        ingredients and product on a daily
        basis.

(iii) Making extensive use of consumer research
        to determine relative consumer accept-
        ability.

However, there remains the obvious gap. We have

"experts" who are sensitive to small changes in product but who do not have a clear, unambiguous terminology to communicate those perceptions effectively,
and we have the consumers who clearly know what they
like but who often do not have the words to say why.
Inevitably, we felt that flavour profiling techniques
could help bridge that gap. We decided to do some
exploratory work using blackcurrant drinks as the
product group. Our reasons for selecting blackcurrant drinks were:

(i)   Major commercial interest.

(ii) Wide range of product types from simple
      flavoured drinks through to high
      quality blackcurrant health drinks.

(iii) Major involvement with the growing, pro-
      cessing and storage of blackcurrants
      to optimise yield, flavour and colour.

Our aim was to develop a method of sensory
analysis of finished products which:

(i)   Allowed full description of the aroma,
      flavour and mouthfeel of blackcurrant
      drinks using defined descriptors.

(ii) Was suitable for product development and
      QC.

(iii) Aided communication within the Company
      and with material suppliers.

(iv) Was cheap, quick and reliable.

These objectives pointed to a level of enquiry
between the original simple profiles described in
the literature and the more complex studies requiring full computer analysis.

ESTABLISHMENT OF PANEL

Because our available internal resources were limited,
we did not use our own employees but set up an external panel. We first recruited a panel leader with
the necessary personal qualities, i.e. sociability,
enthusiasm and the ability to work independently.
She in turn recruited housewives prepared to attend
a regular 1 hour session each week, at a local venue.

About 40 potential subjects were screened for personal
attributes (e.g. interest, ability to communicate)
and for sensory ability. We finally established two
separate groups, each of 7 assessors, who have now
met regularly for 1½ years - or a total of about
60 hours per assessor. The time has been accounted
for by:

(i) Initial training in sensory evaluation
(triangle, ranking tests, etc. of
increasing difficulty).

(ii) Introduction to blackcurrant drinks with
open discussion to generate descrip-
tive terms.

(iii) Detailed discussion to eliminate dupli-
cation and overlap using "spiked"
products and chemical standards.

(iv) Agreement on a chemical standard for
each descriptor.

Table 1 — Odour references for blackcurrant drinks.

Descriptor	Chemical	mg/10 g wax
Natural	–	–
Pastille	benzyl acetate	50
	beta-ionone	10
	iris concrete	5
Sharp	–	–
Sweet	vanillin	50
Caramel	maltol	100
Burnt	2, 5-dimethyl-4-hydroxy-3 (2H) furanone	100
Floral	2-phenylethanol	100
Leafy	cis-3-hexenol	7
	trans-2-hexenol	7
	ethyl acetoacetate	7
Catty	para-menthane-8-thiol-3-one	5
Bushy	blackcurrant bud extract (Pfizer)	200
Woody	Cedarwood oil	100
Earthy	geosmin	0.01
Metallic	–	–

We intended that each descriptor should be
defined by a single pure chemical but inevitably we
have compromised in some cases by using simple mixtures, in others by using complex materials. The
standards (Table 1) are made up as a mixture of the
chemicals in 10 g of paraffin wax in a 100 ml brown
glass bottle. The concentration of each standard
is chosen so as to give a clear, recognizable odour
for all assessors. The odour references are available during group sessions. Some flavour and mouthfeel reference solutions were also made up to assist
training but these are not normally available during
sessions.

Each assessor will score up to four products
per session, each sample being presented coded and in
a black glass beaker to mask colour differences. An
identical control sample is always made available, as
is each assessor's own typical score for the control.
This provides a base-line score over a number of sessions. Control samples are often included blind to
provide an internal reference. To minimise variability, a standard formula is used for the control
and samples are held frozen over a maximum of three
months. After this period a new batch of control
product is made, is compared blind against the old
control to ensure minimal differences and then held
frozen until **required**. An abbreviated form of the
questionnaire in current use is shown in Table 2,
each descriptor being scored on a 0-5 scale. The
full questionnaire provides for several samples.

The format of each session is typically as
follows. Each assessor scores the samples sequen-
tially and independently of the other assessors. On
completion, the panel leader opens discussion on the
samples to identify and hopefully clarify any major
differences in scores between the assessors.

The assessor may then carry out further training or discrimination exercises on blackcurrant pro-
sucts or assess products other than blackcurrant to
provide both variety and useful results in other
areas.

On completion of the assessments the results
are analysed. Though complex analysis would be possible, we simply carry out 2-way analysis of variance
for each descriptor across all samples. This is
followed by Duncan's multiple range test if necessary
to identify samples and/or assessors who are sig-

Table 2 – Questionnaire : blackcurrant drinks.

	Aroma	Flavour	Texture	After taste
Natural			x	
Pastille			x	
Sharp			x	
Sweet			x	
Caramelised			x	
Burnt			x	
Floral			x	
Leafy			x	
Catty			x	
Bushy			x	
Woody			x	
Earthy			x	
Metallic			x	
Bitter	x		x	
Mouthcoating	x	x		x
Astringent	x	x		x
Drying	x	x		x
Body	x	x		x

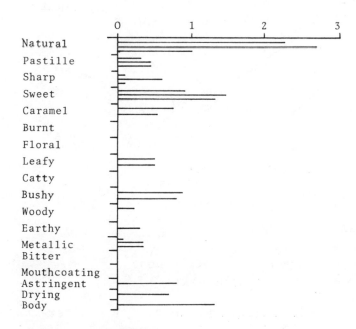

Fig.1 – Sensory profile of Ribena.

nificantly different. We supplement this with a
simple visual inspection which can often be helpful
in understanding the effects of any changes made in
formula or process.

A typical sensory "fingerprint" for standard
Ribena is shown in Figure 1. Each horizontal bar
represents the arithmetic mean score across all the
assessors for each descriptor. In Figures 2 and 3,
results are presented of a comparison of Ribena,
C-Vit and Corona Cordial. These products are clearly
targetted at different consumers and are radically
different in formulation. Ribena is a high quality,
high juice health drink whereas the Cordial is based
on a lower cost formula and is aimed at a different
market; C-Vit lies between the two. For simplicity,
scores are only presented for the descriptors where
analysis of variance showed significant differences
of at least P = 0.05 between products.

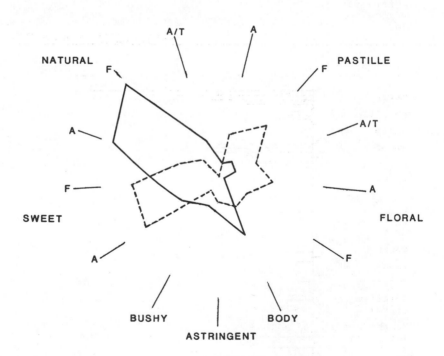

Key: A = Aroma; F = Flavour; A/T = After-taste.

Fig. 2 — Sensory profile — blackcurrant drinks : Ribena (—) and C-Vit (- - - -).

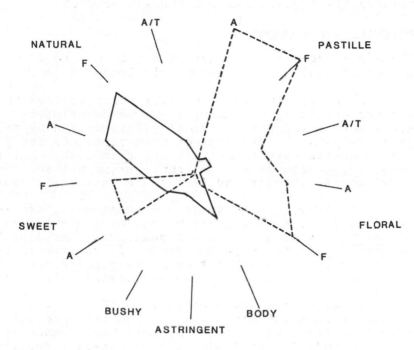

Key: A = Aroma; F = Flavour; A/T = After-taste.

Fig.3 — Sensory profile — blackcurrant drinks : Ribena (—) and Corona Cordial (- - - -).

The results clearly show that the assessors are recognizing and assessing degrees of difference between the products which could be expected from the formula differences between the products.

We have used the panel to evaluate development formulae where differences between samples are much smaller and, in contrast, we have recently used the panel to reassure ourselves that there is no difference between two variants of the same product. For example, we have recently introduced a ready-to-drink (RTD) version of Ribena. This product has the same basic formula as our standard product but has been subjected to further heat processing prior to aseptic filling into carton packs. The RTD product was assessed blind by the panel amongst a series of

formula variants and the product became technically
possible when we found no significant differences
between the traditional and the RTD product.

POTENTIAL APPLICATIONS

The experience on blackcurrant drinks has lead to a
number of observations and conclusions.

Firstly, the use of a small panel trained in
sensory profiling and using a set of descriptive
terms with associated chemical standards can be of
great help in the development situation. It can give
comprehensive results quickly and relatively cheaply.
Moreover, it can be an important bridge between the
development chemist and full-scale consumer research.

Secondly, though there are substantial problems
in setting up, training and maintaining a small panel
of external assessors, such a panel does have the
advantage that it is independent. It can therefore
act as an unbiased arbiter on sensory performance and
that can be very useful in an industrial situation.

Finally, sensory profiling, with descriptors
linked to chemical standards, is probably the only
effective means of defining sensory performance in a
form suitable for inclusion on raw material and finished product specification. The difficulties of
identifying suitable chemical standards will limit
the number of applications but a situation can be
envisaged where more manufacturers will want to include such a sensory "fingerprint" of commercially
or technically important specifications as part of
their commercial contracts.

Chapter 4.9

Comparison between direct similarity assessments and descriptive profiles of certain soft drinks

J. Chauhan, R. Harper and W. Krzanowski
Department of Food Science, and Applied Statistics, University of Reading,
London Road, Reading, UK

SUMMARY

Descriptive profiling using a check list and direct assessment of similarities are compared using 7 soft drinks and a panel of 10 assessors. The profile data were used to generate a matrix of interstimulus-distances, and this and the dissimilarity matrix obtained directly from the similarity assessment were examined using multidimensional scaling approaches (MDS/INDSCAL). The results are compared and discussed. In order to highlight any differences between the two sets of dissimilarity measures, the data were further analysed using the multidimensional unfolding program (METUNF).

The differences between individual assessors are examined and the resulting classification compared with what can be deduced directly from the profiles.

INTRODUCTION

Opinions differ about the value of descriptive profiling as opposed to direct assessments of similarity or dissimilarity of stimuli (products). This study compares both methods. We assessed 7 soft drinks, (i) by descriptive profiling using a check-list, and (ii) in pairs directly for dissimilarity in terms of flavour in the mouth. A matrix of inter-stimuli

Euclidean distances was calculated from each profile
assessment, and this was treated as a dissimilarity
matrix. Multidimensional Scaling was then used to
analyse the dissimilarity matrices obtained from
each method of assessment.

    This study is one of a series carried out over
the last three years. Although we have incorporated
much information derived from earlier work in this
series, the immediate aim is to compare the results
obtained from the profiles of each sample with those
derived from the direct assessment of similarity in
pairs.

PROCEDURE

Seven soft drinks - 5 ginger and 2 citrus-flavoured
drinks - were assessed by 10 assessors (4 female and
6 males ranging in age from 20 to +55);
(i)   individually by descriptive profiling using a
      check-list of some 32 descriptors, each des-
      criptor being scored for intensity on a 0 - 5
      category scale, and
(ii) in pairs directly for dissimilarity in terms of
      flavour in the mouth using a 9 point scale
      (0 = identical, 8 = extremely different).
All assessors were familiar with profiling of soft
drinks but not with direct assessment of dissimilarity. All drinks were assessed twice in replicate.

    A matrix of 28 inter-drink dissimilarities was
obtained from each direct assessment (i.e. including
self-comparison of drinks). Thus, 20 such matrices
were obtained in all (two replicates for each of 10
assessors). To facilitate comparison of the two
methods, each set of profile data was then converted
into a dissimilarity matrix between all pairs of
drinks by computing the Euclidean distance between
their respective scores. This is achieved for any
pair of drinks by taking the square root of the sum
of the squares of the differences in their scores
for each of the 32 descriptors. This yields 21
inter-drink distances for each assessment, as self-
comparison of a drink will always produce a zero
distance. The 20 dissimilarity matrices generated
by each of the two methods were then subjected to
Multidimensional Scaling, using the computer
program INDSCAL [1].

MULTIDIMENSIONAL SCALING

Multidimensional Scaling (MDS) is technically complex [2]. It is primarily a data reduction technique which uses proximities as input, these being numbers which indicate how similar or dissimilar two stimuli are. The output is a geometrical configuration of points, each point corresponding to one of the stimuli, the location of the points on the map being such that the interstimulus distances derived from the map agree as closely as possible with the original assessment of the stimuli dissimilarities. That is, the smaller the perceived distance between two stimuli as shown in the proximities matrix, the closer the corresponding points in the multidimensional space.

The INDSCAL (Individual Differences Scaling) model assumes that all assessors use the same fundamental set of dimensions in making assessments of dissimilarity, but differ with regard to the relative importance or weights given to these dimensions. The distance between stimuli j and k for assessor i, d^i_{jk} is related to the dimensions of a 'group' (i.e. common) stimulus space by the equation:

$$ d^{(i)}_{jk} = \left[\sum_{t=1}^{m} w_{it}(x_{jt} - x_{kt})^2 \right]^{\frac{1}{2}} $$

where m is the dimensionality of stimulus space; x_{it} is the coordinate of the stimulus j on tth dimension of the 'group' stimulus space; and w_{it} is the weight attached to tth dimension by the ith assessor [1]. The interstimulus distances are dependent on the assessors' dimension weights and the stimulus coordinates. The dimension weights for a particular assessor indicate how much each dimension should be stretched or shrunk so that the distances between stimuli will correlate as highly as possible with that particular assessor's dissimilarity ratings. The program aims to determine by means of an interactive least square procedure, the stimulus coordinates and weights for the assessors which will account for as much variance as possible of the dissimilarity data for all assessors.

The individual space for a particular assessor can be thought of as being derived from the group stimulus space by differentially stretching or shrinking the dimensions in proportion to the square

roots of the respective weights of the dimensions.
The weights for each assessor can be plotted in a
separate diagram. This leads to another representation, called the 'weight space', in which assessors
rather than stimuli are denoted by points. The
squared distance from the origin of each assessor in
the weight space gives an indication of how well
each assessor fits the model, and is approximately
equal to the part of variance of that assessor's
data accounted for by the INDSCAL solution.

RESULTS AND DISCUSSION: INDIRECT ASSESSMENT OF SIMILARITY

The four-dimensional INDSCAL solution accounted for
69% of the variance in the dissimilarity matrices
of drinks, as derived by the Euclidean distances
from the profiling data of the 7 drinks; the three-
dimensional solution accounted for 59% and the two-
dimensional 47% of the variance. The coordinate
values for the stimuli in the two-dimensional solution are plotted in Figure 1. These values corresponded exactly to the values of the first two
dimensions of the three-dimensional solution, which
is represented in Figure 2 by plotting dimensions
1 v 3 and 2 v 3. The graphical representation of
these coordinates is the group stimulus space described above. The weights given to each of the two
dimensions for the two-dimensional solution by each
assessor are represented graphically in Figure 3.
This is the weight space described above. In
Figure 3 the replicate assessments made by each
assessor are represented as a and b.

       Test of significance in respect of the dif-
ferences in the configuration of different groups of
samples for INDSCAL are not immediately available.
Consequently the mutual arrangement of the various
samples for the different assessors has to be evaluated in broadly qualitative terms. With this res-
triction in mind, the following interpretation seems
reasonable.

       The group stimulus space for the two dimen-
sional INDSCAL solution shows that the 7 drinks are
differentiated into two separate groups, the ginger
drinks and the citrus-flavoured drinks. Drink 5,
(Ginger Beer) and Drink 2 (Schweppes Dry Ginger Ale)
are seen to be quite distinct, the three other
ginger drinks falling intermediate between the other
two. The three dimensional solution (Fig.2) shows

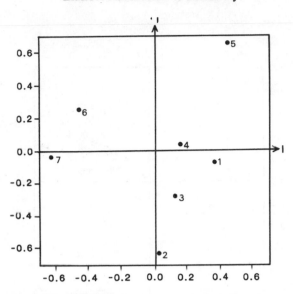

Fig.1 – INDSCAL group stimulus space: a two-dimensional INDSCAL analysis
of 20 matrices of dissimilarities among drinks by indirect assessment.

1. Hunts Dry Ginger Ale; 2. Schweppes Dry Ginger
Ale; 3. Hunts American Ginger Ale; 4. Schweppes
American Ginger Ale; 5. Adris Ginger Beer; 6.
Idris Ginger Beer; 6. Corona Lemonade; 7. Corona
Limeade.

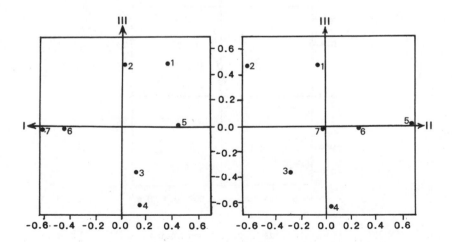

Fig.2 – Indirect assessment of similarity: group stimulus space.

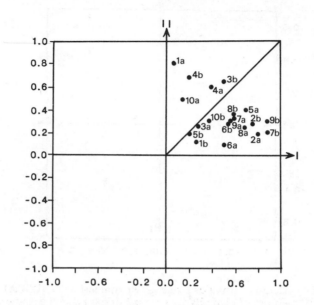

Fig.3 — INDSCAL weight space: dimension weights from a two-dimensional
INDSCAL analysis of 20 matrices of dissimilarities among drinks by
indirect assessment.

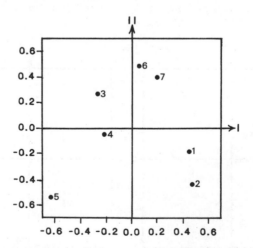

Fig.4 — INDSCAL group stimulus space: a two-dimensional INDSCAL analysis
of 20 matrices of dissimilarities among drinks by direct assessment.

the Ginger Beer to be unique amongst the ginger
drinks, with the two Dry Ginger Ales being differentiated from the two American Ginger Ales. The distance between Drinks 3 and 4 is relatively small compared to that between Drinks 1 and 2 in both two and
three dimensional solutions, indicating the relatively closer similarity between the two American
Ginger Ales than that between the two Dry Ginger
Ales. The American Ginger Ales are relatively closer
to the two citrus drinks also indicating their similarity.

        Individual differences are clearly evident
from the varying weights given to each of the dimensions be the assessors, thus justifying the use of
INDSCAL as a method of analysis. All assessors have
positive weights so there are no aberrant assessors
as far as the theoretical model is concerned. Assessors 2,4,6,8 and 9 show good agreement between the
two replicate assessments of the drinks in contrast
to assessors 1,3,5,7 and 10 whose replicate assessments vary considerably.

RESULTS AND DISCUSSION: DIRECT ASSESSMENT OF SIMILARITY

The four-dimensional INDSCAL solution for the dissimilarity accounted for 66% of the variance in the
original data, the three-dimensional solution accounted for 57% and the two dimensional solution 47%
of the variance. The coordinate values for the stimuli in both two and three dimensional solutions are
represented graphically as for the profile assessment
in Figures 4 and 5. The weight space for the two
dimensional solution is shown in Figure 6.

        The group stimulus space for the two-dimensional
solution shows the 7 drinks to be grouped in pairs:
the two Dry Ginger Ales (Drinks 1 and 2); the two
American Ginger Ales (Drinks 3 and 4); the two citrus
flavoured drinks (Drinks 6 and 7); with the Ginger
Beer (Drink 5) being fairly unique amongst the 7
drinks. The citrus drinks are relatively closer to
the American Ginger Ales than the Dry Ginger Ales
indicating their similarity.

        In the three-dimensional solution (Figure 5)
the grouping of the three pairs of drinks is preserved to some extent, with the exception of the two
Dry Ginger Ales.

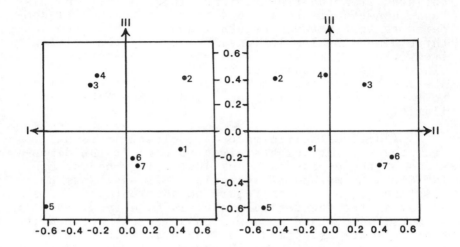

Fig.5 – Direct assessment of similarity: group stimulus space.

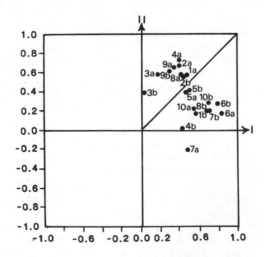

Fig.6 – INDSCAL weight space: dimension weights from a two-dimensional
INDSCAL analysis of 20 matrices of dissimilarities among drinks by
direct assessment.

An appreciable amount of individual variation is evident from the weight space (Fig. 6). Assessors 2,3,5,6,9 and 10 are fairly consistent in their replicate assessments of dissimilarity whereas assessors 1,4,7 and 8 show an alteration in the criteria used to base their assessments of dissimilarity on replication. All assessors have positive weights with the exception of assessor 7 who gives a negative weight to Dimension 11. This suggests that for this assessor certain of those stimuli close to each other in the group stimulus space are perceived to be further apart.

In most instances, cross reference to the original dissimilarity matrices for the different individuals confirms the interpretation of the configuration output by the INDSCAL Analysis.

It is evident from Figures 2 and 6 that assessors 2,6 and 9 are reasonably good at both direct assessment of similarity and profiling of drinks; assessors 3,5 and 10 are relatively better at direct assessments of dissimilarity whereas assessors 4,7 and 8 are better at profiling. Assessor 1 is highly variable in both methods. Comparison of the distribution of dissimilarity ratings given to self-comparisons of the 7 drinks for each of the two replicate assessments indicates a learning effect in assessing dissimilarity. An analysis by individuals clearly indicates assessor 1 to be least consistent. For some individuals estimation of dissimilarity between different stimuli may be just as difficult as describing the characteristics of each stimulus in descriptive terms.

MULTIDIMENSIONAL UNFOLDING

The two assessment methods, direct and indirect, can be compared qualitatively in terms of the group stimulus spaces of Figures 1,2,4 and 5. However, in order to highlight in a formal way, any differences which may exist between the methods, the data have also been analysed using the multidimensional unfolding program METUNF (Lyons, R., unpublished). The theory on which this FORTRAN 1V program is based is given by Schonemann [3], while some illustrative examples of the method are provided in Constantine and Gower [4]. To use multidimensional unfolding, the two dissimilarity matrices obtained from the two methods of assessment are treated as a single matrix, values from one method forming the lower triangle

and values from the other method the upper triangle
of this matrix. The program then produces a group
stimulus space containing two points for each drink,
one point corresponding to each method of assessment.
If these two points are close together, then the two
methods are interpreted as having treated this stimulus comparably. If the points are far apart, however, then the two methods have treated the stimulus
differently. Averages of the 20 matrices for each
method were input to the program to give the configuration shown in Figure 7.

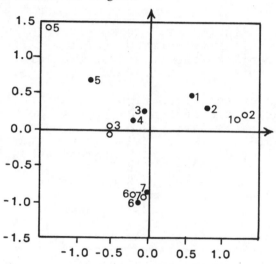

Fig. 7 — Metric multidimensional unfolding using METUNF.

o = indirect assessments; ● = direct assessments.

The overall pattern of the configuration is
similar to that of the group stimulus space output
by INDSCAL solutions: three separate groups of
drinks with the Ginger Beer being unique amongst the
seven drinks. With the exceptions of points representing Drinks 1 and 5, the two points for each of
the other 5 drinks are fairly close together, indicating that the two dissimilarity measures for the
latter 5 drinks are almost equivalent. The differences between the two dissimilarity measures for
Drinks 1 and 5 could be followed up by further analysis.

CONCLUSIONS

The two sets of dissimilarity matrices when subjected
to MDS both yield two dimensional configurations
which lead to broadly similar conclusions. There is
evidence in both INDSCAL solutions, that the 7 drinks
consist of two main groups - the ginger drinks and
the citrus drinks; with two subgroups within the
ginger drinks, the American and Dry Ginger Ales; the
only sample of Ginger Beer is placed uniquely in both
configurations. The two samples of American Ginger
Ales are perceived to be more similar to each other
than the two Dry Ginger Ales, with the former drinks
being relatively more similar to the citrus drinks
than the latter drinks.

The three dimensional INDSCAL solutions for the
data from the direct assessment of similarities
clearly indicates the difference between the two Dry
Ginger Ales; this is not readily discernible from the
corresponding solution for the indirect method. One
possible explanation is that the profile data are
subject to increased variability through the passage
of time. There is also some discrepancy in using
Euclidean distances as dissimilarities since there is
no distinction between minimum and maximum scores
for any two descriptors i.e. the difference between
a descriptor, scored 0 for a particular pair of
drinks and in another instance scored 5, is the same.
In addition, Euclidean distances between replicates
prove to be substantial and not zero. The implications of this warrant further considerations.Ideally,
Euclidean distances imply that the descriptors are
uncorrelated but this is not really so.

A number of alternatives to using Euclidean
distances as dissimilarities exist, one is the correlation measure. However, this is most appropriate
for determining dissimilarities over characteristics
rather than dissimilarities over individual assessors. The use of the correlation measure involves
taking means, no allowance being made for individual
differences. In the present study, Euclidean distances seemed to be the best approach. The multidimensional unfolding solution showed little difference
between the two methods of assessment within the limits of accuracy of the data.

The use of suitable product-orientated terminology is essential in profiling exercises. Ideally,

all descriptors should be clearly understood with minimal ambiguity between assessors. Schiffman [2] considers that in descriptive profiling, assessors are confused by words and their responses biased by preconceived ideas for foods. This author advocates that for interpretation purposes similarity assessments should be followed by the use of words, but the latter should never precede the former. A number of examples are given indicating considerable individual variation in the descriptions of the products but in most of the examples the words are of a non-specific nature covering a wide range. Furthermore, as far as one can tell, the assessors in the studies reported by Schiffman were not trained in the use of words. In any systematic profiling exercise, considerable attention is paid to the words using group discussion, illustration by reference standards and, as far as possible, words which represent every separately identifiable flavour characteristic relevant to the particular product included.

The particular panel of assessors in this study were unfamiliar with assessing dissimilarities but it is clearly evident that an untrained panel can provide meaningful results, although the stimulus spaces and dimensions as derived by MDS analysis are not always easy to interpret. In the case of profiling, descriptors are available for each drink and fine differences between the drinks readily discernible from the profiles themselves.

One of the major disadvantages of the direct assessment of dissimilarity is the number of comparisons involved which with a substantial number of stimuli increases rapidly to unmanageable levels (number of comparisons, including self-comparisons $= (n + 1)/2$ where n is the number of stimuli). Even with only 7 drinks, the paired comparisons assessed in replicate involved the assessors coming in to taste for some 20 days. Fatigue and loss of interest on the part of the assessors are common and could result in unreliable assessments of little value. However, both methods have something to offer in their own rights. The similarity assessments can obviously be very useful for screening individuals for the tests concerned.

ACKNOWLEDGEMENTS

We thank Beecham Products as collaborators in these studies and the assessors, research students and staff of the Department of Food Science for their participation.

REFERENCES

1. Carrol, J.D.; Chang, J.J. Analysis of individual differences in multidimensional scaling via an N-way generalization of 'Eckart-Young' decomposition. Psychometrika, 1970, 35, 283-319.

2. Schiffman, S.; Reynolds, M.L.; Young, F.W. Introduction to Multidimensional Scaling - Theory, Methods and Applications. Academic Press, New York, 1981.

3. Schonemann, P.H. On metric multidimensional scaling. Psychometrika, 1970, 35, 349-365.

4. Constantine, A.G.; Gower, J.C. Graphical representation of asymmetric matrices. Appl. Statistics, 1978, 27, 297-304.

Chapter 4.10

Objective and hedonic sensory assessment of ciders and apple juices

A.A. Williams, S.P. Langron and G.M. Arnold
Long Ashton Research Station, University of Bristol, Long Ashton, Bristol, England

SUMMARY

Over the last decade evaluating sensory quality in beverages has developed along several fronts. Sensory profile techniques have enabled precise descriptive information to be obtained on visual, aroma and flavour characteristics of products. Improvements in the methodology for acquiring information from the consumer have also provided valuable hedonic data permitting both descriptive and analytical information to be related to quality.

As an illustration of current developments in sensory profiling techniques this paper discusses the descriptive assessment of ciders and the use of multivariate statistical analyses to identify the underlying differences between the products of six manufacturers.

Results from a survey to discover the optimum level of sweetness and acidity in apple juices are used to illustrate the use of ratio scaling techniques with the consumer.

INTRODUCTION

The definition of quality in fermented cider and apple juices, as with other products, requires the integration of information from the chemist, the consumer and trained panelist. Chemical information on the compounds potentially giving rise to flavour in these products has increased, with the exploitation of new gas chromatographic and gas chromatographic-mass spectrometric techniques and more recently high performance liquid chromatography. Reference has already been made to polyphenolics in cider and their contribution to bitterness and astringency (see Lea and Arnold, this Symposium). Work on ciders [1,2,] and apple juices [3] using both extraction and headspace collection techniques has also increased our knowledge of the volatile components in these beverages.

This paper, however, will deal with two aspects of the sensory work being carried out at Long Ashton Research Station; these are analytical descriptive analysis by trained judges and the use of ratio scaling in the evaluation of products by the consumer. The first will be illustrated from work on cider and the second from a recent survey aimed at determining optimum levels of sugar and malic acid in apple juices.

THE OBJECTIVE QUANTITIVE DESCRIPTIVE ANALYSIS OF CIDERS

Sensory profile procedures using precisely defined vocabularies were first applied to cider aroma and flavour in 1972 [4]; a vocabulary of 50 terms divided into 11 groups (Table 1) to form a two-tiered system being used. Sub-adjectives within each group defined by standards absorbed into parafin wax, were chosen to produce a gradation of terms within each of the main groups (Fig.1). In operation, each main group. is scored in respect to the intensity of the group

Table 1 — Descriptive groups for assessing cider aroma.

Cough provoking/Irritating
Sharp
Dry/Alcoholic/Fuselly
Musty
Sour/Stale
Sulphurous
Yeasty
Scented
Fruity
Sugary/Cooked
Phenolic/Spicy/Bittersweet

character (0 = no character ⟶ 5 = very intense group
character) and sub-adjectives scored on their appropriateness to the group character (0 = no similarity;
5 = very similar).

```
ODOUR CLASS        (intensity 0-5)   Control   Sample

                   SOUR/STALE        [      ]   [      ]


ADJECTIVE APPROPRIATENESS (0-5)
   Like acetic acid (sour/stale      [      ]   [      ]
                        character)

                       Rancid        [      ]   [      ]

Old horse (2-phenylacetic acid)      [      ]   [      ]

                        Fatty        [      ]   [      ]

                        Soapy        [      ]   [      ]
```

Own description ....

Fig.1 — Example of sub-adjectives within aroma group (sour/stale).

Visual and additional flavour by mouth attributes
were added at a later date, with a similar two tiered
system as used for aroma operating where appropriate.
Main group terms for flavour by mouth are listed in
Table 2.

Table 2 — Main descriptions for assessing cider mouth flavour.

Acidity
Fragrant/Fruity
Alcoholic
Bitterness
Astringency
Body
Balance
Persistency

Since its introduction the vocabulary has been
used to provide general records of samples and to

demonstrate the effect of different cultivars and
processing conditions on the aroma and flavour of
ciders [5]. The application which is discussed in
this paper was aimed at discovering the underlying
differences between the products of different manufacturers.

The analysis of commercial ciders for differences between manufacturers

Sixteen different ciders from six different cider
manufacturers (Table 3) were evaluated by eleven assessors. Each sample was assesssd against a standard
(a Long Ashton Medium Sweet Cider) at each session.
Data were collated with respect to unknown samples
and were examined as absolute scores; results for aroma
and flavour by mouth assessments being treated separately. Typical of the profiles obtained by descriptive analysis is the one shown diagrammatically in
Fig.2. Group terms are shown by the unshaded areas
(the larger the area the more complex the character)
and sub-adjectives by the shaded areas. The greater
the distance from the centre in this diagram, the
greater the intensity of the attribute. With this

Table 3 — Sixteen commercial ciders examined.

Manu-facturer	Sample	Type of cider
1	A	Bottled
2	B	Bottled, produced region 1
	C	Bottled, produced region 2
	D	Bottled, vintage
3	E	Bottled
4	F	Bottled (type 1)
	G	Bottled (type 2)
	H	Bottled (type 3)
	I	Bottled (type 4)
	J	Canned
5	K	Bottled (type 1)
	L	Bottled (type 2)
	M	Bottled (type 3)
	N	Canned (type 3)
	O	Canned (type 4)
6	P	Bottled

particular cider, the dry/alcoholic/fuselly, sulphury and phenolic/spicy/bittersweet characters dominate.

Statistical analyses were carried out using the GENSTAT package [6] available on the ARC Rothamsted computer (ICL System 4, 470).

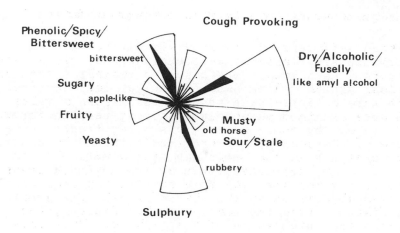

Fig.2 — Cider No. 4.1 aroma profile.

Principal component analyses of the aroma and flavour-by-mouth assessment indicated the main dimensions on which the samples as a whole were being differentiated. With respect to aroma, these were largely the contrast of sulphury and musty aromas with fruity and sugary cooked notes (Component 1), the contrast in sugary cooked aromas with fruity and dry alcoholic notes (Component 2) and the contrast of musty with sulphury, fruity and sugary cooked notes (Component 3). As far as flavour by mouth is concerned, differences in the ciders were largely due to the contrast in the sweet and fruity characters with acidity, bitterness and astringency (Component 1), the contrast in astringency with all the characters, notably sweetness and bitterness (Component 2) and acidity with the other characters, notably bitterness, sweetness and astringency (Component 3). The spatial distribution of the sixteen ciders on these dimensions, e.g. Figures 3 and 4, however, showed no separation according to manufacturers.

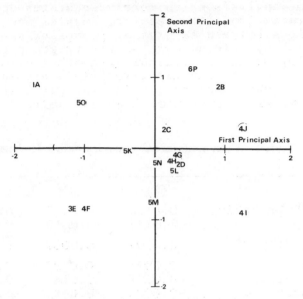

Fig.3   Cider aroma scores, principal components 1 and 2. For identification of ciders see Table 3.

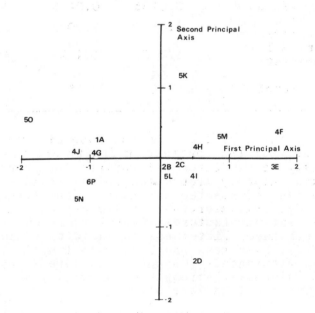

Fig.4 —Cider taste scores, principal components 1 and 2. For identification of ciders see Table 3.

Canonical variate analysis, unlike principal component analysis which merely separates according to the variation accounted for, enables one to optimise differences between samples or groups of samples whilst taking into account sample or group variation. Subjecting aroma and flavour-by-mouth scores of these sixteen ciders to canonical variate analysis gives the significant loadings, using the Bartlett test [7] and the Wilks Λ statistic, shown in Tables 4 and 5.

Table 4 — Cider aroma scores Canonical variate loadings.

	(1)	(2)	(3)
Cough provoking	-0.0118	0.0127	0.300
Sharp	0.0215	-0.0010	0.0792
Dry/Alcoholic/ Fuselly	-0.0207	0.0052	-0.0213
Musty	0.0921	0.0399	0.0200
Sour/Stale	-0.0136	-0.0185	-0.0126
Sulphury	-0.0099	0.0483	-0.0329
Yeasty	-0.0411	-0.0181	0.0120
Scented	0.0216	-0.1024	-0.1167
Fruity	-0.0665	0.0008	0.0082
Sugary/Cooked	0.0256	-0.0448	-0.0148
Phenolic/Spicy/ Bittersweet	-0.0319	0.0002	0.0129
Wilks Λ Test Statistic	172.3	104.29	46.22
df	55	40	27
Sig. level	1%	1%	5%

The first three of these in the case of aroma consisted largely of the contrast of fruity and yeasty aromas with musty notes (Canonical variate 1), scented with musty and sulphury aromas (Canonical variate 2) and the contrast of scented and sharp notes (Canonical variate 3). Differences in taste between the ciders of different manufacturers were largely due to the contrast between bitterness and acidity (Canonical variate 1), sweetness and body with fruitiness, balance and astringency (Canonical variate 2) and balance and alcoholic strength with acidity and fruitiness (Canonical variate 3).

Plots of canonical means with approx. 95% confidence limits over the first two canonical axes for

Table 5 — Cider taste scores Canonical variate loadings.

	(1)	(2)	(3)
Acidity	-0.0297	0.0057	-0.0471
Sweetness	0.0319	0.0504	-0.0009
Fragrant/ Fruity	0.0114	-0.0586	-0.0410
Alcoholic	-0.0123	0.0360	0.0664
Bitterness	0.0642	-0.0129	0.0059
Astringency	0.0117	-0.044	0.0155
Body	0.0023	0.0327	-0.0557
Balance	-0.0066	-0.0535	0.0632
Persistency	-0.0123	-0.0056	0.0309
Wilks Λ Test Statistic	95.17	59.72	35.11
df	49	32	21
Sig. level	1%	1%	5%

the six different manufactureres are shown in Figures
5 and 6. These readily show that the different manufacturers' products can be distinguished in respect
of aroma but less readily so with respect to flavour
by mouth. Cider from manufacturers 3, 4 and 5 are
similar and have more fruity and yeasty aromas than
the others. The cider from manufacturer 6, on the
other hand, is isolated by being much mustier than
the rest. The cider from manufacturer 1, although
similar to those of manufacturers 2, 3, 4 and 5 in
possessing a fruity, yeasty character, differs from
these and 6 by being far more scented.

With respect to taste, cider from manufacturer
3 is significantly more acid and less bitter than
those from the other manufacturers. Cider from manufacturer 6 is also significantly different from
those of 1, 4 and 5 in being sweeter, having less
fruitiness and a poorer balance.

THE HEDONIC ASSESSMENT OF SWEETNESS AND ACIDITY IN CLEAR APPLE JUICES

Small trained panels are ideal for providing objective
descriptions of products. To obtain reliable hedonic
data, however, larger populations representative of
the target market as a whole must be surveyed. There
is little time for training so the questions too have

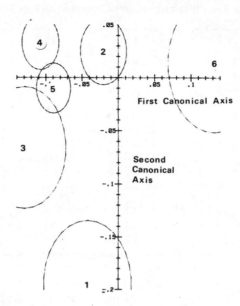

Fig.5 — Cider aroma scores, canonical means (with approx. 95% confidence intervals).

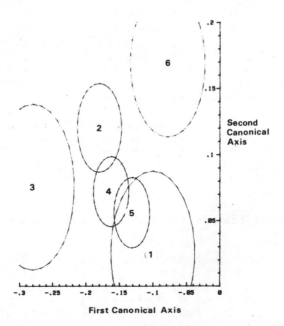

Fig.6 — Cider taste scores, canonical means (with approx. 95% confidence intervals).

to be simple and readily understood, or, alternatively, the attributes assessed defined only in the mind of the person being surveyed.

The following discussion deals with the results of a consumer survey on apple juices in which attributes (not necessarily having the same meaning to all participants) were assessed using ratio scaling techniques (Arnold, G.M. and Williams, A.A. "Apple Juice Consumer Survey, 1981". Unpublished report, Long Ashton Research Station). The results were used to determine the ideal level of malic acid and total sugar (specific gravity) in this beverage.

Seven samples of clear juices, prepared by blending juices made from pure Cox's Orange Pippin and pure Bramley's Seedling apples (Table 6), were examined by visitors (135) to a commercial Agricultural Show. Participants were first presented with the standard sample (a 50:50 blend of Cox's Orange Pippin and Bramley's Seedling juices) for which attributes shown in Figure 7, acidity, sweetness and apple character (not discussed in this paper), were given a score of 100, indicating their intensity in this juice.

Table 6 — Composition of clear apple juices assessed during the pilot survey.

Bramley %	Cox %	SG	Malic acid %
100	0	1.0395	0.78
80	20	1.0410	0.72
60	40	1.0421	0.67
50	50	1.0428	0.64
40	60	1.0428	0.61
20	80	1.0440	0.56
0	100	1.0450	0.50

After assessing this standard sample, participants were presented with the six other juice blends ordered so that for every 15 groups of assessors, position and neighbouring samples were reasonably balanced. Participants were instructed to score the intensity of the three characteristics in these samples in relation to their amounts in the standard, using ratio scaling, ensuring that the meaning of a

FIRST Apple Juice (No....)

Acidity ....100....

Sweetness ....100....

Apple character ..100....

If possible please describe precisely the
apple character you are scoring:

....

Fig.7 — Apple juice : assessment sheet (1).

particular attribute was consistent over all samples.
Having completed their assessment of the six juices
they were then asked to score the intensity of these
characters in their imaginary ideal apple juice on
the same scales.

The scores of each assessor were analysed separately. His or her scores for each attribute in
each juice were subtracted from the scores given to
the ideal, the difference being regressed against
specific gravity in the case of sweetness and % malic
acid in the case of acidity. The point at which the
regression line crossed the analytical data axis gave
the ideal value for that attribute for a particular
person. Respondents for whom the correlation coefficient for this relationship was less than 0.66 were
considered to be either scoring incorrectly or were
not sufficiently sensitive to the attributes for them
to have any real influence on acceptability. Ideal
levels for % malic acid and specific gravity for the
remainder were plotted in respect to the values of
these two parameters. The number of consumers falling
within small regions of the graph were counted and
the information plotted as perspective plots e.g.
Figures 8 and 9 [8], the higher the peak the more
people considering their ideal apple juice to have
that particular sugar acid composition. Although
visually informative, it is difficult to read information from such views, hence a contour plot of this
'landscape' was also constructed (Figure 10) [9].
This latter figure clearly shows the % malic acid
degree of sweetness people want in their apple juice.

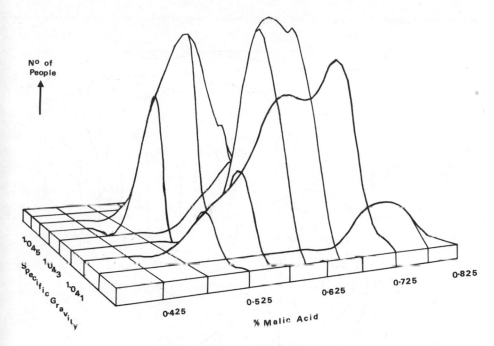

Fig. 8 — Apple juice: perspective plots of ideal acidity and sweetness (i).

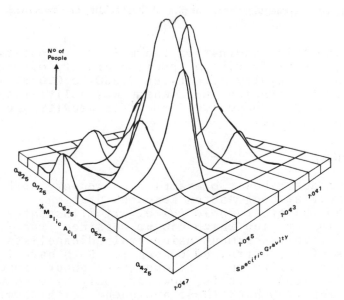

Fig. 9 — Apple juice perspective plots of ideal acidity and sweetness (ii).

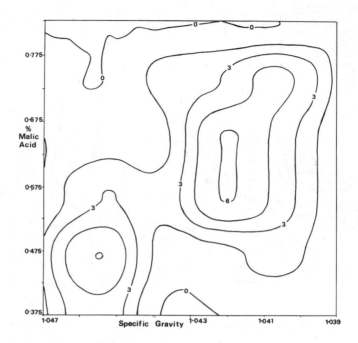

Fig. 10 — Apple juice: contour plot of ideal acidity and sweetness.

From this examination two main sub-populations emerged, one preferring a specific gravity of around 1.042 and an acidity of between 0.550 to 0.675% malic acid, and the other a juice which was a little sweeter and less acid, around 1.045 specific gravity and 0.475% malic acid.

CONCLUSIONS

The paper describes two examples of sensory work being carried out at Long Ashton Research Station, one using cider and the other apple juice. It illustrates the sort of information which can be obtained from formal **objective** assessment using trained panelists, and by means of the untrained consumer. Both have their place in answering specific questions about sensory quality in foods. It is, however, only by combining information from both these approaches with **chemical** and physical data that quality in foods and **beverages** will ultimately be properly understood.

REFERENCES

1. Williams, A.A.; Tucknott, O.G. The volatile
   aroma components of fermented cider: minor
   neutral components from the fermentation of
   Sweet Coppin apple juice. J. Sci. Fd Agric.
   1978, 29, 381-397.
2. Williams, A.A.; May, H.V.; Tucknott, O.G.
   Examination of fermented cider volatiles following concentration on the porous polymer
   Porapak Q. J. Inst. Brew. 1978, 84, 97-100.
3. Williams, A.A.; May, H.V. Examination of an
   extract of cider volatiles using both electron
   impact and chemical ionisation gas chromatography-mass spectrometry. J. Inst. Brew.
   1981, 87, 372-375.
4. Williams, A.A.; Lewis, M.J.; Tucknott, O.G. The
   neutral volatile compounds of cider apple
   juice. Fd Chem. 1980-1981, 6, 139-151.
5. Williams, A.A. The development of a vocabulary
   and profile assessment method for evaluating
   the flavour contribution of cider and perry
   aroma constituents. J. Sci. Fd Agric. 1975,
   25, 567-582.
6. Nelder, J.A. GENSTAT Reference Manual, Rothamsted Experimental Station, 1977.
7. Chatfield, C.; Collins, A.J. Introduction to
   Multivariate Analysis. Chapman and Hall,
   London and New York, 1980, 148-153.
8. Bowyer, A. FORTRAN SOLID 2: A package for the
   production of perspective views of surfaces.
   Bath University, 1981.
9. Thompson, G. FORTRAN Conicon: A package for the
   production of contour plots of smooth surfaces
   Bath University, 1981.

Chapter 4.11

Descriptive analysis and quality of Bordeaux wines

A.C. Noble
Department of Viticulture and Enology, University of California, Davis, CA, USA.
A.A. Williams and S.P. Langron
Long Ashton Research Station, University of Bristol, Long Ashton, Bristol BS18 9AF.

SUMMARY

The major aroma difference among 24 wines (1976 vintage) from 4 Bordeaux communes was attributed to variation in the intensity of the green bean/green olive
character by canonical variates analysis (CVA) of the
aroma descriptor ratings. CVA of flavour by mouth
ratings showed the wines to be discriminated primarily on the basis of astringency and bitterness. In
neither of the configurations derived from the CVAs
were the wines clustered by commune of origin. There
was no significant difference in quality ratings
assigned by Masters of Wine.

INTRODUCTION

Despite the extensive literature on the wines of
Bordeaux, virtually no analytical or sensory evaluations
have been reported. However, numerous claims have
been made about the uniqueness of the wines from
different communes [1, 2, 3]. Wines from St. Estèphe,
a commune in the northern part of the Médoc which is
characterized by heavy clay soil, are reported to be
"higher in acid", "fuller and solider", to have less
perfume [1], to be characterized by deep colour,
"stark, raw, fruity nose" [2], and to be "big, full-
bodied wines" [3]. Wines from Paulillac are often
called "fleshy" [3]. In contrast, wines from St.
Julien are cited for their fruitiness [3], their
"cedary boquet, balance, harmony and elegance" [2].

Wines from Margaux, an area to the south of the Médoc
with well drained gravelly soils, are called less
specifically "refined and exquisite" [1], "renowned
for the beauty of their aroma and softness" [3].

In St. Emilion, where a lower percentage of
Cabernet Sauvignon grapes are used, the wines often
have a higher alcohol content than those from the
Médoc. The wines are described somewhat contradict-
orily as "having the fullest flavour" [1], with a
"less obvious aroma" [3], and as being heavier, darker,
and softer (less tannin) than the Médoc's [3, 4].

Descriptive analysis, a technique for analytic-
ally profiling flavour has been applied to a variety
of beverages, including wines [5, 6, 7], cider [8],
beer [9, 10], and whisky [11], but thus far not to
the wines of Bordeaux.

In this study, Bordeaux wines from four different communes were evaluated by two sensory techniques,
descriptive analysis by trained judges and quality
rating by Masters of Wine.

EXPERIMENTAL

Wines

Twenty wines from the 1976 vintage were selected from
St. Estèphe, St. Julien, Margaux and St. Emilion,
varying in growth designation from unclassed to
second growths. In addition, four 1976 regional wines
were included for comparison. Details of the wines
are given in Table 1.

Descriptive analysis

Following orientation and training sessions, in which
descriptive terms were derived and agreed upon, the
intensities of aroma and flavour-by-mouth attributes
were rated using the scorecard shown in Figure 1. The
wines were scored in duplicate over 16 sessions by
trained judges [12].

Quality rating by Masters of Wine

In one session, Masters of Wine rated the wines for
quality on two criteria: overall quality, "if consumed
immediately", and overall quality, "when ready to

drink". In addition they described the attributes of the wines which influenced their quality ratings.

Data analysis

Analyses of variance (ANOVA) were run on each term rated by the trained judges and on the two quality ratings of the Masters of Wine. The aroma terms and

Table 1 — Commune or district of origin, chateau, growth designation and the price of 1976 Bordeaux wines.

Code	Commune or District of Origin	Château	Growth	£/Case*
1	St. Estèphe	Houissant		49.9
2		Montrose	2nd	82.7
3		Calon Segur	3rd	80.7
4		de Pez		82.4
5		Haut Marbuzet		82.4
6	St. Julien	Lagrange	3rd	66.5
7		Ducru Beaucaillou	2nd	76.8
8		Gloria		58.4
9		Talbot	4th	46.5
10		Léoville Lascases	2nd	77.1
11	Margaux	du Tertre	5th	61.5
12		Brane Cantenac	2nd	76.8
13		Malescot St. Exupéry	3rd	70.8
14		Giscours	3rd	99.0
15		Rauzan Gassies	2nd	70.3
16	St. Emilion	Roudier		39.4
17		Grand-Corbin-Despagne	**	66.0
18		Fombrauge		57.0
19		l'Angelus	**	66.5
20		Canon la Gaffeliere	**	63.2
21	Haut Médoc	Cissac		54.0
22	Haut Médoc	la Tour St. Joseph		42.5
23	Médoc	la Cardonne		44.6
24	Bordeaux	du Pradeau		31.4

*Exclusive of VAT.
**Grand Cru Classé.

the flavour-by-mouth attributes, respectively, were then analyzed by Multivariate Analysis of Variance (MANOVA) using a Genstat program [13] to test whether the wines were significantly different over all attributes. Linear combinations (canonical variates) which maximise the ratio of between to within variance were calculated for both the aroma and flavour-by-mouth terms using the Genstat program [13].

AROMA WINE CODE:			
BERRY (BLACKB/RASPB)			
BLACK CURRANT (CANNED/RIBENA)			
SYNTHETIC FRUIT			
GREEN BEAN/GREEN OLIVE			
SOY/MARMITE			
PHENOLIC/SPICY			
VANILLA			
RAISIN			
ETHANOL			
FLAVOUR BY MOUTH			
SOUR			
BITTER			
ASTRINGENT			
FRUIT (BERRY)			
BLACK PEPPER			

Fig.1 — Scorecard for wine assessments. The intensity of each attribute is scored on a scale from 0 − 9, where 0 = not present, 1 = low, and 9 = high intensity.

RESULTS

Descriptive analysis

When the aroma intensity ratings were analysed by ANOVA, significant differences in intensities between the wines were found for only two terms: blackcurrant ($P<0.05$) and green bean/green olive ($P<0.001$). Inspection of the mean ratings for these terms (Table 2) reveals no regional consistency in the scores. Further, the intensity ratings are uncorrelated ($r = 0.131$, $P>0.05$, df = 22). Significant differences among the wine aroma ratings were also found by MANOVA. By Bartlett's test [14], these differences were shown to occur in at most two dimensions.

The first two canonical variates of aroma data accounted for 30 and 18% of the variance, respectively. In Figure 2, the wine means are plotted for the first two canonical variates together with the standardized attribute loadings. When the standardized attribute loadings are calculated from the loadings by adjusting for differences in variance, the length of each vector reflects the relative importance of the variable. Around each wine mean, the approximate 95% confidence intervals are plotted to indicate which wines are significantly different.

The largest difference among the wine aromas is due to the variation in the green bean/green olive attribute, although differences in the vanilla and soy/marmite character also contribute. In the second dimension, the major source of variation in aroma is attributable to the black currant note. Wines highest in the green bean/green olive character and lowest in the vanilla note were from St. Estèphe (No. 1) and Margaux (No. 12). Conversely, wines No. 23 (Médoc) and No. 10 (St. Julien) were lowest in the vegetative aroma and highest in vanilla. Further, examining the configuration in Figure 2 shows that there is no clustering of wines by commune origin nor by growth designation.

Of the five flavour-by-mouth terms, only two differed significantly across the wines; astringency ($P<0.001$) and bitterness ($P<0.05$). The means for the terms, shown in Table 2, were highly correlated ($r = 0.609$, $P<0.01$, df = 22). By MANOVA, the wines were shown to differ significantly when all attributes were taken together. However, significant differences among the wines were shown to occur in only

one dimension, which alone accounted for 50% of the
variance.

Table 2 — Mean intensity ratings and S.E.D. for blackcurrant aroma, green
bean/green olive aroma, astringency and bitterness.

	Mean Ratings			
Wine No.	Black currant aroma	Green bean/ green olive aroma	Astringency	Bitterness
1	3.90	3.35	3.35	2.85
2	3.85	1.60	4.47	3.18
3	4.60	2.70	3.47	2.79
4	4.50	1.85	4.35	3.03
5	4.80	2.25	4.06	3.21
6	3.90	1.75	3.32	2.50
7	4.50	2.25	4.12	3.21
8	3.75	2.85	3.38	2.74
9	4.50	1.70	3.94	3.12
10	4.00	1.35	3.68	3.00
11	4.80	2.25	3.18	2.74
12	4.10	3.15	3.32	2.53
13	4.65	1.50	3.53	2.71
14	4.80	1.90	4.29	3.27
15	4.50	1.65	3.62	2.94
16	4.10	2.90	3.47	3.09
17	3.00	2.55	3.18	3.50
18	4.30	2.00	4.00	3.59
19	4.80	1.45	3.79	3.09
20	4.65	2.00	3.41	2.82
21	3.70	2.60	4.12	3.32
22	5.15	1.80	3.88	3.44
23	3.65	1.85	3.06	2.68
24	3.25	2.35	3.35	2.62
S.E.D.	0.487	0.433	0.304	0.313

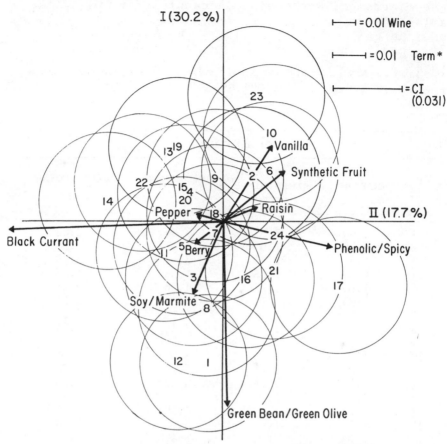

* Term loading adjusted for variance: Loading × $\sqrt{M.S.E.}$

Fig. 2 — Canonical variate scores for 24 Bordeaux wines and adjusted term
loadings for canonical variates I and II from canonical variates analysis
of nine aroma terms (10 judges x 2 replicates).

In Figure 3, the wine means are plotted for the
first two canonical variates, with the standardized
attribute loadings again shown as vectors. The largest variation among the wines' flavour is a function
of astringency and to an extent the bitterness. The
second dimension is primarily attributable to differences in the black pepper by mouth intensity. The
most astringent wines, Nos 2 (St.Estèphe), 14 (Margaux),
and 21 (Haut Medoc) which were analyzed for phenolic

content in a separate study (Noble, A.C., in preparation) contained the highest levels of tannin, expressed as gallic acid, equivalent, respectively, 1900, 2100 and 2100 mg 1^{-1}. The least astringent, wine 23_1 (Médoc) contained the least phenols, i.e. 1300 mg 1^{-1}. As with the configuration from the CVA of the aroma terms, the wines were clustered by commune.

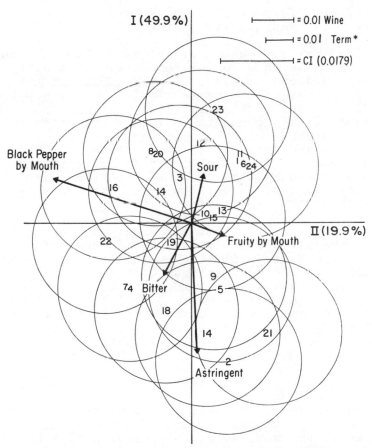

*Term loading adjusted for variance: Loading × $\sqrt{M.S.E.}$

Fig.3 — Canonical variate scores for 24 Bordeaux wines and adjusted term loadings loadings for canonical variates I and II from canonical variates. Analysis of five flavour-by-mouth terms (17 judges x 2 replicates).

Masters of Wine quality ratings

For all wines, the mean scores for the predicted quality of the wines "when ready to drink", were higher than those given for quality "if consumed immediately". However, the wines were not rated significantly different for either rating, nor was there a significant correlation between either quality rating and price: $r = 0.10$ and $r = 0.15$ (df = 22, $\underline{P} > 0.05$), respectively, for correlation of case cost with quality "now" and quality "later".

The quality scores reflect more than anything else, the difference in interpretation of quality among the Masters of Wine. In the ANOVAs of the quality ratings, the Masters of Wine were a highly significant source of variation. Examination of the Masters of Wine's comments indicates the extent of their differences of opinion. One wine was described as "elegant and attractive" and "attractive, has elegance rather than weight, bit too correct and austere" by two Masters of Wine, with the third recording "disagreeable ratty nose, disagreeable wine with nothing to recommend it".

In contrast to their different ways of integrating the attributes of these wines and estimating quality, the Masters of Wine were often consistent in their specific descriptions of the wines. In their descriptive analysis, wine 10 was rated as one of the most intense in berry aroma. Six of the eight Masters of Wine evaluating wine 10 described it as "fruity", with three specific descriptors also being used; "plummy", raisins" and "black currants".

DISCUSSION

This study illustrates well the problems associated with quality judgments. Quality is a composite response to the sensory properties of a wine based on one's expectations for a given wine type. Because each person's experiences and preferences are unique, quality is an individual response. Accordingly, there was no significant difference in the quality ratings among the wines, because of the differences in opinion existing among the Masters of Wine. Furthermore, these differences in the assessment of quality may be attributable to the different styles marketed by the wine companies for which they work.

In contrast, the descriptive analysis of the
wines provides analytical information about the
flavours of the wines.

The largest differences among the wines were
those attributed to variations in the green bean/
green olive and black currant aromas, and in bitterness and astringency, none of which varied as a
function of commune origin, but rather from wine to
wine.

Ideally, the information obtained from descriptive analyses by trained judges should be used to
define the sensory differences in wines shown independently by consumers or wine experts to differ in
preference or quality ratings. Only by coupling the
analytical approach to quality ratings can the reasons
for quality assessments be interpreted in terms of
variation in specific sensory characteristics.

REFERENCES

1. Johnson, H. World Atlas of Wine. Mitchell
        Beazley Ltd., London, 1971,74-92.
2. Broadbent, M. Wine Testing/Enjoying/Understand-
        ing.Cristie's Publication, London, 1977,
        43-44.
3. Durac, J. Wines and the Art of Tasting. E.P.
        Dutton & Co., Inc., New York, 1974, 131-147.
4. Grossman, H.J. Grossman's Guide to Wines, Beers
        and Spirits. Charles Scribner's Sons, New
        York, 1977, 42.
5. Noble, A.C. In "Analysis of Food and Beverages",
        (Charalambous, G., Ed.), Academic Press, New
        York, 1978, 203-228.
6. Williams, A.A.; Baines, C.R.; Arnold, G.M.
        Towards the objective assessment of sensory
        quality in inexpensive red wines. Grape-Wine,
        Centennial Symposium proceedings, University
        of California, Davis, California, USA, 1982,
        322-329.
7. Schmidt, J.O. Comparison of methods of rating
        scales used for sensory evaluation of wines,
        M.Sc. Thesis, University of California, Davis,
        California, USA, 1981.
8. Williams, A.A. Development of a vocabulary and
        profile assessment method for evaluating the
        flavour contribution of cider and perry aroma
        constituents. J. Sci. Fd Agric. 1975, 26,
        567-582.

9. Mecredy, J.M.; Sonnermann, J.C.; Lehmann, S.J.
      Sensory profiling of beer by a modified QDA
      method. Fd Technol. 1974, 28 (11), 36-39.
10. Clapperton, J.F.; Piggott, J.R. Flavour charact-
      erization by trained and untrained assessors.
      J. Inst. Brew. 1978, 85, 275-277.
11. Piggott, J.R.; Jardine, S.P. Descriptive sensory
      analysis of whisky flavour. J. Inst. Brew.
      1979, 85, 82-85.
12. Noble, A.C.; Williams, A.A.; Langron, S.P.
      (submitted for publication).
13. Genstat: A General Statistical Program. Statistics
      Department, Rothamsted Experimental Station,
      Harpenden, Hertfordshire, 1977.
14. Chatfield, C.; Collins, A. Introduction to Multi-
      variate Statistics. Chapman and Hall, London,
      1980, 148-154.

Posters

Chapter 4.12

Influence of storage conditions on the organoleptic quality of apple juice

L. Poll
Department for the Technology of Plant Food Products, Royal Veterinary and Agricultural University, Copenhagen, Denmark.

INTRODUCTION

The organoleptic quality of apple juice is closely related to its apple-like, or fruit-like aroma. To have a high organoleptic quality, a juice should contain considerable fruit-aroma and little off-aroma. In the German DLG system for evaluating fruit juice [1], the positive terms "aromatic", "fruit-like" and "pure" are used to describe aroma and taste of good quality juices.

There are several causes for variation in the organoleptic quality of apple juices, some of the more important factors being listed below.

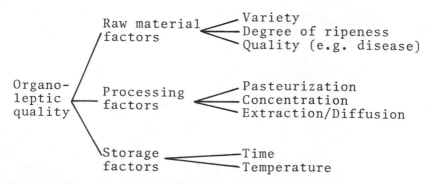

This paper presents results from an evaluation
of some commercial apple juices to illustrate both
the differences in organoleptic quality which may
occur, and also to demonstrate the influence of different storage parameters on the organoleptic quality.

METHODS USED TO EVALUATE JUICES

Organoleptic evaluations

A trained panel of 8 - 10 judges evaluated the juices
for specific aroma characters and in some cases, overall aroma, using a 10 point scale (0 = none of that
character, 10 - strong in that character). The attributes judged were: fruit-aroma; cooked-aroma
(difficult to describe but resembling fresh baked
bread, caramel, and possibly mouldy aromas); off-aroma
(any aroma which could not be described as fruit- or
cooked-aroma).

Hydroxymethylfurfural (HMF)

This is a degradation product of sugars, measured
using Winkler's method [2].

Gas chromatographic analysis

A nitrogen gas purging method was used to transfer
juice volatiles on to Porapak Q. A concentrate from
the ether extract of the Porapak trap was then injected into a packed SP-1000 column (5 m x 3 mm). Column
temperature was held for 10 min at 70°C, and then
programmed from 70°-170°C at 4°C/min; it was then held
isothermal at 170°C. Detection was with a FID; n-
heptanol was the internal standard. Peak identifications were based on retention times.

RESULTS

Evaluation of commercial Danish apple juices

The organoleptic qualities of 12 brands of apple
juices available on the Danish market were evaluated
in 1980 [3]. Juices, in bottles and paper cartons,
were purchased in the Copenhagen area. The organoleptic quality was found to vary considerably; fruit-
aroma ranging from 7.6 to 3.6, off-aroma from 0.1 to
5.7, cooked-aroma from 0 to 3.0, and overall aroma
from 7.4 to 3.3. HMF was found in nine juices, with
values up to 11 mg 1^{-1} No correlation was however
noted between HMF and cooked-aroma (or any of the

other aroma characteristics). Cooked aroma was
greater in juices held in glass bottles than in those
held in paper cartons. Some juices were again purchased six months later; the organoleptic and chemical
analyses showed marked differences for the same brand
bought on these two occasions.

Influence of storage time and temperature on organoleptic quality

Changes in the organoleptic quality of apple juice
are likely to occur during both processing and storage. In processing, an apple juice is likely to be
subjected to high temperatures over short periods of
time, while in storage, temperatures are generally
lower and the time of exposure longer. If a juice
with a strong fruit-aroma and weak cooked- and off-
aromas is exposed to high temperature for a short
time (e.g. $95^{o}C$ for 1 h), the fruit-aroma will fall
while the off- and cooked-aromas will increase. In
addition, the HMF content will increase according to
the extent of the heat treatment. The conditions to
which a juice is exposed during storage could have a
similar effect on the organoleptic quality.

To explore this further, a storage study over
periods of 6 and 12 months at 3 and $20^{o}C$ was conducted
with juices from five apple varieties and concentrates

Table 1 — Organoleptic scores of McIntosh apple juice and concentrate stored for 6 and 12 months at $20^{o}C$ (1979).

	Fruit-aroma	Off-aroma	Cooked-aroma
Juice			
$3^{o}C$, 6 months	7.9	0.7	0.3
$3^{o}C$, 12 "	8.0	0.3	0
$20^{o}C$, 6 "	6.5	1.1	0.8
$20^{o}C$, 12 "	5.7	1.0	2.2
Concentrate			
$3^{o}C$, 12 "	4.4	0.2	0
$20^{o}C$, 12 "	4.2	1.2	3.5

Table 2 — Organoleptic evaluation of juice (McIntosh) stored at 3°C, 10°C, 20°C and 30°C for 12 months, and relative values of volatile compounds in the juices: concentration in juices stored at 3°C = 100, except for furfural (not found in juices stored at 3°C) here 30°C = 100)

	Storage temperature			
	3°	10°	20°	30°
Organoleptic evaluation				
Fruit-aroma (0-10 scale)	6.2	6.0	3.4	3.2
Off-aroma	1.2	1.0	1.0	1.3
Cooked-aroma	0.4	0.5	4.2	3.9
Volatiles by GC				
Aldehydes				
Hexanal	100	34	13	9
Trans-2-hexenal	100	53	31	22
Furfural	0	0	29	100
Esters				
Ethyl butyrate	100	66	25	19
Ethyl 2-methylbutyrate	100	52	24	17
Isopentyl acetate	100	36	12	0
Butyl butyrate	100	44	15	5
Alcohols				
Ethanol	100	152	92	71
Isobutanol	100	97	69	83
Butanol	100	49	64	65
Isopentanol	100	97	69	69
Hexanol	100	99	80	69

(40% s/s) from two of these juices. The results of one series of organoleptic tests (those for McIntosh, a variety of high fruit-aroma) are shown in Table 1. After 6 months, and more so after 12 months, the juice stored at 20°C has less fruit-aroma and more off- and cooked-aromas than juice stored at 3°C. Juice concentrate stored at 20°C for 12 months had more off-aroma and more cooked-aroma than concentrate stored at 3°C. HMF was found only in juices stored at 20°C. No correlation between HMF content and the sensory data was found.

As it is likely that the volatile composition of the juices changed during storage, especially at higher temperatures, a second storage study to investigate the effect of temperature was undertaken. In this, juices of the cultivar McIntosh were held for 12 months at 3°, 10°, 20° and 30°C. Similar results (Table 2) were obtained, e.g. juice stored at 3° and 10°C contained more fruit-aroma and less off- and cooked-aromas than juice stored at 20° or 30°C. The GC investigations showed that the content of the aldehydes, hexanal and trans-2-hexanal, fell sharply with increasing temperature, while furfural was only found in juices stored at higher temperatures. The amounts of the four identified esters also fell with increasing temperature, while the alcohol content remained relatively constant at all four temperatures. Since esters and aldehydes, with the exception of furfural, have fruity-aromas this may explain the lower fruit-aroma found in the juices stored at 20° and 30°C compared to the juices stored at 3° and 10°C. The cooked-aroma, which is found in juices stored at 20° and 30°C, may be due to compounds formed at high storage temperature or as a result of the increased awareness of other aroma characteristics because of low aldehyde and ester content.

CONCLUSION

The results show that when storing apple juices of high organoleptic quality over a long period, the storage temperature should be kept low (under 10°C) if quality is to be maintained.

REFERENCES

1.   Wucherpfennig, K. Das neue DLG-Prüfschema für Fruchtsafte, Fruchtnektare, Fruchtsaftgetranke, Fruchtweine und Fruchtschaumwine. Flüss. Obst 1980, 47, 160-162.
2.   Amerine, M.A.; Ough, C.S. Wine and Must Analysis. John Wiley and Sons, 1974.
3.   Poll, L. Organoleptic and chemical analysis of commercial Danish apple juices. Flüss. Obst. 1981, 48, 572-578.

Chapter 4.13

Sensory and instrumental measurement of quality attributes in apples

S.M. Smith and A. Churchill
Fruit Storage Division, East Malling Research Station, Maidstone, Kent, England.

INTRODUCTION

Until recently, the primary aim of research on the
storage quality of apples was to minimise wastage due
to physiological disorders and rotting and to
preserve the general appearance of the fruit. As
these problems were overcome, more attention began to
be paid to the eating quality of the fruit. Increasing consumer awareness of sensory quality in other
foods and strong competition from imported fruit make
it particularly important that the fruit industry
evaluates any effects on eating quality of new techniques of production and storage, and improves the
eating quality of home produced fruit in general.
When investigating eating quality in apples, the
research worker needs to ascertain whether
differences in fruit quality can be detected by
instrumental and/or sensory methods, and whether
such differences are of any consequence to the
ultimate assessor, the consumer.

VARIATION IN QUALITY ATTRIBUTES

Food scientists working with manufactured or
processed foods are able to start with a uniform
product that will not vary from sample to sample or
over a period of time. They can also create known
differences between products and are only concerned
with whether or not these differences can be detected
by the consumer. Quality tests are usually designed

to include a standard or reference sample, whether
or not designated as such. However, there are two
main reasons why it is not possible to supply a constant reference sample when dealing with fresh
produce. Firstly, there exists an inherent variation
in quality attributes within a sample. For example,
a random sample of 146 Cox's Orange Pippin apples
from one site picked on one date had a mean penetrometer firmness of 4.97 kg, with a standard deviation
of 0.47 and a range from 3.8 kg to 6.1 kg. Secondly,
the quality attributes can vary over a period of
time, as shown (Fig. 1) for changes in instrumental
firmness, total sugars and titratable acidity during
storage of Cox's Orange Pippin. The combined
effects of these two sources of variation could
obscure treatment differences.

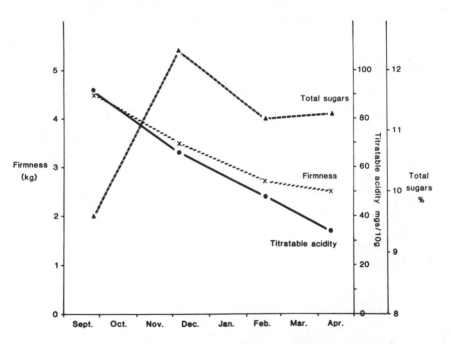

Fig. 1 — Cox's Orange Pippin: changes in firmness, titratable acidity and total
sugars during CA storage ($1\%CO_2:2\%O_2$).

A further variable that must be considered when
using a sensory panel to detect differences, is that
of person-to-person variation. This can be seen
clearly in Figure 2, which shows the results of a

panel training test. In the test, citric acid was
added to commercial apple juice to give five solutions that differed in acidity by known amounts.
The panelists were asked to compare each sample in
turn with a reference sample (i.e. the middle concentration) and state whether they thought it was more
acid (+ or ++), the same as (o) or less acid (- or --).
Although there was a wide distribution of panel
responses, statistical analysis ((Chi)^2 test) still
showed a significant consensus of opinion among the
panelists ($\underline{P}$ = 0.001) that differences existed
between the samples to which acid had been added and
the reference sample. Similar results were obtained
for sweetness where sucrose was added.

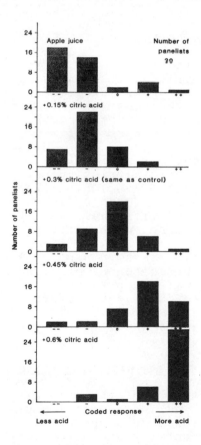

Fig. 2 — Multiple comparison test using commercial apple juice of varying degrees
of acidity.

A paired comparison test is currently being used to compare samples of apples from different orchard management systems for a series of quality attributes which, in the past, have been found to be most important in defining the overall acceptability of apples. Irrespective of person-to-person variation and within sample variation, good agreement between panelists has been achieved, and statistically significant results have been obtained. For example, in a soil management trial, the panel found the addition of extra soil nitrogen fertilizer made the fruit less sweet, less firm and less acceptable; and in a spacing trial, the panel found the fruit from closer-spaced trees to be more acid and less sweet.

INSTRUMENTAL ASSESSMENTS

Having demonstrated that, despite the three sources of variation described, it is possible to obtain sensory data which shows significant differences between samples, the question arises as to whether such differences can be detected instrumentally. Figure 3 shows the changes in firmness, titratable acidity and total sugar in Cox's Orange Pippin harvested from one site at weekly intervals centred on the normal commercial picking period. Statistically significant ($P = 0.05$) differences in the three attributes were found between some picking dates; firmness and titratable acidity declined and total sugars increased with later picking.

Instrumental assessments of quality attributes do not contain the component of person-to-person variation which will be present in sensory assessment. A point to consider, therefore, is whether instrumental assessments are able to detect differences in apple quality which sensory assessments may not detect.

RELATING SENSORY AND INSTRUMENTAL ASSESSMENTS

In order to test whether there is a relationship between sensory and instrumental assessments, Cox's Orange Pippin picked on a number of occasions were assessed instrumentally and organoleptically either immediately after picking or after a further 4 or 14 days 'shelf-life' at 10°C. To overcome between-fruits variation in quality attributes, the instrumental and organoleptic assessments were carried out

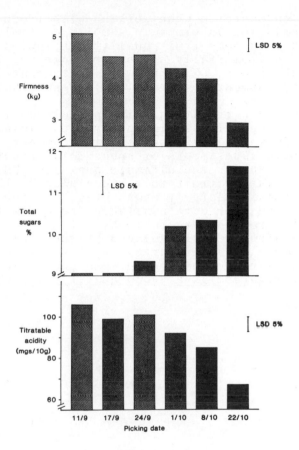

Fig.3 – Cox's Orange Pippin: instrumental assessments of firmness, total sugars and titratable acidity against picking date.

on the same individual fruits. A profile test was used by the sensory panel to assess the fruits for firmness, sweetness and acidity while firmness, total sugars and acidity were assessed instrumentally. Using data from 18 picking date/shelf life combinations, statistically significant ($\underline{P}$ = 0.01) correlations are shown between the instrumental and sensory assessments, with correlation coefficients of 0.94 for firmness, 0.96 for sweetness and 0.94 for acidity.

CONCLUSIONS

Work carried out on the eating quality of apples at East Malling Research Station shows that, despite

problems encountered when working with fresh produce
due to variation inherent in samples of fruit,
differences in some fruit quality attributes can be
detected instrumentally and/or organoleptically.
Relationships also exist between instrumental and
sensory assessments of fruit quality attributes.

Although correlations within individual attributes may be highly statistically significant, it
must be remembered that neither instrumental nor
organoleptic assessments of specific attributes will
necessarily answer the ultimate question: "How
acceptable is the fruit to the consumer?" This
question remains largely unanswered, but the small
amount of consumer data available does show that
sample differences detectable by a trained sensory
panel can also be distinguished by the public.
However, more consumer survey work is now required
to provide more definitive information on what is
generally regarded as a "good quality" apple.

Chapter 4.14

Colour measurement in red wines

P. Bridle
Long Ashton Research Station, University of Bristol, Long Ashton, Bristol BS18 9AF.

Colour is an important indicator of red wine quality and one of the first attributes noted by the consumer. Red wines derive their colour from anthocyanins, the water-soluble pigments present in the skins of black grapes. A single grape variety can contain as many as 16 different types of anthocyanin. The amounts of these and other phenolic compounds found in a young red wine depends on the method of processing as well as the grape cultivar [1]. Simple monomeric anthocyanins from grapes undergo a series of irreversible reactions with other organic components during the aging of wine [2], causing marked colour changes. Thus, the initial red or red-violet colour of a newly made wine is gradually transformed into the characteristic brick-red colour of more mature wines.

These changes in hue which the observer sees are amenable to measurement in the laboratory. Absorbance readings at 520 nm (red) and 420 nm (brown) are used to calculate the amount of colour or "colour density" ($A_{420} + A_{520}$) and the type of colour or "tint" (A_{420}/ A_{520}). Although such information is useful, it lacks precision; also, using this approach small differences in the shades of red are difficult to quantify and colours having no absorbance maxima are not easily described.

More exact data on red wine colour may be obtained by the use of tristimulus colorimetry, a technique which produces results which can be compared more realistically with visual assessments [3]. This method of colour measurement numerically defines any colour in terms of three parameters or tristimulus values [4], L*, a* and b*. L* gives a measure of "lightness" or "brightness" of a colour and is scaled from 0 (black) to 100 (white); and a* and B* are parameters which specify the hue or name of the colour. The a* value describes red and green hues (+a* to -a*) and b* measures yellows and blues (+b* to -b*). The three values define the exact position of any colour in 3-dimensional colour space and are used to calculate:

(i) Hue angle: derived from $\tan^{-1} b*/a*$, defines the spectral shade of the colour thus: red = $0^{\circ} \longrightarrow$ yellow = $90^{\circ} \longrightarrow$ green = $180^{\circ} \longrightarrow$ blue = $270^{\circ} \longrightarrow$ red = $360^{\circ}/0^{\circ}$

(ii) Saturation: derived from $[(a*)^2 + (b*)^2]^{\frac{1}{2}}$ is also known as chroma and measures the purity of colour and is often described by words such as depth, body, intensity or vividness. Highly saturated colours appear as pure hues, whereas colours having low saturation appear to be diluted with grey.

(iii) Colour difference is calculated using the formula $[(\Delta L*)^2 + (\Delta a*)^2 + (\Delta b*)^2]^{\frac{1}{2}}$ and is the amount by which a sample differs from a control or standard colour. It is generally accepted that a colour difference of 0.2 units is just detectable by eye.

With equipment capable of producing data such as this, it is possible to match closely the visual colour assessment of red wine by the human eye.

REFERENCES

1.   Timberlake, C.F; Bridle, P. The effect of processing and other factors on the colour characteristics of some red wines. Vitis, 1976, 15, 37-39.

2.   Timberlake, C.F; Bridle, P.   Interactions
      between anthocyanins, phenolic compounds
      and acetaldehyde and their significance in
      red wines. Amer.J. Enol. Vitic. 1976, 27
      (3), 97-105.

3.   Timberlake, C.F; Bridle, P.   Long Ashton
      Annual Report for 1979, 160.

4.   McKlaren, K.   In "Developments in Food Colours
      - 1" (J.Walford, Ed.). Applied Science,
      London,1980, 36-37.

Chapter 4.15

Browning in white wines

L.F. Burroughs and A.G.H. Lea
Long Ashton Research Station, University of Bristol, Long Ashton, Bristol BS18 9AF, England.

OXIDATION PROCESSES

Browning in white wines is due to oxidation. Phenolic compounds are the main oxidisable substances in grape juices and wines. These normally contain non-flavonoids (approx. 200 mg/l) comprising derivatives of caffeic acid, ferulic acid, p-coumaric acid and gallic acid; and flavonoids (approx. 50 mg/l) comprising d-catechin, l-epicatechin, procyanidins and quercetin (though this is not readily oxidisable) [1].

Oxidation can be either enzymic or chemical. The main reaction is similar in both cases, hydroxyl groups being oxidised to quinones which may then polymerise to give yellow-brown pigments (especially from flavonoids). The oxidation process produces a trace of hydrogen peroxide, which readily oxidises other wine constituents (coupled oxidation) leading to flavour defects, e.g. acetaldehyde by oxidation of ethanol [2].

Enzymic oxidation

This occurs rapidly at crushing and pressing due to polyphenoloxidase (from grape tissue) and sometimes laccase (from Botrytised grapes). Laccase specifically oxidises para-substituted diphenols. Oxidase activity is largely destroyed by yeast action [3], so that very little remains in dry wines [4].

Chemical oxidation

Chemical oxidation (non-enzymic) occurs slowly during wine storage in vat or bottle. Limited oxidation is part of normal wine aging but when excessive gives colour and flavour defects ("maderisation") due to coupled oxidation [2,5].

PREVENTION OF OXIDATION

Oxygen is an essential component so that its exclusion, e.g. by inert-gas protection, prevents oxidation [6].

Free sulphur dioxide prevents enzymic oxidation. It acts both by inhibiting the enzyme itself [7] and also by reducing the quinones (before they polymerise) back to the original phenols [8]. In the latter process, SO_2 is oxidised to sulphate. It also protects a wine against chemical oxidation, by reacting with hydrogen peroxide and preventing "coupled oxidation" of other wine constituents.

Ascorbic acid prevents enzymic oxidation by reducing the quinones back to the original phenols. It does not inhibit the enzymic activity. Similarly it reverses chemical oxidation by the same mechanism, but only temporarily, until all the ascorbate is used up. Unfortunately it is itself subject to chemical oxidation (to dehydro-ascorbic acid - DHA) with the formation of hydrogen peroxide and thus potentiates "coupled oxidation"[2,9]. The DHA formed can itself polymerise to brown pigments [10]. Ascorbic acid can thus act as a catalyst for oxidising certain constituents, rather than as an antioxidant [9].

Polyclar (PVP) treatment preferentially removes flavonoids (catechins and procyanidins) which are the main source of browning [11], and also absorbs brown pigments once formed.

INCREASE IN BROWNING

Prolonged contact with the skin tissues encourages enzyme action and increases the extraction of flavonoids, hence giving more coloured wines [12].

REFERENCES

1.   Singleton, V.L.; Noble, A.C.   In "Phenolic, Sulphur and Nitrogen Compounds in Food

Flavours" Am. Chem. Soc. Sympos. Ser. No. 26, 1976, 47-70.

2.   Wildenradt, H.N.; Singleton, V.L.   Am. J. Enol. Vit.   1974, 25, 119-126.

3.   Kovac, V. Bull. OIV. 1979, 52 (584), 809-826.

4.   Kidron, M.; Harel, E.; Mayer, A.M.   Am. J. Enol. Vit.   1978, 29, 30-35.

5.   Singleton, V.L.; Tronsdale, E.; Zaya, J.   Am. J. Enol. Vit.   1980, 30, 45-54.

6.   Mekhuzla, N.A.   Bull. OIV.   1978, 50 (569-570), 575-581.

7.   White, B.B.; Ough, C.S.   Am. J. Enol. Vit.   1978, 24, 148-152.

8.   Luvalle, J.E.   J. Am. Chem. Soc.   1952, 74, 2970-2977.

9.   Ribereau-Gayon, J.   Am. J. Enol. Vit.   1963, 14, 139-143.

10.   Hiemann, W.; Wisser, K.; Völter, I.   Z. Lebensm. Untersuch. Forsch.   1970, 142, 102-108.

11.   Rapp, A.; Bachmann, O.; Steffan, H.   Bull. OIV.   1977, 50 (553), 167-196.

12.   Singleton, V.L.   Am. J. Enol. Vit.   1980, 31, 14-20.

Chapter 4.16

Evaluating wine quality by the application of statistical methods to analytical GC data

M. Bertuccioli
Instituto Industrie Agrarie, Universita di Perugia
P. Daddi
Instituto di Statistica, Universita di Perugia
A. Sensidoni
Instituto Tecn. Alimentari, Universita di Udine, Italy.

INTRODUCTION

Wines were classified into quality groups based on sensory evaluation and analytical parameters (routine laboratory analytical data and gas chromatographic variables). By stepwise discriminant and multiple regression analyses, it was demonstrated that some components were suitable for determining the sensory quality of the wines.

In general, information about wine quality comes from sensory evaluation. However, it is also possible to make comparisons among different products based on the relationship existing between the concentration of each organoleptic characteristic and sensation [1]. Recent studies on wine have demonstrated a relationship between origin and its volatile constituents [2]. However, the determination of parameters which can be related to the sensory quality of wine (nuances of colour, odour, taste and texture) is more difficult. This paper attempts to identify (independent of grape variety, vintage, or region) the variables which discriminate between wines, given different hedonic ratings in panel tests; using the same variables a multiple regression analysis is developed to predict subjective scores.

MATERIAL AND METHODS

We tested and analysed 47 dry white wines produced

from different grape varieties and wineries and of different vintage and region.

The wines were tested according to the procedure devised by the "Associazione Enotecnici Italiani". The following attributes were assessed; appearance, (out of 20 marks), aroma (32), flavour (48). Scores were then totalled and the wines classified in to three groups;

Group 1 = Excellent   (75.0 - 100.0)
Group 2 = Good   (62.5 - 75.0)
Group 3 = Fair-good   (50.0 - 62.5)

"Objective" data were of two types; the first termed analytical data, included routine measurements such as volatile acids and total phenol, and the second resulted from gas chromatographic analysis of wines (headspace, direct injection and organic extracts).

Stepwise discriminant analysis (SDA) was used to classify the 47 wines into the above three groups by means of a set of rank variables selected according to their capacity to separate one group from the others [3]. Having detected the most significant variables from the point of view of classifying the wines, the same variables were used in a multiple regression analysis [3], applied separately to each group, to derive a predictive relationship between objective data (independent variables) and subjective score (dependent variables).

RESULTS AND DISCUSSION

The components measured and their average concentration for the three groupings are given in Table 1.

Classification according to total scores

Five sets of data: set SA (only GLC variables); set SB (only analytical variables); set SC (SA and SB); set SD (combined variables and variables not included in ratios); set SE (all the variables). Combined variables: $A1=(C+E)/(P+Q+S+T)$; $A2=(D+G+H)/(P+Q+S+T)$; $A3=(C+E)/(D+G+H)$; $A4=N/C4$; $A5=R/C4$; $A6=N/R$; $A7=C13/C4$; $A8=C7/C4$; $A9=C6/C4$; $A10=C14/C6$; $A11=C7/C6$; $A12=C13/C14$; $A13=C2/C12$; $A14=(D+G+H)/(F6+F8+F10)$ were used in the SDA analyses.

Table 1 — GLC and analytical data average of three white wine groups.

Component	Variable	GROUPS		
		1	2	3
		MEAN +/− STANDARD DEVIATION		
ANALYTICAL				
PH	C1	3.303 +/− 0.162	3.157 +/− 0.072	3.243 +/− 0.101
TOTAL ACIDITY (g/l)	C2	6.221 +/− 0.637	6.931 +/− 0.620	6.460 +/− 0.492
VOLATILE ACIDITY (g/l)	C3	0.428 +/− 0.162	0.437 +/− 0.177	0.371 +/− 0.143
FREE SO$_2$ (mg/l)	C4	15.089 +/− 7.987	9.587 +/− 5.457	8.861 +/− 7.408
TOTAL SO$_2$ (mg/l)	C5	112.589 +/− 27.614	118.025 +/− 29.642	114.738 +/− 33.595
COLOR (D.O$_{420}$ x 1000)	C6	81.167 +/− 25.933	83.562 +/− 26.389	107.153 +/− 56.237
TOTAL PHENOL (mg/l)	C7	207.155 +/− 45.483	242.187 +/− 59.814	253.538 +/− 127.415
ETHANOL (VOL. %)	C8	11.893 +/− 0.487	11.910 +/− 0.557	11.968 +/− 0.848
EXTRACT (g/l)	C9	20.822 +/− 1.791	20.518 +/− 2.130	20.277 +/− 1.791
ASH (g/l)	C10	1.707 +/− 0.418	1.496 +/− 0.277	1.703 +/− 0.222
ALKALINITY AОII (meq/l)	C11	17.600 I/ 3.204	16.437 +/− 2.739	17.769 +/− 2.619
MALIC ACID (g/l)	C12	1.770 +/− 1.037	2.345 +/− 0.748	1.657 +/− 1.076
RH	C13	10.926 +/− 4.339	12.456 +/− 3.482	13.069 +/− 0.929
CATECHINS (mg/l)	C14	32.944 +/− 18.675	52.562 +/− 40.740	52.154 +/− 30.973
GAS-CHROMATOGRAPHIC [1]				
i-BUTYL ACETATE *	A	0.566 +/− 0.237	0.489 +/− 0.359	0.421 +/− 0.147
ETHYL BUTIRATE *	B	1.950 +/− 0.718	1.829 +/− 0.842	1.666 +/− 0.748
i-AMYL ACETATE *	C	7.728 +/− 4.205	4.213 +/− 1.398	5.383 +/− 3.592
ETHYL CAPROATE *	D	4.557 +/− 1.868	4.354 +/− 2.054	4.109 +/− 1.970
HEXYL ACETATE *	E	0.624 +/− 0.471	0.342 +/− 0.166	0.443 +/− 0.364
n-HEXANOL *	F	1.237 +/− 0.707	1.226 +/− 0.613	1.258 +/− 0.617
ETHYL CAPHYLATE *	G	5.801 +/− 3.590	4.810 +/− 2.550	4.634 +/− 3.015
ETHYL CAPRATE *	H	1.119 +/− 0.889	0.976 +/− 0.647	0.986 +/− 0.735
DIETHYL SUCCINATE *	I	0.101 +/− 0.118	0.103 +/− 0.112	0.079 +/− 0.034
2-PHENETHYL ACETATE *	K	0.124 +/− 0.082	0.114 +/− 0.108	0.096 +/− 0.057
ETHYL LAURATE *	L	0.128 +/− 0.089	0.118 +/− 0.110	0.121 +/− 0.072
2-PHENETHYL ALCOHOL *	M	0.377 +/− 0.244	0.299 +/− 0.198	0.357 +/− 0.188
ACETALDEHYDE **	N	0.071 +/− 0.019	0.075 +/− 0.025	0.090 +/− 0.040
METHANOL **	O	0.097 +/− 0.119	0.090 +/− 0.129	0.063 +/− 0.015
n-PROPANOL **	P	0.047 +/− 0.014	0.039 +/− 0.016	0.042 +/− 0.012
i-BUTANOL **	Q	0.141 +/− 0.056	0.157 +/− 0.046	0.139 +/− 0.037
ACETOIN **	R	0.022 +/− 0.012	0.014 +/− 0.019	0.011 +/− 0.005
2-METHYL-1-BUTANOL **	S	0.095 +/− 0.038	0.117 +/− 0.036	0.120 +/− 0.040
3-METHYL-1-BUTANOL **	T	0.416 +/− 0.117	0.529 +/− 0.135	0.523 +/− 0.124
2.3 BUTYLEN GLYCOL **	V	0.208 +/− 0.097	0.143 +/− 0.055	0.174 +/− 0.070
GLYCEROL **	X	4.519 +/− 1.090	4.383 +/− 1.102	4.825 +/− 1.763
ETHYL ACETATE **	Y	0.009 +/− 0.025	0.006 +/− 0.018	0.072 +/− 0.034
ETHYL LACTATE **	Z	0.135 +/− 0.095	0.060 +/− 0.053	0.114 +/− 0.093
CAPROIC ACID ***	F6	0.201 +/− 0.077	0.184 +/− 0.072	0.168 +/− 0.090
CAPRYLIC ACID ***	F8	0.578 +/− 0.264	0.502 +/− 0.260	0.435 +/− 0.291
CAPRIC ACID ***	F10	0.173 +/− 0.097	0.113 +/− 0.095	0.111 +/− 0.113

1) EXPRESSED AS $\dfrac{\text{PEAK AREA COMPONENT}}{\text{PEAK AREA INTERNAL STANDARD}}$

*   METHYL BENZOATE
**   3-METHYL-2-BUTANOL
***   ENANTHIC ACID

The results (Table 2) show that almost complete separation can be obtained by using the sets SC and SE. The discriminant variables of these sets are given in Table 3. The canonical plot employing the entered variables of set SE is shown in Figure 1.

Table 2 — Classification of 47 wines into three score groups employing five sets of variables.

(TOTAL SCORE GROUPS)

ACTUAL GROUP	NO. OF CASES	SET SA			SET SB			SET SC			SET SD			SET SE		
		1	2	3	1	2	3	1	2	3	1	2	3	1	2	3
1	18	15	2	1	14	0	4	18	0	0	15	2	1	18	0	0
2	16	1	12	3	0	12	4	0	15	1	1	13	2	0	16	0
3	13	0	4	9	1	2	10	0	0	13	0	2	11	0	0	13

Table 3 — Discriminant variables of sets SC and SE in decreasing order of importance for white wines into three groups.

TOTAL SCORE				ODOUR SCORE				TASTE SCORE			
VARIABLE ENTERED		F - VALUE		VARIABLE INTERED		F - VALUE		VARIABLE ENTERED		F - VALUE	
SC	SE	SC	SE	SC	SE	SC	SE	SC	SE	SC	SE
C9	C9	8.44**	18.84**	C4	A13	18.85**	55.05**	M	I	12.12**	24.00**
E	C6	8.14**	14.97**	I	A4	8.52**	36.42**	C6	A6	10.52**	23.60**
C	C2	7.98**	14.39**	C12	I	7.03**	35.47**	C4	M	9.51**	20.73**
M	F8	6.07**	12.69**	Q	X	6.74**	31.68**	X	A	9.30**	16.25**
C10	N	5.74**	8.83**	C2	F6	6.70**	30.02**	T	C14	8.76**	13.27**
T	P	5.73**	7.80**	C10	B	5.56**	27.57**	L	A3	7.52**	12.80**
C4	A4	5.20**	6.96**	D	C	5.36**	26.37**	H	Q	7.30**	11.91**
I	A7	4.28**	6.69**	N	A5	5.23**	24.68**	F8	A7	7.07**	10.90**
R	K	4.26**	6.31**	B	V	5.18**	24.18**	Y	N	6.01**	10.62**
H	O	3.85**	5.94**	C9	Y	5.17**	23.28**	R	C9	5.57**	7.56**
V	A6	3.38**	5.86**	H	F	5.15**	23.01**	N	C12	5.45**	7.55**
C5	H	2.67*	5.75**	Y	P	4.25**	22.98**	C8	A2	5.27**	6.00**
L	A	2.65*	5.57**	C7	K	4.09**	21.30**	C14	F10	5.02**	5.69**
C12	C10	2.54*	5.04**	C	C5	3.42**	19.89**	F6	C8	4.99**	5.44**
C3	F10	2.42*	4.76**	V	A	3.01**	18.53**	C7	Y	4.86**	4.70**
P	E	2.21*	4.42**	A	N	2.99**	18.11**	C9	A11	4.72**	3.48**
X	C	2.14*	4.30**	E	Q	2.60*	16.41**	S	C2	4.45**	3.45**
O	F	2.13*	3.94**	C14	R	2.39*	16.02**	I	Z	4.36**	3.31**
A	A3	2.00	3.79**	P	C2	2.01	15.58**	C11	A14	2.25*	3.00**
C2	V	1.98	3.74**	F6	O	1.77	11.44**	G	C3	1.62	2.63*
C7	C13	1.92	3.24**	Z	E	1.34	11.33**	F	F8	1.59	2.24*
Y	A5	1.75	2.83**	R	A8	1.29	11.14**	Q	O	1.45	2.21*
C1	I	1.52	1.62	C1	A3	1.19	11.03**	O	F6	1.31	1.32
K	S	1.46	1.56		F8		10.01**	C10		1.29	
F10		1.12			C12		9.14**				
C6		1.04			C7		8.55**				
F8		1.00			C4		8.11**				
					C11		5.06**				
					C1		4.88**				
					C6		2.83*				
					C9		2.79*				
					C13		2.48*				
					A7		1.64				

** = SIGNIFICANT AT P 0.01
* = SIGNIFICANT AT P 0.05

Classification according to odour and taste scores

The summary of the classification results, using two sets of data (SC and SE), is given in Table 4. For the discriminant variables of these sets, see Table 3. Stepwise regression analysis was used to establish the relationship between objective and subjective data.

Table 4 — Classification of 47 wines into three score groups employing two sets of variables (odour and taste score group).

ACTUAL GROUP	NO. OF CASES	SET SC			SET SE		
		1	2	3	1	2	3
ODOUR SCORES							
1	17	17	0	0	17	0	0
2	11	0	10	1	0	11	0
3	19	0	0	19	0	0	19
TASTE SCORES							
1	15	15	0	0	15	0	0
2	17	0	16	1	0	17	0
3	15	0	1	14	0	0	14

Table 5 — Regression with the variable group entered in the discriminant functions of the set SC and SE (standard error shown in brackets).

SET SC

$$^*Y_1 = 73.66 + 5.34\,\mathbf{E} + 18.03\,\mathbf{V}$$
$$\qquad\qquad (1.34)\quad\ (6.40)$$

$$^{***}Y_2 = 50.49 + 9.49\,\mathbf{C10} + 11.07\,\mathbf{M}$$
$$\qquad\qquad (2.54)\qquad\ (3.57)$$

$$^{***}Y_3 = 63.79 - 30.09\,\mathbf{F10} - 0.28\,\mathbf{C4}$$
$$\qquad\qquad (6.26)\qquad\ (0.09)$$

$$^*R^2 = 0.6954;\ ^{**}R^2 = 0.6403;\ ^{***}R^2 = 0.7216$$

SET SE

$$^*Y_1 = 76.12 + 6.61\,\mathbf{E} - 3.44\,\mathbf{A3} + 15.30\,\mathbf{V}$$
$$\qquad\qquad (1.15)\quad\ (1.15)\qquad\ (5.26)$$

$$^{**}Y_2 = 59.30 + 15.63\,\mathbf{C10} + 23.86\,\mathbf{I} - 0.87\,\mathbf{C9}$$
$$\qquad\qquad (3.10)\qquad\ (6.13)\qquad\ (0.39)$$

$$^{***}Y_3 = 30.78 - 25.96\,\mathbf{F10} + 2.30\,\mathbf{C13}$$
$$\qquad\qquad (5.58)\qquad\ (0.68)$$

$$^*R^2 = 0.8142;\ ^{**}R^2 = 0.7259;\ ^{***}R^2 = 0.7631$$

Table 6 — Evaluated and estimated scores (total score, set SE).

	GROUP 1				GROUP 2				GROUP 3		
Wine	Observed	Predicted	Residual	Wine	Observed	Predicted	Residual	Wine	Observed	Predicted	Residual
2	75.8	77.8	−2.0	1	72.0	68.5	+ 3.5	5	61.2	61.8	−0.6
3	77.9	79.9	−2.0	4	64.5	67.5	−3.0	11	62.2	57.3	+4.9
6	79.6	83.0	−3.4	9	74.8	74.7	+0.1	13	58.4	60.3	−1.9
7	79.2	78.4	+0.8	10	64.3	61.4	+2.9	16	52.6	55.3	−2.7
8	86.1	86.3	−0.2	12	72.1	69.9	+2.2	18	61.6	61.3	+0.3
15	77.9	78.7	−0.8	14	65.6	67.0	−1.4	22	58.1	58.8	−0.7
20	78.4	77.9	+0.5	17	66.4	65.9	+05	24	50.3	49.7	+0.6
21	86.1	86.3	−0.2	19	64.0	68.8	−4.8	27	59.6	61.3	−1.7
23	76.8	75.9	+0.9	29	62.6	63.6	−1.0	30	60.8	59.4	+1.4
25	80.2	80.8	−0.6	34	69.2	68.2	+1.0	31	60.0	59.4	+0.6
26	83.2	83.8	−0.6	35	63.5	62.9	+0.6	33	62.1	60.3	+1.9
28	78.5	77.9	+0.6	39	63.9	66.9	−3.0	36	53.2	54.3	−1.1
32	86.1	85.1	+1.0	41	63.6	64.1	−0.5	45	53.8	55.8	−1.0
37	78.0	79.4	−1.4	43	73.2	71.5	+1.7				
38	82.6	79.3	+3.3	46	65.0	64.6	+0.4				
40	79.2	79.2	=0.0	47	72.9	72.1	+0.8				
42	77.0	77.3	−0.3								
44	91.0	90.7	+0.3								

The best regression model for panel acceptability was calculated for each wine group. The results (Table 5), including only two or three variables were considered adequate. Due to the small number of observations within each group, more complex multiple regression models could not be fitted (Table 6).

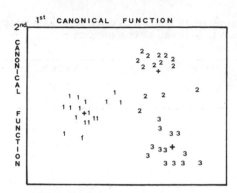

Fig.1 — A canonical plot showing separation of three wine groups on the basis of all the variables.

CONCLUSION

Classification of general wine quality according to objective data requires the inclusion of many variables (both routine analytical and gas chromatographic) (Table 2 and 3). This is in accordance with the complex sensory response evoked by wines. However, by means of stepwise discriminant analysis and multiple regression analysis we have shown that some components are particularly suitable for classifying the wines. Using this data in regression equations, it is possible to estimate the subjective score, within each group.

REFERENCES

1. Dravnieks, A. Approaches to subjective/objective correlations in flavor. ASTM 594 (J.J. Powers, and H.R. Moskowitz, Eds) Philadelphia, 1974, 5-25.
2. Rapp, A.; Hastrich, H.; Engel, L.; Knipser, W. Possibilities of characterizing wine quality and vine varieties by means of capillary chromatography. In "Flavor of Food and Beverages" Academic Press, New York, 1978, 391-417.
3. SPSS - Statistical Package for the Social Sciences. 2nd edn., McGraw-Hill, New York, 1975.

SENSORY AND INSTRUMENTAL METHODS AND THEIR APPLICATION TO SPECIFIC PRODUCTS

(c)   Fish and Meat

Chapter 4.17

Quality of deboned fish flesh

P. Howgate
Ministry of Agriculture, Fisheries and Food, Torry Research Station, PO Box 31,
Aberdeen AB9 8DG, Scotland.

SUMMARY

The main processing factors influencing the sensory
properties of deboned fish flesh are: the quality of
the fish from which the starting material is obtained;
the particular fraction of the fish presented for
deboning and the storage conditions under which the
frozen deboned flesh is held. All three factors influence the flavour of the deboned fish but the last
two mainly affect texture. The colour of the material is almost entirely a function of the fraction
used and depends on the amount of blood pigment present. Any scale of quality has to take into account
the effects on quality of the separate processing
factors. The hedonic rating of fish fingers prepared
from deboned flesh is influenced by all three processing factors.

INTRODUCTION

Deboned flesh is the generic term given to the material obtained from machines designed to separate
meat from bone. In the machine most frequently used
in the UK fish processing industry, fish, or pieces
of fish, are pressed by a moving rubber belt under
tension against a revolving perforated drum. Flesh
is squeezed through the perforations and removed from
inside the drum by a screw conveyor while bones and
skin are retained on the surface of the drum to be
rejected to waste. The perforations can be of various

sizes but 5 mm and 3 mm diameter are most commonly used. The products have the outward appearance and overall texture of a mince and in fact are frequently referred to as minces. Most fish minces are frozen into slabs and later cut up to make fish fingers or other battered or breaded portions; some are made into fish cakes.

The deboning process has been used to recover for higher value use, good quality material which would otherwise go to low value outlets like pet food or fish meal. For example, during the manufacture of bone-free frozen fillet blocks, the fillets are trimmed to cut out parts which contain bones. The flesh in these pieces is of the same quality as the bulk fillets and the bone separator enables this flesh to be recovered, bone-free, and incorporated into the fillet block or frozen as a block of minced flesh. Small fish which would not be big enough for economic filleting can, after heading and cleaning, be processed through the separator to recover the flesh as a mince. The yield of mince by this process is about 55% of the original head-on, gutted fish compared with 40% for skinned fillets.

The use of bone separators in the fish processing industry has increased during the last decade and fish minces are now an established product. At least four conferences [1-4], and one review [5] have been devoted to the processing and utilisation of fish minces. These minces are somewhat different from the usual products of the fish processing industry and their requirements for quality control can also differ from those applied to traditional products. Where minces are prepared and used within a factory, control over raw materials and processing gives good control of quality and a code of practice has been published [6]. Where deboned flesh products are bought and sold, quality standards are required.

This paper considers the factors which influence the sensory properties of fish minces and the problems of measuring and defining quality. Discussion is restricted to minces prepared from white fish, i.e. fish with a very low lipid content.

MAJOR PROCESSING FACTORS INFLUENCING THE QUALITY OF DEBONED FLESH

Between catching the fish and the final consumption of a product made from deboned flesh there are many

handling, storage and processing operations that can
influence the final quality. These influences are
not independent; the effect of any one process interacts with those before and after it. The three major
factors influencing quality of the product are the
nature and quality of the fish as raw material; the
way the fish is butchered and prepared for deboning;
and the way the mince is handled and stored after
preparation.

Nature and quality of the fish

Fish is highly perishable and spoils quite rapidly
even at chill temperatures. Spoilage affects acceptability and the effects are carried through the deboning operation to influence the quality of the
mince. The intrinsic sensory properties of fish, appearance, odour, flavour and the texture, vary according to species, and the sensory properties of the
deboned flesh will reflect these variations.

Preparation of the fish before deboning

The sensory properties of the mince are very dependent on which parts or balance of parts are presented for deboning. Much of the variation is related
to the amount of blood or kidney tissue incorporated
into the mince. Fish can be prepared in many ways,
but the following description summarises the ways
in which the main fractions are prepared.

The first step in filleting fish is to remove
the head at the level of the gill opening and separate the fillets from each side of the backbone. At
the head end of the fillet is a large bone, the lug
bone, and this is cut away along with much of the
thin flap of tissue which forms the wall of the belly
cavity. This part of the fillet is contaminated with
blood leaking from the large blood vessel lying just
behind the gills and which is severed during gutting.
Spoilage of the flesh near the gill cavity and the
belly cavity occurs sooner and proceeds faster than
in the rest of the fillet. The parts cut off at this
stage are called trimmings and they can be passed
through the bone separator as a separate fraction.

The fillet either intact or after trimming can
be passed through the separator although in industrial practice it would be unusual to process fillets
other than from small fish in this way. The separator rejects the skin though the fine belly lining -

black in many species - can be squeezed through and
into the mince.

The backbone with fins attached still contains
a lot of flesh adhering to it and can be passed
through the separator to recover this flesh. There
is a large blood vessel running along the spine and
at the anterior end there is a mass of pulpy, blood-
rich, kidney tissue. The swim bladder is also below
the spine in the belly cavity region. When the backbone is passed through the separator the blood, kidney tissue and swim bladder are squeezed through into
the mince. A better quality mince is obtained by
breaking the backbone just behind the belly cavity
region and presenting the posterior portion to the
separator. However, this still contains blood lost
from the blood vessel below the spine.

Small fish can be headed and gutted then passed
through the separator to give mince equivalent to a
mixture of minces from the separate fractions, just
described. The kidney tissue, swim bladder and belly
lining can be cleared out of the belly cavity before
deboning to improve the quality.

Storage after mincing

Minces spoil faster than intact fillet but in factory
processing the mince is frozen into blocks soon after
preparation. During frozen storage, there are changes
in appearance, flavour and texture, the rate of
change being dependent on temperature, species, the
fraction from which the mince was prepared and probably the freshness of the original fish. Generally,
trimmed fillet material deteriorates least quickly
but is faster with increasing blood or kidney tissue
content. However, there is still much to learn about
the factors which influence cold storage deterioration.

SENSORY PROPERTIES OF DEBONED FLESH

Appearance

Deboned fish flesh loses the flaky appearance of a
fillet and has the texture of a mince. The appearance of minces varies most in colour and this greatly
depends on which part of the dressed fish is passed
through the separator.

Mince from trimmed fillets is similar in background colour to the original fillet though the overall appearance is speckled with reddish brown patches
derived from the brown lateral muscle lying just beneath the skin. Mince from other fractions is darker
and redder as the amount of blood incorporated in it
increases. Mince from entire backbones i.e. still
containing kidney tissue, is very red and appears
almost like minced beef. Even mince from the posterior part of backbones or whole backbones after
cleaning out the kidney portion is still very red.

The colour of the mince is not homogeneous.
In minces prepared from trimmings, whole fillets or
nobbed fish, small black specks of belly lining are
visible. Pieces of white swim bladder and creamy-
white section of spinal cord are dispersed throughout minces from whole backbones and show up strongly
against the dark red background.

Table 1 shows the colour of some types of minces expressed as the L, a,b values derived from
measurements [7] using a tristimulus colorimeter [8],
L expresses the lightness of the product, 100 = white
0 = black, positive b values the amount of yellow
and positive a values the amount of red. The fillet
minces from cod and haddock indicate a light, slightly
yellow product; the backbone minces are darker and
redder but with substantially the same b value. Minces from trimmings and nobbed fish have intermediate
colours reflecting the lower amounts of blood pigments. Saithe flesh is slightly grey compared with
cod or haddock and this is shown by a lower L value
but similar a and b scores.

Icing before preparation or frozen storage
afterwards has only small effects on the colour of
fillet minces. Both these storage conditions tend to
make blood-rich minces browner. Washing the starting
material reduces the degree of discolouration but can
affect flavour and texture.

Flavour

The flavour of cooked minces is affected by all three
major processing stages described above. Each stage
has its own set of flavour (and associated odour)
notes, as summarised in Table 2.

Table 1 — Colour of minces expressed as Hunter L, a, b values. Minces prepared from fish held in ice for two days after catching.

Species	Source of mince	L	a	b
Cod	Fillets	59.8	2.2	9.9
	Trimmings	51.3	5.4	7.6
	Posterior backbones	39.5	10.6	6.8
Haddock	Fillets	59.9	1.3	8.8
	Trimmings	44.3	7.9	7.6
	Nobbed fish	46.5	2.7	7.1
	Total backbones (Cleaned)	40.4	8.6	6.7
Saithe	Fillets	46.3	2.7	8.6

Table 2 — Flavour descriptions associated with different processing stages in preparing and storing deboned flesh.

Process	Flavour/odour terms
Storage before bone separation	sweet, meaty, metallic, green plant, sour, soapy, sweaty, ammonia
The deboning process and the fraction used	raw meat, liver, musty, earthy, boiled milk, cardboard, fish meal
Frozen storage	cardboard, turnips, 'cold store'

Fresh fish has a sweetish, creamy, slightly meaty and sometimes metallic flavour. During chill storage these characteristics are lost and the flavour passes through an insipid stage before spoiled flavours are noticed. The flavour of minces from trimmed fillets resembles that of the original fillets though any fresh flavours are somewhat attenuated. In addition, if the fish is fresh a slightly "cardboardy" note can be detected. Musty, earthy, boiled milk flavours are associated with trimmings and to some extent, with nobbed fish minces. Backbone minces have complex flavours with raw meat and fish meal or fish glue notes. "Cardboardy" flavours that develop during frozen storage are most readily detected in minces from fresh fillets. These flavours are similar to those described in frozen stored fillets and are thought to derive from oxidation of phospholipids [9].

Texture

The texture of fish muscle is very variable [10] but the texture of the cooked flesh in the mouth is usually slightly firm, tender and succulent. The obvious characteristics of a mince, as compared with fillet, are the loss of "flakiness", and its more homogeneous nature. The storage history of the fish before deboning has little effect on the texture of the recovered flesh apart from very stale fish which is slightly softer than fresh. The other two factors, the fraction processed and frozen storage do affect texture.

Mince from trimmed fillets is slightly firmer, tougher and drier than the original fillet. It appears that the mincing process itself has an effect though precisely why is unclear. The texture of trimmings or posterior backbone minces is a little softer, more tender and more succulent than the corresponding fillet mince. It is known from the results of protein fractionation and from hydroxyproline measurements that the collagen content of trimmings and backbone minces is higher than that of fillet and this will produce a more gelatinous texture in the cooked product. Mince from intact backbones is very soft and mushy with noticeable small gelatinous lumps derived from the swim bladder and spinal cord.

During frozen storage the minces become firmer, tougher, drier and more fibrous. The rate at which this occurs depends on the storage temperature, the species and the type of material. Fillet mince is reasonably stable and much more so than trimmings or posterior backbone minces. The characteristic feature of cold-stored minces is the development of a tough rubbery texture. Incorporation of polyphosphates into the minces before freezing makes them more succulent and softer but it is not clear if it slows the development of rubberiness.

MEASUREMENT OF SENSORY PROPERTIES FOR QUALITY CONTROL PURPOSES

When preparing a specification for the quality control of a product it is necessary to state or define the quality criteria included in it along with their levels or intensities. With fish minces as with any food product, sensory properties are important but unfortunately it is difficult to define or quantify them. For a given variety the sensory properties of the fillet are largely dependent on freshness and when relevant the extent of any cold storage deterioration. The sensory properties associated with these storage changes can be measured independently on sensory rating scales [11, 12] and permitted levels can be included in quality specifications. These scales are objective in that sensory properties are described without using value judgements and assessors are trained not to attach subjective value to the terms used to anchor the scale points. The scales, however, can be mapped on to defined subjective quality criteria. There is a requirement for similar scales to be developed for rating the quality of deboned flesh which encompass the various sensory properties which affect that quality.

The colour of foods is difficult to specify and measure by sensory methods and fish mince is no exception. Though small differences in the colour of minces can be detected it is not possible to specify in words the required colours within the tolerances needed for quality assurance. The appearance of minces is not sufficiently close to that of printed shade cards for these to be suitable references, so, we are preparing a series of colour prints to serve as possible standards.

The flavour and associated odour of deboned flesh can be reasonably well described (cf. terms in Table 2). By analogy with the assessment of frozen

fish fillets, a scheme can be visualised whereby the
effects of each of the three main processing parameters are represented on separate scales. A particular sample could then be represented by a point in a
three-dimensional space whose axes are defined by the
three scales. While it would be possible to conceive
of continuous scales for the two storage parameters,
the effects of different fractions presented for deboning are largely discontinuous. In addition there
are interactions among these processing factors and
overlap of the flavours produced. Hence it would
seem necessary to condense these three scales into
one for specifying quality.

**Table 3 — Flavour terms given to deboned flesh grouped in descending order of ·
hedonic pleasantness.**

Class	Flavour terms
1	sweet, creamy, meaty, green plant, met allic
2	raw meat, blood, liver, boiled milk, musty, earthy
3	cardboard, cold store, caramel, sour, soapy, turnipy, cabbage-like, fish meal, fish glue
4	sulphide, burnt, acrid, sweaty, cheese-like, ammonia, high intensities of group three flavours

An approach is illustrated in Table 3. The
terms used to describe flavours were ranked by hedonic value implicit in these terms from most to least
pleasant. The ranking was given by a small group
consisting of sensory analysts from Torry Research
Station and quality controllers in the fish processing industry. The hedonic value of the flavours represented by these terms was considered in the context of fish products. A rating scale has been constructed based on these groupings and is being evaluated in research and industry.

Some aspects of the texture of minces can be measured on bipolar scales already described for fish products [10]. Typically these scales are soft/firm, tender/tough, plastic/rubbery, dry/succulent. Experience has shown that data arising from these scales are highly correlated and just one of them - probably the best is tender/tough - can represent the mechanical aspects of texture. It is somewhat more difficult to represent the geometric and particulate properties of minces. Fillet mince or mince containing a high proportion of flesh tissue is fibrous but mince containing much kidney tissue is mushy though with crumb-like particles. These properties cannot be adequately represented on a continuous scale and are recorded as discrete categories. Though the mechanical aspects of texture can be rated on a tender/tough bipolar scale it is not possible to map this directly on to a quality scale. Each extreme of the texture scale represents low quality with the optimum quality being in between. Quality then is a function of the absolute difference from this optimum texture.

HEDONIC RATING OF DEBONED FISH PRODUCTS

The acceptability of a food product to a consumer is affected by a wide range of factors many of which do not depend on the properties of the food itself. The pleasure which consumption of food gives is influenced greatly by its sensory properties hence the hedonic rating of a product gives an overall measure of these properties. Of course, the relationship between sensory properties and hedonic rating varies from one assessor to another and any conclusions about overall relationships must be based on observations over many assessors.

Table 4 shows hedonic ratings of some fish products served as fish fingers as assessed by members of the staff at Torry Research Station. The absolute values based on such a population may not be representative of a wider population of consumers but the relative values should have meaning. The data are median values of panels of 42 assessors selected from a pool of about 100.

Ratings for fillet minces are usually a little lower than those from the corresponding fillets though for the batch of cod that heads the list they are essentially the same; other batches show a decreased rating on deboning. There is only a small loss

Table 4 — Hedonic rating of fish fingers prepared from some fish products. Scale: 1 = dislike extremely, 9 = like extremely. Panel, n = 42, medium ratings.

Species	Days in ice	Product	Frozen storage	Hedonic rating
Cod	2	fillets	none	7.03
	2	trimmed fillet mince	none	7.10
	2	trimmed fillet mince	18 months at -29°C	6.42
	2	trimmings mince	18 months at -29°C	2.50
	9	fillets	18 months at -29°C	6.77
	9	trimmed fillet mince	18 months at 29°C	5.50
	9	trimmings mince	18 months at -29°C	2.32
Whiting	2	fillets	none	6.97
	2	trimmed fillet mince	none	5.90
	2	nobbed fish mince	none	4.55
	2	trimmed fillet mince	6 months at -15°C	5.01
	2	nobbed fish mince	6 months at -15°C	4.00
Haddock	2	fillets	none	7.13
	2	trimmed fillet mince	none	6.56
	2	nobbed fish mince	none	5.83
	2	trimmed fillet mince	6 months at -15°C	4.52
	2	nobbed fish mince	6 months at -15°C	4.10

in hedonic rating following storage up to 18 months at -29°C. Minces prepared from trimmings are definitely disliked even when they are prepared from fresh fish. This must be predominantly an effect of flavour because the texture of trimmings mince is close to that of fillet mince. The slightly darker colour may also have an effect. Mince from nobbed whiting and haddock is less liked than mince from the corresponding trimmed fillet. Once again there is little difference in texture between these minces and the decrease in acceptability can be attributed to differences in flavour and appearance.

The effect of icing is shown in the cod samples (Table 4). Storage in ice for up to 9 days has a small effect on rating of fillets but a much larger effect on the rating of mince made from the same fillets. (The small effects of storage at -29°C can be ignored here.) This is an example of the effects of interactions between processing and storage factors.

The effects of frozen storage under unsatisfactory conditions - storage temperature of -15°C - are illustrated for the whiting and haddock samples. Frozen storage affects flavour and texture but it is not possible from our trials so far to give weightings to the contributions of each to the change in hedonic rating.

These results show that the hedonic rating of deboned flesh is influenced by the three main processing factors referred to above, and by interactions between them. Similarly, sensory properties are dependent on these factors but as yet without suitable scales for measuring these properties we cannot establish quantitative relationships between hedonic ratings and objective sensory quality.

REFERENCES

1. Martin, R.E. (Ed.), Proceedings of the Conference on the mechanical recovery and utilization of fish flesh, Oak Brook, USA, September 21-22, 1972. National Fisheries Institute,Washington, D.C., 1974

2. Martin, R.E. (ED.), Proceedings of the Second Technical Seminar on Mechanical Recovery and Utilization of Fish Flesh, Boston, USA, June 12-13, 1974. National Fisheries Institute, Washington, D.C., 1976

3. Keay, J.N. (Ed.), Proceedings of the Conference on the Production and Utilization of Mechanically Recovered Fish Flesh (Minced Fish). April 7-8, 1976. Torry Research Station, Aberdeen, Scotland, 1976

4. Martin, R.E. (Ed.), Proceedings of the Third National Technical Seminar on Mechanical Recovery and Utilization of Fish Flesh, Raleigh, North Carolina, USA, December 1-3, 1980. National Fisheries Institute, Washington, D.C., 1982

5. Grantham, G.J. Minced fish technology: a review. FAO Fish. Tech. Paper No. 216. Food and Agriculture Organisation, Rome, 1981

6. Code of practice for minced fish, FAO Fish. Circ. 700. Food and Agriculture Organisation, Rome, 1977

7. Young, K.W., Torry Research Station. (Personal communication.)

8. Hunter, R.S. The Measurement of Appearance. John Wiley and Sons, New York, 1975

9. McGill, A.S.; Hardy, R.; Burt, J.R. Hept-cis-4-enal and its contribution to the off-flavour in cold stored cod. J. Sci. Fd Agric., 1974, 25, 1477-1489

10. Howgate, P. Sensory Properties of Foods (Birch, G.G.; Brennan, J.G.; Parker, K.J., Eds.), Applied Science Publishers, Barking, England, 1977, 249-267

11. Shewan, J.M.; MacIntosh, R.G.; Tucker, C.G.; Ehrenberg, A.S.C. The development of a numerical scoring system for the sensory assessment of the spoilage of wet white fish stored in ice. J. Sci. Fd. Agric., 1953, 4, 283-298

12. Connell, J.J.; Howgate, P. Sensory and objective measurements of the quality of frozen stored cod of different initial freshnesses. J. Sci. Fd. Agric., 1968, 19, 342-354

Chapter 4.18

Sensory and instrumental methods in meat aroma analysis

A.M. Galt and G. Macleod
Department of Food Science and Nutrition, Queen Elizabeth College (University of London),
Campden Hill Road, London W8 7AH, UK

SUMMARY

Twenty-four odour qualities, selected from previously obtained sensory data, were grouped into nine factors by factor analysis. Parallel sensory and instrumental analyses were performed on representative cooked beef aroma isolates obtained by adsorption of the headspace vapours on to Tenax GC. Identification of the aroma components was achieved using combined gas chromatography/mass spectrometry. Heat desorption of the isolates into a heated glass globe - acting as a mixing chamber and fitted with four odour ports - enabled descriptive sensory analysis of the aroma using the previously determined factors and odour qualities. The relevance of heterocyclic compounds in roast beef aroma was established, several thiazoles being important contributors.

INTRODUCTION

The aroma of cooked meat is notoriously complex both in chemical composition and sensory properties [1]. As meat aroma researchers, we are not yet close to being able to state: here is the total chemical data for cooked beef aroma, here is the total sensory data; now let us correlate these to see which compounds contribute to certain aroma qualities. Since statistical correlations are not very meaningful when the data used is incomplete, our present task must be to build up more information, and despite the

many difficulties involved, there is a real need for
parallel instrumental and sensory analyses. With
this frame of mind, our current studies of cooked
beef aroma have had four main objectives. Firstly,
to select relevant sensory descriptors: secondly, to
obtain and analyse chemically, a representative aroma
isolate, which is also amenable to sensory analysis;
thirdly, to describe the isolated aroma sensorially,
and finally to attempt fractionation and therefore
simplification of the complex aroma, in the belief
that complementary chemical and sensory analyses of
fractions would yield useful information. Clearly,
in this short communication, detailed procedures and
results are impossible: they will be published elsewhere. Here, therefore, the main emphasis will be
on methods used. These represent novel applications
in meat flavour research.

SELECTION OF SENSORY DESCRIPTORS

The choice of sensory descriptors was a major problem,
since very few relevant publications exist, e.g. [2,
3], and there is certainly no standard terminology or
recommended vocabularies for cooked meat aromas.
Twenty-four odour qualities (see Table 1) were selected from previously obtained data [3], when 16 cooked
beef samples had been scored by trained assessors
using 41 odour qualities, derived primarily from the
well-known glossary of Harper et al. [4,5] Selection was based on deleting any qualities detected at
low intensity by less than half the panel, and also
those of a subjective nature. An unrestricted factor

Table 1 — Twenty-four selected odour qualities.

ammonia-like	meaty (beef)/raw
animal/goaty	meaty (beef)/boiled
blood-like	meaty (beef)/roast
broth-like	musty/mouldy
burnt	oily/fatty
buttery	paint-like
cool/cooling	pungent
cooked cabbage	spicy
earthy	sweaty
flat/dull	sweet
fragrant	toasted
herbal	vegetables, overcooked

analysis (University of California BMDP4M computer
program [6]; initial factor extraction by principal
components analysis followed by Varimax rotation) was
then applied to the data for these chosen 24 qualities. Nine factors were extracted, explaining approximately 70% of the total variance (see Table 2).

Table 2 — Summarised results of factor analysis.

Factor[a]	Odour quality	Significant[b] factor loading
1 "Meaty" (15.8%)	broth-like	0.851
	meaty/boiled	0.711
	meaty/roast	0.541
	meaty/raw	0.469
2 "Cooked veget-ables" (10.7%)	cooked cabbage	0.855
	overcooked vegetable	0.810
	cool/cooling	0.598
3 "Toasted/Burnt" (8.7%)	toasted	0.817
	burnt	0.743
	meaty/roast	0.602
4 "Ammoniacal" (7.8%)	ammonia-like	0.807
	animal/goaty	0.589
	pungent	0.571
	earthy	0.534
5 "Oily/Fatty" (6.9%)	oily/fatty	0.820
	paint-like	0.660
6 "Spicy/Fragrant" (5.5%)	spicy	0.763
	fragrant	0.752
	sweaty	0.513
7 "Musty/Mouldy" (4.9%)	musty/mouldy	0.812
8 "Flat/Dull" (4.7%)	flat/dull	0.754
	meaty/raw	0.593
	herbal	0.490
9 "Buttery" (4.4%)	buttery	0.868

[a] Figures in brackets denote percentage variance explained.

[b] $p < 0.05$.

Factor 1 was classified as "The meaty factor"; it is
        a general factor denoting meaty aroma qual-
        ities and does not discriminate between
        specific qualities such as raw, boiled and
        roasted aromas.
Factor 2 was classified as "The cooked vegetables
        factor"; it also defined significant cooling
        properties.
Factor 3 was classified as "The toasted/burnt factor"
        and is a specific factor defining roast meat
        qualities.
Factor 4 was classed as "The ammoniacal factor" and
        it defines strong animal/goaty, pungent and
        earthy properties.
Factor 5 was classified as "The oily/fatty factor"
        which had paint-like character.
Factor 6 was classed as "The spicy/fragrant factor".
Factor 7 was classified as "The musty/mouldy factor".
Factor 8 was classified as "The flat/dull factor"
        which had raw meat and herbal associations.
Factor 9 was classed as "The buttery factor".

        In this way, an uncomplicated list of a limited
number of objective aroma qualities was derived.

AROMA ISOLATION AND INSTRUMENTAL ANALYSIS

Aroma isolates were obtained using a modified headspace sampling technique, involving adsorption of

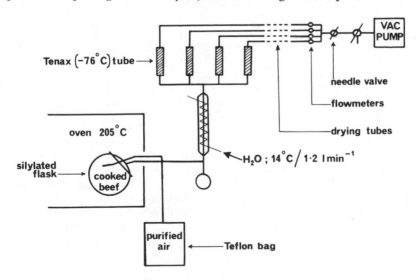

Fig.1 — Aroma isolation apparatus.

cooked beef headspace vapours on to the porous polymer Tenax GC. An idealised diagram of the sampling
system is shown in Figure 1. By means of the vacuum
pump, a highly purified and dried air flow of 500 ml
min^{-1} was used to entrain the volatile components of
the cooked beef (1 kg) headspace through each of the
four "in parallel" sub-ambient Tenax tubes for a sampling time of 5 min. Rapid heat desorption (250°C/
1 min) transferred the volatiles directly on to a gas
chromatography (GC) column for separation, and using
combined gas chromatography/mass spectrometry (GC/MS),
a total of 82 identifications were made, including a
relatively large number of heterocyclic compounds.

SENSORY ANALYSIS OF COOKED BEEF AROMA ISOLATES

Sensory analysis of the isolates was performed using
the apparatus shown in Figure 2. The aroma was heat-
desorbed (250°C/1 min) into a partially evacuated,
silylated and heated (200°C) glass globe (2 1) fitted
with four odour ports on its horizontal circumference.
The desorbed volatiles were flushed into the globe,
which acted as a mixing chamber, by a N_2 flow of
30 ml min^{-1}. By monitoring this flow constantly and
by appropriate use of the tap at position X, the globe
was maintained at, or near, atmospheric pressure.
Four experienced assessors described the aroma perceived at the odour ports, using the previously determined 9 factors and 24 odour qualities — each scored
on a linear 0-5 scale.

The results for an isolate obtained from 1 kg
beef cooked at 205°C for 1 hour are shown in Table 3.
The aroma was strongly roast beef-like, toasted and
burnt - these qualities being represented by factors
F1 and F3; it had moderately strong broth-like,
boiled beef, cooked vegetable-like, flat/dull and buttery qualities represented by F2, F8 and F9, whilst
characteristics defined by F4, F5, F6 and F7 such as
blood-like, sweet, pungent, earthy, ammonia-like,
oily/fatty, spicy, fragrant and musty/mouldy were
weakly present. In particular, the analysis specifically showed that the Tenax had adsorbed and desorbed
(under the analytical conditions used) volatile components which impart cooked beef aroma. The aroma
isolation method and heat desorption techniques were
therefore validated.

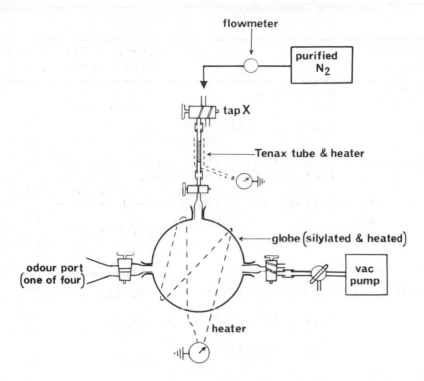

Fig. 2 — The Globe Technique for sensory analysis of heat desorbed aroma isolates.

ATTEMPTED FRACTIONATION OF ISOLATES

Fractionation of isolates was attempted by trapping certain peak combinations on sub-ambient Tenax tubes attached to an outlet splitter on a GC column. Two such fractions contained the relatively low and high boiling components respectively, and their sensory properties were significantly different. Chemical and sensory comparisons of these fractions showed that, when factors 1, 5 and 9 predominated, i.e. when the main sensory properties were *buttery, meaty (beef)/ boiled, broth-like and oily/fatty,* this correlated with the exclusive presence of relatively low boiling components eluting on the PEG 20M column before acetoin - in particular the compounds listed in Table 4. The majority of these are aliphatic compounds; diacetyl and acetoin occur frequently in food

Table 3 — Sensory properties of a cooked beef (1 kg/205°C/1 h) aroma isolate using the Globe Technique.

Intensity	Factors*		Odour qualities* and factor associations	
Strong	Meaty (16)	F1	meaty (beef)/ roast (16)	F1,3
	Toasted/burnt (12)	F3	burnt (14) toasted (14)	F3 F3
Moderate	Cooked veg.(7) Flat/dull (5)	F2 F8	broth-like (7) meaty (beef)/	F1
	Buttery (7)	F9	boiled (5) cooked cabbage (6)	F1,2 F2
			vegetables, overcooked(7)	F2
			flat/dull (5)	F8
			buttery (8)	F9
Weak	Ammoniacal (2)	F4	blood-like (1)	F1,2, 5,7
	Oily/fatty (3) Spicy/ Fragrant (3)	F5 F6	sweet (4) pungent (4)	F2 F4
	Musty/mouldy (4)	F7	earthy (3)	F4,5
			ammonia-like (2)	F4
			oily/fatty (4) spicy (2) fragrant (4) musty/mouldy (2)	F5 F6 F6 F7

* Figures in brackets are panel scores.

aromas and almost certainly explain the very significant buttery note perceived [7,8]. Most of the heterocyclic compounds identified were furanoids.

In the second fraction, Factors 2,3,4 and 6 predominated i.e. the main sensory properties were meaty (beef)/roast, burnt, toasted, cooked vegetable-like, spicy/fragrant, earthy and pungent. This correlated with the presence of relatively high boiling components as shown in Table 5. This time there were relatively few aliphatic compounds. The dimethyl disulphide probably largely explains the cooked veget-

**Table 4 — Compounds identified in a fraction defined predominantly by
Factors 1, 5, and 9.**

Aliphatic hydrocarbons	Sulphur compounds
pentane	methanethiol
hexane	ethanethiol
heptane	carbonyl sulphide
methylpropane	dimethyl sulphide
3-methylpentane	carbon disulphide
a C_{13} hydrocarbon	ethyl methyl disulphide
Alcohols	**Amines**
methanol	trimethylamine
ethanol	a C_4 amine (M73)
butan-1-ol	
pentan-1-ol	**Benzenoids**
	toluene
Aldehydes	
acetaldehyde	**Furanoids**
propanal	furan
hexanal	2-methylfuran
methylpropanal	3-methylfuran
2-methylbutanal	an ethylfuran
3-methylbutanal	2-n-pentylfuran
but-2-enal (crotonaldehyde)	2-methyltetrahydrofuran -3-one
Ketones	
acetone	**Oxazolines**
butanone	2,4-dimethyl-3-oxazoline
pentan-2-one	2,4,5-trimethyl-3- oxazoline
butan-2,3-dione (diacetyl)	
3-hydroxybutanone (acetoin)	
	Thiophens
	a thiophen
	a methylthiophen
	Miscellaneous
	a methylpentanolactone
	a methylpyridine

able-like aroma quality (F2), since it is a major and
characteristic volatile of cooked cabbage. Many
heterocyclic compounds were present and these have
low odour thresholds in general. Several, for example
the pyrazines, have previously been associated with
roasted and earthy aromas (F3 and F4). The thiazoles
are important contributors since both meaty and roasted qualities are associated with some of them e.g.
2,4-dimethyl-5-ethylthiazole   [9,10]. Two thiazoles
(i.e. 2-propyl-4, 5-dimethylthiazole and 2-isopropyl-

Table 5 – Compounds identified in a fraction defined predominantly by Factors 2, 3, 4, and 6.

Aliphatic hydrocarbons
*hept-3-ene

Alcohols
octan-1-ol
dodecan-1-ol

Ketones
decan-2-one

Acids
acetic acid
butanoic acid
hexanoic acid

Sulphur compounds
dimethyl disulphide
dimethyl trisulphide

Benzenoids
a benzenoid compound
benzaldehyde

Furanoids
a furanoid
furfural
(2-furyl)methanol

Pyridines
*2,6-dimethyl-3-ethyl
   pyridine

Pyrazines
2,5-or 2,6-dimethyl
   pyrazine
an ethylmethylpyrazine
a dimethylethylpyrazine
a C_5 sub. pyrazine
*3-isopentyl-2,5-dimethyl
   pyrazine

Oxazoles
a $C_9H_{15}NO$ oxazole

Thiazoles
a $C_7H_{11}NS$ thiazole
a $C_8H_{13}NS$ thiazole
2,4-dimethyl-5-ethyl
   thiazole
*2-isopropyl-4-methyl-
   5-ethylthiazole
*2-propyl-4,5-dimethyl
   thiazole
a C_7 alkylthiazole/an
   acylthiazole
benzothiazole

*Identified for the first time in cooked beef
aroma.

4-methyl-5-ethylthiazole) were identified here for
the first time in cooked beef aroma. Increased substitution in thiazoles confers added nutty, roasted
and meaty qualities [10], and in general, 5-substi-
tuted thiazoles are sulphurous and roasted and some
are meaty [10]. It has previously been shown – and
it was confirmed in this work – that the incorporation of sulphur into ring systems is favoured by prolonged heating periods [11].

ADVANTAGES OF METHODS USED

The methods described offer several advantages in this type of study. Firstly, sensory analysis of aroma isolates can be achieved. This is impossible for many other isolation methods, such as those involving solvent extraction, where solvent odour interferes with sensory assessment. If instrumental and sensory results are to be compared, it is clearly more valid to analyse sensorially the same aroma isolate as is analysed chemically rather than the original food. Secondly, the aroma is isolated by a simple, direct method whereby it is quickly captured and concentrated in one stage using a short sampling time and a procedure which is simulative of normal cooking methods. Thirdly, the Globe Technique allows the totality of an aroma to be analysed by a small panel of assessors, and thereby overcomes an important disadvantage of conventional GC "odour port assessment" methods, in which components are individually assessed such that the effects of masking, synergism etc. on the combined aroma components are not estimated.

CONCLUSION

In conclusion, the aroma profile of cooked meat is due to the sum of all the sensory effects produced simultaneously at the olfactory epithelium by a large number of volatiles of different structures. Heterocyclic compounds, e.g. the thiazoles, are important contributors, and it is likely that many more heterocycles, present in trace amounts, remain to be identified. It is essential, however, in any eager search for characteristic trace volatiles to keep isolation methods as simple and as representative as possible of normally cooked beef, so that artefacts do not cloud the issue.

ACKNOWLEDGEMENTS

We thank the UK Meat and Livestock Commission for financing the work and for a postgraduate scholarship (to AMG); Mr W. Gunn and Mr A. Cakebread for expertise in the operation of the GC/MS and data processing system; Mr R. Taylor, RHM Research Ltd., for statistical and computing help and advice. We acknowledge gratefully the dedication of our assessors.

REFERENCES

1. MacLeod, G.; Seyyedain-Ardebili, M.   Natural and simulated meat flavours (with particular reference to beef).   CRC Crit. Rev. Fd Sci. Nutr. 1981, 14, 309-437.

2. Persson T.; von Sydow, E.; Åkesson, C.   Aroma of canned beef; Sensory properties.   J. Fd Sci. 1973, 38, 386-392.

3. MacLeod, G.; Coppock, B.M.   Sensory properties of the aroma of beef cooked conventionally and by microwave radiation.   J. Fd Sci. 1978, 43, 145-161.

4. Harper, R.; Bate-Smith, E.C.; Land, D.G.; Griffiths, N.M.   A glossary of odour stimuli and their qualities.   Perfum. Essent. Oil Record 1968, 59, 22-36.

5. Harper, R.; Land, D.G.; Griffiths, N.M.; Bate-Smith, E.C.   Odour qualities: A glossary of usage.   Br. J. Psychol. 1968, 59, 231-252.

6. Dixon, W.J.; Brown, M.B.   BMDP Biomedical Computer Programs, P-Series, University of California Press, LA, 1979, 656-684

7. Hirai, C.; Herz, K.O.; Pokorny, J.; Chang, S.S.   Isolation and identification of volatile flavour compounds in boiled beef.   J. Fd Sci. 1973, 38, 393-397.

8. Peterson, R.J.; Izzo, H.J.; Jungermann, E.; Chang, S.S.   Changes in volatile flavour compounds during the retorting of canned beef stew.   J. Fd Sci. 1975, 40, 948-954.

9. Mussinan, C.J.; Wilson, R.A.; Katz, I.; Hruza, A.; Vock, M.H.   Phenolic Sulphur and Nitrogen Compounds in Food Flavours, ACS Symp. Ser. 26 (Charalambous, G.; Katz, I., Eds), ACS, Washington DC, 1976, 133-145.

10. Pittet, A.O.; Hruza, D.E.   Comparative study of flavour properties of thiazole derivatives. J. Agric. Fd Chem. 1974,22,264-269.

11. Schwimmer, S.; Friedman, M.   Genesis of volatile
       sulphur-containing food flavours.   <u>Flavour Ind</u>.
       1972, 3, 137-145.

Posters

Chapter 4.19

Effect of processing changes on the quality of broiler chickens

N.M. Griffiths and J.M. Jones
ARC Food Research Institute, Norwich, UK.

INTRODUCTION

In 1978 approximately 75% of the broiler chickens
processed in the UK were sold frozen; prior to freezing these were chilled by immersion in water at 4°C.
EEC regulations have proposed the introduction of an
alternative cooling method, e.g. air-chilling. At
present 20% of the UK broiler production is air-
chilled and sold fresh. Many UK processors are
familiar with air-chilling but it is not known what
effect air-chilling prior to freezing might have on
quality. Tests were designed to investigate the
effects of frozen storage on the appearance, texture
and flavour of birds chilled by air and immersion
techniques. Broilers were stored at -12°C and -20°C,
the temperatures approximating to those suggested by
the EEC for marketing of frozen and deep-frozen
poultry produce; also at -40°C, for use as "controls"
since broilers have been shown to be stable at this
temperature for 2 years.

APPEARANCE (RAW)

Twenty members of the Food Research Institute staff
who regularly purchased frozen poultry rated the
appearance of the frozen chickens on the scale:
1 = excellent; 2 = very good; 3 = good; 4 = fair;
5 = poor; 6 = unacceptable (Fig.1); they gave
descriptions of each bird.

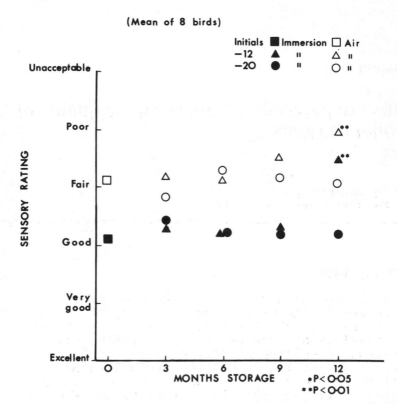

Fig. 1 — Sensory ratings of appearance (raw) of chickens, air- or immersion-chilled before frozen storage.

At the beginning of the work the immersion-chilled birds were rated as good and described as creamy in colour and unblemished; the air-chilled birds were rather red, bruised and wrinkled. Immersion-chilled birds showed no change in appearance when stored for 12 months at -20°C or 9 months at -12°C. All air-chilled had a lower rating than the immersion-chilled birds but only those stored for 12 months at -12°C were significantly different from the original air-chilled samples.

We asked 286 people visiting the Royal Agricultural Show to choose which of two frozen chickens (one air-chilled, one immersion-chilled

they would purchase, giving reasons for their choice.
The birds were matched in weight and sixteen
different pairs were used during the experiment. 70%
preferred the immersion-chilled birds because they
were "plumper", "fresher", "paler"; 30% preferred
the air-chilled because "they didn't look treated".

FLAVOUR

An experienced panel of 14 assessors compared the
air- and immersion-chilled birds stored at -12°C and
-20°C with the immersion-chilled birds stored at
-40°C. The samples were assessed hot, using a form
of multiple comparison test, in which the size of
the difference was rated on the scale 0 = no
difference; 1 = very slight; 2 = slight; 3 = moderate;
4 = large; the quality was also characterised.

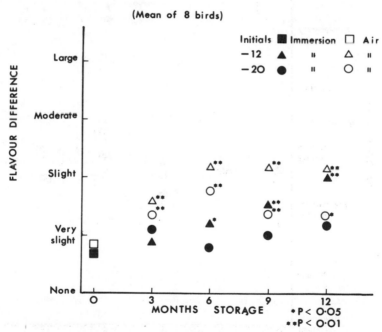

Fig.2 — Flavour difference between chickens, air- or immersion-chilled, prior to
frozen storage.

Immersion-chilled birds stored at -20°C showed no statistically significant change over 12 months storage, but had changed within six months at -12°C. Air-chilled chickens stored at -12°C and -20°C had changed significantly in flavour after only 3 months, those at -12°C more than those at -20°C.

TEXTURE

Fourteen experienced assessors rated the tenderness of the cold meat on the following scale: 1 = extremely tender; 2 = very tender; 3 = moderately tender; 4 = slightly tender; 5 = slightly tough; 6 = moderately tough; 7 = very tough; 8 = extremely tough. Juiciness was rated on a similar scale.

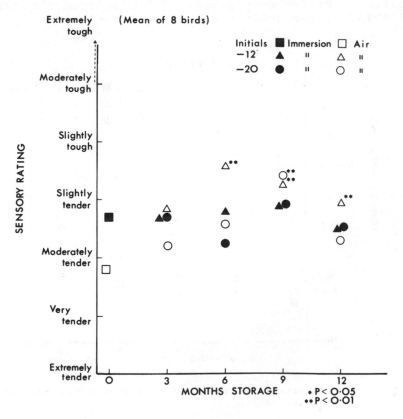

Fig.3 — Sensory ratings of the texture of chickens air- or immersion-chilled before frozen storage.

Although initially the air-chilled birds were
more tender than the immersion-chilled, this difference was not maintained throughout storage. Storage
had no significant effect on the immersion-chilled
birds but the air-chilled birds were slightly tougher
than the initials at 3 months and those stored at
-12°C significantly tougher at 6 months. Within each
group there was large bird-to-bird variation in
texture, e.g. the immersion-chilled birds stored at
-12°C for six months varied from very tender to
moderately tough: this we have observed in other
studies. There was no change in juiciness due to
method of chilling or storage.

CONCLUSION

Using the processing techniques available in the UK
in 1978, the quality of frozen birds cooled by air-
chilling was inferior to those produced by immersion-
chilling. The quality changes were smaller when
birds were stored at -20°C rather than at -12°C.
Preliminary experiments suggest that appearance could
be improved by either equilibration at 1°C or mist
spraying prior to freezing.

Chapter 4.20

Firmness of pig carcass backfat – sensory and instrumental measurements

R.C.D. Jones and E. Dransfield
ARC Meat Research Institute, Langford, Bristol BS18 7DY.

Increasingly, bacon is sold as rindless rashers in vacuum packs. If the fat is soft it appears oily, off-white and definition between rashers is lost. This unsightly defect occurs despite subjective selection of pork for curing. Judgment of carcass subcutaneous fat texture is visual, tactile and kinaesthetic; the most important attribute being hardness-softness by thumb test. In a pilot study testing judges' ability to assess backfat firmness, large differences in discrimination and reproducibility were found.

Finger forces applied to fat, and its deformation, were measured by mounting a finger operated key above the fat. The range of averaged forces was the same between soft and hard fats and between judges (25-40 N). However, all judges used similar average deformations (3-4 mm), while the corresponding range between hard and soft fats was 0.8-7 mm. Judges used similar average deformation rates (2 mm/sec) but with increasing softness the deformation rate increased from 0.5 to 5 mm/sec. The best single predictor of firmness was total deformation, which accounted for 90% of the variation in firmness judged by the experts. Variation in test conditions used by the judges meant that a comprehensive specification for an imitative objective method without feedback was impractical.

   Mechanical properties of cylinders (30 mm diam.)
of backfat compressed uniaxially by 10% in 0.5 sec at
5°C were determined from stress relaxation curves.
Equilibrium Elastic Modulus varied from 1×10^4 to
3×10^5 N/m^2, and its logarithm was related linearly
to sensory firmness. As a practical and objective
alternative to subjective assessment, a stainless steel
probe (3.5 mm diam.) was pushed into backfat at 2mm/sec.
Force at 4 mm travel correlated well (r > 0.8 for
individual judges) with their assessment of firmness.
The ratio of between to within sample variation showed
the probe to be more precise than the best judges.
This objective method could be adapted to standardise
firmness measurement of subcutaneous fat in pork and
bacon production.

Chapter 4.21

Some observations on the role of lipids in meat flavour

D.S. Mottram
ARC Meat Research Institute, Langford, Bristol BS18 7DY.

SUMMARY

The relative contributions of water-soluble and lipid components of muscle to flavour development have been investigated. The triglycerides and the phospholipids were extracted from beef muscle and the aromas of the cooked materials evaluated by a sensory panel. The headspace volatiles from the same cooked meat systems were analysed by GC-MS. Removing triglycerides had little effect on the aroma of the cooked meat, but when both triglycerides and phospholipids were removed marked differences in aroma and headspace volatiles were observed.

INTRODUCTION

Intramuscular fat is believed to be important for the development of flavour during the cooking of meat. Lipids undergo thermal oxidative change producing compounds which can contribute to meat aroma, but lipids or their degradation products may also react with lean tissue components to give other flavour compounds.

To evaluate the relative contributions of lean and lipid components of muscle to flavour development, the triglycerides and phospholipids were removed from beef muscle by selective solvent extraction and the aroma of the remaining material assessed after cooking by a sensory panel. The

headspace volatiles from the same cooked meats were
analysed by GC-MS.

EXPERIMENTAL

Portions of freeze-dried, minced beef (M. semimem-
branosus) were treated as follows:

A.   (Control). Reconstituted to original wet
     weight by addition of distilled water, then
     cooked for 20 minutes on water bath at
     100°C.

B.   Extracted with petroleum spirit (40-60°) for
     10 h in Soxhlet apparatus and vacuum dried.
     Reconstituted and cooked as for A.

C.   As for B except extracted with constant
     boiling chloroform-methanol (87% $CHCl_3$).

D.   Extracted as C, but before reconstituting
     the water-soluble material in the
     chloroform-methanol was extracted and added
     to the meat.

The aromas of the cooked meat samples were
compared by a panel of 13 assessors who were asked
to identify the odd sample in a series of two-way
triangle tests.

The headspace volatiles from the cooked meat
samples (100 g) held at 60°C were entrained on traps
containing 100 mg Tenax GC using nitrogen (50 ml
min^{-1}) for 16 h. The trapped volatiles were therm-
ally desorbed (250°C) onto a cooled CW2OM capillary
column in Finnigan 4000 GC-MS.

RESULTS

The panel were unable to distinguish the aromas of
the control and petroleum spirit defatted samples
(triglycerides and small amount of phospholipids
removed), but found a highly significant difference
when either was compared with the $CHCl_3$ defatted
material (phospholipids removed as well as
triglycerides) (Table 1). When water soluble
material from the chloroform-methanol extract was
added back to the $CHCl_3$ defatted meat, the cooked
aroma was indistinguishable from that of the simple

CHCl$_3$, defatted material. The aromas of control and petroleum spirit defatted samples were both described as meaty, while both types of CHCl$_3$ defatted meat had roast or toasted aromas.

Table 1 — Comparison of aromas of defatted, cooked beef using 2-way triangle tests, showing proportion of panelists correctly choosing odd sample.

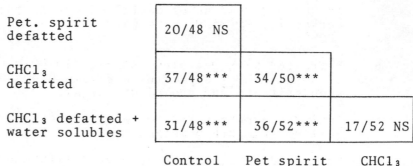

	Control	Pet spirit defatted	CHCl$_3$ defatted
Pet. spirit defatted	20/48 NS		
CHCl$_3$ defatted	37/48***	34/50***	
CHCl$_3$ defatted + water solubles	31/48***	36/52***	17/52 NS

NS = not significant;   *** = $\underline{P}$ < 0.001.

The GC profiles for the headspace volatiles from the control and petroleum spirit defatted samples were similar, and the major components were aliphatic alcohols and aldehydes. The CHCl$_3$ defatted samples had markedly different GC profiles; the quantities of aliphatic aldehydes were considerably reduced and only traces of aliphatic alcohols were found, while large amounts of pyrazines were obtained as well as increased levels of benzaldehyde.

DISCUSSION

Some lipid appears to be essential to give cooked meat aroma, but the phospholipids provide sufficient for the aroma development. Lipid degradation during cooking gives volatile products which contribute to the aroma, but lipid degradation products may also interact with components in the lean. Removing all lipid with chloroform-methanol considerably enhanced pyrazine formation in the cooked material. Pyrazines are formed in the Maillard reaction between amino acids and sugars and it is postulated that during cooking of normal meat, pyrazine formation is inhibited by the interaction of lipids, or their degradation products, with the intermediates of the amino acid-sugar reactions.

SENSORY AND INSTRUMENTAL METHODS AND THEIR APPLICATION TO SPECIFIC PRODUCTS

(d)   Dairy Products

Chapter 4.22

Aspects of sensory quality in milk and unfermented milk products

M.J.A. Schröder
National Institute for Research in Dairying, Shinfield, Reading, UK.

SUMMARY

This paper outlines studies on sensory changes in whole milk under different circumstance and considers briefly, similar changes in the unfermented milk products, skim milk, cream, butter and milk powder. The following causes of potential sensory change in milk are dealt with: accidental contamination with chemicals; milk treatments, in particular thermal processing; and reactions during storage due to microbial growth, and enzymatic or oxidative activity. Some methods, sensory or instrumental, to measure actual or imminent sensory spoilage in milk and unfermented milk products are evaluated.

INTRODUCTION

Fresh cows' milk does not impart any strong sensory impressions. It is slightly sweet and has a typical, but delicate, flavour and no aftertaste. Its whiteness and smooth appearance further reinforce the blandness of its flavour and its tactual smoothness. Because of these characteristics, sensory defects in milk are readily perceived. Milk has a complex structure. It contains about 85% water in which are dissolved salts and carbohydrates and dispersed whey proteins, casein micelles and fat globules. It is also an excellent growth medium for microorganisms. In addition, milk is handled extensively between production and consumption and comes into contact with many plant surfaces, including those of the milking machine, storage tanks, tankers, processing and filling plant and finally the retail container. It is therefore hardly surprising that milk is subject to many potential sensory changes.

EXTERNAL SOURCES OF OFF-FLAVOUR IN MILK

Off-flavour development in milk may start with the cow. For example, the breathing of stale air or the eating of strongly flavoured feeds and weeds within a few hours prior to milking may give rise to taints in the milk. Since it has an aqueous and a fatty phase, milk is a solvent for many substances and also readily absorbs odours. Chemicals such as udder medications used in the treatment of mastitis, boiler compounds and cleaning fluids may accidentally contaminate milk and taint it. An example of this and one which is currently giving some concern is chlorophenol taint [1]. The chlorophenol is generally formed by reaction of phenol with chlorine [2]. The latter is widely used in the sanitization of equipment and the former is a component of some general purpose disinfectant. There is also some danger of domestic abuse of returnable milk containers and this has led to a number of dairies in the USA having to introduce contamination monitoring devices. However, the detectors are not at present fully effective in eliminating containers with signigicant levels of flavour-active chemicals [3]. In addition, plastic milk containers may become a source of off-flavour, especially due to overheating of the material, either during container manufacture or during heat sealing after filling.

In what follows, I shall discuss some important sensory changes that may occur in milk during processing and storage which originate from the milk constituents themselves. These include changes due to heat treatment, microbial growth, lipolysis and proteolysis and oxidative reactions.

HEAT-INDUCED SENSORY CHANGES IN MILK

Milk is heat processed to eliminate pathogenic microorganisms which may be present in the raw milk and to increase the shelf-life. Over 95% of milk consumed in the UK is heated and of this, over 90% is pasteurized [4]. However, in many other European countries milks with a longer life take a far greater share of the market. The three main thermal processes for milk are high-temperature-short-time (HTST) pasteurization, ultra-heat-treatment (UHT) and in-bottle sterilization. The minimum conditions for these processes, as laid down in the UK Milk Regulations, are respectively, $71.7^{\circ}C/15$ s, $132.2^{\circ}C/1$ s and $100^{\circ}C$.

The two most important heat-induced changes in milk that
affect its sensory quality are protein denaturation and the
Maillard reaction between lactose and proteins. However,
neither is important in pasteurized milk. It is the denaturation of the whey protein β-lactoglobulin that is largely
responsible for the typical 'cooked' flavour of fresh UHT milk.
The flavour is the result of the unmasking of sulphydryl (SH)
groups from which volatile sulphides are then produced. Cooked
flavour in UHT milk dissipates with storage time, the rate
depending on the level of oxygen present. When the oxidation
of the SH groups is complete, an underlying 'heated' flavour,
associated with the early stages of the Maillard reaction,
starts to predominate. The reaction continues during the
storage of UHT milk and may lead to some browning [5]. However, the Maillard reaction is far more severe in in-bottle
sterilized milk than in UHT milk, cuasing more pronounced
browning and producing 'caramelized' flavour.

A further effect of UHT and in-bottle sterilization of
milk is an aggregation of certain milk constituents, in
particular whey proteins and salts, which leads to sediment
formation and the sensory defect of 'chalkiness' or
'astringency' [5]. Sedimentation can also occur due to
homogenization of milk [6], and the fact that all milks with
an extended shelf-life have to be homogenized to prevent cream
plugging may contribute to the heat-related problem.

Sediment formation, like browning, increases during
storage, especially at ambient temperatures [5]. Finally,
both UHT and in-bottle sterilized milk may thicken during
storage but this tendency is particularly strong for UHT
milk. Heat-induced changes of the casein micelles and fat
globules are largely responsible, but the exact physico-
chemical processes are not yet understood [5].

Although heat-induced flavours in milk generally lead to
a reduction in acceptability, consumer reactions to the flavours
in this group appear to be relatively diverse. For example,
there is far greater acceptance of UHT milk in mainland Europe
than in the UK and greater acceptance of sterilized milk in the
north than in the south of the UK.

Cooked flavour intensity correlates well with the concentration of SH groups in milk and this can be measured using
chemical techniques which are suitable for control work [2].
One of the first intermediates during the Maillard reaction is hydroxymethyl furfural, and this has been used as an
indicator of thermal stress and the degree of browning [5].
However, a trained taste panel is the most suitable method of
evaluating and monitoring heat-induced sensory changes in milk,
especially since reference milks are readily prepared [2].

SENSORY CHANGES ASSOCIATED WITH MICROBIAL GROWTH (PASTEURIZED MILK)

Neither UHT milk nor in-bottle sterilized milks are necessarily strictly sterile. However, if any heat-resistant spores are present these must not germinate and multiply. In contrast the shelf-life of pasteurized milk is generally determined by the number and activity of the microorganisms present. When milk is pasteurized, only a proportion of the microorganisms present in the raw milk is killed, and a total count of about 10^3/ml, representing heat-resistant bacteria and bacterial spores, remains. These do however multiply only slowly, and sometimes not at all, if the milk is kept under efficient refrigeration, i.e. below 7°C. The spoilage of commercial pasteurized milk is commonly due to the growth of psychrotrophic Gram-negative bacteria whose presence in the milk is the result of post-pasteurization contamination (PPC); PPC generally takes place in the processing plant, especially the fillers. Among this group of organisms, pseudomonads are the most common in refrigerated pasteurized milk. Participation of the heat-resistant microflora of pasteurized milk in growth and spoilage increases with the storage temperature. As temperatures rise to 10°C or more, there is a higher proportion of defects caused by spore formers, e.g. "bitty" cream due to Bacillus cereus.

The off-flavour threshold in refrigerated commercial pasteurized milk with regard to the microbial count is fairly well defined, at about 10^8/ml, and this effectively represents the Gram-negative organisms introduced through PPC. These psychrotrophic bacteria have highly lipolytic and/or proteolytic metabolism and produce off-flavours such as "unclean", due to mixed lipolysis and proteolysis, "bitter" generally caused by proteolysis, and "fruity". The latter is a strawberry-like flavour associated with high levels of Pseudomonas fragi, an organism that produces an esterase as well as lipase [2]. Because of the low handling termperatures of today, lactic acid bacteria, which cause souring owing to their specialized glycolytic metabolism, have become less important in the spoilage of unfermented milk products.

The close relationship between bacterial contamination and sensory spoilage of commercial pasteurized milk means that the non-sensory methods to measure spoilage or predict imminent spoilage are microbiological ones and in some way estimate total count. The total count is obtained either culturally or directly, by microscopy. In addition, there are various indirect methods that respond to the metabolic activity of multiplying microbial cells, some of which give rapid results [7].

As they are heat-sensitive, psychrotrophic Gram-negative bacteria are absent from milk handled aseptically after past-eurization. In some countries, including the USA and The Netherlands, it is reported that such a situation now exists commercially to a greater or lesser degree [8]. Where this is the case, spoilage is generally due to psychrotrophic spore-formers, but at a much later stage than would have been the case if PPC had occurred, and at a slightly lower total count. Typical total growth patterns in milk with and without PPC are illustrated in Figure 1.

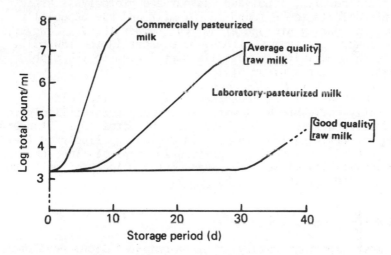

Fig.1 — Typical microbial growth patterns in UK pasteurized milk at 5°C.

Because of the extended shelf-life of pasteurized milk free from PPC, there is also the possibility of spoilage due to non-microbial causes (as discussed below). It should there-fore be apparent that in such milk the total bacterial count is not as good an indicator of spoilage as in milk with PPC.

LIPOLYZED FLAVOURS AND PROTEOLYSIS

Lipolyzed flavours in milk are caused primarily by C-4 to C-12 free fatty acids from the triglycerides which are located in the core of the milk fat globules. In freshly secreted milk, the triglycerides are surrounded, and protected from lipase attack, by the fat globule membrane. However, this membrane is easily ruptured during mechanical or temperature abuse of milk. Agitation and pumping of the raw milk or subjecting it to extreme or rapid changes in temperature increases the risk of damage to the membrane and therefore of lipolysis. The most severe treatment in this respect is the homogenization of raw milk, and immediate heat processing of such milk in order to inactivate the lipase is essential. Native milk lipase is denatured almost completely during HTST pasteurization, although certain bacterial lipases are highly thermostable. Some very important stable enzymes in milk, proteinases as well as lipases, are produced by Gram-negative psychrotrophs, e.g. pseudomonads. The presence of significant concentrations of these enzymes in pasteurized or UHT milk is associated with high levels of these psychrotrophs in the raw milk used.

In practice, because of the short shelf-life of commercial pasteurized milk, lipolyzed flavour and proteolysis are mainly defects to be found in UHT milk and are especially important during storage at ambient temperatures. However, in some cases defects may already be present in the raw milk. Proteinase activity in UHT milk contributes to the problem of gelation during storage [5].

Methods for the measurement of free fatty acids generally correlate well with sensory analysis of lipolyzed flavour, and some of them have been automated [9]. Standards used for training taste panels in evaluating lipolyzed flavour are prepared by inducing lipolysis in samples. Interestingly, the sensitivity of sensory assessment of lipolyzed milk can be increased by lowering the pH [2].

OXIDATIVE FLAVOURS

The most important catalysts of oxidative flavour developments in milk are light and copper. Lipid oxidation sometimes occurs spontaneously,, but this has been linked to naturally high copper levels in those milks [10]. Light-induced oxidations affect either the milk proteins, causing "activated" flavour, or the lipids, causing "oxidized" flavour. For the reactions to take place, oxygen, riboflavin and light of wavelengths around 450 nm, that activate riboflavin, must be present [11]. Activated flavour develops prior to oxidized flavour, i.e. within 10 min in direct sunlight, especially in homogenized milk. It disappears eventually during further light exposure to be replaced by oxidized flavour.

Sulphurous compounds in particular methional, are typical of activated flavour, whilst light-induced oxidized flavour is due mainly to oxidations involving the triglycerides. Copper-induced oxidations also affect the lipid fraction of milk and the resulting flavour is again oxidized. However, in this case it is the phospholipids of the fat globule membrane that are attacked [12]. In contrast to activated flavour, which does not necessarily lead to the rejection of milk, oxidized flavour can become very marked and objectionable, with a strong 'painty' note if light-induced and a 'cardboardy' note when copper-induced.

The level of oxygen in stored milk is important in the development of oxidative flavours. After milking, milk rapidly takes up oxygen until saturation is reached at about 10 ppm, although this depends on the temperature. Only a small proportion of this oxygen is necessary for activated and copper-induced oxidized flavour development. In contrast, light-induced oxidized flavour development relies on relatively large amounts of oxygen. About 7 ppm dissolved oxygen were found insufficient for light-induced oxidized flavour development in UHT and in-bottle sterilized milks [12]. Figure 2 illustrates the situation for in-bottle sterilized milk.

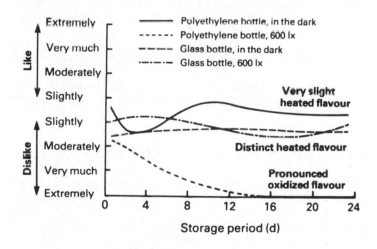

Fig. 2 – Changes in acceptability of in-bottle sterilized milk in relation to light exposure and storage container.

In recent years, light-induced flavours in milk have become a major source of consumer complaint in the USA [13]. The extended shelf-life of milk, use of translucent and oxygen-permeable containers and exposure of milk to fluorescent light in supermarkets have contributed to this trend. Similar conditions apply in Europe, too, although UHT milk is generally packaged in cartons which incorporate an aluminium foil layer, making them both opaque and oxygen-impermeable. In the UK, white polythene bottles are now common for in-bottle sterilization of milk and criticisms as a result of light-induced off-flavours have been on the increase.

In contrast to the light-induced type, copper-induced oxidized flavour, a major problem in the past, is no longer of great commercial importance, although there have been some recent reports of this defect, notably from Scandinavia.

There is at present no suitable instrumental method for the routine evaluation of light-induced flavours, but there are procedures for the preparation of reference samples of activated and copper-induced oxidized flavour for use in taste panel training [2]. Light-induced oxidized flavour can be produced by exposing milk to light for an extended period in the presence of a large oxygen supply. The thiobarbituric acid (TBA) test has been widely used to estimate total oxidation in the copper-induced reaction, but does not correlate well with flavour intensity and does not respond to light-induced lipid oxidation. Chromatographic methods can be used to monitor the concentration of the flavour active compounds, but current methods are unsuitable for routine quality control [9].

Unidentified storage flavours in milk are generally described as "stale", "flat" or "old" and may involve low levels of different types of reaction simultaneously. Such flavours vary in intensity and do not necessarily constitute a serious defect.

SENSORY QUALITY OF SOME UNFERMENTED MILK PRODUCTS

The natural flavour of unfermented milk products, i.e. skim-milk, cream, butter and reconstituted milk powder, can be described in similar terms to that of whole milk, although obviously the different fat levels affect the sensation of richness. In particular, the mouthfeel of butter differs from that of the other products, the original fat-in-water emulsion having been transformed into a water-in-fat emulsion. Un-fermented milk products are also subject to basically the same types of sensory change that occur in whole milk, the main difference being in off-flavours originating from the milk lipids.

Heating-related flavours may form in all four products. Skimmilk and cream, apart from clotted cream, would be sub-jected to one of the thermal processes described for whole milk, and a slight cooked flavour is also typical in butter and milk powder.

Skimmilks vary in fat, and the lower the amount the less likely is the development of flavours originating from the the triglycerides. For example, light-induced oxidized flavour did not develop in fully skimmed milk [12]. Skimmilk

is however not free from phospholipids, and copper-induced
oxidized flavour development is therefore possible. At the
other end of the fat content scale, flavours originating from
the triglycerides are a particular problem in cream and butter.
In these products, the development of taints, especially light
induced oxidized flavour, may start in the surface layer.

In commercially pasteurized cream as in milk, a total
microbial count in excess of 10^7/ml is generally necessary for
off-flavour to develop [14]. Both pseudomonads and bacilli
were present in cream that had spoilt at low temperatures.
The pasteurization conditions applied to cream tend to be
more severe than those for milk and this may lead to increased activation of Bacillus spores.

The sensory quality of cream and butter is related to
their viscosity as well as to flavour, and that of butter, in
addition, to water dispersion. In milk powder, homogeneity
and absence of browning are further aspects of sensory quality.

SENSORY EVALUATION OF MILK AND UNFERMENTED MILK PRODUCTS

Although from much that has been said, routine sensory
evaluation of milk and associated products would seem important to ensure good and uniform flavour, very little appears
to be done, and trained taste panels rarely exist at processing
dairies. In fact, much sensory testing of such products in
the UK appears to be limited to samples which had been rejected and returned by the consumer. However, in the context
of chlorophenol taints, the UK Milk Marketing Board is at
present preparing a code of practice which they hope will not
only provide guidance on the investigation of complaints about
chlorophenol taint, but will also encourage dairies to taste
tankerloads of milk. In some other countries, such as Finland
and some federal states in West Germany, the freedom of raw
milk from off-flavour is a legal requirement and the sensory
evaluation of raw milk therefore obligatory.

Two Standards which are relevant to the sensory evaluation of milk and related products were published in 1980.
The common categories of sensory testing of foods are set out
in the introductory part of a British Standard [15], whilst an
International Dairy Federation Standard provides a code of
practice for the sensory evaluation of dairy products, with
specific guides for butter and milk powder [16]. In addition,
a paper published by a flavour committee of the American Dairy
Science Association on off-flavours in milk [2], and especially
the part where the preparation of sensory reference standards
is described, could help in encouraging more widespread
sensory quality assurance of milk and related products.

REFERENCES

1.   Anon. The nasty taste of tainted milk. Milk Prod.
       1982, 29 (2), 24.

2.   Shipe, W.F.; Bassette, R.; Deane, D.D.; Dunkley, W.L.;
       Hammond, E.G.; Harper, W.J.; Kleyn, D.H.; Morgan,
       M.E.; Nelson, J.H.; Scanlan, R.A. Off flavours in
       milk: nomenclature, standards and bibliography.
       J. Dairy Sci. 1978, 61, 855-869.

3.   Bodyfelt, F.W.; Landsberg, J.D.; Morgan, M.E.
       Implications of surface contamination on multiuse
       milk containers. In "Surface Contamination.
       Genesis, Detection, and Control. Vol.2" (Mittal,
       K.L., Ed.) Plenum Press, New York, USA, 1979,
       1009-1032.

4.   Federation of UK Milk Marketing Boards, U.K. Dairy Facts
       and Figures: 1981.

5.   Blanc, B.; Odet, G. New monograph on UHT milk.
       Appearance, flavour and texture aspects: recent
       developments. Int. Dairy Fed. Bull. Document 133,
       1981, 25-48.

6.   Trout, G.M. Homogenized Milk, Michigan State, College
       Press, East Lansing, USA, 1950.

7.   Pettipher, G.L. Rapid methods for assessing bacterial
       numbers in milk. Dairy Ind. Int. 1981, 46 (11),
       15-22.

8.   Langeveld, L.P.M.; Cuperus, F.; van Breemen, P.; Dijkers,
       J. A rapid method for the detection of post-
       pasteurization contamination in HTST pasteurized
       milk. Neth. Milk Dairy J. 1976, 30, 157-173.

9.   Shipe, W.F. Analysis and control of milk flavor. In
       "The Analysis and Control of Less Desirable flavors
       in Food and Beverages". (Charalambous, G., Ed.),
       Academic Press, New York, 1980, 201-239.

10.   Bruhn, J.C.; Franke, A.A.; Goble, G.S. Factors relating
       to development of spontaneous oxidized flavour in
       raw milk. J. Dairy Sci. 1976, 59, 828-833.

11.   Stull, J.W. The effect of light on activated flavor
       development and on the constituents of milk and its
       products: a review. J. Dairy Sci. 1953, 36,
       1153-1164.

12.   Schröder, M.J.A. The effect of oxygen on the keeping
           quality of milk. I. Oxidized flavour development
           and oxygen uptake in milk in relation to oxygen
           availability. J. Dairy Res. 1982. (In press).

13.   Thomas, E.L. Trends in milk flavours. J. Dairy Sci.
           1981, 64, 1023-1027.

14.   Griffiths, M.W.; Phillips, J.D.; Muir, D.D. Development
           of flavour defects in pasteurized double cream
           during storage at 6°C and 10°C. J. Soc. Dairy
           Technol. 1981, 34, 142-146.

15.   British Standard BS 5929: Part I, Methods for the
           sensory analysis of food, 1980.

16.   International Dairy Federation, International IDF
           Standard 99: Sensory evaluation of dairy products,
           1980.

Chapter 4.23

Flavoured dairy products: sensory and stability problems

W. Grab
Givuadan Dubendorf AG, CH–8600 Dubendorf, Switzerland.

SUMMARY

The influence of various components on sensory and stability properties of flavourings in dairy products (ice-cream, yoghurt, UHT-milk) is discussed with special emphasis on the physico-chemical, physiological, technical and marketing aspects.

INTRODUCTION

Flavour is one important factor to be taken into account when developing a successful food product. The flavour interacts strongly with various factors of a food; other ingredients and technology strongly influence the physico-chemical behaviour of flavour components. Physiology, psychology and the social environment of the consumer influence the perception of the flavour and therefore the acceptance of the food. Marketing combines the needs and wishes of the consumer with the possibilities of product development to launch new products. To be successful, all the above factors must be well balanced. With a few examples from our work, I shall consider some of the problems which have to be considered when developing a new flavour for dairy products.

MARKETING OF DAIRY PRODUCTS

Milk is an important nutritious, healthy and nearly complete food. As a raw material milk is used to produce many different products (Table 1), cheese,

butter and powdered milk being the most important
ones.

Table 1 — Flavoured dairy products

FLAVOURED DAIRY PRODUCTS		MAIN FLAVOUR TYPES	
MILK	PASTEURIZED UHT MILK SHAKE	COCOA	STRAWBERRY VANILLA BANANA
CHEESE	PROCESSED FRESH	HAM	HERBS SPICES
SOUR MILK PRODUCTS	YOGHURT KEFIR	STRAWBERRY	FRUITS
EDIBLE ICE	ICE-CREAM MILK ICE SHERBET SORBET SOFT ICE PRODUCTS	VANILLA	CHOCOLATE STRAWBERRY
SWEET DESSERTS PUDDING	FLAN CREAM CUSTARD MOUSSE	VANILLA	CHOCOLATE CARAMEL

Givaudan is especially interested in flavoured
dairy products, which offer the dairy industry the
opportunity to diversify their product ranges. The
consumption of milk has decreased in many countries
in the last few years [1]. On the other hand, the
consumption of other dairy products is showing progressively increasing sales, especially when flavoured
(Table 2).

In general, the consumer is very conservative
and does not accept all flavour types. Vanilla and
cocoa followed by strawberry are by far the most
important ones as far as dairy products are concerned.
Experiments with other flavours are seldom successful
world-wide.

THE CONSUMER

The consumer is also conservative in his eating habits.
Less than 10% are susceptible to new ideas and will
accept new products instantly. This slow change in
eating habits has however been accelerated by international contacts and by the availability of inter-

national food throughout the year.

Table 2 — Consumption of milk products.

| | PER CAPITA CONSUMPTION | | |
	Fresh Milk kg (1977)	Yoghurt kg (1980)	Ice-Cream l (1978)
France	76 →	9 ↗	4 ↗
W-Germany	70 ↘	7 ↗	7 ↗
Switzerland	115 ↘	14 ↗	7 ↗
UK	139 ↘	4 ↗	6 ↗
USA	126 ↘	2 ↗	24 →

Nostalgia and the housewife's feeling of responsibility towards the family direct her to "natural"
food. "Natural" is to be understood in two ways -
from the legislative standpoint and from the point of
view of providing true to nature sensation when
consumed.

ACCEPTANCE: PHYSIOLOGICAL AND PSYCHOLOGICAL ASPECTS

Many factors influence the individual flavour perception: Momentary mental state (is the body ready to
taste and smell?); Expectations (form and colour
influence your expectations); Experience (do you know
an exotic fruit?); Memory (you can remember the taste
but you cannot correlate it with a food); Environmental factors (the flavour of a wine is perceived
quite differently when you drink it at a dinner or
in a mountain refuge); Attitude; Motivation; Errors;
Attentiveness; Adaptation.

Take strawberry as an example and imagine its
smell and taste. Is it green, ripe, overripe, fresh,
cooked, jam, frozen, thawed, a particular species or
"artificial"?

ADAPTATION

Adaptation protects the brain from the wealth of
information that is continually being provided by
the sensory organs to recognize new situations. All
senses show the phenomenon of adaptation. In flavour

work we use this effect to differentiate between two very similar products. By saturating the nose with one product, and then immediately sniffing another or vice versa we can recognise small differences. A problem arises (from this effect) when testing and comparing different flavours: they influence each other and an objective comparison is occasionally impossible.

INTERACTION WITH FOOD INGREDIENTS

It is important to test flavours in the appropriate food system and at optimal dosage for the product. It is not feasible to screen flavours on blotting-papers like perfumes. Ingredients in a food such as fat, protein, sugar, sweeteners, acids, minerals, additives as well as time of equilibration, strongly influence the perception and the behaviour of a flavour. Stabilizers too, especially gelatine (Table 3), may kill or upset the balance of a flavour.

Table 3 — Stabilizers that adversely affect flavour.

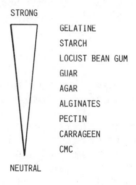

To measure the interactions these compounds have with flavours, we use quantitative headspace analysis techniques. The flavour components are absorbed on small filters, desorbed with a solvent and analyzed by gas chromatography and mass spectrometry. By careful work the standard deviation of the results can be reduced to less than 10%. Quantitative headspace analyses of this nature are very informative instrumental methods for analysing even small sensory changes in a flavour. Two examples of this will be discussed.

The γ-nonalactone content in the headspace of a
single ripening strawberry shows a maximum every day
at noon (Fig.1)[2].

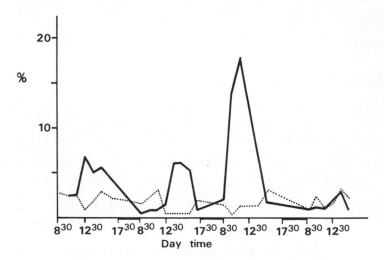

Fig. 1 — Daily variation in the headspace concentration of γ—nonalactone (————)
and butane-2-ol-3-one (. . . . . .) in a strawberry fruit (var. Reife Erdbeere)

Figure 2 show the influence of a food on the headspace concentration of various flavour components.

A high fat content drastically reduces the
headspace concentration. This reduction compares
well with our experience: the dosage of a flavour in
ice-cream is normally double the dosage in milk.
Here we measured a factor of 2 - 4. These components
are unaffected during the first 4 days: measurements
of the headspace concentration show no difference
after 1 day and 4 days. On the other hand, aldehydes
and ethyl-maltol concentrations decline in water, milk
and ice mix after 4 days at room temperature, probably
because aldehydes are prone to oxidation and may react
with proteins.

To get a comparable odour impression in different foods, the quantitative and qualitative composition in the headspace over the food must be the same.
From the different partitions the necessary correction
of the concentration in the liquid phase can be calculated.

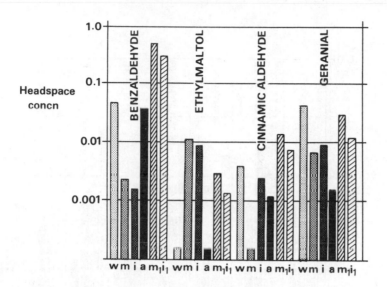

Fig.2 — Effect of food on the headspace concentration of flavour components.

Key: w = water, m = milk, i = ice mix, a = archid oil,
     m_i = milk 1 day, i_i = ice mix 1 day.

During my analytical work I have observed many
types of reaction products of flavour components with
each other, solvents and food ingredients (Fig. 4).

In a natural apple distillate many kinds of
acetals can be identified. These have to be considered
as reaction products of the corresponding aldehydes
and alcohols also present in this substrate. Grape
and mandarin flavours were found to be unstable in
yoghurt. After a short time, a bitter, musty taste
developed. We assume that the common methyl anthran-
ilate of the flavours reacted with the acetaldehyde
of yoghurt to yield this "off-flavour". Similarly,
raspberry flavour developed a strong, sharp "off-note"
which we associate with acetyl crotonate, a reaction
product of ethyl acetoacetate and acetaldehyde. After
long storage a pineapple flavour developed an off-
flavour, which was attributed to benzyl acetate, an
interesterification product of odourless triacetin
with benzyl alcohol.

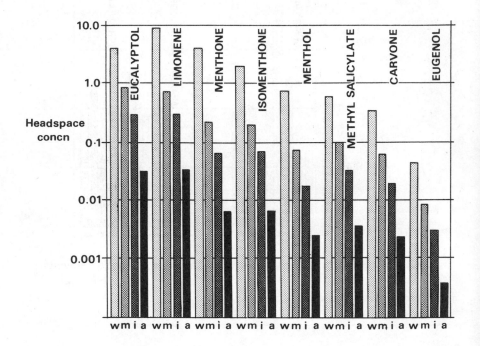

Fig. 3 — Distribution factor between headspace and liquid phase.

All these interactions are time dependant; as a rule therefore, a flavour should not be tested after its application to a food. At such a time it would seem unbalanced and harsh, because flavours are built up to develop during the normal shelf-life of the food. Examples of minimum equilibrium time are given in Table 4.

Table 4 — Minimum equilibrium time.

Sugar water	4 hours
Milk drink, yoghurt	24 hours
Ice-cream, pudding, UHT milk	48 - 72 hours
Cheese	7 days

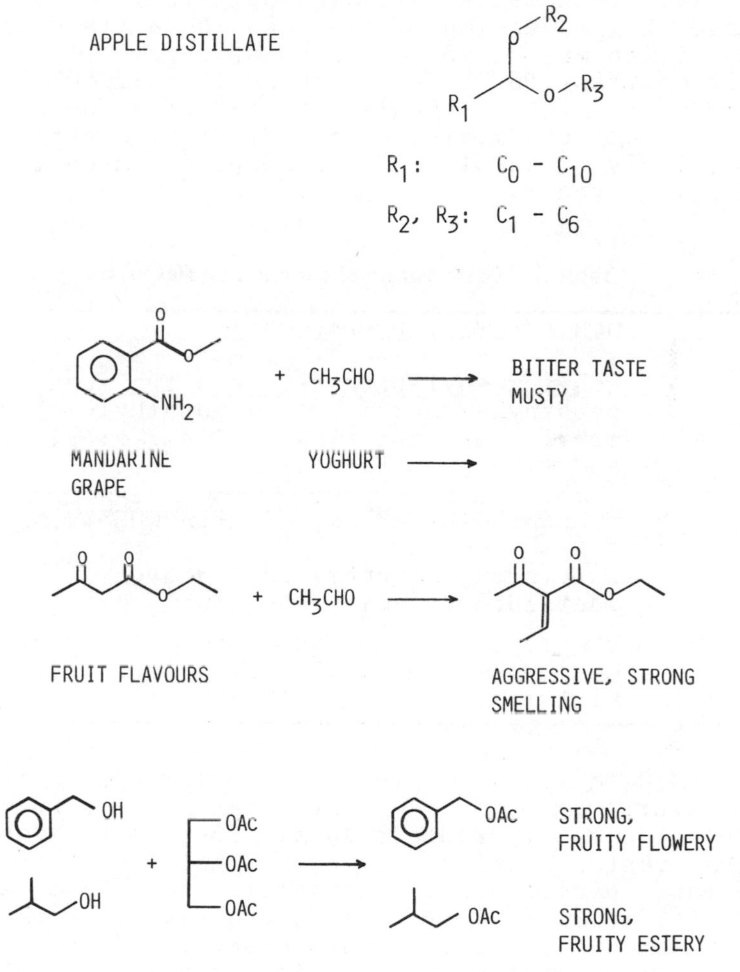
APPLE DISTILLATE
R2
R3
R1
R1: C0 - C10
R2, R3: C1 - C6
NH2
+ CH3CHO
BITTER TASTE
MUSTY
MANDARINE
GRAPE
YOGHURT
FRUIT FLAVOURS
+ CH3CHO
AGGRESSIVE, STRONG
SMELLING
OH
OAc
OAc
OAc
OH
OAc
STRONG,
FRUITY FLOWERY
OAc
STRONG,
FRUITY ESTERY

Fig.4 – Reactions of flavour components.

Another problem in flavour application is the "undesirable flavour" of many food ingredients. In general, a bad odour cannot be neutralized just by adding a flavour. At best, it can be masked by, or incorporated into the flavour. A better solution would be to look for an odourless raw material or to deodorize it before its use.

The trend of the consumer towards "natural" as
opposed to synthetic products has been anticipated by
the flavour industry. Modern analytical techniques
enable the production of flavours whose taste and
composition are close to the natural product. This
is in contrast to "old-fashioned" flavours which were
based on relatively simple mixtures of a few artificial impact chamicals, combined with essential oils.
Table 5 gives examples of the compounds used in old
and new flavours.

Table 5 — Composition of old and new flavours.

OLD ARTIFICIAL FLAVOURS:

Ethyl methyl-phenyl-glycidate; methyl-
naphthyl-ethers; methyl-naphthyl-ketones;
ethyl-vanillin; ethyl-maltol; allyl caproate;
and simple combinations.

MODERN NATURE IDENTICAL FLAVOURS:

saturated, unsaturated aldehydes,
acetaldehyde, cis-3-hexenal.

reactive hydroxy-, sulfur- and nitrogen
compounds; furaneol; mercaptans; complex
mixtures.

Modern flavours are more complex and nearer to
the natural product. A flavourist now has many
nature identical products in his repertory. Some are
rather unstable and reactive, so that new flavours
are more susceptible to instability than "old fashion-
ed" artificial flavours. Today, stringent stability
tests and quality control are essential in the development of a new flavour. It is not only synthetic
materials which cause problems; raw natural materials
also give problems. To comply with rigorous legislative regulations, we looked at and found traces of
"artefacts" in so-called natural raw materials: for
example, ethyl-vanillin in vanilla beans, perfumery
materials in "natural" honey absolute and allyl
caproate in "natural" pineapple essence.

EFFECTS OF PROCESSING

The heat processing of food greatly influences its
flavour. While it can preserve the natural flavour

by careful inactivation of the enzymes, and during concentration and preservation stages, treatments may also
alter flavour in a more or less desirable manner. A
heat-induced flavour as it may occur in UHT milk cannot be neutralized, but it could be incorporated into
the finished flavour. "Brown" flavours, such as
caramel, chocolate, vanilla, nuts are maintained well,
whereas fruit flavours are seldom suitable in over-
heated milk. The UHT process as well as altering the
flavour of the milk can have a strong influence on
flavours: heat treatment and evaporation result in a
loss of 25 - 35% of a flavour. In a UHT-stability
test we check our flavours and see whether the loss
can be corrected by a higher dosage, or whether severe
changes in the flavour character make it unsuitable
for this application. Figure 4 shows a typical test
carried out in our laboratories.

MILK	MILK
ADD 100% FLAVOUR	HEAT
HEAT	ADD 75% FLAVOUR

TRIANGLE PREFERENCE TEST

STABLE	NO DIFFERENCE
STABLE PREFERENCE	DIFFERENCE
NOT STABLE	DIFFERENCE PREFERENCE

Fig.4 — UHT stability test.

In general, a flavour should be added to a food
as late as possible in the technological process.
Even after heat treatment, remaining traces of enzymatic activity can cause loss of flavour during storage.

Fading of the flavour in ice cream during storage
is a phenomenon that is not yet solved. At $-20^{\circ}C$ ice
cream still contains concentrated liquid globules in
the frozen phase. It seems possible that even at this
low temperature, physico-chemical processes are going
on to reduce the flavour perception.

CONCLUSION

The flavour is just one important aspect in a dairy product. The behaviour of the flavour in the food matrix and its perception by the consumer are very complex. Not all the associated phenomena are understood but modern analytical methods like quantitative headspace analysis are helping to solve some of the problems.

ACKNOWLEDGEMENTS

I thank my colleagues, especially Mr R. Schnell, for their help in preparing this manuscript and Mr F. Etzweiler and Mr S. Zehnder for measuring the headspace concentrations.

REFERENCES

1.   Anon. Bulletin of the International Dairy Federation 1963 - 1979.
2.   Grab, W. Changes in strawberry flavour during ripening, processing and storage. Berichte Int. Fruchtsaft-Union, 1978, 15, 213.
3.   Etzweiler, F.; Neuner, N.; Senn, E. Einsatz der quantitativen Headspace Analyse zur Untersuchung des Verhaltens von Riechstoffen in Seifen und Detergentien. Seifen, Oele, Fette, Wachse, 1980, 106, 419.

Poster

Chapter 4.24

Potato-like off flavour in smear coated cheese: a defect induced by bacteria

J.P. Dumont
L.A.O.A., I.N.R.A. 44072 Nantes Cedex, France.
R. Mourgues
L.M.L.G.A., I.N.R.A., 78350 Jouy-en-Josas, France.
J. Adda
Lab. Aromes, I.N.R.A., 21034 Dijon Cedex, France.

SUMMARY

Outbreaks of potato-like off-flavour sometimes occur among smear-coated surface ripened cheeses. Both the volatiles and the live microbial flora from defective samples of the Munster type were investigated. Odour assessments gave evidence that psychrophilic organisms of the *Pseudomonas* family were responsible for the potato smell. Analysis by GC-MS of cheese volatiles and headspaces taken from cultures of the suspected strain made clear that the defect could be associated with 2-methoxy-3-isopropylpyrazine.

INTRODUCTION

Bitterness, excessive pungency and saltiness probably rank as the three main flavour defects found in cheeses. Occasionally, peculiar off-flavours are encountered, some of which are described as catty flavour/ribes-like [1], fruity [2] and stable-like [3].

Although a light earthy note may be desirable in some types of cheese (e.g. Saint Nectaire cheeses made on the farm), most people consider the strong earthy and musty flavour which sometimes develops in smear-coated cheeses as objectionable. This defect, usually referred to as 'potato-like off-flavour' develops suddenly towards the end of the ripening period when most of the wild microbial strains have already died.

The output of the dairy is usually only affected
for a short time but, in some instances, the disease
seems to spread and settle as happened in the Munster
cheese factory from which we obtained the samples
studied. Figure 1 summarises our general approach
in investigating this problem.

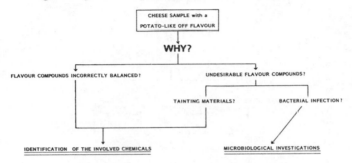

Fig. 1 — Scheme for investigating 'potato-like' off-flavour in cheese.

METHODS AND RESULTS

Volatiles were isolated from the cheese by distillation *in vacuo* [4] and then extracted from the aqueous
distillates by $CFCl_3$ after the pH was adjusted to
either 1 or 9. In this way volatiles were distributed into four fractions (acidic, acidic + neutral,
neutral + basic, basic). Preliminary experiments had
suggested that the potato-like smell was associated
with the basic fractions. In later experiments,
only the basic fraction was investigated.

Concentration and analysis of the $CFCl_3$ extract
was carried out as described previously [5]. Smelling the effluent at the exit port of the GC column
was useful in locating relevant areas in the chromatograms. At first, GC-MS investigations were
hindered by the large quantities of carbonyl compounds in the extracts. For instance, the retention
time of 2-nonanone was very close to that of a compound with a typical potato smell. The reaction of
carbonyl compounds with Girard T reagent which
results in water-soluble derivatives was used to free
the $CFCl_3$ extracts from most of these interfering
components. GC-MS analysis of the refined extracts
revealed that 2-methoxy-3-isopropylpyrazine was the
unknown compound which had co-eluted with 2-nonanone.

In microbiological investigations (outlined in

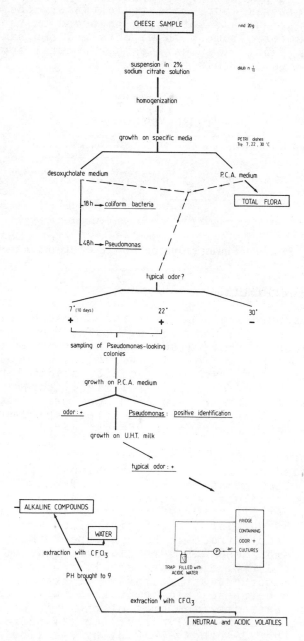

Fig. 2 — Scheme for microbial investigation of the cause of potato-like off-flavour in cheese.

Fig. 2) the criterion used for strain selection
was the ability to produce the potato-like odour.
GC-MS analysis of the volatiles trapped from the
atmosphere of the refrigerator, led to the isolation
and the positive identification of 2-methoxy-3-
isopropylpyrazine.

Further investigations indicated that the alkyl
pyrazine content of the cheese was particularly high.
This agrees with earlier work with Gruyère samples
which had a similar flavour defect [6]. However, no
link has yet been found between alkyl pyrazines and
2-methoxy-3-isopropylpyrazine. The latter compound
is known to possess a very low threshold (around
1 in 10^{-12}) and to have a raw potato-like odour. It
was found for the first time in a foodstuff by
Murray *et al.* [7], and its production by strains of
Pseudomonas has also been reported [8]. According
to the present work, only minute concentrations of
2-methoxy-3-isopropylpyrazine are needed to impart a
typical potato-like off-flavour to cheese. Levels
above the critical threshold level can occasionally
be met as a result of the activity of a psychrophilic flora which can survive in the conditions
used for making cheeses of the smear-coated type.

REFERENCES

1. Badings, H.T.   Causes of ribes flavour in cheese.
   J.Dairy Sci. 1967, 50, 1347-1351.
2. Bills, D.D.; Morgan, M.E.; Libbey, L.M.; Day, E.A.
   Identification of compounds responsible for
   fruity flavour of experimental Cheddar cheese.
   J.Dairy Sci. 1965, 48, 1168-1173.
3. Dumont, J.P.; Roger, S.; Cerf, P.; Adda. J.
   Étude de composés volatils neutres présents
   dans le Vacherin. Lait 1974, 54, 243-251.
4. Dumont, J.P.; Roger, S.; Adda, J.   Étude des
   composés volatils neutres présents dans les
   fromages à pâte molle et à croûte lavée. Lait
   1974, 54, 31-43.
5. Dumont, J.P.; Rousseaux, P.; Adda, J.   Exemple de
   variation de l'arôme à l'intérieur d'un même
   type de fromage : le Comté. Lebensm.-Wiss. u.
   Technol. 1981, 14, 198-202.
6. Dumont, J.P.; Roger, S.; Adda, J.   Mise en
   évidence d'un composé à hétérocycle azoté
   responsable d'un défaut d'arôme dans le Gruyère
   de Comté. Lait 1975, 55, 479-487.

7. Murray, K.E.; Shipton, J.; Whitfield, F.B.
   2-Methoxypyrazines and the flavour of green
   peas. Chem.Ind. (4 July, 1970), 897-898.
8. Morgan, M.E.; Libbey, L.M.; Scanlan, R.A.
   Identify of the musty potato aroma compound in
   milk cultures of *Pseudomonas taetrolens*.
   J.Dairy Sci. 1972, 55, 666.

INFLUENCE OF SENSORY QUALITY ON FOOD CHOICE AND INTAKE

Chapter 5.1

Sensory qualities, palatability of food and overweight

J.E.R. Frijters
Department of Human Nutrition, Agricultural University, Wageningen, The Netherlands.

SUMMARY

As it is often thought that overweight individuals have a "sweet tooth", the evidence for a heightened preference by such people for sweetness has been reviewed. Sensory sensitivity and the perception of intensity of odour and taste stimuli appear to be similar in adult people differing in body fatness. The relationship between body weight and sweetness pleasantness, and food palatability is affected by other variables such as food deprivation and external responsiveness. However, at present there is no single coherent theory to describe sweetness pleasantness on the basis of stimulus attributes and internal physiological and psychological parameters.

INTRODUCTION

There are several popular beliefs on the causes of excess body fatness, and also on the eating habits of people who are overweight. The term, obesity has been introduced to refer to people who are overweight. Overweight and body fatness are readily associated with an intake of more energy than is needed for the performance of physical activities and the maintenance of bodily functions. While it is true, that for some period during the dynamic phase of the development of obesity, a surplus of energy is needed, the majority of laboratory and observational studies have not shown that obese people consume more on one particular occasion than their lean counterparts [1]. The same conclusion can also be drawn from a review [2] of food consumption studies designed to estimate energy intake on the basis of one or more days. Other beliefs about the eating behaviour of overweight people are related to the style and speed of eating, the duration of their meals, and emotional and environmental factors affecting the initiation of eating. Recent literature on these aspects has been reviewed by Spitzer and Rodin [3].

A commonly held belief of the layman is that overweight people have a "sweet tooth". Some investigators [4] have considered the "sweet tooth" to be a potential factor in the genesis of obesity, because a high preference for sweet foods, that is energy-rich foods, would possibly result in a higher intake of energy. Thus, it is appropriate that the taste quality sweetness is the main topic of this paper.

While it may be obvious to the layman what it is to have a "sweet tooth", this concept can be interpreted in at least two ways. It can be considered : (i) as a greater preference for sweet foods by people who are overweight; or (ii) as a greater preference for high than for low sweetness intensities.

ATTITUDES TO SWEET FOODS AND CHOICES OF SUGAR FOODS

The first interpretation, that overweight people have a greater preference for sweet foods than people of normal weight, was studied by Meiselman [5] in a population of 4000 soldiers They were given a list of 378 food items, and were asked to state their preference for each item on a nine category hedonic scale, and the desired frequency for eating each item. It was found that 40% of the 50 top foods were sweet. Further analysis of three weight categories, underweight, normal weight and overweight, showed that there was no difference in the preference for sweet foods such as desserts, beverages and fruits, between the three groups. Meiselman used a question-naire to study food preferences, which reflect attitudes. Most food consumption surveys do not measure attitudes, but only the types and amounts of foods actually consumed by means of self-report questionnaires or diary method.

In two earlier food consumption studies [6,7], no relationship was found betweeen weight and height, and sugar intake which was considered to be a behavioural parameter for sweetness preference. Another investigation [8] reported that the heavier businessmen in a population of 415 had a lower sugar intake than their colleagues of normal weight. This finding was similar for both the group who had deliberately restricted their sugar intake and the group who had not. The daily sugar intake of 4907 adolescents was studies in a Ten

State Nutrition Survey in the USA [9]. The population was divided into three groups on the basis of the triceps skinfold thickness; lean, medium and obese. Foods containing sugar which were surveyed included jams, jellies, icings, candies, honey, and carbonated and non-carbonated soft drink, but desserts were excluded. The population was subdivided into 24 categories according to age, race, sex and fatness. The subsequent statistical analysis did not reveal a significant relationship between fatness and sugar intake.

Food consumption studies of this type are useful, but should be interpreted with caution because of possible confounding variables. For example, overweight people may not accurately report food intakes [10] because of a tendency to give socially desirable responses. In addition, differences between populations with respect to age, social class and subculture make it difficult to generalize from findings of individual studies. Although, the available evidence is not conclusive, there does not appear to be a clear relationship between body fatness and the consumption of foods with a higher sugar content.

SENSORY FACTORS IN SWEETNESS PERCEPTION

The second interpretation of the "sweet tooth", as a greater preference for high sweetness than for low sweetness intensities, has received considerable interest in psychophysical laboratory studies. Unlike the approach of attitude surveys and food consumption studies, the basis of these experiments is that the "sweet tooth" may stem from different sensory functioning in those who are overweight, or from other psychosensory factors. This approach focuses on three closely related aspects; the ability to detect sweetness at low stimulus intensities, the psychophysical function between sugar concentration in a given food and the perceived sweetness intensity, and the psychohedonic relationship between perceived intensity and experienced pleasantness (hedonic or affective value) [cf. 11, 12]. Although a number of studies have been done, only one study [13] has systematically dealt with all three aspects.

Grinker et al. [14] were the first to study sensitivity to sucrose sweetness of normal and obese men and women of various ages. They used a signal detection procedure and one fixed concentration of sucrose of 0.175% (wt/vol) in distilled water at $34^{\circ}C$. After termination of the experiment the mean value of d', a measure of sensory sensitivity or discriminability [15], was calculated. The analysis did not show a significant difference between the value of the group of normal weight and the mean value of the overweight groups.

Frijters and Rasmussen-Conrad [13] studied two groups of women, one of normal weight and the other overweight, in an age range of 24 to 53 years. None of these women were smokers, receiving medication or were dieting at the time of the study. A range of six sucrose solutions in distilled water was prepared. Each concentration was presented three times to each subject together with a sample of distilled water. The discriminability functions for both groups were calculated, and the differential thresholds were determined. The values obtained were not statistically significantly different, being 0.0037 and 0.0040 mol/1 for the normal weight and the overweight women respectively. Recently [16] a value of 0.0036 mol/1 was reported for the sucrose threshold for a normal weight population, age range 20-45 years. It is interesting to note that both studies used a paired-comparison forced-choice procedure. These values, however, are lower than 0.01 mol/1 reported to be the median of values obtained in earlier studies [17].

Malcolm et al. [18] studied detection and recognition thresholds of three groups of subject; juvenile- onset obese, adult-onset obese and normal weight (never been obese). Statistical analysis did not reveal any significant differences between weight groups, even though the numerical values of the mean detection thresholds were not specified in their paper. Thresholds for sodium chloride (salty), hydrochloric acid (sour) and urea (bitter) were also investigated, but no differences between weight groups were observed. Thus from these experiments it may be concluded that body weight is not related to the sensitivity for low taste stimulus intensities.

The relationship between sucrose concentration and perceived sweetness intensity has been subject of several studies. In two of these studies [14, 19], a magnitude estimation procedure was used in combination with a sip and spit procedure to obtain psychophysical functions of the type, $I = kS^n$, in which I is the perceived sweetness intensity, S is the sugar concentration, and k and n are constants to be estimated. There were no significant differences between the psychophysical functions of different weight groups in both studies. From a more recent description [20] of Grinker's original study, the present author has estimated the exponents of the functions from the data in her Figure 1 (Clear Condition). The values obtained are 1.06, 0.96 and 1.20 for, respectively the normal weight, moderately obese and extremely obese group. The psychophysical power function for benzaldehyde odour (food related odour of bitter almonds) for a group of obese and a group of normal weight subjects was also reported not to be different [21].

Frijters and Rasmussen [13] used a similar experimental procedure and found mean individual exponents of 1.40 and 1.51 for, respectively, the normal weight and overweight women. These values are not statistically different; they are within the expected range since it was noted [22] that most exponential values for sucrose obtained with a sip and spit procedure fall within the range of 1.3 - 2.0. It should be noted that the standard deviations of the mean exponents are 0.41 and 0.47 respectively. From this observation it can be concluded that the sensory variability of both weight groups is about the same.

The final conclusion from these scaling experiments is that overweight and normal weight subjects do not differ with respect to neural functioning and sensory processing in the perception of sugar sweetness. This conclusion is supported by the findings in other studies with greater external validity and using other methodology. Rodin [23] had subjects rate the perceived intensities of chocolate milkshakes to which differing amounts of sugar had been added. In another experiment [24], a group of women who were overweight and a group of normal weight were asked to judge the sweetness of glucose concentrations in unsweetened cherry "Kool-Aid". Both studies used a rating-scale procedure, and it was found that the mean intensity ratings for identical concentrations did not differ between the two weight groups. Using a similar method Witherly (unpublished doctoral thesis) found no differences between sucrose sweetness intensities of "Kool-Aid" lemonade obtained from different weight groups. Differences were also not observed between weight groups with respect to oral viscosity responses resulting from the addition of xanthum gum in apricot nectar.

The motivation for sensory studies has come from the assumption that obese and normal weight subjects may differ with respect to sensory physiological or sensory psychological functioning in the perception of taste and odour. The findings of the studies appear to be almost unanimous, that body weight is not related to detection and sensory intensity perception.

PSYCHOHEDONICS OF SWEETNESS PERCEPTION

It was also thought that weight differences are associated with differences in the affective evaluation of perceived intensities or qualities. The findings of studies in infants have supported this approach. Observations of the behaviour of infants during the first few days after birth have shown that the rate of sucking varies with the substance in the feeding bottle, water or a sugar solution [25]. An earlier study [26] showed that the volume of intake varies with the type of sugar (sucrose, dextrose, lactose or fructose) and in addition it was found that the volume of intake is affected by the birth weight of the infant. It was shown [27] that there is a positive relationship between the birth weight of the infant and the amount of sweetened formula consumed: infants weighing more than 3540 g consumed more than infants of normal or low birth weight. In a recent study [28], it was found that normal weight and fat babies had an equal preference for high glucose concentrations, but that thin babies exhibited aversion to these stimuli.

In scaling experiments, numerical responses are obtained for both the intensity and preference associated with a particular stimulus. These responses replace behavioural parameters. To separate sensory from affective factors when explaining affective response patterns of different weight categories, a two-stage research paradigm should be used. Firstly, the relationship between a range of sugar concentrations and the corresponding sweetness intensities should be investigated to obtain the psychophysical function, Secondly, the relationship between these perceived intensities and the corresponding affective values should be studied, so that a psychohedonic function can be obtained [cf.29]. This proposal can be considered to be ideal because in all studies, except one, sweetness pleasantness was studied by establishing a direct relationship between sugar concentration and the hedonic dimension. However, it must be admitted that this approach is acceptable in the light of the evidence available, because the mediating sensory intensity was shown to be independent of body fatness.

It has been shown that the hedonic function for sweetness increases up to a certain point (that is, an ideal point) and then decreases. It is therefore one of the single-peaked preference functions, as referred to by Coombs [30]. Thus, sweetness pleasantness increases with sweetness intensity up to a certain peak value, after which sweetness pleasantness decreases with further increments of sweetness intensity [31-33]. If body fatness is associated with the affectivity for sweetness it can be expected that the psychohedonic functions for sweetness will vary with weight. The "sweet tooth" of obese people would result in a peak of the function at high sweetness intensity.

The first study in which differences between weight groups were reported was based on a paired comparison and on a category rating-scale procedure [14]. Both methods yielded concordant results showing a neutral rating of normal weight subjects for most sucrose concentrations; the most preferred sweetness corresponded to concentrations between 6 and 11% (wt/vol). Obese subjects, however, showed a different response pattern; the sweeter the solution, the more unpleasant

it becomes to the subjects. This observation has been confirmed
by others using a similar category scale procedure [34,35].
In two other studies [36,37], in which a negative correlation
between preference for sweetness and body weight was reported,
only one test concentration was used. Thus, these studies
provide evidence contradictory to the notion that obese
people have a "sweet tooth"

From various other category scaling experiments, it has
been concluded that there is no relationship between body
fatness and sweetness preference. This has been shown with
various substances including; sugar adultered milkshakes [23],
"Kool-Aid" lemonade [24], and sucrose dissolved in water
[18,38]. In addition, it has been shown in four consumer
surveys that there is no relationship between body weight and
the preference for varying concentrations of sugar in foods
such as, apricots, pears, peaches and vanilla ice cream [39].

There is only one experiment using a category rating-
scale procedure that reported a positive correlation between
body weight and sweetness preference [40]. A group of moderately obese and a group of extremely obese women preferred the highest concentration of a glucose range (3 mol/1),
whereas normal weight women showed a maximal preference for
about the middle concentration (1 mol/1). Magnitude estimation
has been used for both intensity and preference measurement
[19], but no differences were observed between normal weight
and obese subjects with respect to the function relating
sucrose concentration to experienced pleasantness.

Frijters and Rasmussen-Conrad [13] also measured the
affective responses to six sucrose concentrations on an un-
structured bipolar scale. A 170 mm line was bisected in the
middle, representing the ideal point of sweetness pleasantness.
If a particular stimulus was considered not to be sweet
enough, the line was marked by the subject to the left of his
ideal point. On the other hand, if a stimulus was judged as
being too sweet, the line was marked to the right of the
individual's ideal point. The distance of a mark from the
ideal point was considered to represent the discrepancy between
the sweetness affectivity of a particular stimulus and the
most preferred sweetness intensity of the individual. This
approach made it possible to determine the psychohedonic
function of each subject in the two weight groups. The
general form of the function is given as:

(i) $A = c \log I + m$.

In this expression I is the perceived intensity, A is the
sweetness pleasantness, and c and m are constants to be
estimated. Since A=0 represents the ideal point, the value

of I corresponding to this point can be calculated. The most preferred sweetness intensity was obtained by setting the equation equal to 0, finding the solution for log I, and then taking the antilogarithm. The most preferred sweetness intensity for each subject is given in Table 1.

As the psychophysical function of each subject was also available, the sucrose concentration corresponding to the most preferred sweetness intensity was easily obtained. The psychophysical function is given as:

$$(ii) \qquad I = kS^n.$$

In this equation, S is sucrose concentration (mol/l), I is perceived sweetness intensity, and k and n are constants. Since A is equal to (i), the following expression was derived;

$$(iii) \qquad A = c(n \log S + \log k) + m$$

Thus, substitution of the psychophysical function into the psychohedonic function produced the preference function that related sugar concentration to the degree of preference, with the ideal point as reference. After calculation of equation (iii) for each subject, A was set equal to 0, in order to obtain the log value of the sucrose concentration corresponding to the most preferred sweetness. The antilogarithms are given in Table 1. From the statistical analyses, it can be concluded that the two weight groups did not differ with respect to the mean most preferred sweetness intensity, and the mean sucrose concentration required to obtain this intensity.

In summary, the overall conclusions of the studies discussed are two-fold. Firstly, the infant studies showed that the heavier babies drank more of a sugar-adultered substance than their lean counterparts. This may indicate a greater preference for sweetness, but it may also be indicative of a better muscular development or other motor skills. It has been noted [41] that birth weight is an inappropriate index of obesity. Secondly, there is not a simple relationship between body weight and sweetness pleasantness; either there is no correlation between body weight and sweetness pleasantness, or obese people have a lower preference for high sweetness intensities than normal weight individuals. This conclusion does not support the notion that obese people have a "sweet tooth"

Several factors may have contributed to the variation of the results reported. Firstly, widely differing methodologies have been used in the individual studies. Secondly, various populations have been used, e.g. students, hospitalized

Table 1 – Details of subjects. Adapted from Frijters, J.E.R. & Rasmussen-Conrad, E.L., J. Gen. Psychol., 1982, in press.

	OVERWEIGHT WOMEN (N=13)				NORMAL WEIGHT WOMEN (N=12)		
Subject nr.	BMI*	Most Pref. Intensity	Most Pref. Sucrose Conc. (mol/l)	Subject nr.	BMI*	Most Pref. Intensity	Most Pref. Sucrose Conc. (mol/l)
1	26.5	7.9	0.3271	14	20.8	2.7	0.0473
2	26.4	0.5	0.0542	15	20.5	3.8	0.1390
3	26.3	7.3	0.2239	16	20.2	8.0	0.2320
4	25.2	10.2	0.2312	17	21.6	4.6	0.1092
5	26.2	0.8	0.0498	18	21.8	10.6	0.2013
6	27.7	14.3	0.2367	19	21.0	28.3	0.4384
7	26.7	28.5	0.2703	20	22.0	5.1	0.1564
8	27.9	130.5	0.9020	21	21.1	6.2	0.0805
9	25.1	6.4	0.2168	22	21.8	7.9	0.1358
10	27.9	5.8	0.1392	23	21.1	16.2	0.2424
11	26.5	0.0	0.0000	24	22.1	6.6	0.1590
12	27.2	5.8	0.1268	25	21.9	16.6	0.1864
13	25.2	11.3	0.2371				
Mean	26.5	7.4**	0.1912**	Mean	21.3	7.8***	0.1542***

* BMI = Body Mass Index = weight (in kg)/ height^2 (in m). ** Geometric Mean, subject 11 excluded. *** Geometric Mean. The standard was 0.2089 mol/1 with I = 10.

and members of weight reduction programmes. Thirdly, different measures and criteria have been used to define weight categories [3, 18].

Little attention has been paid to the pre-experimental attitudes of the subjects to foods with high sugar content and to sweetness, and to the effect subjects attribute to the use of sweet substances on body weight. These and other attitudes to food and body weight may be important confounding factors in the relationship between perceived sweetness intensity and sweetness pleasantness.

In addition to these comments, it should be noted that in some of the studies reviewed, preference for sweetness has tacitly been assumed to be a constant trait of the individual. However, it may equally well be that it is dependent on the momentary bodily state, that is it varies with food deprivation, and with weight increase or weight reduction. This view is the basis of Cabanac's set-point theory of body weight as set out below.

In line with suggestions of Pfaffmann [42] and observations of Pangborn [43], the data of Thompson et al [19] were rearranged on the basis of the individual affective response patterns. Subjects with peak pleasantness ratings between 0.06 and 0.6 mol/1 sucrose were classified as Type 1, and subjects with peak pleasantness ratings above 0.6 mol/1 were classified as Type II. It was observed that a similar percentage of individuals in both weight groups fell into the Type I (curvilinear) and Type II (monotonic rising) response categories. However, Type I responders appeared to be heavier than Type II responders, a conclusion based on a within weight category analysis. It should be noted that the Type I/Type II response patterns were also observed for the pleasantness of benzaldehyde odour, and that these were not related to body weight [21]. In a recent experiment [35] using sucrose dissolved in water, most Type I responders appeared to be obese.

In other more recent experiments]24], four response patterns have been distinguished instead of two [19] or three [43]. Instead of developing a typology based on an arbitrary number of categories, it has been suggested that the peak of a preference or psychohedonic function is a continuous variable lognormally distributed over individuals, irrespective of body weight [13].

SET POINT THEORY OF BODY WEIGHT AND SENSORY PLEASANTNESS

The sweetness pleasantness of a particular sugar solution, or more generally the palatability of a particular·food, was

thought to be dependent not only on the perception of sensory
qualities and intensity, but also on the momentary body weight
of the individual [44-46]. Referred to as the set-point theory,
gustatory and olfactory pleasantness of food and the subsequent
intake are assumed to be sensitive to a particular biological
set-point weight of the body by way of a regulatory ponderostat
analogous to a thermostat. Thus, a subject will rate a
stimulus as pleasant or unpleasant partially on the basis of
its usefulness to the defense of the body weight. This
principle implies that if the momentary weight is lower (or
higher) than the set-point weight to be defended, the taste or
odour of a food is more (or less) pleasant than if the momentary
weight of the subject is at the set-point. The dependence of
stimulus pleasantness on inner state of the subject's body was
called "alliesthesia".

The physiological mechanisms of the ponderostat have not
been identified, and no specifications have been given for the
determination of the set-point weight of an individual. In
their own experiments, Cabanac and co-workers used the
magnitude of weight reduction as a result of dieting as a
measure for the discrepancy between set-point and actual body
weight. Other operational definitions [47] are based on
tables of ideal weight [48], or on weight fluctuations during
a certain period [23,49].

According to Cabanac and co-workers, the actual body
weight of obese individuals should be considered to be below
set-point because of social pressures. In agreement with this
theory, it has been found that the preference for high sweetness was greatly reduced following the ingestion of 200 ml of
25% glucose concentration for normal weight but not for obese
subjects [45, 49]. Thompson et al. [19] obtained similar
results, but interestingly only for Type II obese subjects.
Wooley et al.[38] also obtained identical results using a pre-
load of either noncaloric cyclamate or a caloric 25% glucose
solution. This observation does not support the set-point
theory, because cyclamate has no nutritive value and therefore
it cannot contribute to restoring internal equilibrium.
Negative results have also been reported by Gilbert and Hagen
[50].

Studies on the effect of dieting on sweetness preference
have produced varying results. An increase in preference
for sweetness of high intensities was found [51], but others
showed that dieting had no effect [35,40].

The set-point theory of body weight and the role ascribed
to sensory pleasantness in short-term regulation of food intake by way of a hedonic monitor is intuitively attractive,
but difficult to test empirically. Most of the evidence

available at present does not support the assumption that there
is a simple physiological explanation for the variability in
sweetness pleasantness. The set-point theory has been reviewed recently by Cabanac [52].

PALATABILITY OF FOOD AND OVERWEIGHT

Cabanac's set-point theory stresses the importance of internal
physiological signals affecting the sensory pleasantness of a
perceived food odour or taste. The basic postulate of the
theory is that physiological processes regulate the hedonic
monitor and not the sensory perception of intensity [53,54].

Another theory of the relationship between weight,
eating behaviour and palatability of food is that of Schachter
[55]. It has been observed in several studies [e.g.56] that
obese subjects consumed more food than normal weight subjects,
if the food was experienced as palatable. However, if the
hedonic value was rated as low, no differences in amounts
eaten were observed. This response pattern has been explained
in terms of "internal" and "external" cues. It has been hy-
pothesized that obese subjects are less responsive to "internal"
physiological hunger signals than individuals of normal weight.
Th eating of obese subject is more easily elicited by "external"
food cues such as the perceived taste and odour. This theory
has generated many studies, which have been reviewed by Rodin
[57]. However, the conclusion to be drawn from these studies
is that the distinction between internal and external responsiveness is far too simple; many subjects of normal weight
are externally oriented and the reverse is also true for obese
people.

An alternative theory to explain the obesity-externality
correlation has been based upon the concept of restrained
eating developed by Herman and Polivy [58]. Individuals who
diet consciously restraining their food intake generate a
heightened sensibility to external cues. Thus, individuals
highly responsive to external cues can be found in all weight
classes [e.g. 59].

CONCLUSIONS

From the literature surveyed in this paper it can be concluded that:

-      there is no relationship between sensory sensitivity
       for odour and taste stimuli, and body fatness;

-      there is no relationship between sensory intensity
       perception of odour and taste, and body fatness;

- the relationship between preference for sweetness and body weight is not simple; thus it can be concluded that there is no conclusive evidence to support the popular belief that obesity is associated with a "sweet tooth"

- bodily states resulting from food deprivation can affect sensory pleasantness of sweetness, but as yet a simple relationship with body weight cannot be specified;

- variables such external-internal responsiveness and conscious restrained eating interact with food palatability, and the relationship between palatability and body weight cannot be explained without these mediating variables.

REFERENCES

1.   Rodin, J. Recent Advances in Obesity Research Vol.3 (Björntorp, P; Cairella, M; Howard, A.N., Eds), Libbey and Cie Ltd, London, 1981 106-123.

2.   Osancova, K; Hejda, S. Obesity: Its Pathogenesis and Management (Silverstone, T., Ed.), Publ. Sci. Group Inc., Action, Mass, 1975, 57-91.

3.   Spitzer,L; Rodin, J. Human eating behavior: a critical review of studies in normal weight and overweight individuals.Appetite 1981, 2, 293-329.

4.   Nordsiek, F.W. The sweet tooth: the search for safe means of satisfying the universal craving for sweets continues unabated but so far with limited success. Am. Sci. 1972, 60, 41-44.

5.   Meiselman, H. Taste and Development: The genesis of Sweet Preference (Weiffenbach, J.M., Ed), U.S. Government Printing Office, Washington D.C., 1977 269-279.

6.   Papp, A.O.; Padilla, L; Johnson, A.L. Dietary intake in patients with and without myocardial infarction. Lancet ii,1965, 259-261

7.   Paul, O.; MacMillan, A.; McKean, H.; Park, H. Sucrose intake and coronary heart-disease. Lancet ii, 1968, 1049-1051.

8.   Richardson, J.F. The sugar intake of businessmen

inverse relationship with relative weight. Br.J.Nutr.
1972, 27, 449-460

9.   Garn, S.M., Solomon, M.A.; Cole, P.E. Sugar-food in-
      take of obese and lean adolescents. Econ.Fd Nutr.1980
      9, 219-222.

10.   Beaudoin, R.; Mayer, J. Food intakes of obese and non-
      obese women. J. Am. Diet. Ass. 1953, 29, 29-33.

11.   Ekman, G.; Åkesson, C. Saltness, sweetness and pre-
      ference. Scand. J. Psychol. 1965, 6, 241-253.

12.   Kocher, E.C.; Fischer, G.L. Subjective intensity and
      taste preference. Perc. & Motor Skills 1969, 28, 735-
      740.

13.   Frijters, J.E.R.; Rasmussen-Conrad, E.L. Sensory dis-
      crimination, intensity perception and affective
      judgement of sucrose sweetness in the overweight.
      J. Gen. Psychol. 1982 (in press)

14.   Grinker, J.; Hirsch, J.; Smith, D.V. Taste sensitivity
      and susceptibility to external influence in obese and
      normal weight subjects. J. Pers. Soc. Psychol.
      1972, 22, 320-325.

15.   Green, D.M.; Swets, J.A. Signal Detection Theory and
      Psychophysics. Wiley, New York, 1966.

16.   Moore, L.M.; Nielson, C.R.; Mistretta, C.M. Sucrose
      thresholds: age-related differences. J. Gerontol.
      1982, 37, 64-69.

17.   Cowart, B.J. Development of taste perception in humans:
      Sensitivity and preference throughout the life span.
      Psychol. Bull. 1981, 90, 43-73

18.   Malcolm, R.; O'Neil, P.M.; Hirsch, A.A.; Currey,
      H.S.; Moskowitz, G. Taste Hedonics and thresholds in
      obesity. Int. J. Obesity 1980, 4, 203-212.

19.   Thompson, D.A.; Moskowitz, H.R.; Campbell, R.G. Effects
      of body weight and food intake on pleasantness ratings
      of a sweet stimulus. J. Appl. Physiol. 1976, 41,
      77-82.

20.   Grinker, J. Obesity and sweet taste. Am. J. Clin. Nutr.
      1978, 31, 1078-1087.

21.   Thompson D.A.; Moskowitz, H.R.; Campbell, R.G. Taste and olfaction in human obesity. Physiol. & Behav. 1977, 19, 335-337.

22.   Meiselman, H.L.; Bose, H.E.; Nykvist, W.F. Magnitude production and magnitude estimation of taste intensity. Perc. & Psychoph. 1972, 249-252.

23.   Rodin. J. Effects of obesity and set point on taste responsiveness and ingestion in humans. J. Comp. Physiol. Psychol. 1975, 89, 1003-1009.

24.   Witherly, S.A.; Pangborn, R.M.; Stern, J.S. Gustatory responses and eating duration of obese and lean adults. Appetite 1980, 1, 53-63.

25.   Engen, T..; Lipsitt, L.P.; Peck, M.B. Ability of newborn infants to discriminate sapid substances. Dev. Psychol. 1974, 10, 741-744.

26.   Desor, J.A.; Maller, O.;Turner, R. Taste in acceptance of sugars by human infacts. J. Comp. Physiol. Psychol. 1973, 84 496-501.

27.   Nisbett, R.; Gurwitz, S. Weight, sex and eating behavior in human newborns. J. Comp. Physiol. Psychol. 1970, 73, 245-253.

28.   Milstein, R.M. Responsiveness in newborn infants of overweight and normal weight parents. Appetite 1980, 1, 65-74.

29.   Frijters, J.E.R. Sensory evaluation: a link between food and food acceptance research. Lebensm. Wiss. u Technol. 1975, 8, 294-297.

30.   Coombs, C.H.; Avrunin, G.S. Single-peaked functions and the theory of preference. Psychol. Rev. 1977 84, 216-230.

31.   Pfaffmann, C. Wundt's schema of sensory affect in the light of research on gustatory preferences. Psychol. Res. 1980, 42, 165-174.

32.   Moskowitz, H.R. The sweetness and pleasantness of sugar. Am. J. Psychol. 1971, 84, 387-405.

33.   Moskowitz, H.R.; Kluter, R.A.; Westerling, J.; Jacobs, H.L. Sugar sweetness and pleasantness: evidence for different psychological laws. Science 1974, 583-585.

34.   Underwood, P.J.; Belton, E.; Hulme, P. Aversion to sucrose
       in obesity. Proc. Nutr. Soc. 1973, 32, 93a-94a.

35.   Johnson, W.G.; Keane, T.M.; Bonar, J.R.; Downey, C. Hedonic
       ratings of sucrose solutions: effects of body weight,
       weight loss and dietary restriction. Add. Behav. 1979,
       4, 231-236.

36.   Enns, M.P.; Van Itallie, T.B.; Grinker, J.A.; Contri-
       butions of age, sex, and degree of fatness on preferences
       and magnitude estimations for sucrose in humans. Physiol.
       & Behav. 1979, 22, 999-1003.

37.   Mathieu, A.; Liebermeister, H.; Orlik, P.; Wagner, M.W.
       Unterschiedliche Geschmacksbewertung von Süssungsmitteln
       durch norm-und übergewichtige Probanden. Dtsch.med.Wschr.
       1976, 101, 703-708.

38.   Wooley, O.W.; Wooley, S.C.; Dunham. R.B. Calories and
       sweet taste: effects on sucrose preferences in the obese
       and non-obese. Physiol. & Behav. 1972, 9 765-768.

39.   Pangborn, R.M.; Simone, M. Body size and sweetness
       preference. J. Am. Diet. Ass. 1958, 34, 924-928.

40.   Rodin, J.; Moskowitz, H.R.; Bray, G.A. Relationship
       between obesity, weight loss and taste responsiveness.
       Physiol. & Behav. 1976, 17, 591-597.

41.   Grinker, J.A. Infant taste responses are correlated
       with birthweight and unrelated to indices of obesity.
       Pediat. Res. 1978, 12, 371.

42.   Pfaffmann, C. Nebraska Symposium on Motivation. (Jones,
       M.R. Ed), University of Nebraska Press, Lincoln, 1961,
       71-108.

43.   Pangborn, R.M. Individual variation in affective
       responses to taste stimuli. Psychon. Sci. 1970, 21,
       125-126.

44.   Cabanac, M. Physiological role of pleasure. Science
       1971, 173, 1103-1107.

45.   Cabanac, M.; Duclaux, R. Obesity: absence of satiety
       aversion to sucrose. Science 1970, 168, 496-497.

46.   Cabanac, M.; Duclaux, R.; Spector, N.H. Sensory feedback
       in regulation of body weight: is there a ponderostat?
       Nature 1971, 229, 125-127.

47.   Nisbett, R.E. Hunger, obesity and the ventromedial hypo-
      thalamus. Psychol. Rev. 1972, 79, 433-453.

48.   Metropolitan Life Insurance Company. New weight standards
      for men and women. Stat. Bull. 1959, 40, 1-4.

49.   Guy-Grand, B.; Sitt, Y. Recent advances in obesity
      research,Vol 1. (Howard, A.Ed), Newman Publishing Ltd,
      London, 1975, 238-241.

50.   Gilbert, D.G.; Hagen, R.L. Taste in underweight, over-
      weight, and normal-weight subjects before, during and
      after sucrose ingestion. Add. Behav. 1980, 5, 137-142.

51.   Grinker, J.A.; Price, J.M.; Greenwood, M.R.C. Hunger:
      Basic Mechanisms and Clinical Implications. (Novin, D.;
      Wyrwicka, W.; Bray, G. Eds), Raven Press, New York,
      1976, 441-457.

52.   Cabanac, M. Preference Behaviour and Chemoreception.
      (Kroeze, J.H.A.Ed), I.R.L., London, 1979, 275-289

53.   Moskowitz, H.R.; Kumraiah, J.; Sharma, K.N.; Jacobs,
      H.L.; Sharma, S.D. Effects of hunger satiety and glucose
      load upon taste intensity and taste hedonics. Physiol.
      & Behav. 1976, 16, 471-475.

54.   Mower, G.D.; Mair, R.G.; Engen, T. The Chemical Senses
      and Nutrition. (Kare, M.R.; Maller, O. Eds), Academic
      Press, New York, 1977, pp. 103-118.

55.   Schachter, S. ; Goldman, R.; Gordon, A. Effects of fear,
      food deprivation, and obesity on eating. J. Pers. Soc.
      Psychol. 1968, 10, 91-97.

56.   Nisbett, R.E. Taste, deprivation and weight determinants
      of eating behavior. J. Pers. Soc. Psychol. 1968, 10,
      107-116.

57.   Rodin. J. Current status of the internal-external
      hypothesis for obesity. What went wrong? Amer. Psychol.
      1981, 36, 361-372.

58.   Herman, C.P. Restrained eating. Psychiatr. Clin. North
      Am. 1978, 1, 593-607.

59.   Nisbett, R.E.; Temoshuk, L. Is there an external
      cognitive style? J. Pers. Soc. Psychol. 1976, 33, 36-47.

Chapter 5.2

Marketing and sensory quality

D. Lesser
Lecturer, Department of Agricultural Marketing, University of Newcastle-upon-Tyne.

SUMMARY

The paper asserts that for marketing the only reality
is the aggregate of consumer perceptions. This
orientation has implications for both elements of
sensory testing, discrimination and preference; the
discussion is illustrated by examples mainly related
to meat. The problems are largely problems of
measurement, especially of identifying what to
measure. The solutions are through accurate modelling of consumer perceptions and influence processes.
The conclusion drawn is that marketing sensory
quality is a matter of serving or changing consumer
perceptions of what quality is.

INTRODUCTION

The introductory paper to this conference was on
'A scientist's approach to defining quality'. To
match, my paper could be re-titled 'A marketeer's
approach to defining quality'; and I leap in at once
with a definition "Quality is what the consumer
perceives to be quality".

That there may be a difference in outlook between
'scientist' and 'marketeer' is not a novel idea.
Elrod in a short paper in 1978 on 'bridging the gap
between laboratory and consumer tests' comments
" . . . a marketing person might attribute 25% of the

success of a product to the product itself, 50% to
packaging, promotion, and advertising, and 25% to
distribution and selling. In no way will interest in
the product itself make up 75% of the time and energy
of the Marketing department. Similarly, the advertising agency is more interested in what people think
is so about the product than what really is " [1].
Abei, in a 1979 paper, writes " . . . marketing
experts . . . follow the trend of the majority . . .
the responsible food scientist . . .feels obliged to
design and sell products of equilibrated, comprehensive composition" [2]. My submission is that such comments are based on a fundamental misapprehension, not
about what interests the marketeer or the scientist,
but about what a product really is. A product is
what the consumer thinks it is. The image, the
price, the availability - all are components of the
'product', as real and as inherent as its physical
constituents.

     For marketing, the only reality is the aggregate
of consumer perceptions. The present paper is largely
devoted to establishing and sustaining this interpretation of reality and to examining its implications. The core of the argument can be illustrated
by saying that if a producer knows that what he is
offering is a superior article when measured by some
objective procedure, but if consumers perceive his
product as inferior, then the product actually is
inferior as a product - it is not supplying
adequately the satisfactions consumers want from it.
Conversely, a product dismissed as rubbish by experts
but preferred by the relevant consumers is a better
product. Only from the consumer can you learn what
it is that you are selling. A main focus of sensory
testing studies therefore is the development of ever
better methods of obtaining information from and
about the consumer, methods that are demonstrably
valid, increasingly reliable and increasingly
sensitive.

     This marketing orientation has implications for
both elements of sensory testing, discrimination and
preference.

DISCRIMINATION

For discrimination it implies that differences which
the consumer cannot detect in the circumstances in
which she will normally be exposed to the product,

have no marketing significance. They are merely
embroidery on the perimeter of the marketing reality.
It is because of this that trained or expert panels
have very limited applicability in product testing.
They cannot tell us how the consumer will react; they
cannot even tell us that the consumer will be able to
detect the existence of any attribute or any difference. Only when an expert panel fails to detect a
difference does it lead to any clear conclusion -
that the ordinary consumer too could not detect the
difference. It is a useful role, but confined.

The relevance of 'normal circumstances' was neatly
exposed in the work of Baron and Wright at Newcastle,
on the effects of cooking on meat [3]. They found
that recommendations given in cookery books (assumed
to be a principal source of information for housewives) were imprecise, varied markedly between texts
and often related to larger than typical joints or
steaks; there was little evidence that they drew on
the scientific literature as a basis for recommendations. Housewives, one step further removed from the
laboratory (though only 1 in 4 consulted a book when
cooking) tended to cook joints for longer than
recommended even if in the recommended temperature
range. 'The suggestion', the authors concluded, 'is
that a fair proportion of these joints are being
cooked much more than recommended or modelled in
research procedure.' What is more, 'laboratory
panel tests which attempted to model some of the
survey methods suggest that the apparent cooking
times used by housewives would prevent them detecting
differences between barley beef and mature beef'.
Such a finding calls into question the validity of
much of the laboratory sensory testing of beef
directed at providing a better product for the consumer. Must it not be true that differences, which
are detectable in a laboratory by a trained panel in
meat that has all been cooked in a uniform, measured
fashion, but which are totally camouflaged by the
crude and varied cooking to which meat is subjected
in real life, that such 'differences' are not only
unimportant but, in a real sense, non-existent?

Admittedly if certain classes of meat, even given
the effects of cooking, did turn out on average tenderer (say) than certain other sorts, then it might be
worth striving to produce the tenderer quality.
Differences, however, that do not, even on average,
survive the cooking must be ignored: to spend time

and money in breeding or rearing animals or treating
the meat to obtain such differences is only the self-
indulgence of the specialist. On the other hand,
there might be a minority of cooks able to preserve
differences that others unhappily suppress. Is it
not worth producing the higher quality meat for them?
It would be, provided that there are enough of them
and they care enough to make the production profitable; but then this 'superior' meat should be
marketed to these people and to them alone: it is
wasted on the others.

PREFERENCES

On preferences, the relevance of consumer perceptions, alone, is even more marked. This is indeed
fully acknowledged by sensory testers who would not
normally employ an expert panel to measure preferences. As Olson comments, 'Food scientists probably
possess memory schemata for foods . . . that are
dramatically different from those of ordinary consumers' [4]. And the same is true, though in a lesser
degree, of trained and expert panellists. An expert
is, by definition, not representative of the layman.

     Nevertheless, it often seems to have been the
prejudices of the specialist that have shaped trade or
research practice, instead of the objectively
measured perceptions of the consumer. A good
instance is that of boar pork and bacon. Traditionally young boars have been castrated to prevent the
development of boar taint. Boar taint is a very real
phenomenon; to someone who has ever been closely
acquainted with a mature breeding boar, this odour is
said to be unmistakeable and even a very mild mani-
festation is readily detected. The consequence has
been castration as a standard practice, despite the
fact that not castrating would yield a useful
increase in profit per pig, provided that boar bacon
sold at the same price as castrate bacon. In fact,
it happens that where the experienced nose is alerted
and repelled, the naive consumer mostly doesn't
notice a thing. A considerable body of research (for
example, Rhodes [5] and [6]) has shown that consumers
given the choice are as likely as not to prefer the
boar meat.

     We ourselves at Newcastle conducted a very pre-
cise test on boar bacon for the Ulster Curers' Association and the Northern Ireland Pigs Board who were

considering taking a commercial decision to market
bacon from entire boars [7]. The critical characteristic was identified as strength of aroma during
cooking and eating. We found that only 69 (13%) of
the housewives (who cooked and ate the bacon) marked
the boar aroma as much stronger or very much stronger
than that of their usual bacon. Of those 69 housewives, 55 also classed the aroma of the boar bacon as
much more appetising or very much more appetising.

What I am saying is that, in so far as consumers cannot detect boar taint, it does not exist, not
only in the sense of being of no marketing significance
but also in the more far-reaching sense of not existing at all in terms of boar bacon as a product. Of
course, it does exist in terms of the boar as a farm-
yard animal and of boar bacon as a laboratory
specimen. If consumers, though, cannot tell the
difference between boar and castrate bacon, the two
are identically the same product. If they can
distinguish and prefer the boar, the boar is the
better product.

INFLUENCING CONSUMER PERCEPTIONS

Although at any one time consumer perceptions are, to
the marketeer, a measurable set of objective facts,
these perceptions are continuously shifting; and it
is open to the marketeer to attempt to influence the
directions and degrees of those shifts. It is,
obviously, possible to train people to discriminate
and to educate them in what is good quality. We
spend our lives developing these skills. Rozin and
Fallon, discussing the acquisition of food likes and
dislikes, write, 'The food world of the infant is
its mouth world . . . predominance of the mouth as
the focus for affect extends through adulthood.
However, for many adult interactions with foods, the
mouth serves as an almost incidental conduit to the
body, with actual control passing to more cognitive
systems' [8].

Cognitively-based preferences can be influenced
by personal development and social pressures, and
clearly they are. Who ever liked beer at first
taste? Only years of habituation have enabled some
of us to prefer ale to lemonade, and even then one
notices hard men occasionally backsliding at least
into shandy. The first cigarette for many an
adolescent induced only nausea; to cultivate this

expensive, disagreeable and suicidal addiction
demanded a fair level of dedication. Even tea and
coffee take some getting used to. We learn our
tastes.

What we learn is neither simple nor by any means
solely a function of physiological maturation.
Lundgren, using meat sausage, concluded that perceptions of sensory attributes were 'caused by a complex
set of expectations and attitudes of the subjects'.
[9] We taste what we expect to taste. Indeed when
the actual taste is very different from what is
expected the effect may be disgusting: meat that
tasted of cheese might be uneatable whereas meat with
a cheese sauce or just with cheese is perfectly
acceptable.

Thus what we taste in food is affected by much
more than chemical or physiological interactions.Taste
is, however, only one of the variables that condition
food choice. Perceptions of foods, as of everything
else are based on many different sensations. Schultz
and Wahl comment, 'Food acceptance is a complex
response influenced by psychological and sensory
determinants. The sensory character of a food is a
composite of those physical attributes which are .
sensed by humans, and their integration by the brain
into a total impression of the food' [10]. Following
Hutchings they divide sensory attributes into the
'anticipatory' appearance and the 'participatory'
texture and flavour [11]. The psychological determinants are much wider ranging and tend to precede
the sensory ones. An example is the fact that in
jams and preserves we have begun to associate real
fruit content with a slightly muted colouring which
must be contrary to common sense since manufacturers
adding artificial colouring presumably aim at
realising at least our expectations of the colour the
jam should have. As McKenzie observes, ' . . .
perhaps as a result of some hidden recognition of the
crucial nature of the consumption function, man, in
part at least, also elects to build round food and
eating a whole series of issues in no way related to
health and nutritional status' [12].

Among the many and diffuse influences that bear
upon and help form consumer perceptions of food a major
contribution is made by the marketing activities of
food manufacturers and distributors. Within limits
most of us could be persuaded to consume any of a

wide variety of foods or drinks; the example of beer,
mentioned above, is a case in point. Given that this
is so, the question arises of how much should a
marketing organisation invest in 'educating' consumers into preferring its product. How much should
it spend on marketing sensory quality? To answer
this question, which is central to the analysis of
this paper, we must look briefly at what marketing
is.

MARKETING

Marketing may be defined as the creation and exploitation of monopoly advantages. It needs favoured
access to scarce resources - hence the monopoly
element - and markets in which those resources give
some advantage. If a marketeer can by increasing
consumers' ability to discriminate or by changing
their preferences so increase his monopoly advantage
that the return to him is greater than the cost, then
this training or education is worthwhile; otherwise
it is not. Commonly the most rewarding procedure is
to detect how preferences are changing and just
divert them a little to one side or another making
sure one is in place to catch the flow. In other
words, the aim is to find out what the market will
want and provide it, with just enough distinctiveness
to separate one's own offer from that of the competition, preserving a monopoly element. In some circumstances, however, more dramatic intervention can be
profitable.

The marketing influence on preferences can be
exerted through a range of activities: through development of the physical product, through price changes,
advertising, packaging or any other medium of marketing communication. The choice of activities depends
on what consumer perceptions need to be changed and
on what is the most effective communication for
bringing about that change. This exploitative
approach, this suggestion that to change the pack
changes the product does not seem to be accepted as
axiomatic by some scientists or by consumerists.
Some even are shocked by it. Any outrage, however,
is, I submit, entirely unwarranted. It derives from
the mistaken belief that there is anything more to a
product than what consumers perceive in it.

Even some economists still display uneasiness at
the marketing approach; surprisingly, since that ap-

proach is just an extension of utility analysis. Others
have come to acknowledge that a product is a set of
want satisfactions (see, for example, Baron [13] or
the earlier, seminal paper by Lancaster [14]). The
satisfactions are both physical and psychological.
They are delivered through consumer perceptions.
Philosophically, whether there is a reality that
transcends perception may be a fundamental question;
at the applied level of marketing, that the housewife
tries to buy what she perceives as the product can
hardly be open to doubt. The housewife's perceptions
are based on interpretations of sensory experiences,
and in marketing sensory quality we must be attempt-
ing to alter those perceptions - either the experiences or the interpretations of them (if the
distinction can be validly made).

IMPLICATIONS AND EXAMPLES

The implications of this conclusion can be very
interesting. I should like first to project them on
to one set of products.

        We have recently had brought to the nation's at-
tention the apparently scandalous business of water in
ham. Levels of 30% or more have been detected and
exposed by trading standards officers. The trade has
responded with the weak defence that the addition of
some water is a necessary part of the processing, and
that without the water the ham would be considerably
more expensive. Yet if it is true that the product
is what the consumer perceives then if she perceives
the with-water ham as better, or at least as better
value for money, it is the better product. Were
things otherwise, were there enough housewives eager
to buy more expensive ham with the minimum water content, the signals would, despite market imperfection,
eventually get back to the producers, and they would
respond with a different product: that would be in
their own interest.

        It is not a moral question. If it were then we
concerned thinking people would demand a ham that, as
far as possible, used less of the world's resources,
was less fattening, less poisonous, efficiently re-
cyclable and required as few as possible of our
fellow creatures to be killed. By these standards
the ham that improved upon that with 30% water and a
good proportion of bone and skin, would be the ham
with 40% water and a higher proportion of skin and

and bone. Of course there are other arguments: such
as whether people have the right to know what they
are buying. When all is said and done, though,
within defined limits of health and safety, if the
consumer perceives a product as satisfying her wants,
then it is by definition a good product. The main
deficiency in the 30% water ham may be that it is not
marketed positively enough - perhaps as a low-calorie
ham?

        I do not make the point frivolously. The ethics
of whether we should be told what food contains are a
separate question. Personally I want to know and I
take the view that legislature should ensure my right
to know, but that is by the way. The pertinent point
for us is that the scope for using cheaper additives
instead of real meat or of using any other substi-
tutes instead of the traditional product present a
marketing challenge and a marketing opportunity. The
response must be based on accurage sensory testing
within valid marketing analysis.

        It seems to me that the opportunities are being
missed. Some years back I offered the forecast that
within a decade insistence on eating real meat would
come to be regarded as a rather barbaric eccentricity.
Analogues have, in principle, so many advantages that
only the difficulty of getting them right should
delay their taking over completely from meat. From
its side, of course, the meat industry must employ
powerful and sensitive marketing to help ensure that
consumers want what its product alone provides. At
present, meat is winning hands down. That is perhaps
unexpected since the producers of analogues have
access to marketing skills and experience as good as
any in the world. Perhaps the product is not yet
right: the battle hasn't yet started. To express
the whole argument in personal terms, I am a vegeta-
rian by conviction, but I eat meat because I have
learned to enjoy the experience. If Unilever or
whoever can give me the experience without the
violation, they will be offering a new level of consumer satisfactions.

        To interfere with 'natural' foods is not in prin-
ciple either desirable or undesirable. It is the effects of the individual interference which can be either
good or bad. Adding vitamins or minerals or bran is
probably good, removing them bad; adding salt or
sugar may be bad, removing them perhaps good. But in

these instances we have the criterion of the health
or longevity of the eater. The principle of non-
interference doesn't come into it. The idea that
'natural' is in some way desirable is just that, an
idea - a consumer perception. But perceptions are
what marketing is about, and the 'virtues' of nature
can well be turned into a powerful marketing appeal -
while 'natural' continues to appeal. Nature is,
after all, pretty unpleasant in many respects, and
there was a time when 'untouched by human hand' was
a more effective claim than 'home-made'.

     Apart from health and safety and nourishment,
every other virtue in food is a function of perceived
satisfactions - the interpretation of sensory
quality. Even nourishment is of dubious value for
its own sake. In the Western world, most of us are,
if anything, over-nourished. It is a commonplace
that the ideal of many consumers would be a 'food'
that provided all the satisfactions of eating without
imposing the undesired consequences that most eating
induces. Water ices can cost more than the more
nourishing ice-cream and must therefore have advantages over it. What is intrinsically undesirable
therefore about water ham? Those who maintain that
food choice should properly be based on nourishment
will have triumphed when, and only when, some food
sells on the claim that it contains more calories
per ounce than any other brand.

     Where we have got to so far in the argument is
that in marketing foods, in marketing sensory perceptions, we must aim at providing what are perceived as
satisfactions of what are perceived as wants. We need
to go a step further and include what could be perceived as satisfactions and what could be perceived as
wants. Perhaps the most dazzling manifestations of
the marketeer's art are those in which previously
quite unrecognised wants are uncovered at the same
time as the satisfaction is clamourously unveiled.
When my children were infants, I did not fret that
the towels that dried them at bath-time were not as
soft and gentle as a mother's kiss: what modern
parent can feel comfortable if those towels are not
washed with a conditioner to keep them ultra-soft?
When even younger, I did not swill out with anti-
septic mouth-wash of an early evening: what would-
be lover can today risk the consequences of not doing
so? New needs are created for new products, new
products for new needs. Such marketing may well be

bettered only by that of entrepreneurs who market
tins of scotch mist or lumps of London clay. And the
point is that all these do satisfy consumer wants, do
generate satisfactions as real as those provided by a
motor-car, a baron of beef or a pencil of lipstick.

MEASUREMENT

Within very broad limits therefore the problems are
only those of finding out what the consumer could
want. They are problems of measurement. What,
however, is to be measured?

Sensory perception is much more than taste or
flavour. It obviously includes texture and appearance. Hutchings [11] finds appearance the most
important in determining initial acceptability;
Schultz and Wahl [10] conclude that flavour dominates
but they make the point that all act together. It is
presumably the case that the order of importance of
the attributes differs from product to product.
Also, that for any product there are minimum or
threshhold levels of any attribute which must be
passed before the product is acceptable: beyond that
only particular qualities matter. Though texture may
not be the most important attribute generally, it is
probably the difficulty of getting the texture right
that is the main barrier to acceptance of some food
analogues. In evocations of past food experiences it
is probably flavour that is most temptingly recalled.

The essential point though is made by Booth [15]
'It must be noted that the immediate determinants of
acceptability are not the physical stimuli or conditions as such, but these aspects as perceived
momentarily by the individual consumer.' In turn,
these perceptions are conditioned not only by past
experiences of the direct sensations but by a complex
of cultural, social, psychological and physiological
influences. Rozin and Fallon distinguish psychological categories of food, based on primary reasons
for acceptance or rejection in American culture, as
sensory-effective (flavour), anticipated consequences
(physiological and social) and ideational (appropriateness and effective-transvalued); and they trace
the antogeny of food classification [8]. A more
general and more comprehensive categorisation may be
appropriate, but the underlying common factor must be
that, in marketing food products, or sensory quality,
more information is needed than can be obtained from

direct measurement of sensations.

The analysis that leads to the measurement,
determining what is to be measured, is the definition
of an accurate model of consumer perceptions relevant
to that product, and of the processes through which
those perceptions change and are changed.   The model
must be dynamic because, as Koster observed, even
without outside intervention preferences change as we
become bored, and new stimulation is needed [16].
After sausage and chips for tea every day for a month
the eater would have a very different perception of
sausage and chips from that he held on the first day:
he might have come to hate it, or he might have
developed an addiction, but his perception certainly
would have changed.

Let me offer a practical example of the importance of modelling and of some of the problems that
arise.   At the 1974 Conference of the Market Research
Society, Daniels and Lawford presented a paper on
'The effect of order in the presentation of samples
in paired comparison tests' [17].   The manner of the
test was conventional.   Each of the two variants of
a soup were rated on a hedonic word scale.   Half of
the sample tested variant 'A' first and half variant
'B' first.   There was an order effect: in general
the variant scored more highly when tested first
than when tested second.   On some tests, though,
there was an interaction between the variants and
the order, so strong as to produce the effect that
the scores for 'A' when it was tested first were
higher than the scores for 'B' when that was tested
first, but 'A' tested second scored lower than 'B'
tasted second: there was a cross-over effect, with
the two comparisons giving contradictory results.
The question is that of which test is the more valid.
Does one accept the result when each is tested first
or that when each is tested second?

My memory is that the discussion about this
paper at the meeting mostly supported the validity of
the second test, on grounds expressed by the authors
as 'It can be argued, that the whole purpose of paired comparison testing is to provide respondents with
a reference point for one product to be compared with
another . . . .'   That may be so.   The argument of my
analysis, however, is that the correct answer can
only be gained from the answer to the question 'What
real world situation is our test modelling?'   How

people react in a laboratory (or hall test) is pertinent only for what it reveals about how other
people will react in the real world. The use of the
second test may have implied the model of a world in
which people commonly eat two-course meals with both
courses variants of the same sort of soup: observation leads one to believe that that is a minority
market. It can, on the other hand, be argued that
paired comparison tests compress normal experience
and are thus a more accurate model of long-term
experience than are monodic tests. The point is,
however, that the systematic analysis of which
variables to measure must start from the acknowledge-
ment that we are modelling.

At Newcastle, we faced a related problem in the
test of boar bacon mentioned earlier [7]. Again it was
a standard form of test, a placement test. Bacon was
given to a sample of households in each of two weeks.
Half the sample was given boar bacon in the first
week and castrate in the second; for the others the
order was reversed. In designing the study we had to
consider whether the respondents were to be asked, in
the second week, to compare the bacon with the bacon
given them the previous week; or were they to be
asked in each week, to compare it with their 'usual'
bacon. The comparison with the previous week provided a controlled standard common to all the households; the closer model to what would happen in real
life must be with the 'usual' bacon. Fortunately
there was no reason why both comparisons could not be
asked for, and both were. Fortunately, too, the
results of the two coincided so that even retro-
spectively we did not have to choose. The burden of
my argument though is that had there been a difference, the more valid measurement of what we were
seeking to test was the comparison with the usual
bacon - even though, as was revealed in the analysis,
the bacon given was of a better general quality than
the average of their usual purchases.

THE APPROPRIATE MODEL

What, then should be the model of consumer perceptions appropriate for sensory testing? There is of
course no general model applicable in all circumstances. In each instance the analysis must start by
finding out what the consumer perceives as relevant
and important in choosing among the options for that
particular class of product - what are the salient

dimensions. Only after that need one grapple with
the problems of measuring the products along those
dimensions - with measuring the valences of each
product or variant. In our experiment on boar bacon
we disregarded the first stage and went straight into
the measurement of valences, probably a common enough
practice in sensory testing too. In some cases the
salient dimensions can be distinguished by deduction
or experience and the initial consumer approaches
would be otiose; but was this true of boar taint -
or did we simply not even recognise that there was a
question to be answered?

What is often done is to measure salience retros-
pectively. Having scaled the product on a number of
attributes, the respondent is then required to rank
or rate the importance of the attributes. This does
not, however, reveal any unsuspected criteria the
consumer may have for judging quality.

Moskowitz and Chandler used this pre-structured
assessment in an experiment described in Food
Technology in 1978 [18]. They produced a list of six
foods and seven attributes and asked respondents to
rate (1) the relative importance of each attribute,
and (2) the degree to which products on the market
fulfilled the panellists' desires. Clearly the
second measurement is closely related to marketing.
It is akin to the technique of 'perceptual mapping'
in which brands of a product are located in a multidimensional hyperspace of consumer perceptions;
commonly some ideal of the product is located in the
same space for comparison.

In another experiment described in the same short
paper, the authors apply trade-off analysis to
measure the importance of different sensory attributes. In trade-off measurements the respondent is
presented with several hypothetical products some of
which are better in some respects, others in others;
she is asked to choose among the products and thus to
disclose her preferences among the different levels
of the various attributes, to reveal how much of one
attribute she will trade off for a gain in another.
The trade-off model seems a generally valid one for
consumer decision-making, since in every buying
decision we trade-off product choices against money if
nothing else; there must be scope for its more
frequent application in sensory tasting.

Two other difficulties in representing the market in
sensory tests are raised in the paper by Koster
already referred to [17]. He points out that
researchers commonly record verbal responses to questions rather than observations of behaviour: when
'. . . we put a person in a test booth in our laboratory at eleven in the morning, present him with a
dish of cooked carrots and ask him a series of
questions about the smell, the taste, the mouth feel
and the aftertaste of carrots, we bring him into a
rather unnatural situation. In normal everyday life
we never ask ourselves such questions. We almost
never use our senses of smell and taste in such an
analytical way'. Yet it is only in so far as the
situation mirrors normal everyday life that it has
any applicability at all.

The main topic of Koster's paper, however, is the
very important one of sensory adaption. The effect
of adaption, in fact extends beyond sensory testing
into being one of the most intractable problems in
marketing research generally. How can you in test
marketing or in concept testing measure the ways in
which the consumer will react after numerous and
varied exposures to the physical product, the advertising, the sales promotion, etc.? How can you
measure in advance the effect of an advertising campaign spread over months, even years? The problem
is not different in testing sensory quality - disliked at first taste, the product or varient might
come to be preferred if there is some incentive to
continue using it, or after exposure to the marketing
campaign. We have to ask how, or even whether, we
can compress adaption into a test situation; and if
we cannot, what may be the marketing applicability
of the test.

Blair, suggesting ways to avoid being misled, illustrates the need for care in modelling the market
accurately in sensory testing [19]. He comments on
the need to define correctly the consuming population
and test the product on them; to ensure that the
material tested is a valid sample of what is to be
marketed; and to design the test to take into consideration any effects of in-home preparation. The
foregoing discussion indicates that the greatest
difficulty is that of creating a test situation that
adequately models the consumption reality.

Conclusion

In drawing the threads together perhaps I might be
permitted to follow the example of the organisers of
the conference. The last formal paper, Dr. Harper's,
is on 'Future trends in the evaluation of sensory
quality', on where sensory testing is going. Marketing being a normative discipline, may I offer a
marketeer's suggestion of where it should be going?

        Pearce distinguishes four major areas in which
sensory evaluation can play a role in marketing [20].
One is the development of a product vocabulary
extracted from the consumers and applicable in market
research, concept development and advertising. A
second is the development and maintenance of sensory
data bases; these references can be used both to
decide what characteristics are likely to be acceptable in different products, either one's own or com-
petitors', and can show how preferences are changing.
The third is in relating laboratory data to consumer
data, thus validating laboratory tests. The fourth
is in decreasing the cost and time of bringing a
product to market through indicating when a product
is ready for wider testing. If this may be taken as
the conventional wisdom, then I suggest that the role
of sensory testing is seriously underestimated.
Sensory testing should be much more central to
marketing analysis. If marketing depends on the
delineation of accurate models of consumer perceptions, as I contend it does, then sensory testing,
measuring the sensations that help form those perceptions, must be fundamental. The contribution can
be not only in the findings of the sensory testers
but also in their expertise in scaling and measurement. Sensory testers and marketeers share a common
interest and common challenge in needing to measure
intangibles. Each can contribute to the other.

        On the other hand, there is at least the possibi-
lity that sensory testing could hinder marketing if the
dimensions of testing are not derived from the consumers themselves. My whole argument is that the
purpose of sensory testing in marketing is to help
construct consumer models. That this is not too
often specifically acknowledged may indicate that it
is being taken for granted, but could alternatively
mean that it is being disregarded. In other marketing analyses it is regarded as desirable that the
model be specified. The same must be true of sensory

testing: every test should state how the test situation is supposed to relate to the real world - which,
alone, is of interest.

Relating the test to the real world would define
the role of trained panels. They are not a true but,
as it were, an enlarged reflection of some elements of
reality. Their main application may be in establishing the limits of consumer discrimination. If a
panel cannot detect a difference, the ordinary consumer certainly cannot. Expert panels may also be
used to estimate what consumer education could be
justified in raising the value of the market or a
segment of it; in that case the training of panellists would be used as a model of consumer adaption;
I know of no instances of the systematic application
of this notion. They do also have other marketing
applications, such as in the selection of sample
material for consumer tests.

There may be scope for more emphasis on other
physical attributes of food than taste. Klaui has
commented on aspects of colour in food. Some Cantonese
cuisines balance ingredients of a dish by texture,
and Jellinek has shown that for Americans too
'. . . meanings and associations are attached not
only to complete foods but also to discrete food
attributes, i.e. textures and flavours' [21].
McKenzie suggests a number of relevant 'themes for
the future'.[12].

The methodological challenge must lie not in
measuring what common sense would dictate must be important food variables, not even in measuring what can
by established as the variables that are important to
consumers, but rather in identifying and quantifying
the variables that could profitably be evoked as
important to consumers.

So to end back at the beginning. The marketing
reality is what consumers perceive as reality. In
that a distinction exists between sensing and perceiving, my argument is that whatever it is that can
be described as having a 'quality' must be a matter
of perception rather than of sensing. Perception
includes a complex array of past experiences,
memories and emotional associations, and it is these
factors which the marketeer has to investigate and
operate upon. Marketing sensory quality is a matter
of serving or changing consumer perceptions of what

quality is.

REFERENCES

1. Elrod, J. Bridging the gap between laboratory and consumer tests. Fd Technol. 1978, 32 (11), 63.

2. Abei, H.E. Food acceptance and nutrition: experiences, intentions and responsibilities - an introductory paper. In "Criteria of Food Acceptance" (Solms, J. and Hall, R.L. Eds) Forster Publishing Limited, Zurich, 1981, 3-11.

3. Baron, P.J. and Wright, A.R.I. Cooking Techniques and Consumer Acceptability of Beef. Department of Agricultural Marketing, University of Newcastle Upon Tyne, 1979, Report 25.

4. Olson, J.C. The importance of cognitive processes and existing knowledge structures for understanding food acceptance. In "Criteria of Food Acceptance" (Solms, J. and Hall, R.L. Eds) Forster Publishing Limited, Zurich, 1981 69-81.

5. Rhodes, D.N. J. Sci. Fd Agric., 1971, 22, 485.

6. A marketing trial of pork from boars, Proc, Eur. Meeting of Meat Research Workers, 1977, 21, 178-179.

7. Lesser, D.; Baron, P.J.; Robb, D.J. Boar bacon: a consumer survey, J. Sci. Fd Agric. 1977, 28, 1120-1131.

8. Rozin, P. and Fallon, A.E. The acquisition of likes and dislikes for foods. In "Criteria of Food Acceptance" (Solms, J. and Hall, R.L. Eds) Forster Publishing Limited, Zurich, 1981, 35-48.

9. Lundgren, B. Effect of nutritional information on consumer responses. In "Criteria of Food Acceptance" (Solms, J. and Hall, R.L. Eds) Forster Publishing Limited, Zurich, 1981, 28-33.

10. Schutz, H.G. and Wahl, O.L. Consumer reception of the relative importance of appearance, flavour and texture to food acceptance. In "Criteria of Food Acceptance" (Solms, J. and Hall, R.L. Eds) Forster Publishing Limited, Zurich, 1981, 97-116.

11. Hutchings, J.B. The importance of visual appearance of foods to the food processor and consumer. In "Sensory Properties of Foods", (Birch, G.G.; Bremner, J.G.; Parker, K.J. Eds)

Applied Science Publishers, Barking, 1977, 326.

12. Mc Kenzie, J. Food is not just for eating. In "People and Food Tomorrow" (Hollingsworth, D, and Morse, E. Eds) Applied Science Publishers, London, 1976, 21-31.

13. Baron, P.J. Attitudes - goods characteristics - and the theory of demand. In "Meat Demand and Price Forecasting", Meat and Livestock Commission, Bletchley, 1977.

14. Lancaster, K.J. A new approach to consumer theory, J. Pol. Econ., 1966, 74, 132-164.

15. Booth, D.A. Momentary acceptance of particular foods and processes that change it. In "Criteria of Food Acceptance" (Solms, J. and Hall, R.L. Eds) Forster Publishing Limited, Zurich, 1981, 49-68.

16. Koster, E.P. Time and frequency analysis: a new approach to the measurement of some less-well-known aspects of food preferences. In "Criteria of Food Acceptance" (Solms, J. and Hall, R.L. Eds) Forster Publishing Limited, Zurich, 1981, 240-252.

17. Daniels, P. and Lawford, J. The effect of order in the presentation of samples in paired comparison product tests, Proc. Market Research Society Conference, 1974, 139-152.

18. Moskowitz, H.R. and Chandler, J.W. Consumer perceptions, attitudes and trade-offs regarding flavour and other product characteristics, Fd Technol. 1978, 32 (11), 34-37.

19. Blair, J.R. Interface of marketing and sensory evaluation in product development, Fd Technol., 1978, 32 (11), 61-62.

20. Pearce, J. Sensory evaluation in marketing, Fd Technol., 1980, 34 (11), 60-62.

21. Jellinek, J.S. The meanings of flavours and textures, Fd Technol. 1973, 27 (11), 46-55.

Chapter 5.3

Future trends in the evaluation of sensory quality

R. Harper
Department of Food Science, University of Reading, England.

INTRODUCTION

In order to understand the present and to anticipate
the future a brief account of the past is necessary.
Although it would be justifiable to go back to the
1930's [1] , or even earlier, 1940 has been chosen
as the starting point.   A few important events have
been listed in Table 1.   This is obviously quite
arbitrary and is confined to personal knowledge.
The events selected refer primarily to developments
in the United Kingdom and the United States. Further
details about developments at Davis in the University
of California were reported in 1964   [2] in one of a
series of seventeen different contributions on
sensory evaluation throughout the world.   The first
textbook in the English language was published in
1965 [3].   Reference is also made to the first
official international symposium on 'Principles of
Sensory Evaluation of Food' which took place at the
Swedish Food Institute in Gothenburg in 1968.   The
inaugural address by Tilgner, in which he reviewed
the current state of sensory evaluation and expected
future developments appeared in 1971 [4].   Tilgner
appears to have been the author of the first textbook (in Polish) in the late 1950's. Developments
in the United Kingdom prior to 1977 have been
reported elsewhere   [5] .

Table 1 — Some historical developments.

UK		US
	1940	
		QMF&CI/Chicago Food Acceptance Branch (1943-1963)
Study of skills of Cheesemakers and Cheesegraders, NIRD, Reading (1946-50)	1945	
SCI Symposium: Organoleptic Tests in the Food Industry (1947)		
	1950	Flavour Profile (ADL)
		Beginning of sensory studies at Davis: Univ. California (1951)
Food Rationing in UK ends (Choice demands more than enough)	1955	Manual on Sensory Testing (QMF&CI)
	1960	ASTM Committee E-18 becomes active
		Texture Profile (General Foods)
Studies of Odour Characterisation, FRI, Norwich. (1964-67)	1965	1st Textbook in English (Amerine, Pangborn and Roessler)
BSI Committee FAC/20 (Sensory Analysis) BS Standards: Terminology (1975) Methodology (1980)	1970	1st International Symposium. SIK Sweden (1968) Tilgner's review (1971)
SCI Food Group SENSORY PANEL formed (now 162 Members)	1975	Survey of Services offered: 82 Individuals and Organisations identified
THIS SYMPOSIUM	1980	Sensory Evaluation Division of IFT now over 1000 members
	1985	

Although it is not necessary to go into details about
the entries in Table 1, perhaps the main abbrevia-
tions may need amplification.   Thus:

UK	**US**

NIRD: National Institute
for Research in Dairying

QMF & CI: Quartermaster
Food and Container
Institute for the Armed
Forces, Chicago.   Note
also later work from the
Natick Laboratories.

SCI: Society of Chemical
Industry, London.

ADL: Arthur D. Little
Inc. Cambridge, Mass.

BSI: British Standards
Institution

ASTM E-18: Committee
E-18 (Sensory Evaluation
of Materials and Products)
American Society for
Testing and Materials.

FRI: Food Research
Institute, Norwich.
Established 1964. Both
this and its sister
organisation, the Meat
Research Institute at
Langford, developed out
of the Low Temperature
Research Station,
Cambridge.

IFT: Institute of Food
Technologists.

WHAT IS QUALITY? WHAT IS SENSORY QUALITY?

The word 'Quality' means different things to
different people.   This is evident from the range
of views expressed in this Symposium. Reference to a
dictionary reveals an even greater number of definitions, many of which are not relevant here.   Among
those definitions which are appropriate are the
following:

a)   Degree of excellence
b)   The opposite of quantity
c)   Fitness for intended purpose

A number of other variants could be suggested.   In
the plural, the word 'qualities' refers to sensory
qualities or attributes, with the reservation that
in this context, attributes may vary in intensity or
degree.   (The statistical use of the term is usually
limited to characteristics which are present or absent.)

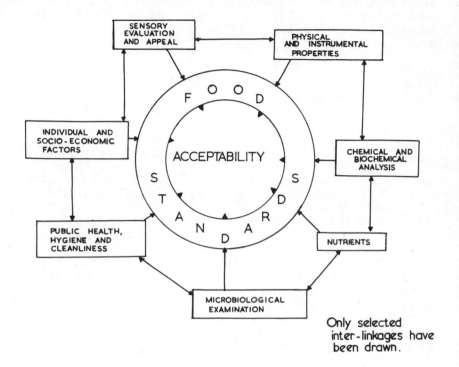

Fig. 1 — Some factors determining quality in food.

Although this Symposium is concerned with sensory quality and its evaluation, a brief note is necessary about quality in general. Some of the factors determining quality in food are illustrated in Fig. 1. This allows us to maintain a proper perspective, sensory quality and acceptability being only a part of the concept of quality as a whole. Treating the component parts graphically, in the form of a circle, avoids the implication that any one aspect is really more important than another. The appropriate weight will have to be given to each aspect and this will differ from one product to another. Each will have associated with it certain limiting conditions, designated here as 'Food standards'. These may be explicit or implicit and must be met before a particular food or drink can reach the central region indicating acceptability.

SENSORY CONSIDERATIONS

The main aims of sensory quality appraisal in foods and beverages include the following:

> Identification and recognition, which include the concept of the brand image, and pattern recognition generally.
>
> Description in terms of the separately identifiable qualities.
>
> Discrimination between different foods and/or between modifications of the same product.
>
> The acceptability of the various sensory qualities, both individually and as a unit (i.e. overall quality), ranging from the avoidance of undesirable qualities to the creation, or addition, of those which are desirable.

Palatability can be manipulated by introducing particular sensory qualities. Indeed, the art of the cook is to blend together an interesting combination of colour, appearance, tastes, odours and textures in the final dish or meal component. These sensory components provide a substantial 'value added component' to the primary raw materials in the development of successful products. Many other considerations play a part in the process of commercial decision-making and market promotion. It is difficult to be sure what the failure rate in new products is, since much depends upon the stage at which a developing product is no longer considered to be viable and on the availability of evidence. However it has been suggested that at least 90 per cent of the proposed developments never succeed or continue to exist. The manufacturer and the market research organiser may ignore the sensory aspects only at their own risks.

From a practical point of view it is clear that sensory qualities cannot be entirely divorced from acceptability, although these two variables must be separated:

> What a particular product is like (i.e. its characterisation in sensory terms) ...

Tells us very little on its own about how
much that food will be liked or dislike.

And vice versa.

This is clearly evident when food is discussed
on radio or TV by people without the necessary expertise and who resort to terms like nice, nasty or
delicious. This fails to convey a definite impression
of the range of sensory qualities which would be
evident from a descriptive profile.

DESCRIPTIVE CHARACTERISATION

The development of descriptive characterisation has
been reviewed elsewhere [6]. Several different
variants exist ranging from spontaneous description,
through the concensus judgments of a group of
specially trained assessors to the independent evaluation by a number of assessors using a pre-established
vocabulary. The term 'assessor' is taken from
BS5098 on terminology [7]. The degree or extent to
which any particular quality is present may be
expressed on any one of several forms of scale,
depending upon the particular version of the profile
method which is being used. Some use a simple category scale (e.g. 0 - 5, or 0 - 9), some use a graphical scale making a mark on a line, while still others
may use magnitude estimation. These methods and
their possible relationships are set out in BS 5929
[8]. See also recent reviews on sensory methods and
their use [9,10].

In directed characterisation the relevant terms
are printed on a form after having been established by
careful investigation. Each list is product-speci-
fic and the number of applications is potentially
unlimited. Expert knowledge about the product and
the processes involved in its production will be
drawn upon in building up such a list of terms.
Detailed knowledge of the chemistry, biochemistry,
microbiology or physics of these processes, and of
the product itself, contribute both to the development and the understanding of such a vocabulary.
Many examples could be quoted including several in
the preceding papers. However, a distinction is
necessary here between the vocabularies representing
the interests of different groups ranging from the
research scientist through the product development
group to market research and the consumer. By no

means all terms can be reduced to the same common
denominator, although a maximum understanding across
all groups is desirable and should be cultivated.

   The number of 'descriptors' required will vary
considerably depending upon the product. An upper
limit of between 40 and 50 is recommended - a limit
set by the number of terms which can be conveniently
printed on a single page - thus avoiding loss of
interest, or boredom. Many products will require a
much smaller number of terms than this. The method
can be applied in principle to the whole range of
sensory qualities. Among the many problems raised
by these descriptive methods is the development and
use of reference standards and the extent to which
different people use the same term with the same
meaning. Individual differences in sensitivity and
sensations in response to the same stimulus cannot
be avoided.

ON PATTERN PERCEPTION

Except in the context of the oversimplified conditions
associated with model systems, and studies in the
research laboratory, perception is a matter of the
perception of objects and things. As such it is a
highly organised complex. The act of picking out
the main 'sensory elements' is not a matter of
selecting independent and pre-existing elements but
involves some form of mental abstraction. On its
own a profile consisting of many such elements does
not necessarily convey the same impression as the
original, spontaneous experience. Many examples
could be given in which a particular odour or flavour is more like itself than any of the separate
terms used to characterise it. This is not to deny
the value of descriptive profiling, but to recognise
its inherent limitations. This should not surprise
us since philosophers, and now linguists, distinguish between verbal definition and ostensive definition (definition by pointing). Definition by
pointing corresponds to the use of reference standards. However this last statement is an over-
simplification because most reference standards -
like objects and things — cannot be characterised
by a single sensory descriptor, other than the name
itself. The importance of pattern perception in
the present context has been recognised for some
time. Its importance in sight and hearing is well
established. Much remains to be done in respect of
the other senses before pattern perception in aroma,

flavour and texture is properly documented and can
be handled technically.   It is a problem which will
not just go away.

It has been suggested that one approach to this
might be the 'non-verbal' evaluation of similarities
(or dissimilarity) taking the various samples to be
appraised in pairs, followed by statistical analysis
using an appropriate computer programme.   The similarity approach involves many more judgements than
the directed profiles, n products involving $n(n - 1)/2$
possible pairs.   Once similarities have been analysed the results need to be interpreted and this is
best done by reference to description of the products.
In any case, it can be argued that the judgment of
similarity is just as complicated as preparing a profile.   In addition, the recent application of multidimensional statistical methods to both types of data
collected in response to the same samples provided
very similar results. [11,12].

ON ACCEPTABILITY

There are differences of opinion on how far the various aspects of acceptability should be included in
the present discussions.   This arises largely from the
terms of reference of the individuals and groups
concerned.   Looked at in the broadest terms, acceptability must be included in the chain of events from
producer to consumer.   However, there are points
within that chain in which acceptability is not the
major concern.   This is especially true of fundamental research, which can be carried on either with
or without considering acceptability, depending on
the scope and aims of the particular study.   In
spite of this observation, an understanding of the
underlying processes of food acceptability has moved
well to the centre of contemporary interests,
whether pure or applied.   Included within this are
the increasing number of studies stressing the individual differences in sensitivity, qualitative
sensory response and affective or hedonic response
to the same stimuli, which have already been mentioned.   The affective, or hedonic response, provide
useful technical terms used in certain professional
or scientific circles as a shorthand for likes and
dislikes or preferences.

In practical terms, it is consumer acceptability,
which ultimately is most important.   Representatives

of the proper consumer group should provide the
essential data.   The sort of differences which are
important here are those which the consumer can
detect.   In order to be representative, the number
of respondents required is greatly in excess of that
required for descriptive information.   Ideally, for
valid information about acceptability, one hundred
respondents from a single homogeneous group are
desirable.   Quite apart from the importance of
individual differences, once it is intended to break
down the data into the responses of the traditional
demographic groups then 1000 - 2000 respondents are
likely to be required.

ORGANISATIONS

Many different organisations, in addition to the
Sensory Panel of the Food Group of the Society of
Chemical Industry, have been responsible for promo-
ting the evaluation of sensory quality in food.   The
Food Group has supported about ten other Symposia in
addition to the present one.   The earliest support
by any national standards organisation, albeit voluntary, is that of Committee E-18 (Sensory Evaluation
of Materials and Products) of the American Society
for Testing and Materials.   This became active in
1960 and from 1968 onwards has issued a number of
special technical publications dealing with different
aspects of sensory evaluation.   The March number of
ASTM Standardisation News contains a review of the
development of these activities as well as reports
on current interests.   The latest STP (No. 758)
deals with guidelines for the selection and training
of sensory panel members.   ASTM E-18 now has 132
members including representatives of 14 major
companies.

Since 1968 the International Standards Organisation has become directly concerned through Sub-
Committee TC 12 (Sensory Analysis) of Technical
Committee 34 on Agricultural Products.   The same year
a number of national committees also became active,
including FAC/20 (Sensory Analysis) of the British
Standards Institution. Two British Standards have
already been issued, dealing respectively with terminology and with methodology. (See above).   The
reader should consult his own standards organization
about activities in his own country.

There is a tendency to be best informed about
activities in one's own country and in the United States.

Therefore it is of interest to note developments in other countries.   For example, Japan has had a well organised approach to sensory evaluation for at least 30 years.   These developments are in the hands of the Japanese Union of Scientists and Engineers. The 'Handbook on Sensory Evaluation in Industry' has been reprinted many times.   The current edition (1973) extends to nearly 900 pages   (Yoshida, personal communication).

These standards organizations clearly have an important part to play in disseminating information on recommended methods. However, in practice, correct diagnosis, followed by matching the appropriate method(s) to what is needed is just as important as standardisation.   In any case, standardisation is not an end in itself and a balance has to be maintained between this and innovation.   These organisations generally function on a consensus principle based on the views of the different experts.   Only occasionally – at least in the present subject area – are the proposals tested experimentally before approval.   ASTM E-18 has just provided an example in which this has been done [13].

Most of the organisations referred to above are concerned with applications. Attention should also be drawn to the European Chemoreception Organisation and to the Association of Chemoreception Sciences for the coordination of fundamental work in this general area.

PRODUCTS

Many different products have been discussed in the preceding papers.   Using the term broadly, products subject to sensory evaluation may range from simple model systems investigated for fundamental reasons to primary products such as wheat, carrots and fruits, on to manufactured products such as fish fingers and soft drinks.   Manufactured products, including those of intermediate product development, can be modified in a controlled manner to appraise the effects of the recipe and its modifications on the final sensory qualities and the acceptability of the product.   Many products have long established scoring systems associated with them.   Most of the traditional systems are complex since they combine both descriptive and evaluative information which some of us, whose interest is primarily scientific,

would wish to separate.   This does not imply that
such complex systems, several of which have been outlined by others, are ineffective for practical purposes.   An interesting example is the scoring
system representing the staling of white fish developed at the Torry Research Station in Aberdeen.
This has long been one of the examples used personally to illustrate the development of and importance
of the specification of quality in sensory terms,
and how this changes.   Perhaps fresh foods - or
foods which should be fresh - constitute a special
case in so far as once they have reached the peak
condition (which is not necessarily at t = zero) the
processes of deterioration set in and become increasingly complex in both sensory and other terms.
For this reason it has been convenient to refer to
this situation pictorially in terms of 'the cone of
quality', with the optimal condition at the peak.
As the base widens with the passage of time, and
loss of quality, the range of sensory qualities and
the variability of the scores given increases.
Acceptability decreases with the progressive intro -
duction of more and more unpleasant notes.

        Many other examples could be discussed, each
with their own special features.   Examples could be
drawn from many different sources and from different
countries.   Changes in external circumstances result
in changes in such systems or the use to which they
are put.   Thus, for example, the comprehensive
system for cheese grading well established in the
UK before World War II degenerated during the period
of rationing into three categories: I, fit for
keeping;   II, fit for immediate consumption;   and
III, fit for processing!   A comprehensive grading
system was re-established c.1957, but with the development of large scale production this has ceased
as an independent activity in England, but not in
Scotland.   It would be of interest to examine why.
Another war-time development of interest, consequent
upon the needs of rationing, was how to make Cheshire
cheese (which is crumbly and therefore not suitable
for a small ration) more like Cheddar (which is firm
and easy to cut into coherent pieces).   This involved research, which had to obtain official permission from the then Ministry of Food, in order to
allow some bad (poor) cheese to be made as a result
of manipulating the process variables well outside
the normal range.

SOME INSTRUMENTAL CONSIDERATIONS

Many different instrumental techniques have been described in the preceding contributions, and there is
little that could usefully be added here.   Suffice
it to recall such techniques as:

> GC/MS ' - HPLC - The measurement of colour using
> the CIE or other systems - and a wide range
> of instruments measuring different aspects of
> texture and consistency.

The advantages and limitations of these and other
techniques in use have been discussed.   Depending
upon circumstances, some instruments involve the
measurement of well-defined physical properties or
the chemical constituents of complex mixtures.
Other instruments have been described as 'empirical'
in the sense that they measure something useful but
highly complex.   Still others copy some form of
human response in appraising or eating foods.   The
dividing lines between these three categories is not
always sharp but the classification is useful.

Eventually, in the present context, it is the
relation between one or more of these instrumental
measurements made on a number of different samples
of foods which is of primary interest.   Ideally,
it would be most desirable to be able to eliminate
the human assessor and to substitute some form of
instrumental data.   However, this can be achieved
only in a limited number of examples.   As already
discussed by others, the critical issue is the
relationship between the instrumental and the sensory information, and its stability in new sets of
data.   Such instruments will always have to be
calibrated against the human response, whether that
is phrased in terms of the sensory qualities of the
product, or its acceptability.   No instrument has
sensations, still less, likes and dislikes or preferences.   The systems of coding and transduction
of impulses in the brain and nervous system
following the processes of stimulation are quite
different from the specific processes involved in
the instrumental measurements.   Thus, although
sensory-instrumental relationships can be established by observation and experiment, these will
usually be empirical rather than precisely reflecting similar processes.   Nevertheless, a few
instruments, such as those measuring texture or

consistency can be selected to simulate the behaviour
of the food in normal use. The importance of this
principle in achieving substantial correlations has
already been noted.

SOME FUTURE DEVELOPMENTS

The following outline of future developments takes
account of the views expressed in the preceding
papers. It is presented in the form of a number of
separate statements or propositions.

- A comprehensive survey of the current state of knowledge and its applications would be most useful,
  although this Symposium provides an interim impression.

- The evaluation of sensory quality will continue to
  expand, especially its industrial and consumer
  applications.

- Although the specification of sensory quality is
  distinct from acceptability, the emphasis on acceptability is already increasing and will continue
  to do so.

- In spite of this many studies, especially those of
  a fundamental or scientific nature, will continue
  to be primarily concerned with description and discrimination (or matching) without immediate reference to consumer acceptability.

- The literature on sensory evaluation and on acceptability is already growing at an increasing rate and
  this process will continue. Several new texts are
  already believed to be in preparation.

- The scope for applications is almost unlimited,
  since practically every product could be examined,
  with a view to producing standard sensory specifications.

- The balance must be maintained between basic research
  and practical applications, the aims of which may
  legitimately differ. Current economic pressures in
  some countries (including the UK) threaten some of
  the fundamental work, but hopefully industrial
  support will help the continuation of such investigations. In this context, reference may be made to
  the Cooperative Awards in Science and Engineering
  offered in support of projects in the United Kingdom

by the Science Research Council, in collaboration
with Industry. Some planned lobbying would not be
out of place.

- The expected expansion, including its continuing
  extension into the consumer area, raise the question
  of education and training in the problems and techniques of sensory evaluation and those of food
  acceptability generally. Such training will be
  required at several levels, gaps being most noticeable at the technician level. This, in turn, implies the need for an increase in available work-
  shops and courses at an appropriate level. Symposia,
  such as the present one, continue to have an important part to play, but they do not meet the training
  needs for those who will be engaged in routine, day
  to day, activities.

- Most of the relevant sensory techniques are probably
  already in existence, but the development and validation of short-cut methods, in contrast to the time
  consuming demands of laboratory studies, needs
  further consideration.

- Rapid recording techniques, which allow response
  data to be entered immediately into the computer,
  are already available. Their use will expand, thus
  reducing the time taken in recording and analysing
  data. These developments will also reduce the bulk
  of the records.

- Interpreting such analyses, which will draw upon an
  even wider range of computer programmes, demands
  knowledge and insight as well as judgment. The
  investigator in charge should be well informed on
  the principles underlying the scientific method,
  thus enabling the distinction to be made between
  extraneous **correlations** and causal relationships.

- There is much scope for improvement in reporting
  experimental/statistical conclusions. Many studies
  suggest that computer print-outs are used without
  proper understanding and results are often quoted to
  a meaningless number of (significant?) figures just
  because these came off the computer, simply representing internal consistency of the arithmetic.

- Many experts believe that there is already too much
  analytical/instrumental work,too little sensory
  testing and too much poor sensory work.

- The expected increase at different levels will call
  for critical examination. This can be accomplished
  in published work by more stringent refereeing.
  However, much applied/industrial work will remain
  confidential and cannot therefore come under the
  same scrutiny. Hopefully, the **increase in** education will help to promote and to maintain high professional and scientific standards. The present
  Symposium will have also contributed to this end.

REFERENCES

1.Punnett, P.W.; Eddy, W.R. What flavour measurements
     reveal about keeping coffee fresh? Fd Ind. 1930,
     2,401-404.

2.Pangborn, R.M. Sensory evaluation in food at the
     University of California. 1964. Lab. Pract. 13,
     1309-13.

3.Amerine, M.A.; Pangborn, R.M.; Roessler, E.B.
     Principles of Sensory Evaluation of Food.
     Academic Press, New York and London, 1965.

4.Tilgner, D.J. A retrospective view of sensory
     analysis and some considerations for the future.
     Adv. Fd Res. 1971, 19, 215-277.

5.Harper, R. Sensory Properties of Foods (Birch,
     G.G.; Brennan, J.G.; Parker, K.J., Eds) Applied
     Sci. Pub., London, 1977, 167-187.

6.Harper, R. Olfaction and Taste V1 (Le Magnen, J.;
     MacLeod, P. Eds) Information Retrieval Ltd.,
     London, 1977, 383-400.

7.BS.5089. Glossary of terms relating to the sensory
     analysis of food. British Standards Institution,
     London, 1975.

8.BS.5929. Methods for the sensory analysis of food.
     Part 1 General Guide to methodology. British
     Standards Institution, London, 1980.

9.Harper, R. Food Flavours (Morton, I.D.; MacLeod
     A.J., Eds) Elsevier Pub. Co., Amsterdam and
     New York, 1982, 79-120.

10.Harper, R. Art and Science in the Understanding
     of Flavour. Food Flavourings, Ingredients,
     Processing, Packaging. (1982) Part 1, 1, 13-15,
     17, 19, 21; Part 2, 2, 17-19, 21, 23. (The
     1981 Bill Littlejohn Memorial Lecture, British
     Society of Flavourists.)

11.Chauhan, J.; Harper, R.; Krzanowski, W. Compari-
     sons between direct similarity assessments and
     descriptive profiles of certain soft drinks.
     (This Symposium.)

12.Schiffman, S.S.; Reynolds, M.L.; Young, F.W.
     Introduction to Multidimensional Scaling,
     Academic Press, New York and London, 1981.

13.Warren, C.B.; Pearce, J.; Korth, B. Magnitude
     estimation and category scaling. ASTM Standard-
     isation News, 1982, 10, 15-16.

Index

A

Absorbtion, light, 124 - 133
Acceptability, 16 - 17, 51, 414, 474
Acids, effect on acceptability, 317 - 322
Alcohols, in apple juice, 339
  in cooked meat aroma, 381
Aldehydes, in apple juice, 339
  in cooked meat aroma, 381
Alkylpyrazines, 199
Analysis of variance (ANOVA), 260, 262, 326, 330, 332
Anthocyanins, co-pigmentation, 143 - 152
  in wines, 140 - 153, 347 - 348
  pH dependence, 142 - 148
  self-association, 143 - 152
Appearance of food products, 121 - 123, 387 - 391, 457
Apple, crispness, 174 - 179
  firmness, 163, 164
  marketing, 36
  sensory quality, 35, 91 - 94, 97, 341 - 346
Apple juices, effect of storage conditions, 336 - 340
  sensory profiling, 317 - 322, 337 - 341
Aroma, descriptive terms, 92, 97, 274, 291, 311, 327, 357
  effect of non-volatiles, 196 - 201
  identification, 191, 192
  of cider, 314, 316
  of meat, 374 - 383
  of watercress, 250 - 253
  separation, 188 - 191, 251 - 255
Ascorbic acid, 351
Asparagus, 179 - 186
Astringency, in ciders, 109 - 114, 203 - 210, 314
  in wines, 328

B

Bacillus cereus, in milk spoilage, 404
Bacon, sensory quality, 392 - 393, 451 - 452, 454 - 456, 460 - 461

Bean, texture profile analysis, 259 - 265
Beef, 97, 100 - 101, 104, 133 - 136, 450
Beer, 51 - 52, 83, 97, 141
Benzyl acetate, 291
Betalaines, 141
Bitterness, in carrots, 243 - 244
  in ciders, 109 - 114, 203 - 210, 314
  in potato, 16
  in wines, 328
  in yoghurt, 417
Blackcurrant, 97
  aroma in wines, 327 333
  drinks, sensory profiling, 287 - 296
  juice pigments, 145
Blanching, 41
Breeding, 17, 35
Broad beans, QAV assessment, 231
Brussels sprouts, 18

C

Cabanac's Set-point theory, 440 - 442
Cabbage, QAV assessment, 230
Caffeine, 198
Canonical correlation analysis, 275
  plots, 358
  variate analysis, 63 - 64, 275, 327, 328, 330 - 331
Capsaicoids, relation to Scoville Index, 266 - 270
Card reader, for sensory profile data, 115 - 116
Carotenoids, 141
Carrots, QC6 assessment, 229
  sensory quality, 18 - 20, 231-233 - 244, 462
Cauliflower, QAV assessment, 230
Cheese, 167 - 168, 477
Chickens, sensory quality, 387 - 391
Chlorogenic acid, 199
Chlorophenol taint, 402, 409
Chromosorb (as absorbant), 189
Ciders, sensory quality, 97, 109 - 114, 141, 203 - 210, 310 - 317

CIE, 121, 123, 124, 478
Coffee, 24, 26, 115
Colour, in beverages, 140 -
    153, 347 - 348
    in fruit and vegetables,
    222 - 223, 229 - 231
    measurements, 121 - 136,
    143 - 152, 478
    natural pigments, 141
    synthetic pigments, 141
Computer, listing of volatiles,
    192
    use in data handling, 83 -
    87, 115 - 117, 237, 480
Consumer, attitude, 59, 474
    discrimination, 449 - 451
    needs, 32
    perceptions, 451 - 454
    response interpretations,
    58 - 62
    surveys, 62, 319
Convenience foods, 42, 43
Co-operatives, 43
Co-pigmentation, 143 - 152
Copper-induced flavour
    changes, 408
Cox's Orange Pippin, 36, 94,
    174 - 179, 319
Crispness, 174 - 179
Cytokinins, 256

D

Dairy products, consumption,
    414
    marketing, 412, 413
    see also Milk
Degree of excellence, 49 -
    53
Descriptive analysis, 55, 61,
    82, 96 - 106, 325, 329,
    472 - 473
    see also Quantitative Des-
    criptive Analysis
Difference testing, 70 - 80
Dimethyl disulphide, 251,
    280 - 281
Discrimination tests, 54
Duncan multiple range test,
    292
Dwarf bean, QC6 assessment,
    227

E

Eating habits and obesity,
    431 - 443

Electrocutaneous stimuli, 98 -
    100, 102 - 104
Electron capture detector, 190
Energy, considerations, 41, 42
Enzymes, activity, 251
    in tomato ripening, 281 -
    285
    oxidation, 250
    in UHT milk, 406
Esters in apple juice, 339

F

Fast foods, 42
Fibrousness, perception in
    fruits and vegetables, 179 -
    186
Firmness of peas, 224 - 225
    see also Texture
Fish (deboned) appearance, 364 -
    365
    colour, 365, 366, 368
    flavour, 365 - 367, 368 -
    369
    hedonic rating, 369 - 372
    preparation, 363 - 364
    texture, 367 - 368, 370
Flavonoids, 141
Flavour, assessment in fruit
    and vegetables, 225 - 227,
    337 - 340
    compounds, 419 - 421
    effects of processing, 420 -
    421
    interaction with food ingred-
    ients, 415
    light-induced changes, 406 -
    408
    terms, 97, 312, 327, 369
    see also Individual products
Flavour profile data, storage and
    retrieval, 115 - 117
    see also Individual products
Food, acceptability, 16
    adulteration, 192
    frozen, 41
    irradiation, 42
    off-flavour, 424 - 427
    palatability, 431 - 443
    safety, 16
    see also Quality
Fruit, quality assessment, see
    Individual species

G

Gas chromatography, 188 - 193,
    196 - 201, 252 - 253, 337,
    354 - 355, 378, 379, 395 -
    396
Gas chromatography - mass spect-
    rometry, 192, 252 - 253, 377,
    395, 425 - 427, 478
Globe trapping/sensory evaluation
    technique, 378, 379, 383
Golden Delicious apples, 35 - 36,
    39
Grading standards, 50
Grape juice colour, 148
Grower requirements, 31

H

Head space volatiles, 189, 196 -
    201, 251 - 252, 374, 377 -
    378, 394, 395 - 396, 425
    in strawberry, 415 - 418
    in wines, 354 - 355
    trapping/evaluation, 378,
    379, 383
High performance liquid chrom-
    atography, 205, 206, 267 -
    269, 478
Hue, 124, 129 - 132, 348
Hunter L,a,b measurements, 129,
    130, 140, 365
Hydroxymethylfurfural, 337 -
    339, 403

I

Ice cream, 413, 418, 457
Illumination (effect of), 122 -
    123, 131, 136
INDSCAL analysis, 91, 96, 101 -
    106, 297 - 307
Infrared spectroscopy, 191
Instron measurements, 263 - 264
Instrumental methods for meas-
    uring sensory quality, 25 -
    26, 121 - 136, 155 - 171,
    173 - 186, 344, 478 - 479
Intensive production, effects
    on fruit quality, 39 - 40
β-Ionone, 251, 291

J

Jam, 32

K

Kubelka-Munk analysis, 121,
    125, 129, 130

L

Light, measurement, 121 - 123,
    129 - 131, 133, 136
Light-induced flavour changes in
    milk, 406 - 410
Lipids, oxidation in milk, 404
    role in meat flavour, 394 -
    396

M

Maillard reaction, in meat, 396
    in UHT milk, 403
Malic acid, 319 - 322
Maltol, 291, 417
Malvidin-3-glucoside, 143 - 147
Marketing, 43, 59 - 62, 447 -
    464, 471
Mass spectrometry, 191, 192, 377
    see also Gas chromatography -
    mass spectrometry
Masters of Wine, 325, 326, 332
Meat, 93, 160, 161, 394 - 396
    colour and opacity, 121, 131 -
    136
    cooked aromas of, 394 - 396
Melanoidin, 141
2-Methoxy-3-isopropylpyrazine,
    424, 427
Microbial-induced off-flavours,
    404 - 406, 427
Milk, copper-induced flavour
    changes, 408
    heat-induced sensory changes
    402 - 403
    light-induced oxidations, 406-
    408
    microbial contamination, 404 -
    406
    off-flavours, 402
    shelf-life, 405 - 407
    UHT, 402 - 403, 406, 421
    see also Dairy products
Modelling consumer perception,
    459, 462
Multi-dimensional scaling, 298 -
    299
Multi-dimensional unfolding
    (METUNF), 305 - 307
Multiple difference testing, 76 -
    80
Multivariate analysis, 233 - 244,
    275, 327
Mushroom, sensory quality, 32 - 34
Myglobin, 121, 133 - 136

N

γ-Nonalactone, 416 - 418
Nuclear magnetic resonance spectroscopy, 191

O

Obesity and eating habits, 431 -
   443
Odour preferences, 24, 25
   terms, 92, 274, 291, 311,
   327, 351, 375, 376
Off-flavours, 402, 404 - 406,
   417, 424 - 427
Opacity, 121, 122, 124, 125
Orange, drink, 121, 125 - 133
   juices, 24, 27
Organic agriculture, 40

P

Packaging, 18, 41, 42
   source of off-flavour,
   402, 407
Panel, responses, 342 - 344
   role, 464
   training of, 84 - 87, 160,
   290 - 292, 296, 337
Paired difference testing,
   70 - 76
Partial Least Squares Regression, 236 - 237, 239 -
   243
Peas, 32, 33, 223 - 225, 231
Pears, texture of, 169 - 170
Phenethyl isothiocyanate,
   251
Phenolics, 141
   effect on flavour volatiles,
   197 - 201
   in white wines, 350 - 351
   see also Procyanidins
Phospholipids, 394 - 396, 406
Pick-your-own outlets, 31, 35,
   43
Pig carcass backfat, 392, 393
Plums, QC6 assessment, 226,
   228
Porapak (as absorbant), 251,
   252, 337
Pork, colour, 135
   see also Bacon
Post-harvest changes, in beans,
   259 - 265
   in tomatoes, 36, 283 - 285
   in watercress, 253 - 256

Potato, grading standards, 37
   firmness, 166
   toxic glycoalkaloids in, 16
Principal Component Analysis,
   236 - 242, 260, 264 - 265,
   275, 314 - 315
Processing, effect on sensory
   quality, 33 - 34, 361 - 372,
   387 - 390, 420 - 421
Procrustes analysis, 90 - 93
Procyanidins, isolation, 204 -
   205
   sensory assessment, 207 -
   209
Product development, 64
Product optimisation (PROP), 52
Protein, in wheat, 38
Pseudomonas, off-flavour in
   cheese, 424 - 427
Pseudomonas fragi, in milk spoilage, 404
Purines, effect on flavour
   volatiles, 197 - 198
Pyrazines, 396 - 397, 427

Q

QAV (Quality Appraisal of Varieties) method, 228 - 232
QC6 (quality appraisal) system,
   220 - 228
Quality appraisal, in fruit and
   vegetables, 219 - 232, 247 -
   250
Quality assurance, 32
Quality control, 32, 53 - 54
Quality, degree of excellence,
   47 - 53
   deviation from standard, 53 -
   55
Quantitative Descriptive Analysis (QDA), 52, 55
   see also Descriptive Analysis
Quinoid (colour), 141
Quinones, 350, 351

R

Ranking procedure, 78 - 80
Reflectance, 121, 124 - 131
Rhubarb, 179 - 186
R - Index, 69 - 80

S

Scaling and scales, 18, 70 - 71,
   75, 93 - 94, 97

Scatter (light), 121, 124 - 136
Scatter diagrams (sensory-phys-
    ical data), 169 - 169
Scoville Index, 264 - 270
Self-association, 143 - 152
Sensory assessment, 50 - 51
Sensory difference testing, 71 -
    80
Sensory evaluation, 48 - 55,
    69 - 80, 82 - 88, 96 - 106,
    155 - 171, 174 - 179, 463,
    464
    historical developments in,
    476   479
    see also Individual attrib-
    utes, techniques and products
Sensory - instrumental data,
    relating, 155 - 170, 176 -
    179, 183, 207, 233 - 244,
    250, 266 - 270, 317 - 322,
    339, 344, 379 - 382, 425
Sensory perception, 27, 458,
    460 - 461
Sensory profiling, 21, 62, 64,
    82, 234, 235, 287 - 296, 297 -
    309, 310 - 322, 345, 370 -
    372, 375 - 383
    see also Individual products
Sensory quality, biological var-
    iation, 22 - 23
    definition, 16, 31, 469 - 470
    degree of excellence, 49 - 53
    deviation from standard, 53 -
    55
    effect of packaging on, 17 -
    18
    future trends, 467 - 481
    manufacturers' view, 49 - 55,
    58 - 64
Signal detection theory, 69
Skim milk, 408 - 409
Sniff evaluation, 192, 378 -
    383
Soft drinks, sensory profiling,
    287 - 296, 297 - 309
Soy sauce, sensory evaluation,
    272 - 276
Spectrophotometry, 126 - 133,
    136
Stabilisers, 415
Standards affecting foods, 409,
    470, 475 - 476
Statistical analyses - see
    Individual methods
Strawberry, breeding, 35
    chilling of, 35
    juice pigments, 149

    marketing needs, 35
    microbially-induced flavour
    in milk, 404
    volatiles, 416
Sugars, in apples, 342
    effect on acceptability,
    317 - 322
Sulphur compounds in cooked
    meat aroma, 381
Sulphur dioxide, 351
Sweetness, in apple juice, 317 -
    322
    in carrots, 244
    perception, 433 - 440

T

Taints - see Off-flavours
Taste, terms, 97, 237, 274,
    291, 312, 327, 369
Tenax GC (as absorbant), 189,
    378, 379, 395
Texture, assessment, 159, 223 -
    225, 458
    measuring instruments, 156 -
    157, 161, 174 - 186, 213 -
    216
    of beans, 259 - 265
    of broiler chickens, 390 -
    391
    of canned peas, 223 - 225
    of canned plums, 224 - 226
    of fruits and vegetables,
    173 - 186
    profiling techniques, 158 -
    159
    see also Fibrousness
Thiazoles, in cooked meat aromas,
    379 - 381
Thin layer chromatography, 204
Tomato, biochemistry of ripen-
    ing, 283 - 285
    effect of growing systems on,
    39 - 40
    handling, 36 - 37
    quality, 36
Translucency, 121, 122, 125 -
    133
Transmission (light), 121, 124 -
    125, 128 - 131
Triglycerides, 394 - 396, 406
Tristimulus measurements, 150 -
    152, 347 - 348

U

UHT milk, 402 - 403, 406 - 407,
    421

V

Vanillin, 291, 420
Vegetables, quality appraisal,
   see Individual species
Volatiles, in apple juices, 339
   in watercress, 249 - 250
   in wines, 354 - 355
   see also Head space volatiles

W

Watercress, aroma compounds of,
   250 - 251
   sensory evaluation, 249 -
   253
   shelf-life, 248 - 249
   storage, 248 - 249, 253,
   256
Wheat, breadmaking, 39
Wine, aroma, 328 - 329
   browning in, 350 - 351
   colour, 149 - 152, 347 -
   349
   flavour, 330 - 331, 356 -
   357
   sensory quality, 152, 324 -
   333, 353 - 358

Y

Yoghurt, 413, 418